Engineering of Software

Peri L. Tarr · Alexander L. Wolf

Editors

Engineering of Software

The Continuing Contributions
of Leon J. Osterweil

 Springer

Editors
Peri L. Tarr
IBM Thomas J. Watson Research Center
P.O. Box 704
Yorktown Heights, NY 10598
USA
tarr@us.ibm.com

Alexander L. Wolf
Imperial College London
Department of Computing
180 Queen's Gate
SW7 2AZ London
United Kingdom
a.wolf@imperial.ac.uk

ISBN 978-3-642-43603-1   ISBN 978-3-642-19823-6 (eBook)
DOI 10.1007/978-3-642-19823-6
Springer Heidelberg Dordrecht London New York

ACM Computing Classification (1998): D.2, F.3.2, K.6

Reprint permission for the individual chapters has been granted with kind permission from
the copyright owners.

Cover photograph: Shaowei Wang
Cover design: deblik

Printed on acid-free paper

Springer is part of Springer Science+Business Media (www.springer.com)

Preface

Software engineering research can trace its roots to a small number of highly influential individuals. Among that select group is Prof. Leon J. Osterweil, whose work has fundamentally defined or impacted major directions in software analysis, development tools and environments, and software process. His exceptional and sustained contributions to the field have been recognized with numerous awards and honors throughout his career.

In honor of Lee's career-long and profound accomplishments, a Festschrift event occurred during the 2011 International Conference on Software Engineering (ICSE) in Honolulu, Hawaii. The event comprised a day-long series of talks by prominent members of the community, followed by a presentation by Lee to respond with his thoughts and reflections.

This book was prepared in honor of that special occasion. It compiles Lee's most important published works to date, together with several new articles exploring the broad impact of his work.

Whether this book provides your first exposure to Lee's groundbreaking vision of software engineering that has helped drive the field from its infancy to a mature discipline, or whether it offers you new insight into the fascinating and important modern impact of his work, we hope you will enjoy and benefit from it as much as we did in assembling it.

It is impossible to produce a work of this magnitude without substantial contributions from others. We would like to give special thanks to our area coordinators, Lori A. Clarke, Matthew B. Dwyer, Wilhelm Schäfer, and Stanley M. Sutton Jr., who did a remarkable job organizing and contributing to their respective parts of the book. We are also very grateful to Richard N. Taylor, the ICSE 2011 General Chair, and Debra A. Brodbeck, the ICSE 2011 Conference Coordinator, for their invaluable help in making the Festschrift a reality.

February 2011   Peri L. Tarr
                                                                Alexander L. Wolf

Contents

Introduction to "Engineering of Software: The Continuing Contributions of Leon J. Osterweil"

Peri L. Tarr and Alexander L. Wolf

Peri L. Tarr is at IBM Thomas J. Watson Research Center, P. O. Box 704, Yorktown Heights, NY 10598 USA, tarr@us.ibm.com

Alexander L. Wolf is at Imperial College London, Department of Computing, 180 Queen's Gate, London SW7 2AZ United Kingdom, a.wolf@imperial.ac.uk

Abstract Software engineering research can trace its roots to a small number of highly influential individuals. Among that select group is Prof. Leon J. Osterweil, whose work has fundamentally defined or impacted major directions in software analysis, development tools and environments, and software process. His exceptional and sustained contributions to the field have been recognized with numerous awards and honors throughout his career. This section briefly reviews his exceptionally distinguished career.

Software pervades our lives today, powering everything from PlayStations® to the Space Station. Entire governments and economies run on software. Businesses differentiate themselves by the quality of their software services. Students learn using software. Food and automobiles and pharmaceuticals are produced using software. Medical devices that give people with a myriad of conditions a new lease on life are powered by software. People collaborate, stay connected, and reap "the wisdom of crowds" [7] using software. It is hard to imagine life without software.

But it wasn't always so. The field of software engineering started from very humble origins as relatively simple aids to productivity, such as mathematical processing packages and small-scale applications to help with back-office functions. Very few could ever have conceived that, one day, the engineering of software would become one of the most important, impactful activities in the world.

Leon J. Osterweil is one of those few. Lee saw past software as a limited aid to corporate and personal productivity, and into a future where it would be possible to engineer large-scale, reliable software that could enhance peoples' effectiveness and enrich their lives. And he went further: he hypothesized that the software processes by which software is engineered could themselves be engineered to help build those game-changing software systems. This doesn't sound like a vision today—it is the reality in which we live—but in the 1970s, when Lee started his exceptionally distinguished career, it was prescient.

Lee has been a major force in driving software engineering from vision to reality. For more than three decades, he has fundamentally defined or significantly af-

P.L. Tarr, A.L. Wolf (eds.), *Engineering of Software*,
DOI 10.1007/978-3-642-19823-6_1, © Springer-Verlag Berlin Heidelberg 2011

fected major approaches to software analysis, development tools and environments, and software process—all critical parts of the software engineering discipline as it is practiced today. The depth and breadth of his work is seen in research, government, academia, and industry. Much of his work and many of his ideas continue to have major influence today—a truly remarkable statement about work in a field in which advances are old in a matter of months or a small number of years. Lee has driven and influenced the field of software engineering in both obvious and subtle ways. He has defined and developed many of the core ideas in the field, and he has also nurtured generations of its practitioners.

Lee started his career in mathematics, receiving the A.B. degree from Princeton University in 1965, and the M.A. and Ph.D. degrees from the University of Maryland in 1970 and 1971, respectively. After graduate school, he became a professor at the University of Colorado at Boulder, where he ultimately served as chair of the Department of Computer Science. During his tenure in Boulder, he and his students produced multiple seminal pieces of research in the analysis of software. Part I of this volume examines the significant and long-lived impact of that work.

It was also during his time in Boulder that Lee's vision of software engineering as a discipline began. After laying the foundation for a study of what would eventually be called "software development environments" with his work on Toolpack (Chapter 11) and Odin (Chapter 12), Lee co-founded the Arcadia Consortium in 1987. Arcadia reflected the group's vision of the engineering of software on a grand scale. Its goal was to perform the research and proof-of-concept development required to make fully integrated, end-to-end software development environments—ones that support all aspects of the engineering of software—a reality. Arcadia was a decade-long joint effort of researchers at the University of Colorado at Boulder, the University of California at Irvine, and the University of Massachusetts at Amherst, and it included participants from TRW, Incremental Systems Corporation, and others. The sheer number and extent of the contributions that came out of Arcadia is overwhelming. Part II examines some of Lee's major contributions in this area.

It was during this time when Lee had the insight that "software processes are software too," [3] which led to his most profound contributions to software engineering to date. In particular, he noticed that the different processes carried out during the course of the engineering of software suffered from many of the same characteristics and problems that software itself does. Processes are frequently erroneously specified, unclear in intent, difficult to debug, and even more difficult to understand. This led him to hypothesize that programming software processes, and subjecting their development to the same, rigorous methods, analyses, and testing to which software is subjected, could benefit processes the same way it had benefited software. Lee's vision radically altered the whole software environments landscape. Even today, *process-centered* software environments—a hallmark of Arcadia—are just emerging in the state-of-the-practice. Part III looks Lee's profound and sustained contributions in the area of software processes.

In 1988, Lee joined the faculty of the University of California at Irvine, where he also served as chair of the Department of Information and Computer Science. While at Irvine, he co-founded the Irvine Research Unit in Software (IRUS), which seeks to advance the state-of-the-art and state-of-the-practice in software engineering by promoting partnerships between academic and industrial participants. IRUS—which continues its invaluable work to this day—is characteristic of Lee: he builds bridges between people with different knowledge and expertise to enable them to find solutions together that none would have found individually.

In 1993, Lee joined the faculty at University of Massachusetts at Amherst, where he remains today. He served as Interim Dean of the College of Natural Sciences and Mathematics from 2001 to 2005. He serves as co-director for the Laboratory for Advanced Software Engineering Research (LASER) and for the Electronic Enterprise Institute. In recent years, he has expanded his research on process definition and analysis to some important domains, including medical safety, dispute resolution, electronic commerce, and e-government, and he has continued to make significant contributions in software testing and analysis.

The pivotal role that software plays in our society means that software engineering practice desperately needs a strong research base on which to draw. The questions inevitably arose: how well have its results supported software engineering practice, and how can it best do so in the future? In 2002, Lee decided to take on these critical questions. He enlisted the help of three colleagues to form the Impact Project [5]. His vision was to produce a series of rigorous, scholarly, and objective studies in various subfields of software engineering, with the goals of assessing past impact and making recommendations to assure future impact. To date, three such studies have been published as peer-reviewed journal articles, authored by teams from both industry and academia, and more are underway. These studies cover the areas of software configuration management [2], modern programming languages [6], and middleware technology [1]. They clearly identify how synergisms among different areas of computer science (e.g., programming languages, distributed systems, database management) and healthy exchanges between academia and industry have sparked key innovation. The Impact Project has been remarkably successful and, indeed, impactful, in affecting both the perception of software engineering research and research agendas in the field.

The Impact Project is just one example of the key and sustained leadership role in the software engineering community that Lee has played throughout his career. His outstanding research contributions have been recognized and honored with awards too numerous to list exhaustively. Lee is a Fellow of the ACM, and he has received the ACM SIGSOFT Outstanding Research Award in recognition of his extensive and sustained research impact. His seminal paper on software process programming was awarded the Most Influential Paper of ICSE 1987, which recognizes it as the paper from that conference which had the most significant impact on the field over the decade that followed its publication. His ICSE 1986 paper on tool integration was selected as the runner-up for the same honor. Lee has served as General Chair for FSE 1998 and ICSE 2006, and Program Chair for many conferences in different areas of software engineering, including ICSE 1994. Lee has been an ACM Lecturer, has been on the board of ACM's Transactions on Software Engineering and Methodology, and has been a member of the Software Engineering Institute's Process Program Advisory Board. He has served on technical advisory boards for, or consulted with, several industrial organizations, including AT&T, Boeing, IBM, SAIC, and TRW.

Lee's research contributions have been so extensive that some people are surprised to learn that he is also a very talented and dedicated educator. He has directed the research of many Ph.D. students who have themselves gone on to achieve significant impact and receive major awards. Lee has also mentored generations of young researchers, guiding them in their careers. He was recently honored with the ACM SIGSOFT Most Influential Educator Award, in recognition of his career-long achievements as an educator and mentor.

Lee's expertise has earned him prominent roles on National Academies Panels, which provide advice to the United States government on key topics in science, engineering, and medicine. In 2007, he co-authored an assessment of the Social Security Administration's electronic service provision [3]. He is currently a member of a National Academies Panel on "Future Information Architectures, Processes, and Strategies for the Centers for Medicare and Medicaid Services."

It has been a privilege and a delight to have the opportunity to assemble the papers in this volume, and to reflect on the distinguished career of someone who laid so much of the foundation for the field of software engineering, and who has done—and continues doing—so much in his career to promote the vitality of the field, its practitioners, and all those whose lives are enriched by it. We hope you enjoy and benefit from this volume as much as we have.

Acknowledgments   We are very grateful to Lori Clarke, Stan Sutton, and Clay Williams for their outstanding feedback and input.

References

[1] Emmerich W, Aoyama M, Sventek, J (2008) The Impact of Research on the Development of Middleware Technology. ACM Trans. Softw. Eng. Methodol. 17(4)
[2] Estublier J, Leblang D, van der Hoek A, Conradi R, Clemm G, Tichy W, Wiborg-Weber D (2005) Impact of software engineering research on the practice of software configuration management. ACM Trans. Softw. Eng. Methodol. 14(4)
[3] Osterweil L (1987) Software Processes are Software Too. In Proc. International Conference on Software Engineering
[4] Osterweil L, Millet L, Winston J (2007) Social Security Administration Electronic Service Provision: A Strategic Assessment. National Academies Press
[5] Osterweil LJ, Ghezzi C, Kramer J, Wolf AL (2008) Determining the Impact of Software Engineering Research on Practice. IEEE Computer 41(3)
[6] Ryder BG, Soffa ML, Burnett, M (2005) The impact of software engineering research on modern programming languages. ACM Trans. Softw. Eng. Methodol. 14(4)
[7] Surowiecki, J (2005) The Wisdom of Crowds. Anchor

Part I: Flow Analysis for Software Dependability

Data Flow Analysis for Software Dependability: The Very Idea

Matthew B. Dwyer

Department of Computer Science and Engineering, University of Nebraska, Lincoln NE 68588-0115, USA. dwyer@cse.unl.edu

Abstract Data flow analysis was developed as a means for enabling the optimization of code generated by source language compilers. Over the past decade the majority of new applications of data flow analysis in published research and in tools for practicing developers have focused on software quality. The roots of the shift from optimization to quality are, perhaps surprisingly, not recent. The very idea of applying data flow analysis to detect potential errors in programs can be traced back to the work of Osterweil and Fosdick (Chapter 5) in the mid-70s. Remarkably, their work outlined the conceptual architecture of nearly all subsequent static analysis techniques targeting software quality, and the application of their approach revealed the key challenges that drive research in practical static software quality tools even today. In this paper, we identify the key insights behind their approach, relate those insights to subsequent approaches, and trace several lines of research that generalized, extended, and refined those insights.

1. From Optimization to Quality

The key concepts that underlie modern compiler optimization were developed in the late 1960s, e.g., [26]. At that time the idea of a control flow graph was already understood as a means of encoding statement sequencing, branching, and looping in programs. Numerous optimizations had been developed and implemented that, for example, simplified arithmetic expression evaluation, eliminated common sub-expressions, and performed loop-invariant code motion. The early '70s witnessed the development of a general framework for formulating data flow analyses whose results are used to trigger the application of code improving transformations. In 1973, Kildall [25] defined what has come to be known as *data flow frameworks* for bit-vector data flow problems and, concurrently, Hecht and Ullman [23] proved that general algorithms for solving such problems were efficient. Kildall's data flow framework, and the Cousot's abstract interpretation framework [12], remain the dominant means of specifying a data flow analysis to this day.

P.L. Tarr, A.L. Wolf (eds.), *Engineering of Software*,
DOI 10.1007/978-3-642-19823-6_2, © Springer-Verlag Berlin Heidelberg 2011

Since their inception, compilers have detected and reported a range of errors, e.g., [2]. Lexical, syntactic, and type errors that prevented compilation were reported and, by the early '70s, sophisticated error recovery techniques were developed that permitted compilers to find multiple errors in a single run of the compiler. The development of optimizing compilers provided additional information about a program's runtime behavior, and early papers anticipated the use of that information to detect errors—for example, mismatches among the units associated with operands in arithmetic expressions [26].

The first system that focused explicitly on the use of compiler techniques to detect errors was Osterweil and Fosdick's DAVE system [29] in 1975. DAVE was developed as a "software validation system"; it did not detect errors as a side-effect of the compilation process. DAVE focused on two patterns that may arise in the sequencing of program variable definitions and references: (1) *undefined references* and (2) *unused definitions*. Sequences of statements that matched the first pattern were reported as errors, whereas those matching the second were reported as warnings—at the very least, they represent inefficient coding.

In its initial form, DAVE did not use the general framework of data flow analysis, even though it targeted anomalous statement sequencing that was related to the flow of data values through the program. DAVE performed a depth-first search of program control flow graph paths attempting to match the two patterns described above. Unlike compiler error reports, DAVE included a path that matched the pattern with each error/warning report, i.e., a witness or counterexample.

DAVE represented a significant step forward in detecting potential runtime errors at compile time, but its developers quickly realized that it could be generalized in two important ways. In 1976, they described how to generalize the class of anomalies that could be analyzed and how an overapproximating analysis of execution behavior could target such anomalies [21].

One proposed extension to DAVE used regular expressions as the means of describing anomalous sequences of variable definitions and references. This permitted them to easily extend DAVE to target errors such as *redundant definitions*, i.e., paths on which two definitions of a variable occur without an intervening reference. The second extension replaced the use of DAVE's depth-first search algorithm with an algorithm that combined the results of live variable and available expression data flow analyses. This new algorithm accounted for all possible paths through the program's control flow graph; thus, if an anomalous execution existed, it would be reported.

2. The Architecture of a Static Program Analyzer

While Fosdick and Osterweil did not highlight the architecture of their analysis approach, in hindsight one can identify the four key elements depicted in Fig. 2.1.

A static program analyzer feeds a specification of undesirable (desirable) behavior and a model of the program's executable behavior to a fixed point computation engine that relates program behavior to the specification and reports behavior that matches (mismatches) the specification.

Fig. 2.1. Conceptual architecture of static behavioral analysis tools

DAVE realized this architecture with regular expression specifications of undesirable behavior, a control flow graph model of program behavior, data flow analysis as the fixed point engine, and control flow graph paths that match the specification as diagnostic reports.

DAVE wasn't just an idea on paper. It was implemented as a 25,000 line FORTRAN program that was applied to a number of FORTRAN codes. The reports of DAVE's application herald a key challenge that is still faced today by developers of static analysis tools. Since DAVE used an overapproximating model of program behavior, it issued *false* error/warning reports. As Osterweil and Fosdick reported, "An obvious and troublesome difficulty is DAVE's copious output...The net effect is that human analysts are often reluctant to pursue all of DAVE's messages" [30]. While multiple strategies for mitigating the false positive problem have been proposed in the literature over the years, the authors of DAVE proposed the first such strategy—the use of *must*, or underapproximating, static analysis to produce error reports that were guaranteed to be feasible [22].

3. Growing Together and Apart

Research on DAVE was a product of the software engineering research community—several of the DAVE papers appeared in general computer science venues and one appeared in the 2nd International Conference on Software Engineering [22]. In the decades that followed the introduction of DAVE, a number of techniques and tools were developed and reported on in the software engineering, programming languages, and (what has come to be known as the) computer aided verification research communities. Many of those techniques shared the architecture established by DAVE.

3.1 Model Checking

To those familiar with model checking, the architecture in Fig. 2.1 will be familiar. The seminal paper on model checking by Emerson and Clarke [19] explains how properties specified using Computation Tree Logic (CTL) can be checked against a semantic model of guarded command programs by means of calculating a fixed point formula. This paper launched an enormously fruitful line of research that has resulted in significant impact in the research community and in industrial practice.

The two most popular tools that implement model checking approaches embody the standard architecture of Fig. 2.1. The SMV model checker, from CMU, implements a form of symbolic model checking [10] that calculates fixed points of the system state transition relation. SMV accepts CTL specifications and produces transition system traces that witness violations of the specification. SPIN [24] accepts Linear Temporal Logic specifications [31] and checks them against a semantic model of systems specified in the Promela language. In SPIN, fixed points are calculated using a nested depth-first search performed on a product construction of the specification and model [36]. As with SMV, traces are produced that witness violations of the specification.

3.2 Typestate and Sequencing Constraint Checking

While work on model checking was enormously active during the '80s and '90s, direct follow-on work to DAVE was rather sparse. The data flow analysis extensions to DAVE described above were further extended by Taylor and Osterweil to support the analysis of concurrent programs [35].

An independent, but related, development by Strom and Yemeni defined the concept of *typestate* [34]. Typestates specify how the sequencing of calls on an interface can lead the underlying implementation into states in which it may permit or reject subsequent calls. While DAVE focused on sequencing of variable definitions and references, typestate lifted the concept of sequencing constraint to the interface level. In subsequent years, Strom and Yellin developed data flow analyses to check typestate specifications against programs [33].

Olender and Osterweil developed the Cecil/Cesar system which extended the DAVE approach in a different direction. Cecil was a general language for specifying sequencing constraints as regular languages [27] and Cesar permitted a data flow analysis to be automatically generated from a given specification [28]. Cecil was used to encode classic typestate properties. For example, a Cecil constraint could specify that the sequence of calls on a file API must lie in the regular language

$$(\text{open}; (\text{read} \mid \text{write})^*; \text{close})^*$$

Such a specification could then be checked against a program with a Cesar generated data flow analysis.

Dwyer and Clarke developed the FLAVERS system in the early '90s. FLAVERS can be viewed as the extension of Cecil/Cesar to concurrent programs along with techniques for enriching the control flow graph model to incorporate information about program values [17].

A number of other projects built on the idea of specifying partial program behavior using typestate and sequencing constraints and checking those specifications against programs using data flow analysis. The ESP project [13, 16] at Microsoft Research and the SAFE project at IBM [20] scaled data flow analyses to reason about typestate conformance to apply them to code bases of hundreds of thousands of lines. A retrospective paper reporting on the SAFE project in this volume (Chapter 3) recounts the key innovations and lessons learned related to scaling typestate analysis for Java programs.

The Vault [14, 15] project at Microsoft Research and the Plural project at CMU [8, 9] sought to enrich typestate specification formalisms and analyses to address the challenges that arise when objects referenced in typestate specifications may be aliased. The technical innovations and practical benefits of Plural are described in this volume (Chapter 4) along with a discussion of the design choices and potential future directions for applying typestate analysis to large library APIs.

3.3 Missed Opportunities

In retrospect, it seems clear that two separate communities were working, largely separately, to develop static system validation techniques and tools. This resulted in missed opportunities to leverage results across community boundaries in the '80s and '90s. The wealth of results on temporal logics could have informed the development of sequencing constraint languages. Exposing the gulf between the imprecise control flow models used in program analysis approaches and the semantic models used in model checking might have given rise to modeling approaches that better balanced the competing desires for improved precision and scalability. Finally, the fact that fixed point computations were at the core of flow analysis and model checking approaches offered a chance for unifying techniques.

4. The Rise of Static Software Validation Tools

By the late '90s researchers had begun to see the connections between results on data flow analysis, abstract interpretation, and model checking. In 1998, Schmidt observed these connections and explained that flow analysis and model checking can be thought of as instances of single framework [32]. Within two years, a number of techniques were developed that began to blend flow analysis and model checking approaches for software validation [3, 11, 37], and that was just the beginning.

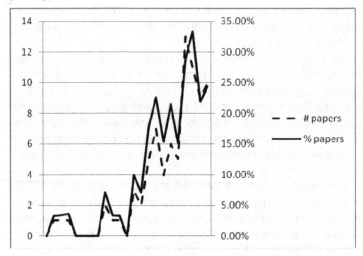

Fig. 2.2. The number (left axis) and percentage (right axis) of software validation papers published in ACM SIGPLAN Conference on Programming Language Design and Implementation from 1990 through 2010.

Throughout the decade beginning in 2000 researchers began to break down the artificial barriers between the software engineering, programming languages, and computer aided verification research communities. It was not uncommon for a research project on software validation to publish and consume results in the major conferences in each of these areas. For example, in 2001 the Microsoft SLAM project published in well-regarded meetings in programming languages [6], computer aided verification [5], and software engineering [4]. This cross-fertilization allowed experts within each of those communities to *see* techniques and application contexts with which they were not familiar and this had the effect of generating more cross-community activity related to static software validation techniques and tools.

This trend is witnessed by the publication record of two of the major meetings in programming languages and computer aided verification. We surveyed all of the papers published between 1990 and 2010 in the proceedings of the ACM SIGPLAN Conference on Programming Language Design and Implementation (PLDI) and the International Conference on Computer Aided Verification (CAV). We read the abstracts of all papers in PLDI and CAV to determine the number and percentage that focus on software validation; Fig. 2.2 and Fig. 2.3 plot that data.

The trend is clear. In both communities there was relatively little work focusing on software validation during the '90s, but beginning in 2000, a clear upward trend was visible.

During the '90s, less than 2% of the papers published in PLDI focused on software validation; the rest focused on foundational issues, optimization, and other topics. Similarly, less than 1% of the papers published in CAV focused on software validation; the rest focused on foundational issues, hardware, communication protocols, and other topics. In contrast, for the decade beginning in 2000 nearly 20% of the papers published in PLDI and CAV addressed software validation.

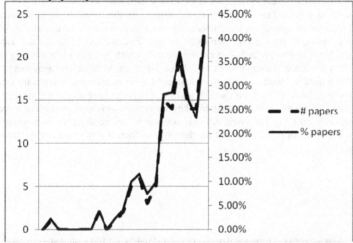

Fig. 2.3. The number (left axis) and percentage (right axis) of software validation and verification papers published in the International Conference on Computer Aided Verification (CAV) from 1990 through 2010.

In the 35 years since Osterweil and Fosdick envisioned the application of data flow analysis to assess software quality there have been an enormous advances. The conceptual architecture of DAVE has been instantiated in numerous research techniques, and several of those techniques have matured into tools that are used daily by software developers. The popular Eclipse integrated development environment [18] adds to the standard Java compiler's undefined reference error messages by providing the unused definition warning that DAVE pioneered. The FindBugs tool checks for a much wider range of anomalies some of which require data flow analysis and others which can be detected by more syntactic analyses. FindBugs is used widely in industry and significant studies of its use at Google have been reported [1]. The Coverity tool suite is a commercial product that builds on a significant body of research on techniques related to static analysis and model checking. The tools have been hardened for industrial use and are now widely deployed [7].

Numerous challenges remain in providing precise scalable static software validation tools for practicing developers. For example, developers still appear to be unwilling or unable to formulate specifications of correctness properties to drive validation. In addition, the problem of copious false positive reports, which was first encountered by Osterweil and Fosdick in applying DAVE, remains a barrier to incorporation of static validation tools in daily build processes. With the continued attention of three energetic research communities, there is good reason to believe that these challenges will be overcome in the coming years.

Acknowledgments It has been fascinating re-reading the literature from the '60s, '70s, '80s, and 90's while researching this article. I encourage my colleagues to go back and re-read the classic papers—they may find some "recent" research results aren't so new after all.

Many people who have helped me as I have moved along with the field of data flow analysis—I started off working on optimizing compilers and moved on to work on static software validation techniques. My colleagues at Intermetrics in the late '80s, and especially Tucker Taft, provided lots of guidance and a rich and open environment in which to learn while working on compilers. I was very fortunate to study under Lori Clarke at UMass-Amherst; she demonstrated and encouraged "high quality'" work and that work happened to be on the topic of software validation. George Avrunin, Jay Corbett, John Hatcliff, and Dave Schmidt have all shaped the way I think about program analysis either by the example they set in their own work or through direct collaboration. Finally, I thank Lee Osterweil, not only because he set the stage for the work that I've done in my career, but because he showed me the value of focusing on important questions and thinking "big".

References

[1] Ayewah N, Hovemeyer D, Morgenthaler JD, Penix J, PughW (2008) Using static analysis to find bugs. IEEE Software 25(5):22–29

[2] Backus JW, Beeber RJ, Best S, Goldberg R, Haibt LM, Herrick HL, Nelson RA, Sayre D, Sheridan PB, Stern H, Ziller I, Hughes RA, Nutt R (1957) The fortran automatic coding system. In: Papers presented at the western joint computer conference: Techniques for reliability, pp 188–198

[3] Ball T, Rajamani SK (2001a) Automatically validating temporal safety properties of interfaces. In: Proceedings of the 8th International SPIN Workshop, pp 103–122

[4] Ball T, Rajamani SK (2001b) Bebop: a path-sensitive interprocedural dataflow engine. In: Proceedings of the 2001 ACM SIGPLAN-SIGSOFT workshop on Program analysis for software tools and engineering, pp 97–103

[5] Ball T, Rajamani SK (2001c) The slam toolkit. In: Proceedings of the 13th International Conference on Computer Aided Verification, pp 260–264

[6] Ball T, Majumdar R, Millstein T, Rajamani SK (2001) Automatic predicate abstraction of c programs. In: Proceedings of the ACM SIGPLAN 2001 conference on Programming language design and implementation, pp 203–213

[7] Bessey A, Block K, Chelf B, Chou A, Fulton B, Hallem S, Henri-Gros C, Kamsky A, McPeak S, Engler D (2010) A few billion lines of code later: using static analysis to find bugs in the real world. Commun ACM 53:66–75

[8] Bierhoff K, Aldrich J (2005) Lightweight object specification with typestates. In: Proceedings of the 10th European software engineering conference held jointly with 13th ACM SIGSOFT international symposium on Foundations of software engineering, pp 217–226

[9] Bierhoff K, Aldrich J (2007) Modular typestate checking of aliased objects. In: Proceedings of the 22nd annual ACM SIGPLAN conference on Object-oriented programming systems and applications, pp 301–320

[10] Burch JR, Clarke EM, McMillan KL, Dill DL, Hwang LJ (1990) Symbolic model checking: 1020 states and beyond. In: Proceedings of the Fifth Annual IEEE Symposium on Logic in Computer Science, pp 428–439

[11] Corbett JC, Dwyer MB, Hatcliff J, Laubach S, Păsăreanu CS, Robby, Zheng H (2000) Bandera: extracting finite-state models from java source code. In: Proceedings of the 22nd international conference on Software engineering, pp 439–448

[12] Cousot P, Cousot R (1977) Abstract interpretation: a unified lattice model for static analysis of programs by construction or approximation of fixpoints. In: Proceedings of the 4th ACM SIGACT-SIGPLAN symposium on Principles of programming languages, pp 238–252

[13] Das M, Lerner S, Seigle M (2002) ESP: path-sensitive program verification in polynomial time. In: Proceedings of the ACM SIGPLAN 2002 Conference on Programming language design and implementation, pp 57–68

[14] DeLine R, Fähndrich M (2001) Enforcing high-level protocols in low-level software. In: Proceedings of the ACM SIGPLAN 2001 conference on Programming language design and implementation, pp 59–69

[15] DeLine R, Fähndrich M (2004) Typestates for objects. In: Proceedings of the European Conference on Object-Oriented Programming, pp 183–204

[16] Dor N, Adams S, Das M, Yang Z (2004) Software validation via scalable path-sensitive value flow analysis. In: Proceedings of the 2004 ACM SIGSOFT international symposium on Software testing and analysis, pp 12–22

[17] Dwyer MB, Clarke LA, Cobleigh JM, Naumovich G (2004) Flow analysis for verifying properties of concurrent software systems. ACM Trans Softw Eng Methodol 13:359–430

[18] Eclipse, The eclipse foundation open source community website. http://www.eclipse.org

[19] Emerson EA, Clarke EM (1980) Characterizing correctness properties of parallel programs using fixpoints. In: Proceedings of the 7th Colloquium on Automata, Languages and Programming, pp 169–181

[20] Fink SJ, Yahav E, Dor N, Ramalingam G, Geay E (2008) Effective typestate verification in the presence of aliasing. ACM Trans Softw Eng Methodol 17

[21] Fosdick LD, Osterweil LJ (1976a) Data flow analysis in software reliability. ACM Comput. Surv. 8(3):305–330 (Reprinted as Chapter 5)

[22] Fosdick LD, Osterweil LJ (1976b) The detection of anomalous interprocedural data flow. In: Proceedings of the 2nd international conference on software engineering, pp 624–628

[23] Hecht MS, Ullman JD (1973) Analysis of a simple algorithm for global data flow problems. In: Proceedings of the 1st annual ACM SIGACT-SIGPLAN symposium on Principles of programming languages, pp 207–217

[24] Holzmann GJ (1997) The model checker spin. IEEE Trans. Software Eng. 23(5):279–295

[25] Kildall GA (1973) A unified approach to global program optimization. In: Proceedings of the 1st annual ACM SIGACT-SIGPLAN symposium on Principles of programming languages, pp 194–206

[26] Lowry ES, Medlock CW (1969) Object code optimization. Commun. ACM 12:13–22

[27] Olender KM, Osterweil LJ (1990) Cecil: A sequencing constraint language for automatic static analysis generation. IEEE Trans. Software Eng. 16(3):268–280 (Reprinted as Chapter 7)

[28] Olender KM, Osterweil LJ (1992) Interprocedural static analysis of sequencing constraints. ACM Trans. Softw. Eng. Methodol. 1:21–52

[29] Osterweil LJ, Fosdick LD (1976a) Dave-a validation error detection and documentation system for fortran programs. Softw. Pract. Exper. 6(4):473–486

[30] Osterweil LJ, Fosdick LD (1976b) Some experience with dave: a fortran program analyzer. In: Proceedings of American Federation of Information Processing Societies National Computer Conference, pp 909–915

[31] Pnueli A (1977) The temporal logic of programs. In: Proceedings of the 18th Annual Symposium on Foundations of Computer Science, pp 46–57
[32] Schmidt DA (1998) Data flow analysis is model checking of abstract interpretations. In: Proceedings of the 25th ACM SIGPLAN-SIGACT symposium on Principles of programming languages, pp 38–48
[33] Strom RE, Yellin DM (1993) Extending typestate checking using conditional liveness analysis. IEEE Trans. Software Eng. 19(5):478–485
[34] Strom RE, Yemini S (1986) Typestate: A programming language concept for enhancing software reliability. IEEE Trans. Software Eng. 12(1):157–171
[35] Taylor RN, Osterweil LJ (1980) Anomaly detection in concurrent software by static data flow analysis. IEEE Trans. Software Eng. 6(3):265–278 (Reprinted as Chapter 6)
[36] Vardi MY, Wolper P (1986) An automata-theoretic approach to automatic program verification. In: Proceedings of the Symposium on Logic in Computer Science, pp 332–344
[37] Visser W, Havelund K, Brat GP, Park S (2000) Model checking programs. In: Proceedings of the 15th international conference on automated software engineering, pp 3–12

The SAFE Experience

Eran Yahav and Stephen Fink

Eran Yahav is at Technion, Israel, yahave@cs.technion.ac.il

Stephen Fink is at IBM T.J. Watson Research Center, sjfink@us.ibm.com

Abstract   We present an overview of the techniques developed under the SAFE project. The goal of SAFE was to create a practical lightweight framework to verify simple properties of realistic Java applications. The work on SAFE covered a lot of ground, starting from typestate verification techniques [18, 19], through inference of typestate specifications [34, 35], checking for absence of null derefences [26], automatic resource disposal [13], and an attempt at modular typestate analysis [42]. In many ways, SAFE represents a modern incarnation of early ideas on the use of static analysis for software reliability (e.g., [21]). SAFE went a long way in making these ideas applicable to real properties of real software, but applying them at the scale of modern framework-intensive software remains a challenge. We are encouraged by our experience with SAFE, and believe that the technique developed in SAFE can serve as a solid basis for future work on practical verification technology.

1. Introduction

Statically checking if a program satisfies specified safety properties (e.g., [21, 14, 29, 28, 8, 12, 5, 22, 20, 4, 30, 11, 17]) can help identify defects early in the development cycle, thus increasing productivity, reducing development costs, and improving quality and reliability.

Typestate [37] is an elegant framework for specifying a class of temporal safety properties. Typestates can encode correct usage rules for many common libraries and application programming interfaces (APIs) (e.g. [39, 1]). For example, typestate can express the property that a Java program should not read data from `java.net.Socket` until the socket is connected.

The SAFE project focused on various aspects of typestate verification and inference with the ultimate goal of being able to verify nontrivial properties over realistic programs.

P.L. Tarr, A.L. Wolf (eds.), *Engineering of Software*,
DOI 10.1007/978-3-642-19823-6_3, © Springer-Verlag Berlin Heidelberg 2011

1.1 Challenges

We focus on sound analysis; if the verifier reports no violation, then the program is guaranteed to satisfy the desired properties. However, if the verifier reports a potential violation, it might not correspond to an actual program error. Imprecise analysis can lead a verifier to produce "false alarms": reported problems that do not indicate an actual error. Users will quickly reject a verifier that produces too many false positives.

Scaling to Real Software. While sophisticated and precise analyses can reduce false positives, such analyses typically do not scale to real programs. Real programs often rely on large and complex supporting libraries, which the analyzer must process in order to reason about program behavior.

Aliasing. There is a wide variety of efficient flow-insensitive may-alias (pointer) analysis techniques (e.g., [10, 24, 36]) that scale to fairly large programs. These analyses produce a statically bounded (abstract) representation of the program's runtime heap and indicate which abstract objects each pointer-valued expression in the program may denote. Unfortunately, these scalable analyses have a serious disadvantage when used for verification. They require the verifiers to model any operation performed through a pointer dereference conservatively as an operation that may or may not be performed on the *possible* target abstract objects identified by the pointer analysis—this is popularly known as a "weak update" as opposed to a "strong update" [6].

To support strong updates and more precise alias analysis, we present a framework to check typestate properties by solving a flow-sensitive, context-sensitive dataflow problem on a *combined domain of typestate and pointer information*. As is well-known [9], a combined domain may yield improved precision compared to separate analyses. Furthermore, the combined domain allows the framework to *concentrate computational effort on alias analysis only where it matters to the typestate property*. This concentration allows more precise alias analysis than would be practical if applied to the whole program.

Using a domain that combines precise aliasing information with other property-related information is a common theme in our work ([17, 33, 18, 19, 34, 35, 26, 42]). Our precise treatment of aliasing draws some ideas from our experience with shape analysis [32]. In the rest of this paper we describe the combined domains we used for typestate verification (Section 2), inference of typestate specifications (Section 3), and verifying the absence of null derefences (Section 4).

Getting Specifications. Typestate verification requires typestate specifications. It is not always easy, or possible, to obtain such formal specifications from programmers. This raises the research question of whether such specification can be obtained automatically. Indeed, much research has addressed *mining specifications* directly from code [1, 2, 7, 38, 40, 41, 25, 16, 23, 27, 15].

Most such research addresses *dynamic analysis*, inferring specifications from observed behavior of representative program runs. Dynamic approaches enjoy the significant virtue that they learn from behavior that definitively occurs in a run. On the flip side, dynamic approaches can learn *only* from available representative runs; incomplete coverage remains a fundamental limitation.

The approach we have taken in SAFE is to obtain specifications using *static client-side specification mining*. The idea in *client-side* specification mining is to examine the ways client programs use that API. An effective static client-side specification mining shares many of the challenges with typestate verification. In particular, it also requires relatively precise treatment of aliasing to track the sequence of events that may occur at runtime for every object of interest.

2. Typestate Verification

Consider the simple program of Fig. 3.1. We would like to verify that this program uses Sockets in a way that is consistent with the typestate property of Fig. 3.2.

As mentioned earlier, we would like our verifier to be sound in the presence dynamic allocation and aliasing. We now informally present a number of abstractions in attempt to verify our example program.

```
1 open(Socket s) { s.connect();}
2 talk(Socket s) { s.getOutputStream()).write("hello"); }
3 dispose(Socket s) { s.close(); }
4 main() {
5     Socket s = new Socket(); //S     { <S,init> }
6     open(s);                          { <S,init>, <S,conn> }
7     talk(s);                          { <S,init>, <S,conn>,
                                           <S,err> }
8     dispose(s);
9 }
```

Fig. 3.1. A simple program using Socket.

Naming Objects in an Unbounded Heap. The idea behind all of our abstraction is to combine aliasing information with typestate information. The first component of our abstraction is a global *heap graph*, obtained through a flow-insensitive, context-sensitive subset based may points-to analysis [3]. This is fairly standard and provides a partition of the set *objects*[#] into abstract objects. In this discussion, we define an *instance key* to be an abstract object name assigned by the flow-insensitive pointer analysis. The heap graph provides for an access path *e*, the set of instance keys it *may* point-to and also the set of access paths that may be aliased with *e*.

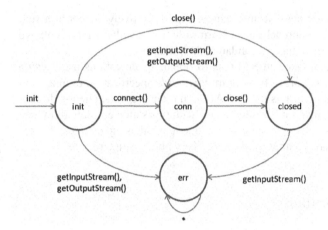

Fig. 3.2. Partial specification for a Socket.

Base Abstraction. Our initial abstraction attempt is an abstraction referred to as a *base abstraction* in [18]. This abstraction tracks the typestate state for every allocation site in the program. The results for this abstraction are shown as annotations in Fig. 3.1. We use a tuple <*Obj, St*> to denote the fact that the abstract state contains an object *Obj* that is in the state *St*. The abstract state is a set of tuples of this form.

In the example of Fig. 3.1, a Socket object is allocated in line 5, leading to an abstract state {<*S, init*>}. After the call to open(s), the abstract state contains two possibilities {<*S, init*>, <*S, connected*>}. This is because when performing the call s.connect(), we do not have sufficient information to perform a *strong update*. The abstract object *S* potentially represents multiple objects of type socket. Invoking s.connect() does not make *all* of these objects change their state to connected. Therefore, to be sound, we have to assume that it is possible for the state to contain other objects, that may be pointed to by *s*, and that remain in their initial state *init*. This sound assumption makes our analysis report a false alarm when invoking talk(s).

Unique Abstraction. The example of Fig. 3.1 actually allocates a single Socket object, and there is no justification for the loss of precision in such simple (and common) cases. To deal with cases in which an allocation site is only used to allocate a single object, we introduce a slightly refined abstraction, tracking tuples of the form <*Obj, Un, St*> representing the fact that the abstract state contains an object *Obj* in the state *St*, and a boolean flag *Un* denotes whether this is the only object allocated at the site *Obj*.

The results of using this abstraction for the simple example program are shown in Fig. 3.3. Tracking the fact that the allocation site *S* only allocates a unique object allows us to perform a strong update on <*S, unique, init*> when connect(s) is invoked. This results in the single tuple <*S, unique, conn*>, and thus with successful verification of this example. However, it is easy to see that whenever an allocation site is executed inside a loop, the unique abstraction may be insufficient and result in false alarms similar to the ones we had with the base abstraction. We therefore introduce a family of abstractions that integrate typestate information and flow-sensitive must (and may) points-to information enabling to handle destructive updates on non-unique abstract objects.

```
1 open(Socket s) { s.connect();}
2 talk(Socket s) { s.getOutputStream()).write("hello"); }
3 dispose(Socket s) { s.close(); }
4 main() {
5    Socket s = new Socket(); //S        { <S,U,init> }
6    open(s);                             { <S,U,conn> }
7    talk(s);                             { <S,U,conn> }
8    dispose(s);
9 }
```

Fig. 3.3. A simple program using Socket with Unique abstraction.

2.1 Integrating Typestate and Must Points-to Information

The simple abstractions presented earlier are used as preceding phases of the SAFE analyzer to dismiss simple cases. The real strength of SAFE comes from the integrated verifier that tracks must points-to information using access paths and combines it with typestate information.

Technically, our abstract semantics uses a combination of two representations to abstract heap information: (i) a global heap-graph representation encoding the results of a flow insensitive points-to analysis; (ii) enhanced flow-sensitive must points-to information integrated with typestate checking.

2.1.1 Parameterized Typestate Abstraction

Our parameterized abstract representation uses tuples of the form: $<o,unique,typestate,AP_{must},May,AP_{mustNot}>$ where:

- o is an instance key.
- *unique* indicates whether the corresponding allocation site has a single concrete live object.
- *typestate* is the typestate of instance key o.
- AP_{must} is a set of access paths that must point-to o.
- *May* is true indicates that there are access paths (not in the must set) that may point to o.

- $AP_{mustNot}$ is a set of access paths that do not point-to o.

This parameterized abstract representation has four dimensions, for the *length* and *width* of each access path set (must and must-not). The length of an access path set indicates the maximal length of an access path in the set, similar to the parameter k in k-limited alias analysis. The width of an access path set limits the number of access paths in this set.

An abstract state is a set of tuples. We observe that a conservative representation of the concrete program state must obey the following properties:

a. An instance key can be indicated as unique if it represents a single object for this program state.

b. The access path sets (the must and the must-not) do not need to be complete. This does not compromise the soundness of the staged analysis due to the indication of the existence of other possible aliases.

c. The must and must-not access path sets can be regarded as another heap partitioning which partitions an instance key into the two sets of access paths: those that a) must alias this abstract object, and b) definitely do not alias this abstract object. If the must-alias set is non-empty, the must-alias partition represents a single concrete object.

d. If *May=false*, the must access path is complete; it contains all access paths to this object.

```
1  class SocketHolder { Socket s; }
2    Socket makeSocket() {
3    return new Socket(); // A
4  }
5  open(Socket t) {      { <A, ¬U, init,{} ,May, {}> }
6  t.connect();          { <A, ¬U, init,{}, May, {¬t}>,
                           <A, ¬U, conn,{ t }, May, {}> }
7  }
8  talk(Socket s) {
9  s.getOutputStream()).write( hello );
10     { <A, ¬U, init, {}, May, {¬g, ¬s}>,
       { <A, ¬U, conn, { g, s }, May, {}> }
12 main() {
13   Set<SocketHolder> set = new HashSet<SocketHolder>();
14   while( ) {
15     SocketHolder h = new SocketHolder();
16     h.s = makeSocket();
17     set.add(h);  { <A, U, init, { h.s }, May, {}> }
18   }
19   for (Iterator<SocketHolder> it = set.iterator(); ) {
20     Socket g = it.next().s;
21     open(g);
```

```
22      talk(g);       { <A, ¬ U, init, {}, May, {¬ g }>,
                         <A, ¬ U, conn, { t }, May, {}> }
23  }
24 }
```

Fig. 3.4. A program using Sockets stored inside a collection.

The focus operation. A key element of SAFE's abstraction is the use of a *focus* operation [32], which is used to dynamically (during analysis) make distinctions between objects that the underlying basic points-to analysis does not distinguish.

We now describe the focus operation, which improves the precision of the analysis. As a motivating example, consider the statement t.connect() in line 6 of the example. Since this statement is invoked on sockets coming from the iterator loop of lines 20-23, we have an incoming tuple representing all of the sockets in the collection, and, hence, we cannot apply a strong update to the tuple, which can subsequently cause a false positive.

The *focus* operation replaces the single tuple with two tuples, one representing the object that t points to, and another tuple to represent the remaining sockets. Formally, consider an incoming tuple $<o,unique,typestate,AP_{must},true,AP_{mustNot}>$ at an observable operation $e.op()$, where $e \notin AP_{must}$, but e may point to o (according to the flow-insensitive points-to solution). The analysis replaces this tuple by the following two tuples:

$$\langle o,unique,typestate,AP_{must} \cup \{e\},true,AP_{mustNot} \rangle$$

$$\langle o,unique,typestate,AP_{must},true,AP_{mustNot} \cup \{e\}\rangle$$

In our example under consideration, the statement t.connect() is reached by the tuple $<A,\neg U,init,\varnothing,May,\varnothing>$. Focusing replaces this tuple by the following two tuples:

$$\langle A,\neg U,init,\{t\},true,\varnothing \rangle$$

$$\langle A,\neg U,init,\varnothing,true,\{t\}\rangle$$

The invocation of t.connect() is analyzed after the focusing. This allows for a strong update on the first tuple and no update on the second tuple resulting in the two tuples:

$$\langle A,\neg U,conn,\{t\},true,\varnothing \rangle$$

$$\langle A,\neg U,init,\varnothing,true,\{t\}\rangle$$

We remind the reader that the *unique* component tuple merely indicates if multiple objects allocated at the allocation site o may be simultaneously alive. A tuple such as $<A,false,conn,\{t\},\varnothing>$, however, represents a single object at this point, namely the object pointed to by t, which allows us to use a strong update.

The analysis applies this *focus* operation whenever it would otherwise perform a weak update for a typestate transition. Thus, focus splits the dataflow facts tracking the two typestates that normally result from a weak update.

3. Static Specification Mining

Static analyses for specification mining can be classified as *component-side*, *client-side*, or both. A component-side approach analyzes the implementation of an API, and uses error conditions in the library (such as throwing an exception) or user annotations to derive a specification.

In contrast, client-side approaches examine not the implementation of an API, but rather the ways client programs use that API. Thus, client-side approaches can infer specifications that represent how a particular set of clients uses a general API, rather than approximating safe behavior for all possible clients. In practice, this is a key distinction, since a specification of non-failing behaviors often drastically over-estimates the intended use cases.

The SAFE approach provides static analysis for client-side mining, applied to API specifications for object-oriented libraries.

```
1  class SocketChannelClient {
2    void example() {
3      Collection<SocketChannel> channels = createChannels();
4      for (SocketChannel sc : channels) {
5        sc.connect(new InetSocketAddress
                            ("tinyurl.com/23qct8",80));
6        while (!sc.finishConnect()) {
7          // ... wait for connection ...
8        }
9        if (?) {
10         receive(sc);
11       } else {
12         send(sc);
13     }
14   }
15   closeAll(channels);
16 }
17   void closeAll(Collection<SocketChannel> chnls) {
18     for (SocketChannel sc : chnls) { sc.close(); }
19   }
20   Collection<SocketChannel> createChannels() {
21   List<SocketChannel> list
        = new LinkedList<SocketChannel>();
22   list.add(createChannel("http://tinyurl.com/23qct8", 80));
23   list.add(createChannel("http://tinyurl.com/23qct8", 80));
24   // ...
25   return list;
26 }
```

```
27 SocketChannel createChannel(String hostName, int port) {
28   SocketChannel sc = SocketChannel.open();
29   sc.configureBlocking(false);
30   return sc;
31 }
32 void receive(SocketChannel x) {
33   File f = new File("ReceivedData");
34   FileOutputStream fos = new FileOutputStream(f,true);
35   ByteBuffer dst = ByteBuffer.allocateDirect(1024);
36   int numBytesRead = 0;
37   while (numBytesRead >= 0) {
38     numBytesRead = x.read(dst);
39     fos.write(dst.array());
40   }
41   fos.close();
42 }
43 void send(SocketChannel x) {
44   for (?) {
45     ByteBuffer buf = ByteBuffer.allocateDirect(1024);
46     buf.put((byte) 0xFF);
47     buf.flip();
48     int numBytesWritten = x.write(buf);
49   }
50 }
51 }
```

Fig. 3.5. A simple program using APIs of interest.

Consider the program of Fig. 3.5. We would like to extract the specification of how this program uses objects of type SocketChannel. The central challenge is to accurately track sequences that represent typical usage patterns of the API. In particular, the analysis must deal with three difficult issues:

- **Aliasing.** Objects from the target API may flow through complex heap-allocated data structures. For example, objects in the program of Fig. 3.5 are passed through Java collections.
- **Unbounded Sequence Length.** The sequence of events for a particular object may grow to any length; the static analysis must rely on a sufficiently precise yet scalable finite abstraction of unbounded sequences. For example, Fig. 3.6 shows a sample concrete history for the program of Fig. 3.5.
- **Noise.** The analysis will inevitably infer some spurious usage patterns, due to either analysis imprecision or incorrect client programs. A tool must discard spurious patterns in order to output intuitive, intended specifications.

We present a two-phase approach consisting of (1) an *abstract-trace collection* to collect sets of possible behaviors in client programs, and (2) a *summarization* phase to filter out noise and spurious patterns.

In this paper we focus on the abstract trace collection phase, details about summarization can be found in [34, 35]. Experimental results in [34, 35] indicate that in order to produce reasonable specifications, the static analysis must employ sufficiently precise abstractions of aliases and event sequences. Based on experience with the prototype implementation, we discuss strengths and weaknesses of static analysis for specification mining. We conclude that this approach shows promise as a path to more effective specification mining tools.

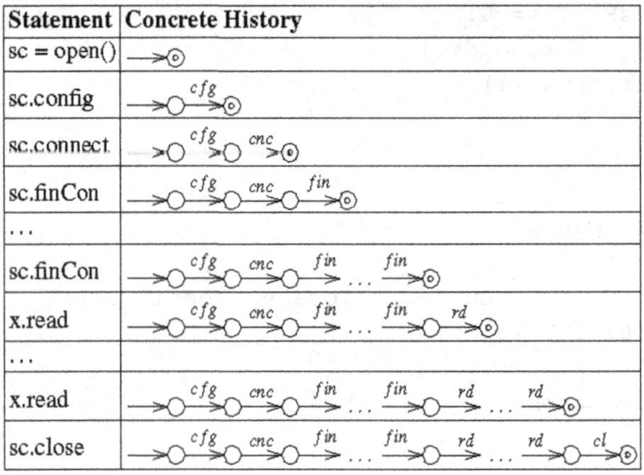

Fig. 3.6. Example of concrete histories for an object of type SocketChannel in the example program.

3.1 Abstract Trace Collection

The abstract trace collection requires abstraction on two unbounded dimensions: (i) abstraction of heap-allocated objects; (ii) abstraction of event sequences.

The abstraction we use for specification mining is based on the abstraction used for verification as described in Section 2. Both verifying a typestate property, and mining it, require precise reasoning on the sequences of events that can occur during program execution. The main difference is that mining typestate properties requires recording traces of events, where typestate verification only requires tracking of the state in a known typestate property.

An abstract program state consists of a set of tuples, called "factoids." A *factoid* is a tuple $<o, heap\text{-}data, h>$, where

- o is an instance key.

- *heap-data* consists of multiple components describing heap properties of o (described below).
- *h* is the abstract history representing the traces observed for o until the corresponding execution point.

An abstract state can contain multiple factoids for the same instance key o, representing different alias contexts and abstract histories.

The *heap-data* component of the factoid is crucial for precision; we adopt the *heap-data* abstractions of [18], as described in Section 2. Technically, the *heap-data* component of the factoid uses tuples of the form: $<unique, AP_{must}, May, AP_{mustNot}>$ as described earlier. Intuitively, the heap abstraction relies on the combination of a preliminary scalable (e.g. flow-insensitive) pointer analysis and selective predicates indicating access-path aliasing, and information on object uniqueness. Informally, a factoid with instance key o, and with *heap-data* = *{unique=true, must={x.f}, mustNot={y.g}, may=true}* represents a program state in which there exists exactly one object named o, such that $x.f$ must evaluate to point to o, $y.g$ must *not* evaluate to point to o, and there *may* be other pointers to o not represented by these access-paths. Crucially, the tracking of *must point-to* information allows *strong updates* [6] when propagating dataflow information through a statement.

While a concrete history describes a unique trace, an abstract history typically encodes multiple traces as the language of the automaton. Different abstractions consider different history automata (e.g. deterministic vs. non-deterministic) and different restrictions on the current states (e.g. exactly one current state vs. multiple current states). We denote the set of abstract histories by $\mathcal{H}$.

The remainder of this section considers semantics and variations of history abstractions.

Abstracting Histories. In practice, automata that characterize API specifications are often simple, and further admit simple characterizations of their states (e.g. their ingoing or outgoing sequences). Exploiting this intuition, we introduce abstractions based on quotient structures of the history automata, which provide a general, simple, and in many cases precise, framework to reason about abstract histories.

Given an equivalence relation R, and some *merge criterion*, we define the quotient-based abstraction of R as follows.

- The abstraction h_0 of the empty-sequence history is $Quo_R(h_0^\natural) = h_0$, i.e. the empty-sequence history.
- The *extend transformer* appends the new event σ to the current states, and constructs the quotient of the result. More formally, let $h=(\Sigma, Q, init, \delta, \mathcal{F})$. For every $q_i \in \mathcal{F}$ we introduce a fresh state, $n_i \notin Q$. Then $extend(h,\sigma)=Quo_R(h')$, where $h' \triangleq (\Sigma, Q \cup \{n_i \mid q_i \in \mathcal{F}\}, init, \delta', \{n_i \mid q_i \in \mathcal{F}\})$ with $\delta'(q_i,\sigma) = \delta(q_i,\sigma) \cup \{n_i\}$ for every $q_i \in \mathcal{F}$, and $\delta'(q',\sigma') = \delta(q',\sigma')$ for every $q' \in Q$ and $\sigma' \in \Sigma$ such that $q' \notin \mathcal{F}$ or $\sigma' \neq \sigma$.

- The *merge operator* first partitions the set of histories based on the given *merge criterion*. Next, the merge operator constructs the union of the automata in each partition, and returns the quotient of the result.

To instantiate a quotient-based abstraction, we next consider options for the requisite equivalence relation and merge criteria.

3.2 Past-Future Abstractions

In many cases, API usages have the property that certain sequences of events are always preceded or followed by the same behaviors. For example, a `connect` event of `SocketChannel` is always followed by a `finishConnect` event.

This means that the states of the corresponding automata are characterized by their ingoing and/or outgoing behaviors. As such, we consider quotient abstractions w.r.t. the following parametric equivalence relation.

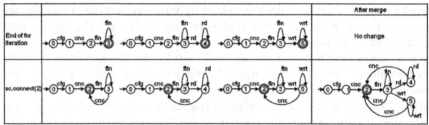

Fig. 3.7. Abstract interpretation with past abstraction (Exterior merge).

Definition 3.1 (Past-Future Relation) *Let $q1, q2$ be history states, and $k_1, k_2 \in \mathbb{N}$. We write $(q_1, q_2) \in R[k_1, k_2]$ iff $in_{k_1}(q_1); out_{k_2}(q_1) \cap in_{k_1}(q_2); out_{k_2}(q_2) \neq \emptyset$, i.e., q_1 and q_2 share both an ingoing sequence of length k_1 and an outgoing sequence of length k_2.*

We will hereafter focus attention on the two extreme cases of the past-future abstraction, where either k_1 or k_2 is zero. Recall that $in_0(q) = out_0(q) = \{\varepsilon\}$ for every state q. As a result, $R[k,0]$ collapses to a relation that considers ingoing sequences of length k. We refer to it as R_{past}^k, and to the abstraction as the *k-past abstraction*. Similarly, $R[0,k]$ refers to outgoing sequences of length k, in which case we also refer to it as R_{future}^k. We refer to the corresponding abstraction as the *k-future abstraction*. Intuitively, analysis using the k-past abstraction will distinguish patterns based only on their recent past behavior, and the k-future abstraction will distinguish patterns based only on their near future behavior. These abstractions will be effective if the recent past (near future) suffices to identify a particular behavioral sequence.

Merge Criteria. Having defined equivalence relations, we now consider merge criteria to define quotient-based abstractions. A merge criterion will determine when the analysis should collapse abstract program states, thus potentially losing precision, but accelerating convergence.

We consider the following merge schemes.

- *None:* each history comprises a singleton set in the partition. This scheme is most precise, but is impractical, as it results in an exponential blowup.
- *Total:* all histories are merged into one.
- *Exterior:* the histories are partitioned into subsets in which all the histories have compatible initial states and compatible current states. Namely, histories h_1 and h_2 are merged only if (a) $(init_1, init_2) \in R$; and (b) for every $q_1 \in F_1$ there exists $q_2 \in F_2$ s.t. $(q_1, q_2) \in R$, and vice versa.

Intuitively, the total criterion forces the analysis to track exactly one abstract history for each "context" (i.e. alias context, instance key, and program point).

The exterior criterion provides a less aggressive alternative, based on the intuition that the distinguishing features of a history can be encapsulated by the features of its initial and current states. The thinking follows that if histories states differ only on the characterization of intermediate states, merging them may be an attractive option to accelerate convergence without undue precision loss.

Example. Fig. 3.7 presents abstract histories produced during the analysis of the single instance key in our running example, using the 1-past abstraction with exterior merge. The first row describes the histories observed at the end of the first iteration of the `for` loop of `example()`.

These all hold abstract histories for the same instance key at the same abstract state. Each history tracks a possible execution path of the abstract object.

Although these histories refer to the same instance key and alias context, exterior merge does not apply since their current states are not equivalent. The second row shows the result of applying the extend transformer on each history after observing a `connect` event.

Fig. 3.8 presents the corresponding abstract histories using the 1-future abstraction with exterior merge (in fact, in this case total merge behaves identically). Unlike the case under the past abstraction, merge applies at the end of the first loop iteration, since the initial and current states are equivalent under the 1-future relation. As a result, the analysis continues with the single merged history. The second row shows the result of applying the extend transformer on it after observing a `connect` event.

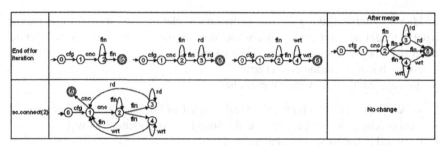

Fig. 3.8. Abstract interpretation with future abstraction (Exterior merge).

4. Verifying Dereference Safety

Null-pointer dereferences represent a significant percentage of defects in Java applications. Furthermore, a null dereference is often a symptom of a higher-level problem; warning the programmer about a potential null dereference may help in exposing the more subtle problem. The general approach presented in the previous sections can be used to address the problem of verifying the safety of pointer dereferences in real Java programs.

We present a scalable analysis via lazy scope expansion. Unlike most existing bug-finding tools for detecting null dereferences our analysis is *sound*.

Our abstract domain is a product of three domains: (i) the abstract domain used for the may-alias analysis, (ii) the abstract domain used for the must-alias analysis, and (iii) a set AP_{nn} of access paths that are guaranteed to have a non-null value. We guarantee that the abstract domain is finite by placing a (parameterized) limit on the size of the AP_{nn} sets and on the maximal length of the access paths that they may contain.[1] We refer to the size of the access path set AP_{nn} as the *width* of AP_{nn} and to the maximal length of an access path $ap \in AP_{nn}$ as the *length* of AP_{nn}.

Note that domains (i) and (ii) above *are the same ones* used for typestate verification and specification mining in Sections 2 and 3.

For details on how elements of the third domain are updated, see [26]. Here, we wish to focus on another aspect, which is the notion of *expanding scopes*.

The idea is to break the verification problem into modular sub-problems. Specifically, our analysis operates on program *fragments*, and gradually expands the analysis scope in which a fragment is considered when additional context information is required. While this idea has been presented in [26] in the context of verifying dereference safety, it is applicable to all of the other analyses we presented here, and in particular to the typestate verification and typestate mining of the previous sections.

---

[1] The length of access path $<v,<f_1,...,f_k>>$ is defined to be $k+1$.

Expanding-Scope Analysis. We present a *staged* analysis that adapts the *cost* of the analysis to the difficulty of the verification task. Our analysis breaks the verification problem into multiple subproblems and adapts the analysis of each subproblem along two dimensions: the *precision* dimension and the *analysis-scope* dimension. Our analysis adapts the *precision* (and thus the expected cost) of the abstract interpretation [9] to the difficulty of verifying the subproblem. In this aspect, it is similar to the staging in [18].

The novelty of our approach lies in its ability to adapt the *scope* of the analyzed program fragment to the difficulty of the verification task. Unlike existing staged techniques, which analyze whole programs (e.g., [18]), our analysis operates on program *fragments*. The basic idea, inspired by Rountev et. al. [31], is to break the program into fragments and analyze each fragment separately, making conservative assumptions about the parts of the program that lie outside the fragment. However, if the property cannot be verified under the conservative context assumptions, our approach provides for gradually *expanding the scope* of the analyzed fragment.

The premise of this approach is that a large percentage of the potential points of failure in a program can be verified by (i) using a scalable imprecise analysis that conservatively approximates context information, and (ii) employing more precise analyses that consider a limited scope, which may be expanded as needed.

Our approach is based on the principle of expanding scopes; it applies this principle to the problem of dereference safety, which is particularly challenging due to its dependence on aliasing information.

Another approach to modular analysis, that is based on symbolic representation of procedure summaries, can be found in [42].

5. Conclusion

In this paper, we surveyed some of the techniques developed in the SAFE project. Despite the sophisticated techniques used, the end result is that scalability of the approach remains limited. One of the main difficulties remains the sound treatment of large libraries. This is becoming more of a hurdle as software is becoming heavily based on framework code. We believe that practical success lies in the combination of static and dynamic techniques, as well as in moving to higher level languages that enable modular reasoning.

References

[1] Alur R, Cerny P, Madhusudan P, Nam W (2005) Synthesis of interface specifications for java classes. SIGPLAN Not. (40)1:98–109

[2] Ammons G, Bodik R, Larus JR (2002) Mining specifications. In: POPL '02: Proceedings of the 29th ACM SIGPLAN-SIGACT symposium on Principles of programming languages

[3] Andersen LO (1994) Program Analysis and Specialization for the C Programming Language. Dissertation, DIKU, Univ. of Copenhagen

[4] Ashcraft K, Engler D (2002) Using programmer-written compiler extensions to catch security holes. In: Proc. IEEE Symp. on Security and Privacy

[5] Ball T, Rajamani SK (2001) Automatically validating temporal safety properties of interfaces. In: SPIN 2001: SPIN Workshop

[6] Chase D, Wegman M, Zadek K (1990) Analysis of pointers and structures. In: Proc. ACM Conf. on Programming Language Design and Implementation.

[7] Cook JE, Wolf AL (1998) Discovering models of software processes from event-based data. ACM Trans. Softw. Eng. Methodol. 7(3):215–249.

[8] Corbett J, Dwyer M, Hatcliff J, Pasareanu C, Robby, Laubach S, Zheng H (2000) Bandera: Extracting finite-state models from Java source code. In: Proc. Intl. Conf. on Software Eng.

[9] Cousot P, Cousot R (1979) Systematic design of program analysis frameworks. In: Proc. ACM Symp. on Principles of Programming Languages

[10] Das M (2000) Unification-based pointer analysis with directional assignments. In: Conference on Programming Language Design and Implementation (PLDI)

[11] Das M, Lerner S, Seigle M (2002) Esp: Path-sensitive program verification in polynomial time. In: Proc. ACM Conf. on Programming Language Design and Implementation

[12] DeLine R, Fähndrich M (2001) Enforcing high-level protocols in low-level software. In: Proc. ACM Conf. on Programming Language Design and Implementation

[13] Dillig I, Dillig T, Yahav E, Chandra S (2008) The CLOSER: Automating resource management in Java. In: ISMM '08: International Symposium on Memory Management

[14] Dwyer MB, Clarke LA (1994) Data flow analysis for verifying properties of concurrent programs. In: Proc. Second ACM SIGSOFT Symp. on Foundations of Software Engineering

[15] Engler D, Chen DY, Hallem S, Chou A, Chelf B (2001) Bugs as deviant behavior: a general approach to inferring errors in systems code. In: SOSP '01: Proceedings of the eighteenth ACM symposium on Operating systems principles

[16] Ernst MD, Cockrell J, Griswold WG, Notkin D (2001) Dynamically discovering likely program invariants to support program evolution. IEEE Transactions on Software Engineering 27(2):99–123

[17] Field J, Goyal D, Ramalingam G, Yahav E (2003) Typestate verification: Abstraction techniques and complexity results. In: *SAS* '03: 10th International Static Analysis Symposium

[18] Fink S, Yahav E, Dor N, Ramalingam G, Geay E (2006) Effective typestate verification in the presence of aliasing. In: ISSTA '06: Proceedings of the 2006 international symposium on Software testing and analysis (Best paper award)

[19] Fink SJ, Yahav E, Dor N, Ramalingam G, Geay E (2008) Effective typestate verification in the presence of aliasing. ACM Transactions on Software Engineering and Methodology 17(2):1–34.

[20] Flanagan C, Leino KRM, Lillibridge M, Nelson G, Saxe JB, Stata R (2002) Extended static checking for java. In: Proc. ACM Conf. on Programming Language Design and Implementation

[21] Fosdick LD, Osterweil LJ (1976) Data flow analysis in software reliability. ACM Comput. Surv. 8 (Reprinted as Chapter 5)

[22] Foster JS, Terauchi T, Aiken A (2002) Flow-sensitive type qualifiers. In: Proc. ACM Conf. on Programming Language Design and Implementation

[23] Hangal S, Lam MS (2002) Tracking down software bugs using automatic anomaly detection. In: Proc.24th International Conference on Software Engineering

[24] Heintze N, Tardieu O (2001) Ultra-fast aliasing analysis using CLA: A million lines of C code in a second. In: Conference on Programming Language Design and Implementation

[25] Livshits VB, Zimmermann T (2005) Dynamine: Finding common error patterns by mining software revision histories. In: Proc. 13th ACM SIGSOFT International Symposium on the Foundations of Software Engineering

[26] Loginov A, Yahav E, Chandra S, Fink S, Rinetzky N, Nanda MG (2008) Verifying dereference safety via expanding-scope analysis. In: ISSTA '08: International Symposium on Software Testing and Analysis

[27] Nanda MG, Grothoff C, Chandra S (2005) Deriving object typestates in the presence of inter-object references. In: OOPSLA '05: Proceedings of the 20th annual ACM SIGPLAN conference on Object oriented programming, systems, languages, and applications

[28] Naumovich G, Avrunin GS, Clarke LA (1999) Data flow analysis for checking properties of concurrent java programs. In: Proc. Intl. Conf. on Software Eng.

[29] Naumovich G, Clarke LA, Osterweil LJ, Dwyer MB (1997) Verification of concurrent software with FLAVERS. In: Proc. Intl. Conf. on Software Eng.

[30] Ramalingam G, Warshavsky A, Field J, Goyal D, Sagiv M (2002) Deriving specialized program analyses for certifying component-client conformance. In: Proc. ACM Conf. on Programming Language Design and Implementation

[31] Rountev A, Ryder BG, Landi W (1999) Data-flow analysis of program fragments. In: ESEC / SIGSOFT FSE

[32] Sagiv M, Reps T, Wilhelm R (2002) Parametric shape analysis via 3-valued logic. ACM Trans. Program. Lang. Syst. 24(3):217–298.

[33] Shaham R, Yahav E, Kolodner EK, Sagiv M (2003) Establishing local temporal heap safety properties with applications to compile-time memory management. In: SAS '03: 10th International Static Analysis Symposium

[34] Shoham S, Yahav E, Fink S, Pistoia M (2007) Static specification mining using automata-based abstractions. In: ISSTA '07: Proceedings of the 2007 international symposium on Software testing and analysis (Best paper award)

[35] Shoham S, Yahav E, Fink S, Pistoia M (2008) Static specification mining using automata-based abstractions. IEEE Transactions on Software Engineering (TSE) 34(5)

[36] Steensgaard B (1996) Points-to analysis in almost linear time. In: Conference record of OPL '96, 23rd ACM SIGPLAN-SIGACT Symposium on Principles of Programming Languages

[37] Strom RE, Yemini S (1986) Typestate: A programming language concept for enhancing software reliability. IEEE Trans. Software Eng. 12(1):157–171

[38] Weimer W, Necula G (2005) Mining temporal specifications for error detection. In: TACAS

[39] Whaley J, Martin M, Lam M (2002) Automatic extraction of object-oriented component interfaces. In: Proceedings of the International Symposium on Software Testing and Analysis

[40] Whaley J, Martin MC, Lam MS (2002) Automatic extraction of object-oriented component interfaces. In: Proceedings of the International Symposium on Software Testing and Analysis

[41] Yang J, Evans D, Bhardwaj D, Bhat T, Das M (2006) Perracotta: mining temporal API rules from imperfect traces. In: ICSE '06: Proceeding of the 28th international conference on software engineering

[42] Yorsh G, Yahav E, Chandra S (2008) Generating precise and concise procedure summaries. In: POPL '08: Proceedings of the 35th annual ACM SIGPLAN-SIGACT symposium on Principles of programming languages

Checking Concurrent Typestate with Access Permissions in Plural: A Retrospective

Kevin Bierhoff, Nels E. Beckman, and Jonathan Aldrich

Kevin Bierhoff is at Two Sigma Investments, kevin.bierhoff@cs.cmu.edu

Nels E. Beckman is at Google Pittsburgh, nbeckman@cs.cmu.edu

Jonathan Aldrich is at Carnegie Mellon University, jonathan.aldrich@cs.cmu.edu

Abstract Objects often define usage protocols that clients must follow in order for these objects to work properly. In the presence of aliasing, however, it is difficult to check whether all the aliases of an object properly coordinate to enforce the protocol. Plural is a type-based system that can soundly enforce challenging protocols even in concurrent programs. In this paper, we discuss how Plural supports natural idioms for reasoning about programs, leveraging *access permissions* that express the programmer's design intent within the code. We trace the predecessors of the design intent idioms used in Plural, discuss how we have found different forms of design intent to be complimentary, and outline remaining challenges and directions for future work in the area.

1. Introduction

Many libraries and components define *usage protocols*: constraints on the order in which clients may invoke their operations. For example, in Java one must first call `connect` on a `Socket`, after which data may be read or written to the socket. Once `close` is called, reading and writing is no longer permitted.

A recent corpus study of protocols in Java libraries showed that protocol definition is relatively common (in about 7% of types) and protocol use even more so (about 13% of classes) [2]. By comparison, only 2.5% of the types in the Java library define type parameters; thus, the commonality of protocol definition compares well to the use of an important Java language feature. Protocols also cause problems for developers in practice: Jaspan found that almost 20% of the understandable postings in an ASP.NET help forum were related to protocol constraints [10].

Over the past 6 years, we have been developing Plural, a type-based system for specifying and enforcing correct protocol usage. The primary goal of Plural is to

P.L. Tarr, A.L. Wolf (eds.), *Engineering of Software*,
DOI 10.1007/978-3-642-19823-6_4, © Springer-Verlag Berlin Heidelberg 2011

make modular protocol checking practical for realistic object-oriented programs. Preliminary evidence suggests that we have made substantial progress towards this goal: Plural has been applied to multiple open source programs totaling 100kloc+, assuring hundreds of protocol uses and finding many protocol errors and race conditions in well-tested code [4,2].

In this paper, we reflect on the key design characteristics that have enabled Plural to effectively verify realistic software. Many real program designs use substantial aliasing, which provides many design benefits, but which also makes reasoning about protocols difficult, as the multiple clients of an abstraction must coordinate to obey the protocol. Central to the success of our approach was drawing inspiration from how software developers naturally reason about protocols in the presence of aliasing. In order to provide scalability and modularity, our approach also provides natural ways for developers to express their design intent when specifying and verifying protocol usage.

In the next section, we will look at the historical development of protocol checking ideas, with a particular focus on design intent and developer reasoning. Section 3 describes how we further developed these ideas, reviewing the design of the Plural tool from earlier work. Section 4 reflects on our experience with Plural, both in terms of our successes in verifying usage protocols in challenging contexts, and in terms of the limitations we have observed in the methodology. We close in Section 5 with a discussion of future research directions that may enable protocol checking to become a routine part of software development practice.

2. Historical Context

The idea that checking sequences of events is important in software reliability has a long history. Fosdick and Osterweil [13] (reprinted in Chapter 5) were the first to suggest applying program analysis techniques to address the challenges of software reliability. Their Dave system used data flow analysis to detect "data flow anomalies" that are symptomatic of programming errors. These anomalies, such as dead stores to variables or uses of undefined variables, were expressed as problematic sequences of access to a variable: e.g., a read after creation, or two writes with no intervening read. Of course, an anomaly is not necessarily an error; Fosdick and Osterweil state that "a knowledge of the intent of the programmer is necessary to identify the error." Given the context, Fortran programming in the 1970s, it was "unreasonable to assume that the programmer will provide" that design intent. Still, the remark foreshadowed subsequent work that focused on how to make descriptions of limited design intent practical.

A major step in the direction of providing design intent regarding protocols came a decade later, when Strom and Yemini [26] proposed a *typestate* abstraction for enforcing protocol constraints. Their programming language, NIL, allowed the gradual initialization of data structures to be tracked statically. In order to make analysis modular, they proposed that programmers declare a simple form of design intent, specifying the initialization state of these data structures at procedure boundaries.

Olender and Osterweil [24] (reprinted in Chapter 7) observed that it is insufficient to only track fixed properties like data initialization, saying "a flexible sequence analysis tool was needed." Their Cecil specification system allowed the analyst to define which events he or she wished to reason about, to correlate those events to program statements, and then to specify a regular expression that describes a valid sequence of events. The Cesar analysis tool could then verify that the program obeyed the Cecil specification.

Because of the frequent aliasing in object-oriented programs, an application of typestate or sequence analysis in that context required significant advances in specifying and reasoning about aliases. The Turing language included an annotation (now commonly called unique) specifying that a particular argument to a function may not be aliased [16], meaning that program analysis tools need not worry about interference when tracking the state of an object. Hogg proposed the idea of *borrowed* arguments, which may not be stored in fields, and thus help to maintain uniqueness. In addition to borrowing, Hogg proposed read-only method arguments (which we call pure), which allow tools to assume that a method does not change the state of the passed-in object [15]. Noble et al. proposed immutable as a stronger version of pure, specifying that the referenced object cannot be changed through any reference in the program [23]. Following others, we use share to indicate an unrestricted reference, which may be aliased arbitrarily.

These three ideas—a programmer-defined sequence of events, an expression of sequencing design intent via typestate, and an expression of aliasing intent via alias annotations—first came together in DeLine and Fähndrich's Vault [11] project for verifying low-level software. Their later Fugue system [12] adapted protocol checking to the object-oriented setting, developing a methodology for modular typestate checking in the presence of inheritance. Despite these advances, however, Fugue was limited to reasoning about the state of unique objects; it was not able to help developers in the relatively common case of aliased objects with typestate. Our work was motivated by the need to overcome this limitation.

3. Typestate Protocols with Access Permissions

The goal of Plural is to modularly check protocols in realistic object-oriented programs. Checking realistic programs means that we need some way of reasoning about the aliasing that occurs in these designs. Modular checking means we would like to check code one method at a time, using only the specifications of other objects; this requires us to describe the protocol and aliasing state of objects at method boundaries. We accomplish both tasks using access permissions [6], which we have implemented in Plural [7], an automated tool for checking permission-

based typestate protocols in Java. This section is a review of previously published
work [6, 3, 7].

3.1. Access Permissions

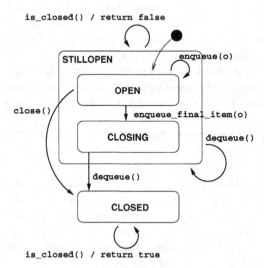

Fig. 4.1. Simplified `Blocking_queue` protocol. Rounded rectangles denote states refining
another state. Arches represent method calls, optionally with return values.

Our static, modular approach to checking API protocols is based on access permissions ("permissions" for short). Permissions are predicates associated with
program references describing the abstract state of that reference and the ways in
which it may be aliased.

In our approach, developers start by specifying their protocol. Figure 1 shows a
simplified protocol for a concurrent blocking queue `Blocking_queue`.[1] Its protocol is modeled as a Statechart [14]. Blocking queues can be used to hand work
items from one producer thread to multiple consumer threads. We will use this
protocol as a running example.

We allow developers to associate objects with a *hierarchy* of typestates, similar
to Statecharts [14]. For example, *OPEN* and *CLOSING* (no more items can be enqueued) can be summarized into *STILLOPEN*, which is the state needed for consumer threads to `dequeue` an item (Fig. 4.1). Hierarchy serves to naturally encode design intent regarding the structure of the state space; we have found it to be
essential for expressing complex protocols compactly [5].

---

[1] We are very grateful to Allen Holub for allowing us to use this example.

Methods correspond to state transitions and are specified with *access permissions* that describe not only the state required and ensured by a method, but also how the method will access the references passed into the method. We distinguish exclusive (unique), exclusive modifying (full), read-only (pure), immutable, and shared access (Table 4.1). Furthermore, permissions include a *state guarantee*, a state that the method promises not to leave [6].

Access through	Current permission has ...	
other permissions	Read/write access	Read-only access
None	unique	unique
Read-only	full	immutable
Read/write	share	pure

Table 4.1. Access permission taxonomy.

Permissions are associated with object references and govern how objects can be accessed through a given reference [6]. They can be seen as rely-guarantee contracts [18] between the current reference and all other references to the same object: permissions provide guarantees about object accesses through other references *and* restrict the current reference to not violate other permissions' assumptions. Thus our permissions encode a natural form of reasoning that has been used in concurrent systems, but adapt it to reason in the context of aliasing in addition to concurrency. Permissions capture three kinds of design intent:

1. *What kinds of references exist?* Our system distinguishes read-only and modifying access, both through the current reference and (if applicable) other references. The resulting 5 permissions (shown in Table 4.1) cover the space of possibilities in a more systematic way than previously described permission systems, and enable natural reasoning based on who is in control of a protocol.
2. *What state is guaranteed?* A guaranteed state supports natural reasoning about agreements ensuring that the multiple clients of an object do not interfere with each other. A client can rely on this guaranteed state even if the referenced object may be modified by other clients.
3. *What do we know about the current state of the object?* Every operation performed on the referenced object can change the object's state. In order to enforce protocols, we ultimately need to keep track of what state the referenced object is currently in.

Permissions can only co-exist if they do not violate each other's assumptions. Thus, the following aliasing situations can occur for a given object: a single reference (unique); a distinguished writer reference (full) with many readers (pure); many writers (share) with many readers (pure); and only readers (immutable and pure) with no writers.

Permissions are linear in order to preserve this invariant. But unlike linear type systems [27], they allow aliasing. This is because permissions can be *split* when aliases are introduced. For example, we can split a unique permission into a full and a pure permission, written unique ⇛ full ⊗ pure, to introduce a read-only alias. Using *fractions* [9] we can also *merge* previously split permissions when aliases disappear (e.g., when a method returns). This allows us to recover a more powerful permission. For example, full ⇛ ½ · share ⊗ ½ · share ⇛ full

3.2. Plural: Access permissions for Java

Our tool, Plural[2], is a plug-in to the Eclipse IDE that implements a previously developed type system [6,3] as a static dataflow analysis for Java [7]. In the remainder of this section, we show example annotations and explain how permissions are tracked and API implementations are verified.

Developer annotations. Developers use Java 5 annotations to specify method pre- and post-conditions with access permissions. Fig. 4.2 shows the Blocking_queue specification with Plural annotations (compare to Fig. 4.1). We use @States to declare two parallel *state dimensions*, *protocol* and *structure*, which represent orthogonal parts of object state (the need for two dimensions in this example will be explained in the next section). Permission-named annotations on methods specify *borrowed* permissions for the receiver. Borrowed permissions are returned to the caller when the method returns. The optional attribute "value" specifies the dimension which the permission gives access to. For example, close borrows a full permission to operate only on the *protocol* dimension. Additionally, a required (or ensured) state must hold when the method is called (or returns), as illustrated by close. Boolean *state tests* such as is_closed can additionally be annotated with the state implied by each return value. Finally, we use @Perm annotations to declare permissions required and ensured by a method separately, such as in the constructor (which "produces" a receiver permission) or enqueue_last_item (which "consumes" a permission).

Permission tracking and local permission inference. Fig. 4.3 shows a simple consumer thread that pulls items of a blocking queue. Plural is able to check whether this code respects the protocol declared for the Blocking_queue interface in Fig. 4.2. This program is buggy! Plural complains that the blocking queue referenced by q is not *STILLOPEN* when dequeue is called. The program seemingly just established that fact when entering the while loop, but because only a pure permission is used for testing the queue's state, Plural rightly assumes that other threads could have closed the queue in between the two calls to q in Fig. 4.2. Plural will no longer issue a warning after the addition of a synchronized block.

---

[2] http://code.google.com/p/pluralism

```
@Refine({
  @States(dim="structure", value={"STRUCTURESTATE"}),
  @States(dim="protocol", value={"CLOSED", "STILLOPEN"}),
  @States(value={"OPEN", "CLOSING"}, refined="STILLOPEN")})
class Blocking_queue {
  // fields omitted
  @Perm(ensures="unique(this) in OPEN,STRUCTURESTATE")
  Blocking_queue() { ... }

  @Share(value="structure")
  @Full(value="protocol", requires="OPEN", ensures="OPEN")
  void enqueue(Object o) { ... }

  @Share(value="structure")
  @Perm(requires="full(this, structure) in OPEN")
  void enqueue_final_item(Object o) { ... }

  @Share(value="structure")
  @Pure(value="protocol", requires="STILLOPEN")
  Object dequeue() { ... }

  @Pure(value="protocol")
  @TrueIndicates("CLOSED") @FalseIndicates("STILLOPEN")
  boolean is_closed() { ... }

  @Full(value="protocol", ensures="CLOSED")
  void close() { ... }
}
```

Fig. 4.2. Simplified `Blocking_queue` specification in Plural (using the typestates from Fig. 4.1).

Notice that we use the same annotations for annotating method parameters in client code that we used for declaring API protocols in the previous section. Plural applies intra-procedural analysis and uses these annotations to track permissions across method calls. Conversely, Plural needs no annotations inside method bodies: based on the annotations provided, Plural infers how permissions flow through method bodies fully automatically. Since Plural is based on a dataflow analysis, it computes the fixed point of a loop without requiring the programmer to write a loop invariant. Local variables, variables of primitive type, and method parameters whose protocols we do not wish to check need not be annotated at all.

API implementation checking. Plural not only checks whether a client of an API follows the protocol required by that API, it can also check that the implementation of the protocol is consistent with its specification. The key abstraction for this is the *state invariant*, which we adapted from Fugue [12]. A state invariant associates a typestate of a class with a predicate over the fields of that class. In our approach, these predicates usually consist of access permissions for fields and look similar to the contents of @Perm annotations (see Fig 4.2).

```
public void consumerThread(
  @Share("structure") @Pure("protocol")
  Blocking_queue<String> q)
{
  while ( !q.is_closed() ) {
    String s = q.dequeue(); //Error! q may have been closed
    System.out.println("I received the message " + s);
  }
  // Thread continues...
}
```

Fig. 4.3. Simple Blocking_queue client with concurrency bug that is detected by Plural.

4. Reflections on Permissions

After six years of verifying object protocols with access permissions, we can reflect on Plural's position in the larger design space of typestate checkers, some of the ways in which the approach is successful, and other ways in which it is not. In this section we will reflect upon some of the more interesting things we have noticed during our experience using Plural.

4.1. Design Space

Typestate checking with Plural represents a compromise between many conflicting goals including expressiveness, the amount of developer input required, and the precision and scale at which Plural is able to perform typestate checking.

- *Expressiveness* here means the ability to express the rules that API designers would like API clients to follow. Plural specifications are by design not as expressive as behavioral specification languages like the JML [19], to keep developer input low and performance at a level acceptable for interactive use. On the other hand, we were repeatedly surprised that access permissions let us encode protocols we didn't think could be encoded with finite state machines. In particular, we found that Plural can express protocols involving multiple objects, such as collections and iterators over them [6], which were previously not expressible in modular typestate checkers [22].

- *Developer input* is the amount of help Plural needs to do its job. Plural limits developer input to Java annotations for method parameters and instance fields (and infers permissions inside methods). We empirically found that about 2 annotations per method are sufficient [4]. This is far less than what full-fledged program verification requires [19]. On the other hand, we decided not to make Plural an inter-procedural analysis (like [22]). That allows Plural to check individual source files quickly, improves analysis precision (in particular for challenging protocols like iterators over collections), and lets Plural check library code for compliance to its advertised protocols [4].
- *Analysis precision* is the amount of false positives (spurious protocol violation warnings) and false negatives (missed actual protocol violations) reported by Plural. Plural is envisioned to work like a typechecker and hence sound [6,3] so false negatives cannot occur. Empirically we found Plural's false positive rate to be less than 6 false positives per kloc in sample open-source programs [7].
- *Scalability* refers to Plural's ability to produce verification results for large programs. Plural performs an intra-procedural dataflow analysis, which can suffer in performance for large methods. On the other hand, dataflow analysis allows Plural to reduce developer input by inferring loop invariants etc. In practice, Plural checked sample open-source programs in less than 200 ms per method (with a 3.2 GHz CPU and 2 GM of RAM) [4]. Since methods are checked individually, Plural scales to programs with arbitrarily many methods.

As suggested above, typestate checking involves compromises. The following subsections explore some of the difficulties and benefits of our approach.

4.2. Difficulties

Even with the introduction of flexible aliasing permissions, the fact remains that verification in the face of aliasing can be quite difficult. One interesting, if unsurprising, observation is that the difficulty associated with verifying a piece of code is directly proportional to the permission types that are used. Code using immutable permissions is almost trivial to verify, as such objects do not change state, and their permissions can be freely duplicated. This nicely lines up with the statements made by those in the functional programming community, who have long argued that effect-free programs are easier to reason about. Our system provides such benefits, while still making the verification of imperative code possible when necessary. Next, unique permissions are quite easy to verify when the relevant objects are unaliased. Permissions give us the freedom to reason about these objects locally, even as side-effecting methods are called. At the other end of the spectrum are share and pure permissions. They can be quite difficult to use because of their limited guarantees. Both essentially say, "all bets are off," with respect to the behavior of an object.

In fact, the share permission is worthy of particular discussion since it was widely used throughout our case studies. In practice, typical methods in an object-oriented program consist of a series of method calls, and often little else! Unfortunately, such methods are poorly suited for verifying share permissions. In the Plural methodology, at any call-site, what we know about states of all the share permissions in the static context must be "forgotten," downgraded to the guaranteed state. This is because of the potential that such objects are modified through a different alias. In a method with numerous call sites, this means that the state of an object of share permission may not persist from the line where it is established to the line where it must be used. As discussed in the next section, state guarantees serve to make share and pure permissions more powerful, but when a state cannot be guaranteed, these permissions can be quite difficult to use.

It was intriguing to see that fractions, one of the most technically interesting pieces of our approach, were not needed terribly often. Fractions are useful for reassembling weak permission pieces together in order to recreate stronger permissions. However, in our experience, most objects in an object-oriented program are either designed to be aliased or unaliased. After initialization, their level of aliased-ness does not typically change much, and if it does, correct performance of the program does not depend on reestablishing stronger permissions. One of the most important use cases for fractional permissions is in concurrent programs, where a number of threads take reference to a shared object, read from the object in parallel and then *join* together, so that the single remaining thread has unique permission. However, with the exception of a few scientific-style applications, such thread forking and joining is not typical in object-oriented programs. In our experience, programs rarely depend on all other references being dropped. This has important implications, because the theoretical and engineering machinery necessary to make fractions work is vast. Doing away with such machinery would leave a system that is more practicable.

4.3. Surprising Power

Fortunately, despite some of the issues we encountered, we found the access permissions approach to be quite powerful, including in some ways we found surprising. First, and as previously mentioned, we got an extraordinary amount of leverage out of state guarantees. Guarantees make even the weakest permissions useful. Such a feature does not exist in other verification systems, in which very little can be done with arbitrarily aliased objects. Often, such permissions will be completely outside of the verification methodology, as in Fugue [12]. Such guarantees are only useful because of state hierarchies, a feature that is novel to our typechecking approach. Hierarchies allow simultaneous references to the same object with varying levels of precision.

A recurring theme in our case studies was an interplay between states and permissions in verification. In our initial conception, we developed a hierarchical system of states expressive enough to model many of the most intricate protocols we observed in the Java standard library. Then, in order to verify such models in the face of aliasing, the system of access permissions was developed. In other words, the specification of protocols and aliasing were conceived as two orthogonal issues. But in practice, there was an interesting interplay between the two. Features designed for the specification of state machines helped in alias-control, and vice-versa.

As an example, consider the specification of the blocking queue in Fig. 4.2. This class is specified with a **structure** dimension, into which the underlying linked list is mapped. This allows both producer and consumer threads, each of which have a **share** permission to this dimension, to modify the linked list, while at the same time, only the producer thread has modifying rights to the **protocol** dimension, which contains the queue's actual protocol. Dimensions were initially conceived for use in classes that define multiple orthogonal state machines. In this case, however, the **structure** dimension defines a protocol that is completely uninteresting; it consists of a single state. It is, rather, because we can map fields into dimensions, and hand out permissions to those dimensions independently, that the queue is given a second dimension at all! Thus, in this example, dimensions serve to naturally encode the intuition that anyone can modify the queue, but the producer is in charge of determining when it can be closed; without dimensions, verifying the queue would be impossible in our system.

Dimensions have proved themselves to be quite a powerful abstraction. In numerous cases we found it useful to store a permission to an object inside the object itself. In order to do this, a permission to one dimension is stored inside another dimension. Consider the `enqueue_final_item` method of the `Blocking_queue` class. When this method is called, the producer is conceptually stating that no further items will be enqueued, but that the consumers are free to dequeue all of the items waiting in the queue. When the last item is dequeued, that consumer is responsible for actually closing the queue. The question arises, "how can a consumer thread call the `close` method when it requires full permission and consumers have only pure?" The answer is that when the producer calls the method to enqueue the final item, it must forfeit its full permission. This permission is then stored in the **structure** dimension, and is used by the consumer thread when the last item is dequeued. This idiom can be thought of as encoding the intuition that permission to do something—closing the queue in this case—is carried through the queue from the producer to the consumer along with the last element.

As another example of the interplay between permissions and states, consider that programs often may pass through various "phases" of aliasing. For example, in one phase an object may be completely unaliased as it is being initialized. Later on, aliases may be created in an unrestricted fashion. Such phases do not exist by coincidence. Developers use these phases to reason about their own programs, to tell themselves what must be true at any given point in the program. It turns out that these phases nicely correspond to abstract states in an object protocol, and permissions can be used in a natural way to express design intent and to aid in verification even in situations where objects do not define protocols in the typical sense. Many times we used such a pattern: an object referencing one or more fields would be constructed in an "uninitialized" state. The invariants associated with this state indicate that the fields are unaliased, perhaps also in their own initialization states. Later on, after all fields have been set up, and the object is in the "initialized," it is legal to call its getter methods, which return aliases to the internal objects.

5. Conclusion and Ongoing Research

Verifying protocols is important due to their ubiquity in modern software development, yet it is difficult in the presence of aliasing. The Plural system has achieved some success by leveraging access permissions, which express design intent with respect to how an object is aliased and how it is used through those aliases. The different features of access permissions were designed to capture the natural forms of reasoning that engineers are using anyway to think about protocols. We have found that the concepts in access permissions are complementary in surprising ways, allowing fairly simple mechanisms to verify quite complex examples.

A number of current research projects have been inspired by Plural and related permissions systems. These projects build on the themes of natural reasoning and design intent, and promise to increase the impact of permissions and extend their benefits into new application areas:

Permission-Based Type Systems. What benefits might there be from designing the type system of a programming language around Plural-like permissions? The Plaid language is an attempt to explore this research question [1]. In Plaid, not only can the interface of an object change (as in typestate), but the representation (fields) and behavior (method implementations) can change as well. Closer integration into the language appears to smooth over some rough edges of Plural (such as syntax and the handling of inheritance) while reducing functionality overlaps (such as duplicate parameterization mechanisms for permissions and Java types). It also opens intriguing new possibilities, such as the ability to test permissions with a run-time cast that can verify, for example, that a reference to an object is really unique.

In looking at permission-based type systems, we have also begun to explore the idea of merging the permission kind and typestate parts of a specification into a single abstraction, and providing customized rules for how different permission abstractions can be split and merged [21]. This design may eventually provide more flexibility compared to the 5 fixed permission kinds in Plural.

Impact Analysis. An innovative use of Plural that does not involve API protocols at all is impact analysis [25], where it can be used to understand implicit state dependencies between components (in contrast to dependencies due to explicit messages being passed between components). When changing a component that has read-only access to shared state then the change cannot impact other component with access to the same state. Plural's distinction between read-only and read-write references allows making this determination, increasing impact analysis precision.

Program Verification. Plural employs fractional permissions [9] specifically for typestate reasoning. But fractions are more broadly useful for reasoning about program behavior under aliasing [8]. More expressive program verification tools that incorporate fractional permissions have since been developed [17, 20]. Plural and these tools show that fractional permissions—which were originally proposed for reasoning about data races—are not only useful for reasoning about concurrent programs but also well-suited for reasoning about sequential programs. In particular, permissions provide new ways to express how different objects collaborate [6].

Acknowledgments We would like to thank the many people who have given us feedback and encouragement over the years, including John Boyland, Frank Pfenning, and Ciera Jaspan. We are also very thankful to Matthew Dwyer for giving us the opportunity to present this article. This work was supported in part by DARPA grant #HR0011-0710019 and NSF grant CCF-0811592. While at Carnegie Mellon University, the second author was supported by a National Science Foundation Graduate Research Fellowship (DGE-0234630).

References

[1] Aldrich J, Sunshine J, Saini D, Sparks Z (2009) Typestate-oriented programming. In: Onward!

[2] Beckman NE (2010) Types for Correct Concurrent API Usage. Dissertation, Carnegie Mellon University

[3] Beckman NE, Bierhoff K, Aldrich J (2008) Verifying correct usage of atomic blocks and typestate. In: Object-Oriented Programming, Systems, Languages & Applications

[4] Bierhoff K (2009) API Protocol Compliance in Object-Oriented Software. Dissertation, Carnegie Mellon University

[5] Bierhoff K, Aldrich J (2005) Lightweight object specification with typestates. In: Joint European Software Engineering Conf. and Symp. on the Foundations of Software Engineering

[6] Bierhoff K, Aldrich J (2007) Modular typestate checking of aliased objects. In: Object-Oriented Programming, Systems, Languages & Applications

[7] Bierhoff K, Beckman NE, Aldrich J (2009) Practical API protocol checking with access permissions. In: European Conference on Object-Oriented Programming

[8] Bornat R, Calcagno C, O'Hearn P, Parkinson M (2005) Permission accounting in separation logic. In: Principles of Programming Languages

[9] Boyland J (2003) Checking interference with fractional permissions. In: International Symposium on Static Analysis

[10] Jaspan C (2010) Proper Plugin Protocols. Thesis proposal, Carnegie Mellon University

[11] DeLine R, Fähndrich M (2001) Enforcing high-level protocols in low-level software. In: Programming Language Design and Implementation

[12] DeLine R, Fähndrich M (2004) Typestates for objects. In: European Conference on Object-Oriented Programming

[13] Fosdick LD, Osterweil LJ (1976) Data flow analysis in software reliability. ACM Computing Surveys 8(3):305–330 (Reprinted as Chapter 5)

[14] Harel D (1987) Statecharts: A visual formalism for complex systems. Science of Computer Programming 8(3):231–274

[15] Hogg J (1991) Islands: Aliasing Protection in Object-Oriented Languages. In: Object-Oriented Programming, Systems, Languages & Applications

[16] Holt RC, Matthews PA, Rosselet JA, Cordy JR (1988) The Turing Language: Design and Definition. Prentice-Hall

[17] Jacobs B, Piessens F (2008) The VeriFast program verifier. Technical Report CW-520, Department of Computer Science, Katholieke Universiteit Leuven

[18] Jones CB (1983) Tentative steps toward a development method for interfering programs. ACM Trans. Programming Languages and Systems 5(4):596–619

[19] Leavens GT, Baker AL, Ruby C (1999) JML: A notation for detailed design. In: Behavioral Specifications of Businesses and Systems. Kluwer Academic Publishers, Boston

[20] Leino, KRM, Müller P (2009) A basis for verifying multi-threaded programs. In: European Symposium on Programming

[21] Militão F, Aldrich J, Caires L (2010) Aliasing control with view-based typestate. In: Formal Techniques for Java-like Programs

[22] Naeem N, Lhoták L (2008) Typestate-like analysis of multiple interacting objects. In: Object-Oriented Programming, Systems, Languages & Applications

[23] Noble J, Vitek J, Potter J (1998) Flexible Alias Protection. In: European Conference on Object-Oriented Programming

[24] Olender KM, Osterweil, LJ (1990) Cecil: A sequencing constraint language for automatic static analysis generation. IEEE Trans. Software Engineering 16(3):268–280 (Reprinted as Chapter 7)

[25] Popescu D, Garcia J, Bierhoff K, Medvidovic, N (2009) Helios: Impact analysis for event-based systems. Technical Report USC-CSSE-2009-517, University of Southern California

[26] Strom RE, Yemini S (1986) Typestate: A programming language concept for enhancing software reliability. IEEE Trans. on Software Engineering 12(1):157–171

[27] Wadler P (1990) Linear types can change the world! In: Programming Concepts and Methods

Data Flow Analysis In Software Reliability[1]

Lloyd D. Fosdick and Leon J. Osterweil

Department of Computer Science, University of Colorado, Boulder, Colorado 80809

Abstract The ways that the methods of data flow analysis can be applied to improve software reliability are described. There is also a review of the basic terminology from graph theory and from data flow analysis in global program optimization. The notation of regular expressions is used to describe actions on data for sets of paths. These expressions provide the basis of a classification scheme for data flow which represents patterns of data flow along paths within subprograms and along paths which cross subprogram boundaries. Fast algorithms, originally introduced for global optimization, are described and it is shown how they can be used to implement the classification scheme. It is then shown how these same algorithms can also be used to detect the presence of data flow anomalies which are symptomatic of programming errors. Finally, some characteristics of and experience with DAVE, a data flow analysis system embodying some of these ideas, are described.

Introduction

For some time we have believed that a careful analysis of the use of data in a program, such as that done in global optimization, could be a powerful means for detecting errors in software and otherwise improving its quality. Our recent experience [27, 28] with a system constructed for this purpose confirms this belief. As so often happens on such projects, our knowledge and understanding of this approach were deepened considerably by the experience gained in constructing this system, although the pressures of meeting various deadlines made it impossible to incorporate all of our developing ideas into the system. Moreover, during its construction advances were made in global optimization algorithms that are useful to us, which for the same reasons could not be incorporated in the system. Our purpose in writing this paper is to draw these various ideas together and present them for the instruction and stimulation of others who are interested in the problem of software reliability.

The phrase "data flow analysis" became firmly established in the literature of global program optimization several years ago through the work of Cocke and Allen [2, 3, 4, 5, 6]. Considerable attention has also been given to data flow by Den-

---

[1] This work supported by NSF Grant DCR 75-09972.

Lloyd Fosdick and Leon J. Osterweil, "Data Flow Analysis in Software Reliability,"
ACM Computing Surveys 8:3 September 1976.
DOI: 10.1145/356674.356676, © 1976 ACM, Inc. Reprinted with permission

nis and his co-workers [9, 29] in a different context, advanced computer architecture. Our own interpretation of data flow analysis is similar to that found in the literature of global program optimization, but our emphasis and objectives are different. Specifically, execution of a computer program normally implies input of data, operations on it, and output of the results of these operations in a sequence determined by the program and the data. We view this sequence of events as a flow of data from input to output in which input values contribute to intermediate results, these in turn contribute to other intermediate results, and so forth until the final results, which presumably are output, are obtained. It is the ordered use of data implicit in this process that is the central object of study in data flow analysis.

Data flow analysis does not imply execution of the program being analyzed. Instead, the program is scanned in a systematic way and information about the use of variables is collected so that certain inferences can be made about the effect of these uses at other points of the program. An example from the context of global optimization will illustrate the point. This example, known as the live variable problem, determines whether the value of some variable is to be used in a computation after some designated computation step. If it is not to be used, space for that variable may be reallocated or an unnecessary assignment of a value can be deleted. To make this determination it is necessary to look in effect at all possible execution sequences starting at the designated execution step to see if the variable under consideration is ever used again in a computation.

This is a difficult problem in any practical situation because of the complexity of execution sequences, the aliasing of variables, the use of external procedures, and other factors. Thus a brute force attack on this problem is doomed to failure. Clever algorithms have been developed for dealing with this and related problems. They do not require explicit consideration of all execution sequences in the program in order to draw correct conclusions about the use of variables. Indeed, the effort expended in scanning through the program to gather information is remarkably small. We discuss some of these algorithms in detail, because they can be adapted to deal with our own set of problems in software reliability, and turn to these problems now.

Data flow in a program is expected to be consistent in various ways. If the value of a variable is needed at some computation step, say the variable α in the step

$$\gamma \leftarrow \alpha + 1,$$

then it is normally assumed that at an earlier computation step a value was assigned to α. If a value is assigned to a variable in a computation step, for example to γ, then it is normally assumed that that value will be used in a later computation step. When the pattern of use of variables is abnormal, so that our expectations of how variables are to be used in a computation are violated, we say there is an anomaly in the data flow. Examples of data flow anomalies are illustrated in the following FORTRAN constructions. The first is

```
   ...
X=A
X=B
```

...

It is clear that the first assignment to X is useless. Why is the statement there at all? Perhaps the author of the program meant to write

    X=A
    Y=B

Another data flow anomaly is represented by the FORTRAN construction

...

    SUBROUTINE SUB(X, Y, Z)
    Z=Y+W

...

Here W is undefined at the point that a value for it is required in the computation. Did the author mean X instead of W, or W instead of X, or was W to be in COMMON? We do not know the answers to these questions, but we do know that there is an anomaly in the data flow.

As these examples suggest, common programming errors cause data flow anomalies. Such errors include misspelling, confusion of names, incorrect parameter usage in external procedure invocations, omission of statements, and similar errors. The presence of a data flow anomaly does not imply that execution of the program will definitely produce incorrect results; it implies only that execution may produce incorrect results. It may produce incorrect results depending on the input data, the operating system, or other environmental factors. It may always produce incorrect results regardless of these factors, or it may never produce incorrect results. The point is that the presence of a data flow anomaly is at least a cause for concern because it often is a symptom of an error. Certainly software containing data flow anomalies is less likely to be reliable than software which does not contain them.

Our primary goal in using data flow analysis is the detection of data flow anomalies. The examples above hardly require very sophisticated techniques for their detection. However, it can easily be imagined how similar anomalies could be embedded in a large body of code in such a way as to be very obscure. The algorithms we will describe make it possible to expose the presence of data flow anomalies in large bodies of code where the patterns of data flow are almost arbitrarily complex. The analysis is not limited to individual procedures, as is often the case in global optimization, but it extends across procedure boundaries to include entire programs composed of many procedures.

The search for data flow anomalies can become expensive to the point of being totally impractical unless careful attention is given to the organization of the search. Our experience shows that a practical approach begins with an initial determination of whether or not any data flow anomalies are present, leaving aside the question of their specific location. This determination of the presence of data flow anomalies is the main subject of our discussion. We will see that fast and effective algorithms can be constructed for making this determination and that these algorithms identify the variables involved in the data flow anomalies and provide rough information about location. Moreover, these algorithms use as their basic

constituents the same algorithms that are employed in global optimization and require the same information, so they could be particularly efficient if included
within an optimizing compiler.

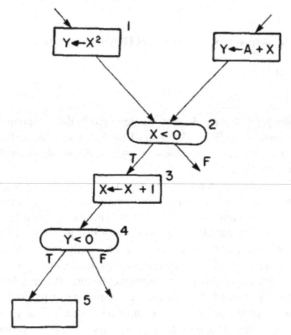

Fig. 5.1. The path in this segment of a flow diagram represented by visiting the boxes in the sequence 1, 2, 3, 4, 5 is not executable. Note that $Y \geq 0$ upon leaving box 1 and this condition is
true upon entry to box 4, thus the exit labeled T could not be taken.

Localizing an anomaly consists in finding a path in the program containing the
anomaly; this raises the question of whether the path is executable. For example,
consider Fig. 5.1 and observe that although there is a path proceeding sequentially
through the boxes 1, 2, 3, 4, 5, this path can never be followed in any execution of
the program. An anomaly on such a nonexecutable path is of no interest. The determination of whether or not a path is executable is particularly difficult, but often can be made with a technique known as symbolic execution [8, 19, 22]. In
symbolic execution the value of a variable is represented as a symbolic expression
in terms of certain variables designated as inputs, rather than as a number. The
symbolic expression for a variable carries enough information that if numerical
values were assigned to the inputs a numerical value could be obtained for the variable. Symbolic execution requires the systematic derivation of these expressions.
Symbolic execution is very costly, and although we believe further study will lead
to more efficient implementations, it seems certain that this will remain relatively
expensive. Therefore a practical approach to anomaly detection should avoid
symbolic execution until it is really necessary. In particular, with presently known

algorithms the least expensive procedure appears to be: 1) determine whether an anomaly is present, 2) find a path containing this anomaly, and then 3) attempt to determine whether the path is executable.

We show that the algorithms presented here do provide information about the presence of anomalies on executable paths. While they do not identify the paths, the fact that they can report the presence of an anomaly on an executable path without resorting to symbolic execution is of considerable practical importance.

While an anomaly can be detected mechanically by the techniques we describe, the detection of an underlying error requires additional effort. The simple examples of data flow anomalies given earlier make it clear that a knowledge of the intent of the programmer is necessary to identify the error. It is unreasonable to assume that the programmer will provide in advance enough additional information about intent that the errors too can be mechanically detected. We visualize the actual error detection as being done manually by the programmer, provided with information about the anomalies present in his program. Obviously, many tools could be provided to make the task easier, but in the end it must be a human who determines the meaning of an anomaly.

We like to think of a system which detects data flow anomalies as a powerful, thorough, tireless critic, which can inspect a program and say to the programmer: "There is something unusual about the way you used the variable α in this statement. Perhaps you should check it." The critic might be even more specific and say, "Surely there is something wrong here. You are trying to use α in the evaluation of this expression, but you have not given a value to α."

The data flow analysis required for detection of anomalies also provides routine but valuable information for the documentation of programs. For example, it provides information about which variables receive values as a result of a procedure invocation and which variables must supply values to a procedure. It identifies the aliasing that results from the multiple definition of COMMON blocks in FORTRAN programs. It identifies regions of the program where some variables are not used at all. It recognizes the order in which procedures may be invoked. This partial list illustrates that the documentation information provided by this mechanism can be useful, not only to the person responsible for its construction, but also to users and maintainers.

We are ready now to enter into the details of this discussion. We begin with a presentation of certain definitions from graph theory. Graphs are an essential tool in data flow analysis, used to represent the execution sequences in a program. We follow this with a discussion of the expressions we use to represent the actions performed on data in a program. The notation introduced here greatly simplifies the later discussion of data flow analysis. Next, we discuss the basic algorithmic tools required for data flow analysis. Then we describe both a technique for segmenting the data flow analysis and the systematic application of this technique to detect data flow anomalies in a program. We conclude with a discussion of the experience we have had with a prototype system based on these ideas.

Basic Definitions—Graphs

Formally a graph is represented by $G(N, E)$ where N is a set of nodes $\{n_1, n_2, \ldots, n_k\}$ and E is a set of ordered pairs of nodes called the edges, $\{(n_{j1}, n_{j2}), (n_{j3}, n_{j4}), \ldots, (n_{jm-1}, n_{jm})\}$, where the n_{ji}s are not necessarily distinct. For example, for the graph in Fig. 5.2,

$$N = \{0, 1, 2, 3, 4\},$$
$$E = \{ (0, 1), (0, 2), (2, 2), (2, 3), (4, 2),$$
$$(1, 4), (4, 1) \}.$$

The number of nodes in the graph is represented by $|N|$ and the number of edges by $|E|$. For the graph in Fig. 5.2, $|N| = 5$ and $|E| = 7$. For any graph $|E| \leq |N|^2$, since a particular ordered pair of nodes may appear at most once in the set E.

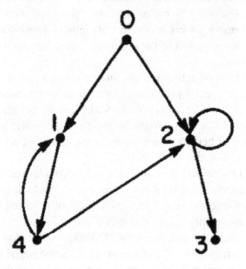

Fig. 5.2. Pictorial representation of a directed graph. The points, labeled here as 0, 1, 2, 3, 4, are called nodes, and the lines joining them are called edges.

For the graphs that will be of interest to us it is usually true that $|E|$ is substantially less than $|N|^2$; in fact it is customary to assume that $|E| \leq k|N|$ where k is a small integer constant.

For an edge, say (n_i, n_j), we say that the edge goes from n_i to n_j ; n_i is called a predecessor of n_j, and n_j is called a successor of n_i. The number of predecessors of a node is called the in-degree of the node, and the number of successors of a node is called the out-degree of the node. For the graph shown in Fig. 5.2, 0 is the predecessor of 1 and 2, the out-degree of 0 is two; 0 is not a successor of any node, it has the in-degree zero. In this figure we also see that 4 is both a successor and a predecessor of 1, and 2 is a successor and predecessor of itself. A node with no predecessors (i.e., in-degree = 0) is called an entry node, and a node with no successors (i.e., out-degree = 0) is called an exit node; in Fig. 5.2, 0 is the only entry node and 3 is the only exit node.

A path in G is a sequence of nodes $n_{j_1}, n_{j_2}, \ldots, n_{j_k}$ such that every adjacent pair $(n_{j_l}, n_{j_{l+1}})$ is in E. We say that this path goes from n_{j_1} to n_{j_k}. In Fig. 5.2, 0, 2, 3 is a path from 0 to 3; 1, 4, 1, is a path from 1 to 1. There is an infinity of paths from 1 to 1: 1, 4, 1; 1, 4, 1, 4, 1; etc. The length of a path is the number of nodes in the path, less one (equivalently, the number of edges); thus the length of the path 0, 1, 4, 1, 4, 2, 3 in Fig. 5.2 is six. $n_{j_1}, n_{j_2}, \ldots, n_{j_k}$ is a path p, then any subsequence of the form $n_{j_i}, n_{j_2}, \ldots, n_{j_k}$ for $1 \leq i < k$ and $1 \leq m \leq k - i$ is also a path, p'; we say that p contains the path p'.

If p is a path from n_i to n_j and $i = j$, then p is a cycle. In Fig. 5.2 the paths 1, 4, 1; 1, 4, 1, 4, 1, and 2, 2 are cycles. The path 0, 1, 4, 1, 4, 2, 3 contains a cycle. A path which contains no cycles is acyclic, and a graph in which all paths are acyclic is an acyclic graph.

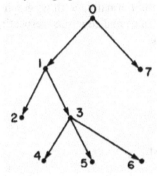

Fig. 5.3. Pictorial representation of a tree rooted at 0. Each node has a unique predecessor except the root which has no predecessor.

If every node of a connected graph has in-degree one and thus has a unique predecessor, except for one node which has in-degree zero, the graph is a tree $T(N, E)$. The graph in Fig. 5.3 is a tree, and if the edges (4, 1), (4, 2), and (2, 2) in Fig. 5.2 are deleted, then the resulting graph is also a tree. The unique entry node is called the root of the tree and the exit nodes are called the leafs. It will be recognized that there is exactly one path from the root to each node in a tree; thus we can speak of a partial ordering of the nodes in a tree. In particular, if there is a path from n_i to n_j in a tree, then n_i comes before n_j in the tree; we say that n_i is an ancestor of n_j and n_j is a descendent of n_i. In Fig. 5.3 every node except 0 is a descendent of 0, and 0 is the ancestor of all of these nodes. Similarly 1 is an ancestor of the nodes 2, 3, 4, 5, 6; on the other hand, 7 is not an ancestor of these nodes. A tree which has been derived from a directed graph by the deletion of certain edges, but of no nodes, is called a spanning tree of the graph.

These elementary definitions are commonly accepted, but they are not universal. Graph theory seems to be notorious for its nonstandard terminology. Additional information on this subject can be found in various texts such as Knuth [24], and Harary [13].

The use of flowcharts as pictorial representations of the flow of control in a computer program dates back to at least 1947 in the work of Goldstine and von Neumann [11], and the advantage of the systematic application of graph theory to computer programming was pointed out in 1960 by Karp [21]. In recent years this approach has been actively developed with numerous articles appearing in the *SIAM Journal on Computing*, the *Journal of the ACM*, and many conference proceedings, especially those of the ACM Special Interest Group on the Theory of Computing. We now introduce some ideas and definitions drawn from this literature pertinent to the subsequent discussion.

When a graph is used to represent the flow of control from one statement to another in a program, it is called a flow graph. A flow graph must have a single entry node, but may have more than one exit node, and there must be a path from the entry node to every node in the flow graph. Formally, a flow graph is represented by $G_F(N, E, n_0)$, where N and E are the node and edge sets, respectively, and n_0, an element of N, is the unique entry node.

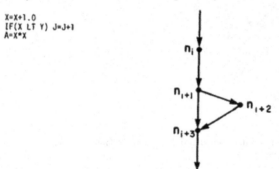

Fig. 5.4. Graph representation of a segment of a FORTRAN program. Node n_i represents the statement X = X + 1.0, node n_{i+1} represents the first part of the IF statement IF(X.LT.Y), node n_{i+2} represents the second part of the IF statement J = J + 1, and node n_{i+3} represents the statement A = X*X.

Generally the nodes of a flow graph represent statements of a program and the edges represent control paths from one statement to the next. In data flow analysis the flow graph is used to guide a search over the statements of a program to determine certain relationships between the uses of data in various statements. Thus before data flow analysis can begin, a correspondence between the statements of a program and the nodes of a flow graph must be established. Unfortunately, difficulties arise in trying to establish this correspondence because of the structure of the language and the requirements of data flow analysis.

Statements in higher level languages can consist of more than one part, and not all parts may be executed when the statement is executed. This is the case with the FORTRAN logical IF, as in

IF(A .LE. 1.0)J = J + 1,

where execution of the statement does not necessarily imply fetching a value of J from storage and changing it. For the purpose of data flow analysis it is desirable to separate such statements into their constituent parts and let each part be represented by a node in G_F as illustrated in Fig. 5.4 for this IF statement.

Statements which reference external procedures pose a far more serious problem. Such statements actually represent sequences of statements. If a node in a flow graph is used to represent an external procedure, then some ambiguities in the data flow analysis arise because the control structure of the represented external procedure is, so to speak, hidden. On the other hand, if we permit this control structure to be completely exposed by placing its flow graph at the point of appearance of the referencing statement, then we invite a combinatorial explosion. Later we will discuss mechanisms for propagating critical data flow information across procedure boundaries in such a way as to avoid a combinatorial explosion, but at the price of losing some information. An important construction used here is the call graph.

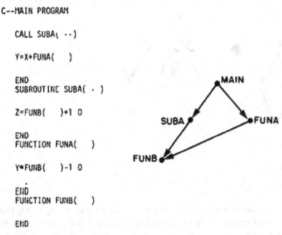

Fig. 5.5. Illustration of the call graph for a FORTRAN program. The nodes have been labeled to identify the program unit represented.

Formally a call graph, which we represent by $G_c(N, E, n_0)$ is identical to a flow graph. However the nodes and edges have a different interpretation: using FORTRAN terminology, the nodes in a call graph represent program units (a main program and subprograms); an edge (n_i, n_j) represents the fact that execution of the program unit n_i will directly invoke execution of the program unit n_j. This is illustrated in Fig. 5.5. In data flow analysis the call graph is used to guide the analysis from one program unit to another in an appropriate order.

In data flow analysis, transformations are sometimes applied to a flow graph to reduce the number of nodes and edges, with nodes in the resulting graph representing larger segments of the program. One of these transformations is illustrated in Fig. 5.6. Here all nodes along paths from a node with a single exit to a node with a single entry and containing only paths with this property are collapsed into a single node. The nodes in the transformed graph are called basic blocks [4, 6, 31]. The important and obvious fact about a basic block is that it represents a set of statements which must be executed sequentially; in particular if any statement of the set is executed, then every statement of the set is executed in the prescribed sequence. Maximality is implicit in the definition of a basic block, i.e., no additional nodes can be collapsed into the node representing a basic block, and the single entry, single exit condition is preserved. It follows easily that in a flow graph in which every node is a basic block, either $E = \emptyset$ (the empty set) or for every $(n_i, n_j) \in E$ either the out-degree of n_i is greater than 1, or the in-degree of n_j is greater than 1, or both of these conditions are satisfied.

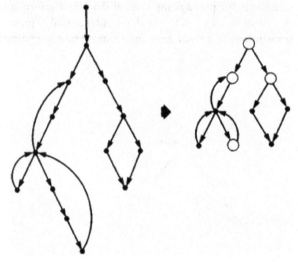

Fig. 5.6. Illustration of a transformation which replaces paths consisting of a single entry and a single exit by a node. In the transformed graph open circles have been used to identify nodes representing paths in the original graph.

Since there are no branches or cycles in a basic block, the analysis of data flow in it is particularly simple. In some situations the reduction of a flow graph in which nodes are statements to one in which the nodes are basic blocks results in a significant reduction in the number of nodes. In such cases there is a practical advantage in performing the data flow analysis on the basic blocks first, then reducing the flow graph to one in which the nodes are the basic blocks and continuing the data flow analysis on the reduced graph. However, we have found that the average reduction in the node count for FORTRAN programs is about 0.56. Thus for FORTRAN it is not clear that a significant advantage can be obtained by this initial preprocessing of basic blocks and reduction of the graph. In global optimization it is customary [4, 6, 31] to use basic blocks, since an intermediate language, close to assembly language, is used and the reduction in node count is significant.

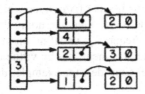

Fig. 5.7. Data structure for the graph in Fig. 5.2. This is a linked successor list representation. The numbered entries could be replaced by pointers to a node table carrying ancillary information.

Knuth [24] is the standard reference for data structures to represent graphs. Hopcroft and Tarjan [17] describe a structure that is particularly efficient for the search algorithms described here and is illustrated in Fig. 5.7. In this structure there is an ordered list of $|N|$ elements, each representing a node and pointing to a linked sublist of successors of that node. The storage cost for this structure is $|N| + 2|E|$ words if we assume that one word is used to store an integer. In practice it is necessary to associate information of variable length with each node so we need to allow for a second pointer with each of the nodes, bringing the storage cost to $2(|N|+|E|)$, so that if $|E| \leq k|N|$, the cost is less than or equal to $2(1 + k)|N|$.

Basic Definitions—Path Expressions to Represent Data Flow

When a statement in a program is executed, the data, represented by the variables, can be affected in several ways, which we distinguish by the terms *reference, define*, and *undefine*. When execution of a statement requires that the value of a variable, say α, be obtained from memory we say that α is referenced in the statement. When execution of a statement assigns a value to a variable, say α, we say that α is defined in the statement. In the FORTRAN statement

A = B + C

B and C are referenced and A is defined, and in the FORTRAN statement

I = I + 1

I is referenced and defined. In the statement

A(I) = B + 1.0

B and I are referenced and A(I) is defined. The undefinition of variables is more complex to describe, and we note here only a few instances. In FORTRAN the DO index becomes undefined when the DO is satisfied, and local variables in a subprogram become undefined when a RETURN is executed. In ALGOL local variables in a block become undefined on exit from the block.

We will want to associate nodes in a flow graph with sets of variables which are referenced, defined, and undefined when the node is executed.[2] In doing this the undefinition operation requires special attention. Frequently, undefinition of a variable occurs not by virtue of executing a particular statement, but by virtue of executing a particular pair of statements in sequence. Consider, for example, the following FORTRAN segment:

```
      ...
      DO 10 K = 1, N
      X = X + A(K)
      Y = Y + A(K)**2
10 CONTINUE
      WRITE---
      ...
```

The DO index K becomes undefined when the WRITE statement is executed after the CONTINUE statement, but it does not become undefined when the statement X = X + A(K) is executed after the CONTINUE statement. Thus it would be more appropriate to associate the undefinition with an edge in the flow graph rather than with a node. However, for consistency we prefer to associate undefinition with nodes, therefore in the example above we would introduce a new node in the flow graph on the edge between nodes for the CONTINUE and the WRITE and would associate with this node the operation of undefinition of K. Similar situations in other languages can be handled in the same way. In the discussion which follows we assume that the undefinition of variables takes place at specific nodes introduced for that purpose and that at such nodes no other operation, reference or definition, takes place. Thus, in particular for a flow graph representation of a FORTRAN subroutine, we would introduce a node which would not correspond to any statement but would represent the undefinition of all local variables on entry to the subroutine. Similarly, at the subroutine exit a node representing undefinition of local variables would be introduced.

Array elements pose a problem, too. While it is obvious that the first element of A is referenced in the FORTRAN statement

```
      B = A(1) + 1.0
```

no particular conclusion can be drawn about which element is referenced in the statement

```
      B = A(K) + 1.0
```

without looking elsewhere. That may be hopeless if the program includes

```
      ...
      READ(5, 100)K
      B = A(K) + 1.0
      ...
```

---

[2] Here and elsewhere we speak of nodes as if they were the objects they represent, thus avoiding cumbersome phrasing such as—"... when the statement represented by the node is executed."

For this reason we adopt the convenient, but unsatisfactory, practice of treating all elements of an array as if they were a single variable.

The abbreviations r, d, and u are used here to stand for reference, define, and undefine, respectively. To represent a sequence of such actions on a variable these abbreviations are written in left-right order corresponding to the order in which these actions occur; for example, in the FORTRAN statement

A = A + B,

the sequence of actions on A is rd, while for B the sequence is simply r. In the FORTRAN program segment

A = B + C
B = A + D
A = A + 1.0
B = A + 2.0
GO TO 10

the sequence of actions on A is drrdr and on B it is rdd. We call these sequences *path expressions*. Habermann [12] has used this same terminology in a different context. The path expressions $\rho u r \rho'$, $\rho dd \rho'$, $\rho du \rho'$ where ρ and ρ' stand for arbitrary sequences of r's, d's, and u's, are called anomalous because each is symptomatic of an error as discussed earlier. Our goal is to determine whether such path expressions are present in a program.

The problem of searching for certain patterns of data actions is common in the field of global program optimization, a subject which receives extensive treatment in a recent book by Schaeffer [31]. Recent articles by Allen and Cocke [6] and Hecht and Ullman [16] discuss aspects of this problem that have particular relevance to our discussion. We focus on two problems in global optimization: the live variable problem and the availability problem. We will show that algorithms used to solve these problems can also be used for the efficient detection of anomalous path expressions.

The live variable problem has already been sketched in the introduction to this paper. The availability problem arises when one seeks to determine whether the value of an expression, say $\alpha + \beta$, which may be required for the execution of a selected statement actually needs to be computed, or may be obtained instead by fetching a previously generated and stored value for it. Since our specific interest in these problems arises in the context of software reliability rather than global optimization, we prefer to characterize and define these problems in a general setting which we now develop.

Consider a flow graph $G_F(N, E, n_0)$. With this flow graph we associate a set known as the token set, denoted by *tok*, consisting of elements $\alpha, \beta, ...$ With every node, $n \in N$, we associate three disjoint sets: $gen(n)$, $kill(n)$, and $null(n)$, subsets of *tok*, with $gen(n) \cup kill(n) \cup null(n) = tok$. This association is illustrated in Fig. 5.8. Informally, one may think of the tokens as representing variables in a program, and the sets $gen(n)$, $kill(n)$, and $null(n)$ as representing certain actions performed on the tokens; for example, if the first action performed on α at node n is a definition then $\alpha \in gen(n)$, if no action is performed on α at node n then

$\alpha \in null(n)$, etc. The specific association of these sets with elements of the program will depend on the problem under consideration, as we illustrate later. For the time being we simply assume that the sets $gen(n)$, $kill(n)$ and $null(n)$ are given.

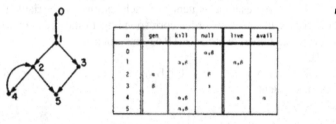

n	gen	kill	null	live	avail
0			α,β		
1		α,β		α,β	
2	α		β		
3	β		α		
4		α,β		α	α
5		α,β			

Fig. 5.8. Illustration of *gen*, *kill* and *null* sets assigned to the nodes of a simple flow graph. The derived *live* and *avail* sets are shown in the last two columns.

For a path p and a token α we are interested in the sequence of sets containing α along the path. We traverse the path, and as each node n is visited we write down g if $\alpha \in gen(n)$, k if $\alpha \in kill(n)$, and 1 if $\alpha \in null(n)$. The resulting sequence of gs, ks, and ls is a path expression for α on p which we denote by $P(p; \alpha)$. Here the alphabet used is $\{g, k, 1\}$ instead of $\{r, d, u\}$. Referring to Fig. 5.8, the path expression α on $p = 0, 1, 2, 4, 2, 5$ is

$$P(0, 1, 2, 4, 2, 5; \alpha) = 1kgkgk,$$

and similarly,

$$P(0, 1, 2, 5; \beta) = 1k1k.$$

We use the notation of regular expressions (e.g., [18, p. 39]) to represent sets of path expressions. For example, the set of path expressions for α on the set of all paths leaving node 1 in Fig. 5.8 is

$$P(1 \rightarrow; \alpha) = g(kg)^*k + 1k,$$

where it is to be noted that the k associated with node 1 is not included. Similarly, the set of path expressions for α on the set of all paths entering node 5 in Fig. 5.8 is

$$P(\rightarrow 5; \alpha) = 1kg(kg)^* + 1k1,$$

where it is to be noted that the k associated with node 5 is not included. These too are called path expressions. We say a path expression is simple if it corresponds to a single path. It is evident that a simple path expression will not contain the symbols * or +.

Path expressions are concatenated in an obvious way. Thus, referring again to Fig. 5.8,

$$P(1; \alpha)P(1 \rightarrow; \alpha) = k(g(kg)^*k + 1k)$$

and

$$P(\rightarrow 5; \alpha)P(5; \alpha) = (1kg(kg)^* + 1k1)k.$$

Two path expressions representing identical sets of simple path expressions are equivalent. Thus, using the last path expression above, it is easily seen that

$$(1kg(kg)^* + 1k1)k \equiv 1kg(kg)^*k + 1k1k.$$

Furthermore, two path expressions differing only by transformations of the form

$$1g \to g, 1k \to k, g1 \to g, k1 \to k, 11 \to 1,$$
$$\text{and } 1 + 1 \to 1$$

are equivalent. For example

$$1 + 1^*gk + kk1 + 11 \equiv gk + kk + 1.$$

The final step in this general development is to introduce the sets *live(n)* and *avail(n)*, subsets of *tok*. For each $\alpha \in tok$ and each $n \in N$ of $G_F(N, E, n_0)$.

$$\alpha \in live(n) \quad \text{if and only if} \quad P(n \to; \alpha) \equiv g_\rho + \rho'$$

and

$$\alpha \in avail(n) \quad \text{if and only if} \quad P(\to n; \alpha) \equiv \rho g,$$

where ρ and ρ' stand for arbitrary path expressions. In words, $\alpha \in live(n)$ if and only if on some path from n the first "action" on α, other than null, is g; and $\alpha \in avail(n)$ if and only if the last action on α, other than null, on all paths entering n is g. These definitions are illustrated in Fig. 5.8, where the *live* and *avail* sets are shown.

The live variable problem is: given $G_F(N, E, n_0)$, *tok*, and, for every $n \in N$, *kill(n)*, *gen(n)*, and *null(n)* determine *live(n)* for every $n \in N$. The availability problem is: given $G_F(N, E, n_0)$, *tok*, and for every $n \in N$, *kill(n)*, *gen(n)*, and *null(n)* determine *avail(n)* for every $n \in N$. While one might solve these two problems directly in terms of the definitions, that is by deriving the path expressions and determining if they have the correct form, such an approach would be hopelessly slow except in the most trivial cases. Instead, these problems are attacked by using search algorithms directly on G_F which avoid explicit determination of path expressions, but which do provide enough information about the form of the path expression to solve the live variable problem and the availability problem. These algorithms are discussed in the next section.

Before closing this section we show how these tools are helpful with a simple example. In this example the problem is to detect the presence of path expressions (now in terms of references, definitions, and undefinitions) of the form $\rho dd\rho'$. Assume that we can construct a flow graph for the program in which the nodes are statements or parts of statements, so that the following rules of membership for tokens representing variables can be trivially applied at every node:

1) $\alpha \in kill(n)$ if α is referenced at n, or undefined at n;
2) $\alpha \in gen(n)$ if α is defined at n and $\alpha \notin kill(n)$;
3) $\alpha \in null(n)$ otherwise.

After these sets have been determined, suppose the live variable problem is solved. Now if α is defined at n and if $\alpha \in live(n)$ it follows easily that there is a path expression of the form $\rho dd\rho'$ in the flow graph. The truth of this conclusion is seen from the fact that $\alpha \in live(n)$ implies $P(n \to; \alpha) \equiv g_\rho + \rho'$ and since g stands for a definition

$$P(n \to; \alpha) \equiv d_\rho + \rho',$$

hence

$$P(n; \alpha)P(n \to; \alpha) \equiv dd_\rho + \rho''.$$

Conversely, if at every node at which α is defined $\alpha \epsilon \, live(n)$, then one may similarly conclude there is no path expression of the form $\rho dd \rho'$; i.e., there are no data flow anomalies of this type.

Algorithms to Solve the Live Variable Problem and the Availability Problem

In the last section the live variable problem and the availability problem were defined and a simple example was given to show how a solution to the live variable problem can be used to determine the presence or absence of data flow anomalies. In this section we describe particular algorithms for solving the live variable problem and the availability problem. Several such algorithms have appeared in the literature [6, 16, 23, 31, 35]. The pair of algorithms we have chosen for discussion do not have the lowest asymptotic bound on execution time. However, they are simpler and more widely applicable than others and their speed is competitive.

The algorithms involve a search over a flow graph in which the nodes are visited in a specific order derived from a depth first search. This search procedure is defined by the following algorithm, where it is assumed that a flow graph $G_F(N, E, n_0)$ is given, and a push down stack is available for storage.

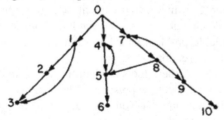

Fig. 5.9. Numbering of the nodes of a graph in the order in which they are first visited during a depth first search. This numbering is called preorder.

Algorithm *Depth First Search*:
1. Push the entry node on a stack and mark it (this is the first node visited, nodes are marked to prevent visiting them more than once).
2. While the stack is not empty do the following:
   2.1 While there is an unmarked edge from the node at the top of the stack, do the following:
   2.1.1 Select an unmarked edge from the node at the top of the stack and mark it (edges are marked to prevent selecting them more than once);
   2.1.2 If the node at the head of the selected edge is unmarked, then mark it and push it on the stack (this is the next node visited);

2.2 Pop the stack;
   3. Stop.

In Fig. 5.9 the nodes of the flow graph are numbered in the order in which they are first visited during the depth first search. We follow the convention that the leftmost edge (as the graph is drawn) not yet marked is the next edge selected in step 2.1.1; thus the numbering of the successor nodes of a node increases from left to right in the figure. The ordering of the nodes implied by this numbering is called preorder [24]. The order in which the nodes are popped from the stack during the depth first search is called postorder [16, 24]. In Fig. 5.10 the nodes are numbered in postorder. This numbering could be generated in the following way. Introduce a counter in the depth first search algorithm and initialize it to 0 in step 1. In step 2.2, before popping the stack, number the node at the top of the stack with the counter value and then increment the counter. If each postorder node number, say k, is complemented with respect to $|N|$, i.e., $k' \leftarrow |N| - k$, then the new numbering represents an ordering known as r-postorder [16]. This numbering is shown in parentheses in Fig. 5.10.

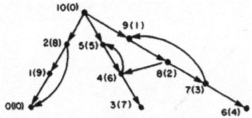

Fig. 5.10. Illustration of postorder and r-postorder numbering of the nodes of a graph. The r-postorder numbers are in parentheses.

The depth first spanning tree [33] of a flow graph is an important construction for the analysis of data flow. This construction can be obtained from the depth first search algorithm in the following way. Add a set E' which is initialized to empty in step 1. In step 2.1.2 put the selected edge in E' if the head of the selected edge is unmarked. After execution of this modified depth first search algorithm, the tree $T(N, E')$ is the depth first spanning tree of $G_F(N, E, n_o)$, the flow graph on which the search was executed. The depth first spanning tree of the flow graph in Fig. 5.9 is shown in Fig. 5.11. The edges in the set $E - E'$ fall into three distinct groups:

    1) forward edges with respect to T: $e \in E - E'$, is in this group if this edge goes from an ancestor to a descendant of T;

    2) back edges with respect to T: $e \in E - E'$, is in this group if this edge goes from a descendant to an ancestor of T, or if this edge goes from a node to itself;

    3) cross edges with respect to T: $e \in E - E'$, is in this group if this edge goes between two nodes not related by the ancestor-descendant relationship.

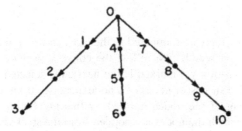

Fig. 5.11. Depth first spanning tree of the flow graph shown in Fig. 5.9. Nodes are numbered in preorder.

These edges are shown in Fig. 5.12 for the flow graph in Fig. 5.9 and for the tree shown in Fig. 5.11 derived from it. Tarjan [34] has shown that it is possible to perform a depth first search, number the nodes in preorder, determine the number of descendants for each node in the depth first spanning tree, and determine the backedges, forward edges, and cross edges, all in $O(|N| + |E|)$ time.

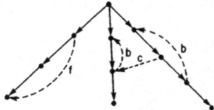

Fig. 5.12. Forward edges, back edges, and cross edges marked by dashed lines and lettered f, b, e, respectively. This grouping is with respect to the tree shown in Fig. 5.11.

This way of characterizing the edges in a flow graph is particularly valuable for an analysis of data flow patterns. It is to be noted in particular that if the back edges are deleted in Fig. 5.12, then the resultant graph is acyclic. This is true in general. The cycles in a graph cause the major complication in the analysis of data flow. All of the data flow analysis algorithms would have $O(|E|)$ execution times if cycles were absent, but with cycles present they have execution times which generally grow faster than linearly in $|E|$ as $|E| \to \infty$. By focusing attention on back edges one can more easily see how cycles add to the complexity of a data flow analysis algorithm. Some data flow analysis algorithms require the flow graph to be reducible. This property is characterized in the theorem below, which follows from results of Hecht and Ullman [15]:

THEOREM. G_F is reducible if and only if n_i dominates n_j in G_F for each back edge (n_j, n_i), where $j \neq i$, with respect to a depth first spanning tree of G_F.

The notion of dominance which is introduced here is defined as follows. Given a pair of nodes n_i and n_j in G_F, n_i dominates n_j if and only if every path from n_0 to n_j contains n_i. It can be easily seen from this theorem that the flow graph in Fig. 5.9

is not reducible. Notice that the edge (5, 4) is a back edge (cf. Fig. 5.12) with respect to the spanning tree in Fig. 5.11. On the other hand, node 4 does not dominate node 5; notice the path 0, 7, 8, 5. If this back edge is deleted, then the remaining graph is reducible. The frequently mentioned paradigm of a nonreducible flow graph is shown in Fig. 5.13.

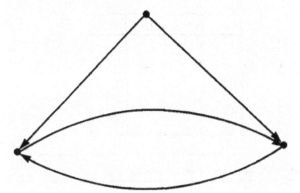

Fig. 5.13. Paradigm of a nonreducible graph.

Some experiments [6, 25] have led to the general belief that flow graphs derived from actual programs often are reducible. For flow graphs with this property, particularly fast algorithms have been developed [1, 23, 35] for the live variable problem and the availability problem. Recently two algorithms for solving these problems on any flow graph were presented by Hecht and Ullman [16]. While these algorithms are not always as fast as the others, they are competitive and they have the distinct advantages of simplicity and generality (they are not restricted to reducible flow graphs). These algorithms are described below.

The following algorithm [16] determines the *live* sets of a flow graph. This algorithm assumes that the nodes have been numbered 0, 1, ..., n in postorder and refers to the nodes by the postorder number.

Here $S(j)$ denotes the set of successors of node j, and $\emptyset$ denotes the empty set.
Algorithm LIVE:
> **for** $j \leftarrow 0$ **to** n **do** $live(j) \leftarrow \emptyset$;
>> *change* $\leftarrow$ **true**;
>> **while** *change* **do**
>>> **begin**
>>>> *change* $\leftarrow$ **false**;
>>>> **for** $j \leftarrow 0$ **to** n **do**
>>>>> **begin**
>>>>>> *previous* $\leftarrow live(j)$;

(*) $live(j) \leftarrow \underset{k \in S(j)}{\cup} \big((live(k) \cap (tok - kill(k)) \big) \cup gen(k))$

>>>>>> **if** *previous* $\neq live(j)$ **then**

```
                change ← true;
            end
        end
    stop
```

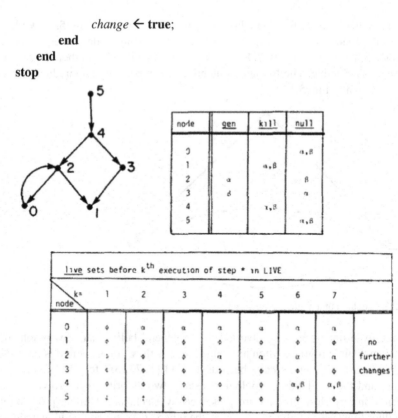

Fig. 5.14. Illustration of the steps in the creation of the *live* sets by algorithm LIVE for a simple flow graph. Nodes are numbered in postorder. The correct *live* sets are obtained after five executions of step *, however seven more executions are required before no change to the sets is recognized which then terminates execution.

We refer to the paper by Hecht and Ullman [16] for a proof of correctness of this algorithm. Its operation is illustrated in Fig. 5.14 where the *live* sets are indicated before each execution of the step labeled by (*). It is easily verified that the total number of times step (*) is executed in this example is twelve: first the **for** loop is executed six times, making one pass over the six nodes, then since there was a change to the *live* sets a second pass is made, during which no change occurs to the *live* sets, and this completes execution.

The correctness of the algorithm does not depend on the order in which the nodes are visited, but the execution time does. In the simple example just considered it is easily verified that if the nodes were visited in the order 5, 4, 2, 3, 0, 1 then eighteen executions of step (*) would be required; note that in this case α is not put in the *live* set of node 2 during the first pass. The nodes are visited in postorder to ensure a relatively rapid termination of the algorithm. In particular, if the flow graph is acyclic, then after the **while** loop is executed once all *live* sets are correct; one more execution of the **while** loop is required to establish that there are no further changes to the live sets. Thus for an acyclic flow graph the step (*) is executed $2 \mid N \mid$ times. If there is one back edge, then the effect of a *gen* can be propagated to a lower numbered (in postorder) node, and it is not too difficult to see that upon completion of the second (at most) execution of the **while** loop all *live* sets will be correct. Thus for a flow graph with one back edge the step (*) is executed $3 \mid N \mid$ times at most. Hecht and Ullman [16] have shown that if τ is the number of times the step (*) is executed, then

$$\tau \leq (2 + d)|N|,$$

where d is the largest number of back edges in any acyclic path in the graph. For a reducible flow graph it has been shown [15] that the back edges are unique, but if the flow graph is not reducible then the back edges will depend on the depth first spanning tree. The d appearing above refers to the back edges with respect to the spanning tree generated to establish the postorder numbering of the nodes.

We now present an algorithm [16] to determine the *avail* sets of a flow graph. This algorithm assumes that the nodes have been numbered 0, 1, ..., n in r-postorder and refers to the nodes by the r-postorder number. Here $P(j)$ denotes the set of predecessors of node j, and $\emptyset$ denotes the empty set.

Algorithm AVAIL:

$avail\ (0) \leftarrow \emptyset$;

for $j \leftarrow 1$ **to** n **do** $avail(j) \leftarrow tok$;

$change \leftarrow$ **true**;

while $change$ **do**

  begin

    $change \leftarrow$ **false**

    for $j \leftarrow 1$ **to** n **do**

      begin

        $previous \leftarrow avail(j)$;

        $avail(j) \leftarrow \bigcap_{k \in P(j)} \big(\big(avail(k) \cap \big(tok - kill(k)\big)\big) \cup gen(k)\big)$;

        if $previous \neq avail(j)$ **then**

          $change \leftarrow$ **true**

      end

  end

stop

We refer again to the paper by Hecht and Ullman [16] for a proof of correctness of this algorithm. Its operation is illustrated in Fig. 5.15 where the *avail* sets are indicated before each execution of the step labeled by (*). Here, as with the example for LIVE it is easy to verify that step (*) is executed twelve times. With the exception of the entry node, which is treated separately, it does not matter in what order the remaining nodes are visited in the **while** loop so far as correctness is concerned, but it does matter for the execution time. Again, the back edges are a critical factor. With τ and d as defined before, Hecht and Ullman [16] show that

$$\tau \leq (2 + d)(|N| - 1).$$

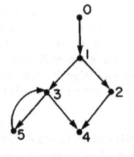

node	gen	kill	null
0	β		α
1		α,β	
2	α,β		
3	α		β
4		α,β	
5			α,β

avail sets before k^{th} execution of step * in AVAIL

k= node	1	2	3	4	5	6	7	
0	φ	φ	φ	φ	φ	φ	φ	
1	α,β	β	β	β	β	β	β	no
2	α,β	α,β	φ	φ	φ	φ	φ	further
3	α,β	α,β	α,β	φ	φ	φ	φ	changes
4	α,β	α,β	α,β	α,β	α	α	α	
5	α,β	α,β	α,β	α,β	α,β	α	α	

Fig. 5.15. Illustration of the steps in the creation of the *avail* sets by algorithm AVAIL for a simple flow graph. Nodes are numbered in *r*-postorder. The correct *avail* sets are obtained after five executions of step *, however seven more executions are required before no change to the sets is recognized which then terminates execution.

Empirical evidence obtained by Knuth [25] leads Hecht and Ullman [16] to the conclusion that in practice one can expect $d \le 6$ and on the average $d \le 2.75$ for FORTRAN programs. However, it is to be noted that there are pathological situations, as shown in Fig. 5.16, for which the execution time is much larger than these numbers indicate.

Segmentation of Data Flow

Normally a program consists of a main program and a number of subprograms or external procedures. This segmentation of the program is a natural basis for the segmentation of the data flow analysis. Here we describe how this is done in such a way as to permit detection of data flow anomalies on paths which cross procedure boundaries. We will see that the system for doing this naturally includes the detection of data flow anomalies on paths which do not cross procedure boundaries. In this section we describe the identification and representation of the data flow, and in the next section we describe the detection of anomalous data flow.

Fig. 5.16. Pathological situation in which the execution time for the availability algorithm is unusually long. Here $d = |N| - 3$, $\tau = (|N| - 1)^2$ assuming $\alpha \in gen(n_i)$ and $\alpha \in kill(n_j)$ and is not in any other *gen* or *kill* sets.

We make several assumptions at the outset. The first concerns aliasing, the use of different names to represent the same datum. In crossing a procedure boundary the name of a datum typically changes from the so-called actual name used in the invoking procedure to the so-called dummy name used in the invoked procedure. It is assumed here that the aliases for a datum are known and that a single token identifier is used to represent them. Thus, in particular, in our notation for representing actions on a token α along some path p we use $P(p; \alpha)$ even when p crosses a procedure boundary and the datum represented by α is known by different names in the two procedures. The second assumption we make is that the procedures under consideration have a single entry and a single exit. We could permit multiple entries and multiple exits, but it would complicate the discussion without adding anything really important to it. While we will discuss the segments as if they were procedures, it will be obvious that the discussion applies equally well to any single-entry, single-exit segment of a program. Our most restrictive assumption is that the call graph for the program is acyclic. This excludes recursion. We will discuss this restriction later.

Let us consider a flow graph $G_F(N, E, n_0)$ in which some node invokes an external procedure, as illustrated in Fig. 5.17. In order to analyze the data flow in $G_F(N, E, n_0)$ it is necessary to know certain facts about the data flow in the invoked procedure. In particular we need to know enough about the data flow in the invoked procedure to be able to detect anomalous patterns in the flow across the procedure boundaries. Referring to G_F in Fig. 5.17 and considering a single token α, it becomes evident that we need to recognize three cases to detect anomalous patterns of the form $\rho u r \rho'$ on paths crossing the procedure boundary:

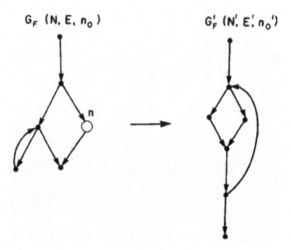

Fig. 5.17. At node n in $G_F(N, E, n_0)$ an external procedure is invoked. The flow graph of the invoked procedure is represented by $G_F'(N', E', n_0')$.

a) $P(\rightarrow n; \alpha) \equiv \rho u + \rho'$,
   $P(n; \alpha) \equiv r_\rho + \rho'$;
b) $P(n; \alpha) \equiv \rho u + \rho'$,
   $P(n \rightarrow; \alpha) \equiv r_\rho + \rho'$;
c) $P(\rightarrow n; \alpha) \equiv \rho u + \rho'$,
   $P(n; \alpha) \equiv 1 + \rho'$;
   $P(n \rightarrow; \alpha) \equiv r_\rho + \rho'$.

Thus all we need to know about the data flow in the invoked procedure is whether $P(n; \alpha)$ has one of the following three forms: $r\rho + \rho'$, $\rho u + \rho'$, $1 + \rho'$. The last form represents the situation in which there is at least one path through the invoked procedure on which no reference, no definition, and no undefinition of α takes place. It is evident that a particular $P(n; \alpha)$ could have more than one of these forms, e.g., $ru + 1$ has all three forms. Similar consideration of the problem of detecting anomalous path expressions of the form $\rho dd\rho'$ and $\rho du\rho'$ leads to the conclusion that the following additional forms for $P(n; \alpha)$ need to be recognized: $d\rho + \rho'$, $\rho d + \rho'$, $u\rho + \rho'$.

We now wish to extend these ideas to permit recognition of situations where an anomalous path expression exists on all paths entering or leaving a node. This recognition is important because it permits us to conclude something about the presence or absence of anomalous path expressions on executable paths. Fig. 5.1 makes it clear that some paths in a flow graph may not be executable, and it is evident that anomalous path expressions on them are not important. Only anomalous path expressions on executable paths are important as indicators of a possible error. Unfortunately, the recognition of executable paths is difficult[3], but if we make the reasonable assumption that every node is on some executable path, then if all paths through a node are known to be anomalous we may draw the very useful conclusion that there is an anomalous expression on an executable path. Certain additional forms for path expressions need to be distinguished to achieve this. We observe, for example, that if

$$P(\to n; \alpha) \equiv \rho u \quad \text{and} \quad P(n; \alpha) \equiv r\rho',$$

then on every path in G_F of the form $n_0, \ldots, n, \ldots$ there is an anomalous path expression $\rho u r \rho'$. Thus it would be desirable to be able to distinguish the form $r\rho$. Notice also that if

$$P(\to n; \alpha) \equiv \rho u, \quad P(n; \alpha) \equiv r\rho' + 1,$$
$$P(n \to; \alpha) \equiv r\rho',$$

then the same conclusion can be drawn, so it is also desirable to distinguish the form $r\rho + 1$. Similar considerations show the need for recognizing the forms ρu, $\rho u + 1$, 1 and similar considerations for anomalous expressions of the form $\rho dd\rho'$, and $\rho dup'$ lead to corresponding forms involving d and u.

label	path expression
A_x	$x\rho$
B_x	$x\rho + 1$
C_x	$x\rho + \rho'$
D_x	ρx
E_x	$\rho x + 1$
F_x	$\rho x + \rho'$
I	1

Fig. 5.18. Seven forms for path expression in single-entry, single-exit flow graphs and labels used to identify them. The parameter x stands for r, d, or u.

Collecting these results leads to the seven forms for path expressions shown in Fig. 5.18. Corresponding sets $A_x(n)$, $B_x(n)$, ..., $I(n)$ which are subsets of the token set are defined as follows:

$$\alpha \in A_x(n) \quad \text{if} \quad P(n; \alpha) \equiv x\rho;$$
$$\alpha \in B_x(n) \quad \text{if} \quad P(n; \alpha) \equiv x\rho + 1;$$
$$\ldots$$
$$\alpha \in I(n) \quad \text{if} \quad P(n; \alpha) \equiv 1(n).$$

These sets are called *path sets*. Although this classification scheme was developed for situations in which n represents a procedure invocation as illustrated in

---

[3] Indeed this problem is not solvable in general, for if we could solve it we could solve the halting problem [18].

Fig. 5.17, it will be recognized that it applies when n is a simple node representing, say, an assignment statement. For example if n represents $\alpha \leftarrow \alpha + \beta$ and $tok = \{\alpha, \beta, \gamma\}$, then

$$\alpha \in A_r(n), \quad \alpha \in C_r(n) \quad \beta \in A_r(n),$$
$$\beta \in C_r(n) \quad \alpha \in D_d(n), \quad \alpha \in F_d(n)$$
$$\gamma \in I(n).$$

In such simple cases membership in the sets can be determined by rather obvious rules. On the other hand, when the node represents a procedure invocation, determination of membership in the path sets requires an analysis of the data flow in the procedure. It is this problem to which we now direct our attention.

Suppose the path sets for node n' are to be determined. We assume that n' represents the invocation of an external procedure with flow graph G_F and that the path sets for the nodes of G_F have been determined already. (Our focus of attention now shifts to the invoked procedure and to avoid an excess of primes we have switched the role of primed and unprimed quantities shown in Fig. 5.17.) We also assume that no data actions take place at the entry node and exit node of G_F; thus

$$I(n_0) = tok \text{ and } I(n_{exit}) = tok.$$

This assumption is not restrictive since we can augment G_F by attaching a new entry node and new exit node with these properties without affecting the data flow patterns. The algorithms for determining the path sets are presented informally below. They are presented in alphabetic order; however, as will become apparent, a different order is required for their execution. A satisfactory execution order is $A_x(n'), C_x(n'), B_x(n'), D_x(n'), F_x(n'), E_x(n'), I(n')$.

Algorithm *Determine $A_x(n')$*

1) for all n such that $n \in N - \{n_{exit}\}$ do
   $$null(n) \leftarrow I(n) \cup B_x(n);$$
   $$kill(n) \leftarrow A_x(n);$$
   $$gen(n) \leftarrow tok - (kill(n) \cup null(n));$$
2) $null(n_{exit}) \leftarrow \emptyset;$
   $kill(n_{exit}) \leftarrow \emptyset;$
   $gen(n_{exit}) \leftarrow tok;$
3) execute LIVE on G_F;
4) $A_x(n') \leftarrow tok - live(n_0);$
   {comment--the *null* sets are not explicitly needed but are included here for clarity}.

Algorithm *Determine $B_x(n')$*

1) for all n such that $n \in N$ do
   $$null(n) \leftarrow I(n) \cup B_x(n);$$
   $$kill(n) \leftarrow A_x(n);$$
   $$gen(n) \leftarrow tok - (kill(n) \cup null(n));$$
2) execute LIVE on G_F;
3) $B_x(n') \leftarrow (tok - live(n_0)) \cap (tok - A_x(n')) \cap C_x(n').$

Algorithm *Determine* $C_x(n')$
  1) for all n such that $n \in N$ do
     $gen(n) \leftarrow C_x(n)$;
     $kill(n) \leftarrow (A_y(n) \cup A_z(n))$;
       { comment—x, y, z is any permutation of r, d, u }
     $null(n) \leftarrow tok - (gen(n) \cup kill(n))'$;
  2) execute LIVE on G_F;
  3) $C_x(n') \leftarrow live(n_0)$.

Algorithm *Determine* $D_x(n')$
  1) for all n such that $n \in N$ do
     $gen(n) \leftarrow D_x(n)$;
     $kill(n) \leftarrow (F_y(n) \cup F_z(n))$;
       { comment—x, y, z is any permutation of r, d, u }
     $null(n) \leftarrow tok - (gen(n) \cup kill(n))$;
  2) execute AVAIL on G_F;
  3) $D_x(n') \leftarrow avail(n_{exit})$.

Algorithm *Determine* $E_x(n')$
  1) for all n such that $n \in N - \{n_0\}$ do
     $gen(n) \leftarrow D_x(n)$;
     $kill(n) \leftarrow F_y(n) \cup F_z(n)$;
       { comment—x, y, z is any permutation of r, d, u }
     $null(n) \leftarrow tok - (gen(n) \cup kill(n))$;
  2) $gen(n_0) \leftarrow tok$;
     $kill(n_0) \leftarrow \emptyset$;
     $null(n_0) \leftarrow \emptyset$;
  3) execute AVAIL;
  4) $E_x(n') \leftarrow avail(n_{exit}) \cap (tok - D_x(n')) \cap F_x(n')$.

Algorithm *Determine* $F_x(n')$
  1) for all n such that $n \in N - \{n_0\}$ do
     $gen(n) \leftarrow D_y(n) \cup D_z(n)$;
       { comment—x, y, z is any permutation of r, d, u }
     $kill(n) \leftarrow F_x(n)$;
     $null(n) \leftarrow tok - (kill(n) \cup gen(n))$;
  2) $gen(n_0) \leftarrow tok$;
     $kill(n_0) \leftarrow \emptyset$;
     $null(n_0) \leftarrow \emptyset$;
  3) execute AVAIL;
  4) $F_x(n') \leftarrow tok - avail(n_{exit})$.

Algorithm *Determine* $I(n')$

1) $I(n') \leftarrow \bigcap_{n \in N} I(n)$.

Since LIVE and AVAIL terminate, it is obvious that these algorithms terminate. Proofs of correctness for some of these algorithms are presented below.

Proof *Determination of $A_x(n')$ is correct*

Let $\alpha \in tok$. By step 4 of the algorithm $\alpha \in A_x(n')$ if and only if $\alpha \notin live(n_0)$. Take the "if" part first:

$$\alpha \notin live(n_0) \Rightarrow P(n_0 \to; \alpha) \not\equiv g\rho + \rho'$$
$$\Rightarrow P(n_0 \to; \alpha) \equiv k\rho \text{ or } P(n_0 \to; \alpha) \equiv k\rho + 1,$$

or $P(n_0 \to; \alpha) \equiv 1$. The last two alternatives are ruled out because by step 2 of the algorithm $gen(n_{exit}) = tok$. Consequently, because of the construction of the *kill* sets in step 1, $\alpha \notin live(n_0) \Rightarrow P(n_0 \to; \alpha) \equiv x\rho$. We observe $(n' \to; \alpha) = P(n_0 \to; \alpha) \, P(n_0 \to; \alpha) = P(n_0 \to; \alpha)$, the last equality following from the fact that no data action takes place at n_0. Thus $\alpha \notin live(n_0) \Rightarrow P(n'; \alpha) \equiv x\rho$; i.e., $\alpha \in A_x(n')$. Now consider the "only if" part. $\alpha \in live(n_0) \Rightarrow P(n_0 \to; \alpha) \equiv g\rho + \rho'$. Consequently, because of the construction of the *gen* sets $P(n_0 \to; \alpha) \equiv y\rho + \rho'$ where $y \neq x$. (Note that $\alpha \in gen(n)$ implies, by step 1, $P(n; \alpha) \equiv x\rho + 1, P(n; \alpha) \equiv 1$.) Consequently, $\alpha \in live(n_0) \Rightarrow P(n'; \alpha) \equiv y\rho + \rho' \not\equiv x\rho$; i.e., $\alpha \notin A_x(n')$. ■

Proof *Determination of $B_x(n')$ is correct*

Let $\alpha \in tok$. By step 3 of the algorithm $\alpha \in B_x(n')$ if and only if $\alpha \notin live(n_0)$ and $\alpha \notin A_x(n')$ and $\alpha \in C_x(n')$. Take the "if" part first: $\alpha \notin live(n_0) \Rightarrow P(n_0 \to; \alpha) = k\rho$ or $P(n_0 \to; \alpha) = k\rho + 1$ or $P(n_0 \to; \alpha) = 1$. The first and last alternatives are excluded by the conditions $\alpha \notin A_x(n')$ and $\alpha \in C_x(n')$. This leaves only $P(n_0 \to; \alpha) = k\rho + 1$ and using $\alpha \in kill(n) \Rightarrow P(n; \alpha) \equiv x\rho$ gives $P(n_0 \to; \alpha) = x\rho + 1$. Finally

$$P(n' \to; \alpha) = P(n_0; \alpha) \, P(n_0 \to; \alpha)$$
$$\equiv P(n_0 \to; \alpha)$$
$$\Rightarrow P(n'; \alpha) \equiv x\rho + 1;$$

i.e., $\alpha \in B_x(n')$. Now consider the "only if" part.

$$\alpha \in live(n_0) \Rightarrow P(n_0 \to; \alpha) = g\rho + \rho'.$$

From step 1 it is seen that

$$\alpha \in gen(n) \Rightarrow P(n; \alpha) \equiv y\rho + \rho', y \neq x.$$

Hence $\alpha \in live(n_0) \Rightarrow P(n_0 \to; \alpha) = y\rho + \rho', y \neq x$, and from this it is easily concluded that $\alpha \notin B_x(n')$. It is immediately evident that $\alpha \in A_x(n') \Rightarrow \alpha \notin B_x(n')$ and that $\alpha \notin C_x(n') \Rightarrow \alpha \notin B_x(n')$. ■

Proof *Determination of $D_x(n')$ is correct*

Let $\alpha \in tok$. By step 3 of the algorithm $\alpha \in D_x(n')$ if and only if $\alpha \notin avail(n_{exit})$. Take the "if" part first. $\alpha \in avail(n_{exit}) \Rightarrow P(\to n_{exit}; \alpha) \equiv \rho g$. Hence

$$P(n'; \alpha) = P(\to n_{exit}; \alpha) \, P(n_{exit}; \alpha) \equiv \rho g.$$

Now using the fact that $\alpha \in gen(n) \Rightarrow P(n; \alpha) = \rho x$ we conclude that

$$\alpha \in avail(n_{exit}) \Rightarrow P(n'; \alpha) \equiv \rho x; \text{ i.e., } \alpha \in D_x(n').$$

Now take the "only if" part.

$$\alpha \notin avail(n_{exit}) \Rightarrow P(\to n_{exit}; \alpha) \equiv \rho k + \rho'$$

$$\text{or } P(\to n_{exit}; \alpha) \equiv 1,$$

Since $\alpha \in kill(n)$ implies $P(\to n; \alpha) \equiv \rho y + \rho', y \neq x$, it easily follows that $\alpha \notin avail(n_{exit}) \Rightarrow P(n'; \alpha) \not\equiv \rho x$; i.e., $\alpha \notin D_x(n')$. ∎

The last item to be discussed in this section is the initiation and progressive determination of the path sets for a program. Consider the call graph shown in Fig. 5.5. Since the subprogram FUNB invokes no other subprogram, the algorithms just presented are unnecessary in the determination of the path sets for the nodes of the flow graph representing FUNB. In this flow graph each node will represent a simple statement or part of a statement having no underlying structure, so the path set determination can be made by inspection. Once this is done the path sets for the nodes of the flow graph representing SUBA can be determined, since the path sets are known for the only subprogram it invokes. The same remarks apply to the flow graph representing FUNA. Finally, after these path sets are determined it is possible to determine the path sets for the nodes of the flow graph representing MAIN. Thus by working backwards through an acyclic call graph it is possible to apply the algorithms just described. We call this backward order the leafs-up subprogram processing order. We have restricted our attention to acyclic call graphs because this procedure breaks down if a cycle is present in the call graph. One way to solve this problem if cycles are present might be to carry out an iterative procedure, as suggested by Rosen [30], in which successive corrections are made to some initial assignment of path sets but we have not pursued this idea.

Detecting Anomalous Path Expressions

It will be recalled that we have defined an anomalous path expression to have one of the forms: $\rho ur\rho'$, $\rho dd\rho'$, or $\rho du\rho'$. Let us assume now that the path sets have been determined for every node of a flow graph $G_r(N, E, n_o)$. It should be evident that if $(n, n') \in E$ and $\alpha \in F_u(n)$ and $\alpha \in C_r(n')$, then there is a path expression of the form $\rho ur\rho'$: $\alpha \in F_u(n), \alpha \in C_r(n') \Rightarrow P(nn'; \alpha) \equiv \rho ur\rho' + \rho''$. Note, however, that the undefinition and reference do not necessarily occur on nodes n and n' respectively. Indeed, these data actions may not even occur on nodes of this flow graph: they might occur on nodes of other flow graphs representing invoked procedures. We only know that on some path which includes the edge (n, n') there is an anomalous path expression. Also this anomalous path expression may not be on an executable path, but if $\alpha \in D_u(n)$ and $\alpha \in A_r(n')$, then we may reasonably conclude that the path expression $\rho ur\rho'$ occurs on an executable path. In this case our assumptions imply that on every path which includes the edge (n, n') there must be an anomalous path expression: $\alpha \in D_u(n), \alpha \in A_r(n') \Rightarrow P(nn'; \alpha) \equiv \rho ur\rho'$. We assume at least one of these paths is executable. In this section these ideas are expanded to include the detection of anomalous path expressions on paths which go through a selected flow graph.

Assume that the path sets have been constructed for a flow graph G_F, and we wish to determine whether

$$P(n; \alpha)\, P(n \to; \alpha) \equiv \rho xy\rho' + \rho''$$

or

$$P(n; \alpha)\, P(n \to; \alpha) \equiv \rho xy\rho'$$

for each $n \in N$ and each $\alpha \in tok$. For anomaly detection we are interested in those cases when $x = $ u, $y = $ r or $x = $ d, $y = $ d, or $x = $ d, $y = $ u, but there is no need to fix the values of x and y now. A similar, but not equivalent, pair of problems is to determine whether

$$P(\to n; \alpha)\, P(n; \alpha) \equiv \rho xy\rho' + \rho'' \quad \text{or}$$
$$P(\to n; \alpha)\, P(n; \alpha) \equiv \rho xy\rho'$$

for each $n \in N$ and each $\alpha \in tok$. The discussion of the last section should make it apparent that the first pair of problems can be attacked with the algorithm LIVE and the second pair of problems can be attacked with the algorithm AVAIL. Indeed, the algorithms presented in the last section have, in effect, solved these problems.

Consider the algorithm to determine $A_x(n')$. After execution of step 3, suppose we construct the sets

$$A_x(n \to) = tok - live(n)$$

for all $n \in N$. Note that in step 4 we did this for the entry node only. It is evident that $\alpha \in A_x(n \to)$ implies $P(\to n; \alpha) = x\rho$, and conversely. Hence if $\alpha \in D_y(n)$ and $\alpha \in A_x(n \to)$ we know that

$$P(n; \alpha)\, P(n \to; \alpha) \equiv \rho xy\rho'$$

and so if $y = $ u and $x = $ r, an anomalous path expression of the form $\rho u r\rho'$ is known to be present.

Now, using the idea and notation suggested in the last paragraph assume that we augment the last step in the algorithm for $A_x(n')$, $C_x(n')$, $D_x(n')$, and $F_x(n')$ described in the last section to construct the sets $A_x(n \to)$, $C_x(n \to)$, $D_x(\to n)$, $F_x(\to n)$. Using them we construct the set intersections: $F_x(n) \cap C_y(n \to)$, $D_x(n) \cap A_y(n \to)$, $F_x(\to n) \cap C_y(n)$, and $D_x(\to n) \cap A_y(n)$. Then it is seen that:

$$\alpha \in F_x(n) \cap C_y(n \to)$$
$$\Leftrightarrow P(n; \alpha)P(n \to; \alpha) \equiv \rho xy\rho' + \rho'';$$
$$\alpha \in D_x(n) \cap A_y(n \to)$$
$$\Leftrightarrow P(n; \alpha)P(n \to; \alpha) \equiv \rho xy\rho';$$
$$\alpha \in F_x(\to n) \cap C_y(n)$$
$$\Leftrightarrow P(\to n; \alpha)P(n; \alpha) \equiv \rho xy\rho' + \rho'';$$
$$\alpha \in D_x(\to n) \cap A_y(n)$$
$$\Leftrightarrow P(\to n; \alpha)P(n; \alpha) \equiv \rho xy\rho';$$

The proofs of these assertions, which we omit, are essentially the same as those given in the previous section, Segmentation of Data Flow, for the determination of the sets $A_x(n')$, ...

It will be recognized that the segmentation scheme described in the previous section permits exposure only of the first and last data actions on paths entering or leaving a flow graph. Therefore, if we are to detect the presence of all anomalous path expressions in an entire program by the method just described, we must apply it systematically to the flow graphs for each of the subprograms in the entire program. In practice this would be done in the order dictated by the call graph, as already discussed in connection with constructing the path sets. Indeed, these two processes would be done together while working through the subprograms. To illustrate, consider the call graph shown in Fig. 5.5. The steps performed would be as follows:

1) For FUNB determine the sets $A_x(n') \dots I(n')$, $A_x(n \rightarrow)$, $C_x(n \rightarrow)$, $D_x(\rightarrow n)$, $F_x(\rightarrow n)$;

2) For FUNB construct the sets $F_x(n) \cap C_y(n \rightarrow)$, $\dots$, $D_x(\rightarrow n) \cap A_y(n)$ and report anomalies;

3) Repeat steps 1 and 2 for SUBA;

4) Repeat steps 1 and 2 for FUNA;

5) Repeat steps 1 and 2 for MAIN.

The time required to do the detection of anomalous path expressions is essentially controlled by the time required to execute LIVE and AVAIL. Step 1 of the example described above requires nine executions of LIVE (A_x, B_x, C_x for $x =$ r, d, u), and nine executions of AVAIL (D_x, E_x, F_x for $x =$ r, d, u), plus a small additional amount of time proportional to the number of nodes in the flow graph. We are assuming that the set operations can be done in unit time so there is no dependence on the number of tokens. In practice this assumption has only limited validity. Step 2 of the example described above requires a time proportional to the number of nodes (in particular 4(|N|-2) where the -2 term arises because we can ignore the entry and exit nodes). Therefore, if a call graph has $|N_c|$ nodes and $|\bar{N}|$ is the average number of nodes in each flow graph represented by a node of the call graph, the time τ to detect all anomalous path expressions may be expressed as

$$\tau = |N_c|(9\tau_{LIVE} + 9\tau_{AVAIL} + k|\bar{N}|),$$

where τ_{LIVE} and τ_{AVAIL} are execution times for LIVE and AVAIL. If we use the results given in the section Algorithms to Solve the Live Variable Problem and the Availability Problem for the execution times for LIVE and AVAIL, we see that in practical situations we can expect to detect the presence of all anomalous path expressions in a program in a time which is proportional to the total number of flow graph nodes. While the constants of proportionality might be large and there would be a substantial overhead to create the required data structures, the important point is that a combinatorially explosive dependence on |N| has been avoided.

The principal reason why a combinatorial explosion has been avoided is that we have not looked explicitly at all paths. The loss of information resulting from this does not prevent us from detecting the presence of anomalous path expressions, but it greatly restricts our knowledge about specific paths on which the anomalous path expression occurs. Thus if $\alpha \in F_u(n) \cap C_r(n \rightarrow)$, we know that on some path starting at n we will find an expression of the form $\rho u r \rho'$, but we do not know which path and we do not know which nodes on the path contain the actions u and r on α. This problem can be attacked directly by performing a search over paths starting at node n. This search can be made quite efficient if we deal with one token at a time. The idea is to use a depth first search but to restrict it so that we avoid visiting any node n' such that $\alpha \notin C_r(n' \rightarrow)$. While this strategy does not preclude backtracking, it tends to reduce it and generally restricts the number of nodes visited in the search. It seems certain that more efficient schemes for localizing the anomalous path expression can be constructed.

The information gathered for the detection of anomalous path expressions is valuable for other purposes. For example, it determines which arguments need initialization before execution of a procedure—thus it could be used to supply this information as a form of automatic documentation. Alternatively, this information can be used to verify assertions by the programmer concerning arguments needing initialization.

Similarly, it is possible to determine the arguments which are assigned values by a procedure, i.e., the output arguments. However, unlike the case for initialization where the set $C_i(n')$ identifies the arguments requiring initialization, none of the path sets is sufficient for this purpose. Notice in particular that $F_d(n')$ is not satisfactory because $P(n'; \alpha) \equiv \rho dr$ obviously implies that α is an output for the procedure represented by n' yet $\alpha \notin F_d(n')$. However, it is not difficult to construct an algorithm for this purpose. Indeed, we only need to modify one step in the algorithm for $F_x(n')$; in particular, replace $gen(n) \leftarrow D_y(n) \cup D_x(n)$ by $gen(n) \leftarrow D_u(n)$.

Then after step 4, $\alpha \in F_d(n')$ implies α is an output for the procedure represented by n'. It will be recognized that this excludes tokens for which $P(n'; \alpha) \equiv \rho dr^*u$. This is reasonable, since the definition is destroyed by the subsequent undefinition, and no value is actually returned to the invoking procedure. Thus we have a mechanism for providing automatic documentation about procedure outputs, or for verifying assertions about which procedure arguments are output arguments.

Conclusion

As noted in an earlier section of this paper, we have implemented a FORTRAN program analysis system which embodies many of the ideas presented here. This system, called DAVE, [27, 28] separates program variables into classes that are somewhat similar to those shown in Fig. 5.18. DAVE also detects all data flow anomalies of type $\rho ur\rho'$ and most of the data flow anomalies of types $\rho dd\rho'$ and $\rho du\rho'$. DAVE carries out this analysis by performing a flow graph search for each variable in a given unit, and analyzing subprograms in a leafs-up order, which assures that no subprogram invocation will be considered until the invoked subprogram has been completely analyzed. An improved version of DAVE would continue to analyze the subprograms of a program in leafs-up order, but would use the highly efficient, parallel algorithms described here to either detect or disprove the presence of data flow anomalies. The variable-by-variable depth first search currently used in DAVE exclusively, would be used only to generate a specific anomaly bearing path, once the more efficient algorithms had shown that an anomaly was present. Such a system would have considerably improved efficiency characteristics and, perhaps more important, could be readily incorporated into many existing compilers which already do live variable and availability analysis in order to perform global optimization.

The apparent ease with which our anomaly detection scheme could be efficiently integrated into existing optimizing compilers is a highly attractive feature and a strong argument for taking this approach. Other methods for carrying out anomaly detection can be constructed, but most that we have studied lack efficiency and compatibility with existing compilation systems. One such method, which is quite interesting for its strong intuitive appeal, involves symbolic execution of the program. Symbolic execution, a powerful technique which has recently found applications in debugging, program verification, and validation [8, 19, 22], involves determining the value of each program variable at every node of a flow graph as a symbolic formula whose only unknowns are the program's input values. These formulas of course depend upon the path taken to a given node. A notation similar to regular expression notation could be used to represent the set of symbolic expressions for a variable at a node, corresponding to the set of paths to the node. If these expressions were to be stored at their respective nodes, a flow graph searching procedure could be constructed which would be capable of detecting all the anomalies described here by careful examination of the way the expressions evolved along paths traversed by a single flow graph search. Moreover, because the symbolic execution carried along far more information than does our proposed system, even more powerful diagnostic results are possible.

The relative weaknesses of such a method are its lack of efficiency and the difficulty of incorporating it into existing compiling systems. Although it seems reasonable to suppose that sophisticated representation schemes could be used to reduce the very large time and space requirements of the symbolic execution system, it also seems clear to us that even such reduced requirements would necessarily greatly exceed those of our proposed system. We have finally concluded that symbolic execution systems currently seem more attractive as stand-alone diagnostic systems where their greater level of detail can be used to carry out more extensive program analysis, but at greater cost. We believe, moreover, that our proposed data flow analysis scheme can and should be integrated into compilers in order to provide highly useful error diagnosis at small additional cost. The diagnostic output of a system such as ours would then be useful input to a symbolic execution system.

Much has been learned from our experiences with the current version of DAVE. Believing that similar systems should be used in state-of-the-art compilers, we now summarize these experiences in order to place in better perspective the problems and benefits to be expected.

Certain programming practices and constructs which are present in FORTRAN and common to a number of other languages cause difficulties for data flow analysis systems such as DAVE. The handling of arrays, as mentioned earlier, is one such example. Problems arise when different elements of the same array are used in inherently different ways and hence have different patterns of reference, definition, and undefinition. Static data flow analysis systems such as DAVE are incapable of evaluating subscript expressions and hence cannot determine which array element is being referenced by a given subscript expression. Thus, as stated earlier, in DAVE and in many other program analysis systems arrays are treated as though they were simple variables. This avoids the problem of being unable to evaluate subscript expressions, but often causes a weakening or blurring of analytic results. As an example, consider the program shown in Fig. 5.19. Suppose n' is the node of $G_{MAIN}(N, E, n_0)$, the flow graph of the main program, which invokes SQUARE. Denote by $R(\bullet, 1)$ and $R(\bullet, 2)$ arbitrary elements of column 1 and column 2 respectively of array R. Now clearly $R(\bullet,1) \in A_d(n')$ and $R(\bullet,2) \in A_r(n')$. In addition, it is clear that $R(\bullet,1) \in D_d(\to n')$ and $R(\bullet,2) \in D_u(\to n')$. Hence $P(\to n'; R(\bullet,1))P(n'; R(\bullet,1)) \equiv \rho dd\rho'$, and $P(\to n'; R(\bullet,2))P(n'; R(\bullet,2)) \equiv \rho ur\rho'$, and we see there are two data flow anomalies present. DAVE, however, treats R as a simple variable and determines that $R \in A_d(n')$, $R \in D_d(n')$, $R \in D_d(\to n')$ and $R \in A_r(n' \to)$. Thus $P(\to n'; R)P(n'; R) \equiv \rho dr\rho'$ and $P(n'; R)P(n' \to; R) \equiv \rho dr\rho$, and no data flow anomalies will be detected. This loss of anomaly detection power is worrisome, and it is seemingly avoided only when programmers call functionally distinct subarrays by separate names.

There are also certain difficulties involved in determining the leafs-up subprogram processing order referred to earlier. This order is important, because it ensures that each subprogram will be analyzed exactly once, yet that data flow anomalies across subprogram boundaries will be detected. If subprogram names are passed as arguments, this order may become difficult to determine. This difficulty can arise because the name used in a subprogram invocation may not be the name of a subprogram, but rather can be a variable which has received the subprogram name, perhaps through a long chain of subprogram invocations. All such chains must be explored in order to expose all subprogram invocations and then determine the leafs-up order. Recent work by Kallal and Osterweil [20] indicates that the AVAIL algorithm can be used to efficiently expose all such invocations.

Recursive subprograms pose another obstacle to determining leafs-up order. Although recursion is not allowed in FORTRAN, it is a capability of many other languages. Moreover, it is possible to write two FORTRAN subprograms such that each may invoke the other, but such that no program execution will force a recursive calling sequence. Such a program would be legal in FORTRAN, but would not appear to have sufficient leaf subprograms (i.e., those that invoke no others) to allow construction of the complete leafs-up order. This problem is not adequately handled by DAVE, however no FORTRAN programs with this construction have been encountered. In any case current work indicates that recursive programs can be analyzed using the methods described here.

```
        DIMENSION R(100,2)

        READ(5,10)(R(I,1),I=1,100)

10      FORMAT(F10.2)

        CALL SQUARE(R)

        WRITE(6,20)(R(I,2),I=1,100)

20      FORMAT(1X,F10.2)

        STOP

        END

        SUBROUTINE SQUARE(R)

        DIMENSION R(100,2)

        DO  10  I=1,100

10      R(I,1)=R(I,2)**2

        RETURN

        END
```

Fig. 5.19. A program in which failure to distinguish between the differing patterns of reference, definition and undefinition of different array elements prevents detection of data flow anomalies.

Finally it should be observed that subprogram invocations involving the passing of a single variable as an argument more than once may be incorrectly analyzed. This occurs because DAVE assumes that all subprogram parameters represent different variables as it analyzes subprograms in leafs-up order.

Despite these limitations, the DAVE system has proven to be a useful diagnostic tool. We have used DAVE to analyze a number of operational programs and it has often found errors or stylistic shortcomings. Among the most common of these have been: variables having path expressions equivalent to purp' (referencing uninitialized variables), and pdup' (failing to use a computed value) occurring simultaneously, usually due to a misspelling; subprogram parameters having path expressions equivalent to 1, caused by naming unused parameters in parameter lists; and COMMON variables having path expressions equivalent to purp' or pdup' usually due to omitting COMMON declarations from higher level program units.

The cost of using DAVE has proven to be relatively high, partly due to the fact that it is a prototype built for flexibility, and not speed, and partly due to the failure to use the more efficient algorithms described here. We have observed the execution speed of the system to average between 0.3 and 0.5 seconds per source statement on the CDC 6400 computer for programs whose size ranged from several dozen to several thousand statements. The total cost per statement has averaged between 7 and 9 cents per statement for these test programs using the University of Colorado Computing Center charge algorithm. It is, of course, anticipated that these costs would decline sharply if a production version of DAVE were to be implemented.

Based on these experiences and observations, we believe that systems like DAVE can serve the important purpose of automatically performing a thorough initial scan for the presence of certain types of errors. It seems that the most useful characteristics of such systems are that 1) they require no human intervention or guidance and 2) they are capable of scanning all paths for possible data flow anomalies. A human tester need not be concerned with designing test cases for this system, yet can be assured by the system that no anomalies are present. In case an anomaly is present, the system will so advise the tester and further testing or debugging would be necessary. Clearly such a system is capable of detecting only a limited class of errors. Hence further testing would always be necessary. Through the use of a system such as DAVE, however, the thrust of this testing can be more sharply focused. It seems that these systems could be most profitably employed in the early phases of a testing regimen (e.g., as part of a compiler) and used to guide and direct later testing efforts involving more powerful systems that employ such techniques as symbolic execution. Towards this end, further work should be done to widen the class of errors detectable by means such as those described in this paper.

Acknowledgments We want to close with a grateful recognition of the stimulating and valuable discussions we have had on this subject with our colleagues and students—especially Jim Boyle, Lori Clarke, Hal Gabow, Shachindra Maheshwari, Carol Miesse, and Paul Zeiger—and the helpful comments of the referees. Finally, we gratefully acknowledge the financial assistance provided by the National Science Foundation in this work.

References

[1] AHO, A. V.; and ULLMAN, J. D. "Node listings for reducible flow graphs," in *Proc. of the 7th Annual ACM Symposium on Theory of Computing*, 1975, pp. 177-185.

[2] ALLEN, F.E. "Program optimization," in *Annual Review in Automatic Programming*, 1969.

[3] ALLEN, F.E. "A basis for program optimization," in *Proc. IFIP Congress 1971*, North-Holland Publ. Co., Amsterdam, The Netherlands, 1972, pp. 385-390.

[4] ALLEN, F. E.; AND COCKE, J. *Graph-theoretic constructs for program control flow analysis*, IBM Research Report RC3923, T. J. Watson Research Center, 1972.

[5] ALLEN, F. E. "Interprocedural data flow analysis," in *Proc. IFIP Congress 1974*, North Holland Publ. Co., Amsterdam, The Netherlands, 1974, pp. 398-402.

[6] ALLEN, F. E.; AND COCKE, J. "A program data flow analysis procedure," *Comm. ACM* 19, 3 (March 1976), 137-147.

[7] BALZER, R. M. "EXDAMS: Extendable debugging and monitoring system," in *Proc. AFIPS 1969 Spring Jr. Computer Conf.*, Vol. 34, AFIPS Press, pp. 567-580.

[8] CLARKE, L. *A system to generate test data and symbolically execute programs*, Dept. of Computer Science Technical Report #Cu-CS-060-75, Univ. of Colorado, Boulder, 1975.

[9] DENNIS, J.B. "First version of a data flow procedure language," in *Lecture notes in computer science 19*, G. Goos and J. Hartmanis (Eds.), 1974, pp. 241-271.

[10] FAIRLEY, R.E. "An experimental program testing facility," in *Proc. First National Conf. on Software Engineering*, 1975, IEEE #75CH0992-8C, IEEE, New York, 1975, pp. 47-55.

[11] GOLDSTINE, H. H.; AND VON NEUMANN, J. Planning and coding problems for an electronic computing instrument," in *John von Neumann, collected works*, 1963, pp. 80-235.

[12] HABERMANN, A.N. *Path expressions*, Dept. of Computer Science Technical Report, Carnegie-Mellon Univ., Pittsburgh, Pa., 1975.

[13] HARARY, F. *Graph theory*, Addison-Wesley Publ. Co., Reading, Mass., 1969.

[14] HECHT, M. S.; AND ULLMAN, J. D. "Flow graph reducibility," *SIAM J. Computing 1*, (1972), 188-202.

[15] HECHT, M. S.; AND ULLMAN, J.D. "Characterizations of reducible flow graphs," *J. ACM 21*, 3 (July 1974), 367-375.

[16] HECHT, M. S.; AND ULLMAN, J. D. "A simple algorithm for global data flow analysis problems," *SIAM J. Computing 4* (Dec. 1975), 519-532.

[17] HOPCROFT, J.; AND TARJAN, R. E. "Efficient algorithms for graph manipulation," *Comm. ACM 16* (June 1973), 372-378.

[18] HOPCROFT, J. E.; AND ULLMAN, J.D. *Formal languages and their relation to automata*, Addison Wesley Publ. Co., Reading, Mass., 1969.

[19] HOWDEN, W.E. "Automatic case analysis of programs," in *Proc. Computer Science and Statistics*: 8th Annual Symposium on the Interface, 1975, pp. 347-352.

[20] KALLAL, V.; AND OSTERWEIL, L. J. *Constructing flowgraphs for assembly language programs*, Dept. of Computer Science Technical Report Univ. of Colorado, Boulder, 1976.

[21] KARP, R.M. "A note on the application of graph theory to digital computer programming," *Information and Control 3* (1960), 179-190.

[22] KING, J. C. "A new approach to program testing," in *Proc. Internatl. Conf. on Reliable Software*, 1975, IEEE #75CH0940- 7CSR, IEEE, New York, 1975, pp. 228-233.

[23] KENNEDY, K.W. "Node listings applied to data flow analysis," in *Proc. of 2nd ACM Symposium on Principals of Programming Languages*, 1975, ACM, New York, 1975, pp. 10-21.

[24] KNUTH, D. E. *The art of computer programming, Vol. I fundamental algorithms*, (2d Ed.), Addison Wesley Publ. Co., Reading, Mass., 1973.

[25] KNUTH, D. E. An empirical study of FORTRAN programs, *Software—Practice and Experience 1*, 2 (1971), 105-134.

[26] MILLER, E. F., JR. *RXVP, FORTRAN automated verification system*, Program Validation Project, General Research Corp., Santa Barbara, Calif., 1974, pp. 4.

[27] OSTERWEIL, L. J.; AND FOSDICK, L D. "DAVE—a FORTRAN program analysis system," in *Proc. Computer Science and Statistics: 8th Annual Symp. on the Interface*, 1975

[28] OSTERWEIL, L. J.; AND FOSDICK, L. D. "DAVE—a validation, error detection and documentation system for FORTRAN programs," *Software—Practice and Experience*, 1976.

[29] RODRIGUEZ, J. D. *A graph model for parallel computation*, Report MAC-TR-64, Project MAC, MIT, Cambridge, Mass., 1969.

[30] ROSEN, B. *Data flow analysis for recursive PL/I programs*, IBM Research Report RC5211, T. J. Watson Research Center, Yorktown Heights, New York, 1975.

[31] SCHAEFFER, M. *A mathematical theory of global program optimization*, Prentice-Hall Inc., Englewood Cliffs, N. J., 1973.

[32] STUCKI, L. G. "Automatic generation of self-metric software," in *Proc. IEEE Symposium on Computer Software Reliability*, 1973, IEEE, pp. 94-100.

[33] TARJAN, R. E. "Depth-first search and linear graph algorithms," *SIAM J. Computing* (Sept. 1972), 146-160.

[34] TARJAN, R. E. "Testing flow graph reducibility," *J. Computer and System Sciences 9*, 3 (Dec. 1974), 355-365.

[35] ULLMAN, J. D. "Fast algorithms for the elimination of common subexpressions," *Acta Informatica 2* (1973), 191-213.

Anomaly Detection in Concurrent Software by Static Data Flow Analysis[1]

Richard N. Taylor and Leon J. Osterweil

Richard N. Taylor is at Space and Military Applications Division, Boeing Computer Services Company, Seattle, WA 98124.

Leon J. Osterweil is at Department of Computer Science, University of Colorado, Boulder, CO 80309.

Abstract Algorithms are presented for detecting errors and anomalies in programs which use synchronization constructs to implement concurrency. The algorithms employ data flow analysis techniques. First used in compiler object code optimization, the techniques have more recently been used in the detection of variable usage errors in single process programs. By adapting these existing algorithms, the same classes of variable usage errors can be detected in concurrent process programs. Important classes of errors unique to concurrent process programs are also described, and algorithms for their detection are presented.

I. Introduction

Data flow analysis has been shown to be a useful tool in demonstrating the presence or absence of certain significant classes of programming errors [1]. It is an important software verification technique, as it is inexpensive and dependably detects a well-defined and useful class of anomalies. Work to this point has been directed at the analysis of single-process programs. Investigation of the applicability of data flow analysis to concurrent programs is just beginning [8], [13], [15]. Concurrency causes difficulty in the detection of most errors which occur in single-process programs; it also creates the possibility of new classes of errors.

One of the simplest errors which can occur in both categories of programs is referencing an undefined variable. (The authors recognize that this error can be eliminated by requiring that all variables be declared and given initial values at the point of declaration. Most programming languages do not have this requirement, however. Moreover, the presentation and discussion of this error is useful for pedagogical purposes.)

---

[1] This work was supported by the National Aeronautics and Space Administration under Contract NAS1-15253 and by the National Science Foundation under Grant MCS77-02194.

Richard N. Taylor and Leon J. Osterweil, "Anomaly Detection
in Concurrent Software by Static Data Flow Analysis,"
IEEE Transactions on Software Engineering 6:3, May 1980. © 1980 IEEE

Another programming anomaly which may occur in both categories is a dead variable definition. This occurs when a variable is defined twice without an intervening reference, or if a variable is defined, yet never subsequently referenced. (The notion of an anomaly is described in more detail in [1] and [7].)

In concurrent software, these types of anomalies and errors can occur in more subtle ways than in single-process programs. For example, within a system of concurrent processes, one process may reference a shared variable while a parallel process may be redefining it. It is clearly desirable that such errors and anomalies be analytically detected or shown to be absent from programs.

In this paper, the authors show that data flow analysis can reliably demonstrate the presence or absence of these and other programming anomalies for both single-process and concurrent programs. While the anomalies are of interest in themselves, they are particularly important because experience has shown that consideration of why they arose in the program's construction often leads to the detection of significant design errors.

II. Example and Basic Definitions

A. Programming Language Description

In order to clarify the types of errors being addressed, several examples are needed. The interest here is in designing analytic techniques which may be applied to a variety of languages supporting concurrent programming, such as Concurrent Pascal [2], Modula [3], and Jovial. The languages which are currently used for real-time, concurrent process programming display a variety of techniques to allow synchronization and communication. Some are more error-resistant than others (to say the least). Still more constructs and techniques are being proposed. For example, Ada [4], the new, proposed, common higher order language for embedded applications developed for the Department of Defense displays a number of new techniques. We have attempted to avoid language and methodology dependence in developing analytic techniques, so that they will remain as current as possible. Only the existence of a few constructs common to nearly all contemporary concurrent languages has been assumed, because tools are needed now for the languages which are already in use. It appears likely, however, that the techniques designed in creating these tools will not be made obsolete by new language designs or concurrency constructs.

The programming language which forms the basis for this presentation is derived from HAL/S, an algorithmic language designed for the production of real-time flight software [5]. HAL/S was developed for use on the Space Shuttle and is employed elsewhere within NASA for a variety of tasks [6]. The authors have extracted a simple yet powerful subset of this language and slightly altered the syntax and semantics of several of its constructs.

HAL/S bears many similarities to Algol 60 and PL/I. Hence, the syntax and semantics of these languages can generally be safely used in understanding the examples in this paper. Of particular interest, however, are the following language constructs which will be analyzed and with which the examples will be formed.

1) Assignment statement. This statement is of the form

    variable = expression;

In executing this statement, the expression is evaluated and the result is then assigned to the variable.

2) Process declaration statements (**program, task,** and **close**). The declaration of each process begins with a declaration statement. The main program begins with a **program** declaration statement. Other processes begin with a **task** declaration statement. The end of a process declaration is marked with a close declaration statement.

3) Schedule statement. The execution of any process except for the main program is enabled through execution of a **schedule** statement. Execution of a **schedule** does not guarantee that the specified process will begin immediately; it merely indicates that the process is ready for execution. The actual time of initiation of a process is determined by the system scheduler. Any number of processes may be enabled for concurrent execution, but a process may not be scheduled to execute in parallel with itself. The schedule statement explicitly names the process or processes to be started; run-time determination of processes to be scheduled is not allowed.

4) Wait statement. This statement causes the executing process to wait for another process (or processes) to terminate before continuing with its own execution. A process has *terminated* when it has completed its execution and no longer resides in the system scheduler's "ready" queue. As with the **schedule** statement, the process(es) waited for is (are) named explicitly in the declaration; run-time determination is not allowed. The statement may be formulated two ways:

    wait for process_name$_1$ **and** process_name$_2$...

or

    wait for process_name$_1$ **or** process_name$_2$...

When the process names are joined through logical disjunction, the wait is interpreted as **wait**-for-any. As soon as one of the named processes has terminated, the waiting process may proceed. When the process names are joined by logical conjunction, *all* of the named processes must terminate before the waiting process may proceed. This is referred to as a **wait**-for-all statement.

5) Shared variables. Program variables have associated with them Algol-like scoping rules. This scoping exists at the program level, meaning that two processes may both access the same variable. We assume that no protection mechanism exists.

6) Transput. Input to a program is accomplished through a **read** statement. Values are output via a **write** statement.

B. Example

Using the above constructs, a sample program (Fig. 6.1) is presented which contains several anomalies.

```
1       Main: program;

2           declare integer x,y;
            /* x,y are global variables known
            throughout the main program and all tasks */
3           declare boolean flag ;

4           T1: task;
5               write x ;
6               wait for T3 ;
7           close T1 ;

8           T2: task;
9               x = 5 ;
10              y = 6 ;
11          close T2 ;

12          T3: task;
13              read x ;
14          close T3 ;

            /* end of declarations */

15          schedule T1 ; /* first executable
            statement of Main*/
16          schedule T2 ;
17          read flag ;
18          if flag then x = 8 ;
19          write x ;
20          y = 9 ;
21          wait for T2 ;
22          if flag then y = 10 ;
23          write y ;
24          wait for T2 ;
25          schedule T1 ;

26      close Main ;
```

Fig. 6.1. Sample program with several data flow and synchronization anomalies.

A few of the anomalies are listed below.

1) An uninitialized variable (x) may be referenced at line 5, as task T1 may execute to completion before task T2 begins.

2) The definitions of y as found in task T2 (line 10) and the main program (line 20) may be "useless," since y may be redefined at line 22, before y is ever referenced.

3) y is defined by two processes which act in parallel—thus the reference at line 23 may be to an "indeterminate" value.

4) Variable x is assigned a value by task T2 (line 9) while simultaneously being referenced by the main program at line 19.

5) There is a possibility that task T1 will be scheduled in parallel with itself at line 25 since there is no guarantee that T1 terminated after its initial scheduling.

6) The **wait** at line 24 is unnecessary, as T2 was guaranteed to have terminated at line 21, and it has not subsequently been rescheduled.

7) The **wait** at line 6 will never be satisfied as T3 was never scheduled.

C. Event Expressions

Clearly, many of these error phenomena are interrelated. Hence, a more precise categorization and definition system is desirable. Some notions employed in [7] are modified here to gain this precision. In [7] errors were described in terms of anomalous or illegal sequences of events occurring along a path through a program.

For instance, the events "reference" (accessing a value from a variable), "define" (setting a value into a variable), and "undefine" (causing the value of a variable to become undefined, such as by satisfying the running index of a loop) are the significant ones in the detection of undefined variable references and dead variable definitions. Thus, in determining the presence or absence of these errors in a given program, the execution of the program is modeled as the set of all potential execution sequences of these three events happening to each of the program variables. In a single-process program, any path traceable through the program's flowgraph is taken to represent a potential execution.

Now denote the events "reference," "define," and "undefine" by r, d, and u, respectively. Then clearly an undefined variable reference can occur within a program if and only if there is a path subsequence of the form "ur" for some variable and some potential execution. Similarly, a dead variable definition is indicated by either a "dd" or "du" path subsequence. In a concurrent program, it is more difficult to determine the potential executions and hence the potential sequences of events. Different processes may be executing simultaneously on different CPU's, or in some nondeterminable interleaved order on a single CPU. If these processes operate on shared data, then the sequence of events happening to that data cannot be predicted, even though the code for each process is known. All that can be safely assumed is that every interleaving of the statements of all processes which can act concurrently must be considered a potential execution. Hence, the set of execution sequences for a given concurrent program is the set of all possible sequence of events which could result from a potential execution of the program.

Thus, for example, in Fig. 6.1, noting that all variables are initially undefined and that a **write** is a reference, variable x may have the sequence "urd," "udr," "ud," "ur," or "u" by the time line 17 is reached. "urd" corresponds to task T1 acting first, then T2; "udr" corresponds to T2 actually executing before T1 (there is nothing in the program prohibiting this); "u" corresponds to tasks T1 and T2 both being ready to execute, but not actually having done so.

D. Error Categorization and Definitions

Using the notation developed above, definitions may now be formulated for the errors in which we are interested. The following are anomalies which we wish to detect in all programs. Their detection is more complicated in programs using concurrency constructs.

1) Referencing an uninitialized variable. An execution during which this error occurs will have an event sequence of the form "purp'" for some program variable, where p and p' are arbitrary event sequences.

2) A dead definition of a variable. An execution during which this anomaly occurs will have an event sequence the form "pddp" for some variable.

The following are errors and anomalies to be detected in concurrent code. In the following, the schedule event will be denoted by an "s," the wait by a "w." All processes will be assumed to be in state "u," unscheduled, when not scheduled.

3) Waiting for an unscheduled process. This anomaly is represented by the event expression "puwp'."

4) Scheduling a process in parallel with itself. This anomaly is represented by the event expression "pssp'."

5) Waiting for a process guaranteed to have previously terminated. The expression "pwwp'" is symptomatic of this condition.

6) Referencing a variable which is being defined by a parallel process. There exists a **schedule** s_0 such that for some variable both the event sequence "ps_0rdp'" and the event sequence "ps_0drp'" are possible.

7) Referencing a variable whose value is indeterminate. There exists a **wait** w_0 and two separate definition points for a given variable, d_1 and d_2, such that both the event expressions "$pd_1d_2w_0r$" and "$pd_2d_1w_0r$" are possible.

For each of the above anomalies, an interesting determination will be whether they exist in the event expression *at* a statement (i.e., the event expressions consisting of the preceding events concatenated with the current event), or in the event expression which represents the transformations undergone after *leaving* a statement. In addition, it will be important to distinguish between errors which are *guaranteed* to occur and those which *might* occur.

E. Program Representation

At the heart of data flow analysis are algorithms which operate on an annotated graphical representation of a program. Single process programs may be represented by a flowgraph [7]. As introduced in [8], communicating concurrent process programs may be represented by a *process augmented flowgraph*, or PAF. A PAF is formed by connecting the flowgraphs representing the individual processes with special edges indicating all synchronization constraints. In the sample languages given here, an edge must be created for each ordered pair of nodes of the type (**schedule** p_name, **task** p_name) and (**close** p_name, **wait for** p_name).

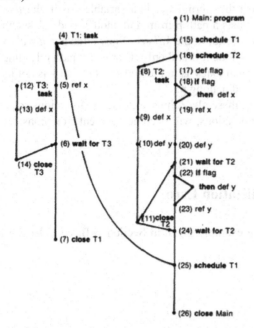

Fig. 6.2. Process-augmented flowgraph for the program of Fig. 6.1.

Fig. 6.2 is a PAF for the example program of Fig. 6.1. The creation of the PAF for programs in the sample language is quite straightforward. It is important to note, however, that most actual languages incorporate synchronization constructs which greatly complicate the construction of the PAF. In fact, it is impossible to create a fixed static procedure capable of constructing the PAF of any program written in a language which allows run-time determination of tasks to be scheduled and waited for. These issues will be discussed later in this paper.

F. Data Flow Analysis Algorithms

Data flow analysis algorithms arose out of research in global program optimization [9], [10]. The function of these algorithms, described in detail in [7] and [1], is to infer global program variable usage information from local program variable usage information. Our usage of them has a different objective from program optimization, however. The global usage information will be used to infer verification and error detection results.

The local variable usage is represented by attaching two sets of variables, *gen* and *kill*, to each program flowgraph node. The global data usage is represented by attaching two sets, *live* and *avail*, to each node. The algorithms presented in the references cited assure that when they terminate: 1) a variable v is in the *live* set for node n, if and only if there exists a path p from n to another node n', such that v is in the *gen* set at n', but that v is not in the *kill* set of any node along path p; 2) a variable v is in the *avail* set for node n if and only if for every path p leading up to n there exists a node n' on p, such that v is in the *gen* set at n', but v is not in the *kill* set for any node between n' and n along p.

The implications and usage of these algorithms, and the modifications required as a result of concurrency considerations, will become apparent from considering some examples.

III. Detection of Uninitialization Errors

Before examining the extensive example given in Section II-B, consider the following one:

```
1 Main: program;
2     declare integer x;
3     declare boolean flag;

4     T1: task;
5             write x;
6     close Tl;

7     T2: task;
8             write x;
9     close T2;

10    schedule TI;
11    read flag;
12    wait for TI;
13    if flag then read x;
14    schedule T2;

15 close Main;
```

The PAF for this program is given in Fig. 6.3. All the nodes are annotated corresponding to the program statements.

Now consider the uninitialization errors which are present and how they may be detected.

Two uninitialization errors are present in the program. When task T1 is executed, the write statement will reference uninitialized variable x. (It is not possible that x was initialized, even by the main program which operates in parallel with the task.) When task T2 is executed, there exists a *possibility* for referencing x as uninitialized. If "flag" has the value **true**, then x will be initialized and no error will occur. If, however, flag is **false**, x will still be uninitialized. Thus, there is an instance of an error which "must" occur and an instance of an error which "might" occur. In addition, each of these anomalies may be detected at two different places: the point of variable reference, or at the start node. Thus, there are four different subcategories of the uninitialized variable reference error.

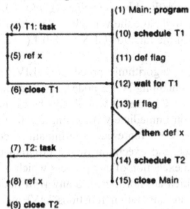

Fig. 6.3. PAF for program with two uninitialization anomalies.

The balance of this paper will be devoted to specifying algorithms for detecting the various subcategories of this error and a variety of other errors and phenomena of interest in the analysis of concurrent software. These algorithms will, in general, involve the use of the LIVE and AVAIL procedures described in Section II-F of this paper. It will be shown that a diversity of diagnostic algorithms can be fashioned by using a variety of criteria for marking the nodes of the program flow graph with *gen* and *kill* notations, and choosing suitable criteria for interpreting the output of the LIVE and AVAIL procedures.

For these reasons, it should be apparent that the algorithms presented here are much involved with placing *gen* and *kill* annotations of flowgraph nodes and interpreting *live* and *avail* annotations that subsequently appear on flowgraph nodes. This annotation information will be represented by means of bit vectors, denoted in the following way:

$$\text{AVAIL}(n) = \textbf{intersect } (\text{GEN}(n_i) \textbf{ union } (\text{AVAIL}(n_j) \textbf{ intersect not } \text{KILL}(n_i)))$$
$$\text{all } n_i,$$
$$\text{immediate}$$
$$\text{predecessors}$$
$$\text{of } n$$

If an annotation criterion dictates that a particular variable, say x, is "*gen*'ed" at a node n, this will be indicated by setting the value of the function *gen*(n, x) to 1.

Otherwise, the value of *gen*(n, x) is 0. The function *kill*(n, x) is defined similarly. (The difference between the two functions is that for a given application of the analysis algorithms, one annotation criterion will determine at which nodes each variable is *gen*'ed, while a different criterion will determine at which nodes each variable is *kill*ed. A sample criterion might be "Is variable x defined at this node?")

Assume that the program unit being analyzed has v variables, and that a one-to-one function f has been defined, mapping the variables of the program unit onto the integers $(1, \ldots, V)$. Hence, a bit vector is defined by the values $(gen(n, x_1), \ldots, gen(n, x_i), \ldots, gen(n, x_v))$, where x_i is used to denote the variable x for which $f(x) = i$. This bit vector is used as the definition of the function GEN(n). KILL(n) is defined similarly.

It will also be assumed that there exists algorithmic procedures, LIVE and AVAIL, which operate upon a flowgraph containing $N + 2$ nodes, and annotation functions GEN and KILL defined on the $N + 2$ nodes. It will always be assumed that node 0 represents an initialization action immediately preceding the first executable statement of a program unit. Node $N + 1$ represents a termination action immediately following all statements which end execution of the program unit (i.e., the **close** of the main program), or end execution of any process which is not **waited** for (i.e., all process **close** nodes which are not joined to any **wait** nodes). LIVE and AVAIL, when executed, compute annotation functions LIVE(n) and AVAIL(n), respectively, defined on the $N + 2$ nodes. The values of LIVE(n) and AVAIL(n) are V-bit vectors for n between 0 and $N + 1$. The bits of LIVE(n) and AVAIL(n) are defined by $live(n, x_i)$ and $avail(n, x_i)$, respectively, where x_i is the variable x for which $f(x) = i$.

As described in Section II-F of this paper, the AVAIL algorithm is devised to assure that at termination, a variable x will be *avail* at n if and only if for every possible execution of the program leading up to n, there is a previous *gen* of x without an intervening *kill* of x. For single process programs, AVAIL(n) is computed correctly at every flowgraph node n, provided that the following equality is achieved at termination of the AVAIL algorithm.

The LIVE algorithm is devised to assure that at termination, a variable x will be *live* at n if and only if there exists an execution sequence beginning at n, such that there is a *gen* of x before there is a *kill* of x. For single process programs, LIVE(n) is computed correctly at every flowgraph node n, provided that the following equality is achieved at termination of the LIVE algorithm.

$$\text{LIVE(n)} = \textbf{union} \ (\text{GEN}(n_i) \ \textbf{union} \ (\text{LIVE}(n_i) \ \textbf{intersect not} \ \text{KILL}(n_i)))$$
$$\text{all } n_i,$$
$$\text{immediate}$$
$$\text{successors}$$
$$\text{of } n$$

If $live(n, x) = 1$, then "variable x is *live* at node n." If $avail(n, x) = 1$, then "variable x is *avail* at node n."

An algorithm for detecting all statements at which an uninitialized variable reference "must" occur appears in Fig. 6.3. This algorithm is designed to detect that the reference to x at statement 5 is a "must" uninitialized reference error. For this and subsequent algorithms, the functions REF(n) and DEF(n) must be defined on the nodes of the flowgraph. These functions will be used as annotation criteria in establishing the *gen* and *kill* notations for a particular application of the analysis algorithms. REF(n) is a V-bit vector whose i-th component is defined by $ref(n, x_i)$. $ref(n, x_i)$ is 1 if and only if the statement represented by node n involves a reference to the variable x which is mapped by f onto index value i. Otherwise, $ref(n, x_i)$ is 0. DEF(n) is defined similarly. $def(n, x_i)$ is 1 if and only if the statement represented by node n defines the variable x which is mapped by f onto the index value i. Otherwise, $def(n, x_i)$ is 0. Also, 0 is defined as a V-bit vector, all of whose components are 0. 1 is a V-bit vector all of whose components are 1.

Algorithm 1:

```
/* initialize bit vectors */
for n := 1 to N + 1 do
    GEN(n) := 0;
    KILL(n) := DEF(n); /* DEF is the criterion employed
    in establishing the KILL sets */
od;
GEN(0) := 1; /* all variables are in the GEN set of the start node */
KILL(0) := 0; /* no variables are in the KILL set of the start node */
/* invoke analysis algorithm */
call AVAIL;
/* generate error messages */
for n := 1 to N do /* loop through program nodes */
    for i := 1 to V do /* check all variables at each node */
        if ref(n, i) = 1 and avail(n, i) = 1 /* the error condition */
            then print ("an uninitialized reference to", f⁻¹(i),
                "must occur at node", n);
        fi;
    od;
od;
```

It is important to observe that Algorithm 1 is designed to assure that the error message will only be generated when a particular variable cannot possibly be initialized by any execution sequence leading up to the reference at the node to which the message pertains. In particular, it is important for the reader to verify that this algorithm correctly analyzes the program, in Fig. 6.3. Fig. 6.4 shows the contents of each set (*gen*, *kill*, etc.) at each node upon termination of Algorithm 1. Note that variable x is in the *avail* set at the write node in task T1. Also note that x is not in the *avail* set at the write in task T2. Thus, an error message will definitely be produced for the reference to x at statement 5, but not for the reference at statement 8.

NODE	REF	DEF	GEN	KILL	AVAIL
0			x,flag		x,flag
1					x,flag
2	---	---	---	---	---
3	---	---	---	---	---
4					x,flag
5	x				x,flag
6					x,flag
7					
8	x				
9					
10					x,flag
11		flag		flag	x,flag
12					x
13	flag	x		x	x
14					
15					
16					

Fig. 6.4. Contents of the data flow analysis sets for the PAF of Fig. 6.3.

An algorithm is now presented for detecting "may" uninitialized variable reference errors at a node. This algorithm is designed to detect a variable reference occurring at a statement for which there exists an execution sequence that leads up to the statement and does not initialize the variable. Referring to Fig. 6.3 again, such an error clearly occurs at statement 5, but of more interest there is also such an error at statement 8. Algorithm 1 does not detect the error at statement 8, but Algorithm 2 will.

Before presenting Algorithm 2, a necessary modification to the AVAIL algorithm must be explained.

Suppose n_w is a flowgraph node which represents a **wait** statement. In the PAF G of the program containing n_w, n_w will be the head of some edges which are usual flow of control edges, and the head of at least one edge whose tail represents the termination activity for a concurrent task. Suppose now that the set of usual flow of control edges whose heads are n_w is given by, $((f_1, n_w), (f_2, n_w), \ldots, (f_F, n_w))$, and that the set of concurrent task termination edges which have n_w as their heads is given by $((p_1, n_w), (p_2, n_w), \ldots, (p_P, n_w))$. Now, create a new graph node n_w', delete the edges $((f_1, n_w), \ldots, (f_F, n_w))$ and replace them by the edges $((f_1, n_w), \ldots, (f_F, n_w'), (n_w', n_w))$. Suppose this is done for every **wait** node in G. Denote the resulting graph by G'. Now compute AVAIL(n) as usual, except use the following equilibrium condition at the **wait**-for-any nodes of G' only.

(*) $\text{AVAIL}(n_w) = \textbf{intersect } \text{AVAIL}(p_i) \textbf{ union } \text{AVAIL}(n_w') \ (p_i)_{i=1}^{P}$

This condition allows a variable to be computed as *avail* at a **wait**-for-any only if it will be *avail* regardless of which task completes first (and thus satisfies the **wait**).

A different equilibrium condition is required at **wait**-for-all nodes.

$$(*)\ \text{AVAIL}(n_w) = \textbf{union}\ \text{AVAIL}(p_i)\ \textbf{union}\ \text{AVAIL}(n'_w)\ (p_i)_{i=1}^{P}$$

A variable will be *avail* here if it is *avail* on any one of the tasks which feed into the **wait** (as the **wait**-for-all guarantees that all the tasks will have executed before the **wait** is satisfied).

The resulting AVAIL(n) bit vectors will be quite useful here. Thus, denote the algorithm which employs the starred formulas as the equilibrium conditions for all of the wait nodes of G' as AVAIL*. In all the algorithms which follow, it is assumed that graph G' has been created and that the analysis takes place on that graph.

Algorithm 2:
```
/* initialize the bit vectors, but differently from 3.1 */
for n := 1 to N + 1 do
    KILL(n) := 0;
    GEN(n) := DEF(n);
od;
KILL(0) := 1;
GEN(0) := 0;
/* invoke the revised analysis algorithm */
call AVAIL*;
/* generate error messages as before */
for n := 1 to N do
    for i := 1 to V do
        if ref (n, i) = 1 and avail(n, i) = 0 /* note the
                        revised error condition */
            then print ("an uninitialized reference to",
                        f¹(i), "may occur at node", n);
        fi;
    od;
od;
```

Using a different algorithm, the event sequence associated with this anomaly may be indicated to the programmer. Unfortunately, many such event sequences are unexecutable. This problem and partial remedies to it are discussed elsewhere [12]. In the example here, variable x is not in the *avail* set at either write statement in task T1 or T2. Thus, the potential for error is reported at both nodes. In this case, the associated event sequences are clearly executable.

An algorithm is now presented for detecting at the start node all the "must" uninitialization errors. In the example of Fig. 6.3, interest is again in detecting the error which occurs at the reference to x in statement 5, except in this case the point of detection (and error message generation) will be the start node of the program.

Analogous to the presentation of Algorithm 2, a necessary modification to the LIVE algorithm must be explained. For concurrent programs, it is useful to define a different equilibrium condition than that presented earlier. This revised condition is applied only at **schedule** nodes.

(*) LIVE(n) = **intersect** (GEN(n_i) **union** (LIVE(n_i) **intersect not** KILL(n_i)))

all n_i,

immediate

successors

of n

Since an error should be signaled only if a definition is encountered on both the scheduling process and all the scheduled processes, the intersection of the live sets on all successors of the **schedule** is taken.

The algorithm which creates the *live* sets, employing (*) at all **schedule** nodes of G, is denoted by LIVE*. (A graph G' is not required in this case, as a schedule node only has a single control flow edge leaving it. All others lead to a **task** initialization node.)

Algorithm 3:

```
/* initialize bit vectors */
for n := 0 to N do
    GEN(n) := DEF(n);
    KILL(n) := REF(n);
od;
GEN(N + 1) := 1;
KILL(N + 1) := 0;
/* invoke the revised analysis algorithm */
call LIVE*;
for i := 1 to V do /* now check all the variables
    at the start node */
    if live(0, i) = 0 /* the error condition */
            then print ("an uninitialized reference to", f⁻¹(i),
                "will occur");
    fi;
od;
```

In Fig. 6.3, variable x will be missing from the *live* set at the start, due to the *kill* present at line 5. (The *live* set at the **wait** node does contain x, however, as the error in task T2 is dependent on the execution sequence taken.)

The detection of *possible* errors is achieved through the following algorithm.

Algorithm 4:

```
/* initialize the bit vectors, same criteria at all nodes */
for n := 0 to N + 1 do
    GEN(n) := REF(n);
    KILL(n) := DEF(n);
od;
/* use the standard analysis algorithm */
```

```
    call LIVE;
    for i := 1 to V do /* check for errors at the start node */
        if live(0, i) = 1 /* a different error condition from 3 */
                then print ("an uninitialized reference to", f⁻¹(i),
                        "may occur"); )
        fi;
    od;
```

In this example, variable x is in the *live* set at the start because of the references in both tasks. (Now note that the **wait** node has x in its *live* set, indicating that there is an execution sequence following which encounters a reference before any initialization. An error in that execution sequence would depend on x not being initialized before the **wait**, which of course it is not.)

To summarize briefly, two basic algorithms are involved. One computes *live* sets; the other *avail* sets. With suitably created *gen* and *kill* sets attached to the PAF and special rules applied at **wait** nodes during the computation of avail and at **schedule** nodes during the computation of *live*, a comprehensive set of programming anomalies may be detected in concurrent process programs.

That is not the end of the problem, however.

IV. Parceling of Analysis Activities

Now return to the example of Section III and modify the program slightly. In that example, task T2 performed the same actions as task T1. There was no need to declare two tasks, except that it made the analysis simpler. The program shown below is written with only a single task declaration.

```
1 Main: program;

2       declare integer x;
3       declare boolean flag;

4       T1: task;
5           write x;
6       close TI;

7       schedule TI;
8       read flag;
9       wait for TI;
10      if flag then read x;
11      schedule TI;
12 close Main;
```

The PAF for this program is given in Fig. 6.5. As before, the nodes are numbered and annotated with the corresponding statements. Note that the PAF has been drawn with two edges entering the task's start node.

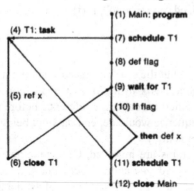

Fig. 6.5. PAF for program with two uninitialization errors, written with a single task.

Suppose now that "must" uninitialization errors should be located and detected at the point of reference. The concern, therefore, is to compute the *avail* sets as described in Algorithm 1. Using this algorithm on the graph as shown will result in x not being in the *avail* set at the reference (at line 5). Thus it cannot be stated that whenever this node is executed an uninitialization error will result. Indeed, this is a correct statement when applied to the second time the task is scheduled: there is only the possibility for an error at this line. This is somewhat unsatisfactory, though, as it is clear that the first time T1 is scheduled an error will occur, regardless of the execution sequence.

The strength of the analysis may be improved in this regard by parceling the PAF and detecting the error not at the reference, but at the point where the task is scheduled. One disadvantage to doing this is that one will not be able to point directly to the statement in the task at which the error occurs.

The method for doing this is based on the technique presented by Fosdick and Osterweil for handling external procedures when performing data flow analysis on single-process programs [7]. Their technique abstracts the data flow in each procedure using the LIVE and AVAIL algorithms, and attaches this abstracted information to all invoking nodes for each procedure. Data flow analysis can then be performed on the invoking procedure. This technique is adapted here to the analysis of tasks for anomalous event sequences. The data usage patterns within each task are determined using LIVE and AVAIL. These abstractions are attached to all **schedule** and **wait** nodes referring to each task. Analysis of this remarked ("trimmed") graph then proceeds as described previously.

For the example of Fig. 6.5, the analysis will proceed roughly as follows. The algorithms 1-4 would be run for the local variables in task T1 first. (Since there are no local variables, this step is omitted.) Next, T1 is annotated as described in Algorithm 3 for global variables (in this case, x). The LIVE algorithm is run, giving the result that x is *live* at the **task** node, 4. Consequently, nodes 7 and 11 are labeled with $ref(n, x) = 1$, indicating that execution of node 7 or node 11 always results in a subsequent reference to x. Algorithms 1-4 can now be run for the variables local to Main. Algorithm 1 will show that x is *avail* at 7, indicating an uninitialized reference to x will always occur as a consequence of executing node 7. Ideally, the resulting error message will indicate that the error actually occurs "somewhere" in the scheduled task. Determination of the error's precise location would be relegated to a separate (depth-first) scan of the task.

Clearly, it is possible to continue passing up data usage abstractions through an arbitrary number of levels of task scheduling. The restriction that must be imposed on the program in order to adopt this technique is that the process invocation graph be acyclic. In the single-process program situation there is an analogous restriction that the subroutine call graph be acyclic; recursion is prohibited. This prohibition exists for multiprocess programs as well, but the process invocation graph is also required to be acyclic. This is a stronger restriction, as it is possible to have a cyclic process invocation graph which does not involve any recursion, either on the process or the subroutine level. For the moment we are satisfied that a significant class of programs is nevertheless being addressed, but further investigation is clearly called for here.

V. Additional Reference/Definition Anomalies

A. Referencing a Variable While Defining It in a Parallel Process

Reconsider the example of Section II-B. At line 5, in task T1, there is a reference to variable x which, in the absence of a "fortunate" sequencing of events, will be uninitialized when the task is first scheduled. If Algorithm 1 is run on the PAF corresponding to this program (Fig. 6.2), an "always" uninitialization error will be detected at the reference. (It is assumed that the analysis is carried out in the parceled manner described in the preceding section, as the second time the task is scheduled the possibility exists that x is defined.)

Would it be proper to report this as an always error? What is termed a "fortunate" sequence really makes this an anomaly. It is conceivable that known operating environment conditions guarantee that the initialization performed by task T2 transpires before the reference in task T1. A "sometimes" error message is unsatisfactory, though, as such "guarantees" are outside the domain of the program. This confusion is due to the referencing and defining of a variable by two processes which may be executing in parallel. This construction, besides impairing the other analyses in the manner described, seems inherently dangerous and should be reported as an anomaly in its own right.

This anomaly may be detected in a rather naive manner, given that it can be determined which sections of the program may be operating concurrently. Assume that the PAF is parceled into S subgraphs, G_i. Each section corresponds to a task or a portion of a task. Briefly, section boundary nodes are **program, task, close,** and **wait** nodes. (The notion of a section is roughly equivalent to that of a task which contains no **wait** statements.) Also, assume that a Boolean function, PARALLEL, is available which determines which sections can execute in parallel. That is, PARALLEL defines a function of two variables, i and j, such that PARALLEL(i,j) is **true** if and only if G_i and G_j represent sections which might execute in parallel. It is important to note that the algorithm for determining this is not trivial. Indications of how such an algorithm can be constructed may be found in [13] and [14]. Based on these assumptions, an algorithm can be presented for detecting the possibility of referencing and defining a variable from parallel tasks or sections.

Suppose the nodes of graph G_i are numbered from $n_{i,0}$, the logical predecessor to the sections start node, to $n_{i,1i}$ the logical successor to the sections final node. For clarity, also assume as before that f maps all the variables of the program onto the integers 1-V.

Algorithm 5:

  for i = 1 **to** S **do** /* loop through each section */

    for j = 1 **to** 1_i **do** /* annotate the start node within the
    section according to the actions at each node within
    the section */

      $REF(n_{i,0}) := REF(n_{i,0})$ union $REF(n_{i,j})$;
      $DEF(n_{i,0}) := DEF(n_{i,0})$ union $DEF(n_{i,j})$;

    od;

  od;

  for i := 1 **to** S **do** /* examine every possible section/section pair */

    for j := 1 **to** S **do**

      if i ≠ j

        then if PARALLEL(i, j)

          then if $REF(n_{i,0})$ intersect $DEF(n_{j,0}) \neq 0$

            then print ("the following may be referenced",
            "and defined in parallel by sections", i, "and", j);

              for v := 1 **to** V **do** /* check each variable */

                if $ref(n_{i,0}, v) = 1$ **and**
                    $def(n_{j,0}, v) = 1$

                  then print $(f^{-1}(v))$;

                fi;

            od;

          fi;

        fi;

      fi;

    od;

  od;

This algorithm detects the possibility of references and definitions occurring in parallel. An algorithm can also be constructed that determines when this error must occur, regardless of the execution paths within the process. The only change required to Algorithm 5 is in the creation of the REF and DEF sets at the nodes $n_{i,0}$. The REF sets at $n_{i,0}$ would be computed by an algorithm similar to 3, and the DEF sets by an algorithm similar to 1.

B. Unused Variable Definitions

A programming anomaly that is not truly erroneous, but which often indicates the presence of a design error, is an unused variable definition. The example of Section II-B contains such an anomaly. Variable y is defined both by task T2 and by the main program (at line 20). Y is then possibly redefined at line 22, before ever being referenced. (The anomalous situation which occurs at the reference to y (line 23) will be examined in the next section.)

This anomaly may be detected by techniques very similar to those presented in Section III. Here, as with uninitialization errors, there are four cases to examine: detecting errors which always occur through examining all possible event sequences which follow a node, detecting the possibility of such errors, detecting errors which always occur through examining all event sequences preceding a node, and detecting possible errors by examining the preceding event sequences. The algorithm presented here is only for determining the anomalous situation where a variable v is defined at node n, yet on all paths leading to n, v has been previously defined without any intervening reference. Algorithms for the other three related anomalous situations should be derivable by analogy. Note that the presence of reference-definition in parallel anomalies may impair the quality of the analysis here, as it did before.

The procedure given here assumes that the program graph has been parceled into task subgraphs, that the process invocation graph is acyclic, and that the labeling used in Algorithm 5 is used. This particular error also requires that a new equilibrium condition be defined for application during the computation of the AVAIL sets at **wait** nodes. The new condition is as follows:

(**) $\text{AVAIL}(n_w) =$

    intersect $\text{AVAIL}(p_i)$ **union** $\text{AVAIL}(n_w') - $ **intersect** $\text{REFED}(p_i)$

    $(p_i)_{i=1}^P$ $(p_i)_{i=1}^P$

This condition applies at **wait**-for-anys. At **wait**-for-alls:

(**) $\text{AVAIL}(n_w) =$

    union $\text{AVAIL}(p_i)$ **union** $\text{AVAIL}(n_w') - $ **union** $\text{REFED}(p_i)$

    $(p_i)_{i=1}^P$ $(p_i)_{i=1}^P$

AVAIL** will denote the algorithm which employs the double-starred formulas as the equilibrium conditions for all the **wait** nodes of G'. REFED(n) is a V-bit

vector used during the computation of AVAIL**, which is used to save the value
of some intermediate AVAIL sets.

Algorithm 6:

```
declare bit vector PROCESSED (1: S);
PROCESSED := 0; /* nothing has been processed yet */
while PROCESSED ≠ 1 do /* loop until all processes analyzed */
    for i := 1 to S do /*find an un-analyzed process*/
        if processed_i = 0 and processed_t = 1 for all tasks, t,
                for which G_i waits /* ensure all the processes G_i
                waits for are analyzed */
        then
                processed_i := 1; /* mark this process as analyzed */
                for j = 1 to 1_i do /* annotate the processes nodes */
                  GEN(n_{i,j}) := REF(n_{i,j});
                  KILL(n_{i,j}) := 0;
                od;
                KILL(n_{i,0}) := 1; /* block off any references which
                occur before this section */
                call AVAIL*;
                /* a variable is now avail if it is referenced along paths */
                REFED(n_{i,1i}) := AVAIL(n_{i,1i} 1); /* save the avail sets */
                /* remark the graph */
                for j := 1 to 1_i do
                  GEN(n_{i,j}) := DEF(n_{i,j});
                  KILL(n_{i,j}) := REF(n_{i,j});
                od;
                KILL(n_{i,0}) :=1; /* block any definitions which
                precede the start node of the section */
                call AVAIL**; /* this algorithm used the REFED vector */
                for j : = 1 to 1_i do /* generate the messages */
                  if DEF(n_{i,j}) intersect AVAIL(n_{i,j}) ≠ 0
                  then print ("the definition(s) at node", n_{i,j},
                        "is always immediately preceded by another",
                            "definition. The variable(s) is (are): ");
                  for k := 1 to V do
                            if def(n_{i,j},k) = 1 and avail(n_{i,j},k) = 1 then print(f^{-1}(k)); fi;
                  od;
                fi;
            od;
        fi;
    od;
od;
```

C. Referencing a Variable of Indeterminate Value

In the above presentation, the anomalous data flow situation existing at the reference to variable y, occurring at line 23 of the sample program in Section II-B was not discussed. Y is defined by task T2 at line 10, by the main program at line 20, possibly again in the main program at line 22. If, for the moment, the definition at line 22 is ignored, then it is indeterminate whether the definition from the task or from the main program is referenced at line 23. If the presence of the definition at line 22 is acknowledged, depending on the event sequence (namely, whether variable flag is true), the reference at line 23 may be to an indeterminate value.

The algorithm now presented is designed to detect indeterminate reference anomalies which will occur, regardless of execution sequence. The anomalies will be detected at the point of indeterminate reference.

Algorithm 7:

declare bit vector PROCESSED (1:S); /* will indicate which sections
have been processed */
PROCESSED : = 0;
while PROCESSED $\neq$ 1 **do** /* loop until all sections processed */
   for i := 1 **to** S **do** /* seek an unprocessed section */
     if processed$_i$ = 0 and processed$_t$ = 1 for all tasks, t,
       for which G$_i$ waits /* the condition for processing */
   then
     processed$_i$:= 1; /* mark this section as processed */
     for j :=1 **to** 1$_i$ **do**
         GEN(n$_{i,j}$) := DEF(n$_{i,j}$);
         KILL(n$_{i,j}$) := 0;
     od;
     KILL(n$_{i,0}$) := 1; /* block off the effects of definitions
     prior to execution of this section */
     call AVAIL*;
     /* if a variable is *avail* at section i's stop node, its
     value must have been set as the result of executing
     task i */
     DEFED(n$_{i,1i}$) = AVAIL(n$_{i,1i}$); /* this information is
     needed for processing other tasks which wait for this
     task */
     for j :=1 **to** 1$_i$ **do**
         GEN(n$_{i,j}$) := 0; KILL(n$_{i,j}$) := DEF(n$_{i,j}$);
         /* GEN will be reinitialized below. KILL is set to
         1 iff there is a definition local to this task which
         could supercede definitions in other tasks */
     od;
     for all w$_{i,a}$, **wait** nodes in G$_i$ **do**

```
COUNT := 0;
for all predecessor nodes, p_{i,a,b}, of w_{i,a} do
    COUNT := COUNT plus AVAIL (p_{i,a,b});
od;
/* COUNT now contains, for each variable, the
number of different tasks which may set the
value of the variable immediately before execution
resumes at node w_{i,a} */
GEN(w_{i,a}) : = 0;
for v := 1 to V do
    if COUNT_v greater than 1
    then GEN(w_{i,a},v) := 1; /* potential for error
    exists */
    fi;
od;
```

od;
```
call AVAIL;
/* avail is 1 iff on no path will a necessarily
multiple definition be screened by an unambiguous
local (to this task) definition */
for j := 1 to 1_i do
    if AVAIL(n_{i,j}) intersect REF(n_{i,j}) ≠ 1
    then print ("indeterminate reference at", n_{i,j});
    fi;
od;
AVAIL(n_{i,1i}) := DEFED(n_{i,1i}); /* label this
task's stop node with reference information
needed by tasks which wait for it */
```
fi;
od;
od;

VI. Process Synchronization Anomalies

As an outgrowth of the author's investigation into the detection of data flow anomalies in concurrent process software, it became clear that some forms of synchronization errors could be detected in essentially the same manner. The nature of these errors was alluded to in the Introduction. They will now be considered in detail. Note that in form the synchronization anomalies are analogous to data flow anomalies. In addition, as with data flow, many of the anomalies are not strictly errors, but they are conditions which may be interpreted as erroneous in the sense of indicating deeper problems. At the very least, they represent conditions which should be clearly documented.

A. Waiting for an Unscheduled Process

This anomaly is perhaps the most apparent, and the closest in form to the data flow anomalies already discussed. The example of Section II-B contains such an error at line 6 in task T1. Task T3 is never scheduled, yet T1 waits for it. The analogous data flow anomaly is an uninitialized variable. As such, Algorithm 1 is rewritten to detect this anomaly. Thus, the interest here is in detecting anomalies which must occur, and the anomaly is to be detected at **wait** nodes. Our notation requires the introduction of functions SCH(n), WAIT_ALL(n), and WAIT_ANY(n). All function values are T-bit vectors. It will be assumed that the program unit being analyzed has T processes, and that a one-to-one function g has been defined, mapping the process names onto the integers $(1, ..., T)$. The i-th component of SCH(n) is defined by $sch(n, t_i)$. $sch(n, t_i)$ is 1 if and only if the statement represented by node n schedules the task t, which is mapped by the function g onto index value i. WAIT_ALL and WAIT_ANY are similarly defined for the two types of **wait** statements in this language.

Algorithm 8:

```
for n := 1 to N+1 do
  GEN(n) := 0;
  KILL(n) := SCH(n);
od;
GEN(0) := 1;
KILL(0):= 0;
call AVAIL;
for n := 1 to N do
  for i := 1 to T do
    if (wait all(n, i) 1 or wait any(n, i) = 1)
      and avail(n,i) = 1
    then print ("the reference to process", g⁻¹(i),
       "at node", n, "is to a process which has not been scheduled.");
    fi;
  od;
od;
```

In Fig. 6.2, task T3 will be in the *avail* set at the node corresponding to line 6. Thus the error will be detected.

As may be expected, there is also an analogue to the reference-definition in parallel condition here. The following program presents such a condition.

    1 Main: **program**;

```
2   T1: task;
3     schedule T2;
4   close T1;

5   T2: task;
6     /* do something */
7   close T2;
8   schedule T1;
9   /* do something */
10  wait for T2;

11  close Main;
```

In this program, there is the possibility that task T2 will be scheduled before the **wait** at line 10 is encountered. The analysis described above will cause an "always" message to be generated. Thus, a "schedule/wait in parallel" analysis must be performed to give a complete description of the situation. This would be performed in a manner analogous to that of reference/definition in parallel analysis.

B. Waiting for a Process Guaranteed to Have Already Terminated

The example of Section II-B still has errors that must be considered. At line 24, the main program waits for task T2 to complete. Yet, the task was already assured to have terminated at line 21. The second **wait** is therefore superfluous and possibly misleading. Since the language syntax used here enables specification of **wait**-for-all and **wait**-for-any, one must be careful to distinguish the errors which will be detected and the algorithms which apply in each case.

To indicate the nature of the technique, a single case will be considered: looking for constructs which, regardless of event sequence, assure us that at least one of the processes named in a **wait**-for-all has in fact already terminated at a previous **wait**.

   Algorithm 9:
```
   for n := 1 to N+1 do
      KILL(n) := SCH(n);
      GEN(n) := WAIT_ALL(n);
      if the statement represented by node n is
         a task statement for t_i
            then gen(n, t_i) := 1;
      fi;
   od;
   GEN(0) := 1;
   KILL(0) := 0;
```

```
call AVAIL;
for n := 1 to N do
  for i := 1 to T do
    if avail(n, i) = 1 and wait all(n, i) = 1
      then print ("termination has already been
        ensured for task", g⁻¹(i), "at node", n);
    fi;
  od;
od;
```

In Fig. 6.2, task T2 is in the *avail* sets of all predecessor nodes of the node corresponding to the first **wait** (line 21), but is in only one of the *avail* sets of the predecessor nodes of the wait at line 24. Thus, the first **wait** is correct, while the second is anomalous.

The algorithm presented here may be easily modified to detect the possibility of anomalies. To detect anomalies occurring at **wait**-for-anys, new procedures must be developed to account for situations such as:

> **wait for** T1 or T2;
>   ...
> **wait for** T1 or T2;

In the absence of other synchronization statements, the second wait is spurious; satisfaction of the first wait guarantees immediate satisfaction of the second.

C. Scheduling a Process in Parallel with Itself

The last synchronization anomaly which will be examined is that of scheduling a process to execute in parallel with an already active incarnation of the same process. In the example of Section II-B, there is an instance of this error at line 25, where task T1 is scheduled for the second time (the first being at line 15). At no point in any process, let alone before the second **schedule**, has TI been guaranteed to have terminated.

An algorithm will be presented for detecting situations where, regardless of event sequence, termination has not been assured by the time a **schedule** is reached.

Algorithm 10:
```
for n :=1 to N+1 do
  GEN(n) : = SCH(n);
  KILL(n) := WAIT_ALL(n) union WAIT_ANY(n);
od;
KILL(0) := 1;
GEN(0) := 0;
call AVAIL*;
```

```
for n :=1 to N do
  for i :=1 to T do
    if sch(n, i) = 1 and avail(n, i) = 1
      then print ("termination of process", g⁻¹(i),
        "has never been ensured before the schedule at node", n);
    fi;
  od;
od;
```

If this algorithm is applied to the example, an error will be detected at line 25.

As may be expected, if a **schedule** may be performed in parallel with a **wait** (on the same process) the quality of this analysis is impaired. In particular, if such a condition exists, Algorithm 10 will detect a "for sure" error, where in fact there is an event sequence where termination takes place.

VII. Conclusion

A. Summary

In this paper we have presented several algorithms useful in the detection of data flow and synchronization anomalies in programs involving concurrent processes. Data flow is analyzed on an interprocess and interprocedural basis. The basis of the technique is analysis of a process augmented flowgraph, a graph representation of a system of communicating concurrent processes. The algorithms have excellent efficiency characteristics, and utilize basic algorithms which are present in many optimizing compilers. A procedure is outlined which allows analysis to proceed on "parcels" of the subject program. Only the most basic synchronization constructs have been considered, however.

B. Open Problems

Several matters discussed in this presentation clearly warrant further investigation. The most pressing need now is a consideration of additional synchronization and communication constructs. These will introduce new classes of errors and may require that changes be made to the algorithms presented here.

One issue not addressed here is the creation of correct process-augmented flowgraphs. In the sample language presented in this paper this was a relatively trivial task, but as additional (real) synchronization constructs are added significant problems are anticipated. It is not clear at this point if "correct" PAF's can always be generated. The analysis schemes may require alteration to accommodate such a situation.

Dynamic determination of synchronization paths has not been considered at all here, but work has been done in this area [15]. Likewise, recursive procedures and processes have been precluded. Work has been done in data flow analysis of recursive routines [16], but it appears inadequate for the analysis performed here.

References

[1] L. J. Osterweil and L. D. Fosdick, "DAVE—A validation, error detection, and documentation system for FORTRAN programs," *Software—Practice and Experience*, vol. 6, 1976.

[2] P. Brinch Hansen, "The programming language concurrent Pascal," *IEEE Trans. Software Eng.*, vol. SE-1, pp. 199-207, June 1975.

[3] N. Wirth, "Modula: A language for modular multiprogramming," *Software—Practice and Experience*, vol. 7, pp. 3-35, Jan. 1977.

[4] DoD Requirements for High Order Computer Programming Languages, STEELMAN, 1978.

[5] F. H. Martin, "HAL/S—The avionics programming system for shuttle," in *Proc. AIAA Conf Computers in Aerospace*, Los Angeles, CA, Nov. 1977, pp. 308-318.

[6] T. A. Straeter, et al., "Research flight software engineering an MUST-An integrated system of support tools," in *Proc. COMPSAC 77*, Chicago, IL, Nov. 1977, pp. 392-396.

[7] L. D. Fosdick and L. J. Osterweil, "Data flow analysis in software reliability," *Computing Surveys*, vol. 8, pp. 305-330, Sept. 1976. (Reprinted as Chapter 5)

[8] R. N. Taylor and L. J. Osterweil, "A facility for verification, testing, and documentation of concurrent process software," in *Proc. COMPSAC 78*, Chicago, IL, Nov. 1978, pp. 36-41.

[9] F. E. Allen, "Program optimization," *Annu. Rev. Automatic Programming*, 1969.

[10] F. E. Allen and J. Cocke, "A program data flow analysis procedure," *Commun. Ass. Comput. Mach.*, vol. 19, pp. 137-147, Mar. 1976.

[11] M. S. Hecht and J. D. Ullman, "A simple algorithm for global data flow analysis problems," *SIAM J. Computing*, vol. 4, pp. 519-532, Dec. 1975.

[12] L. J. Osterweil, "The detection of unexecutable program paths through static data flow analysis," Dep. Comput. Sci., Univ. Colorado, Tech. Rep. #CU-CS-110-77, 1977.

[13] W. Riddle, G. Bristow, C. Drey, and B. Edwards, "Anomaly detection in concurrent programs," in *Proc. 4th Int. Conf. Software Eng.*, Munich, Germany, Sept. 1979.

[14] J. L. Peterson, "Petri nets," *Computing Surveys*, vol. 9, pp. 223-252, Sept. 1977.

[15] J. H. Reif, "Data flow analysis of communicating processes," in *Proc. 6th Annu. ACM Symp. Principles of Programming Languages*, Feb. 1979.

[16] J. M. Barth, "A practical interprocedural data-flow analysis algorithm," *Commun. Ass. Comput. Mach.*, vol. 21, pp. 724-736, Sept. 1978.

Cecil: A Sequencing Constraint Language for Automatic Static Analysis Generation[1]

Kurt M. Olender and Leon J. Osterweil

K. M. Olender was with the Department of Computer Science, University of Colorado, Boulder, CO 80309. He is now with the Department of Computer Science, Colorado State University, Fort Collins, CO 80523.

L. J. Osterweil was with the Department of Computer Science, University of Colorado, Boulder, CO 80309. He is now with the Department of Information and Computer Science, University of California, Irvine, CA 92717.

Abstract This paper presents a flexible and general mechanism for specifying problems relating to the sequencing of events and mechanically translating them into dataflow analysis algorithms capable of solving those problems. Dataflow analysis has been used for quite some time in compiler code optimization. It has recently gained increasing attention as a way of statically checking for the presence or absence of errors and as a way of guiding the test case selection process. Most static analyzers, however, have been custom-built to search for fixed, and often quite limited, classes of dataflow conditions. We show that the range of sequences for which it is interesting and worthwhile to search is actually quite broad and diverse. We create a formalism for specifying this diversity of conditions. We then show that these conditions can be modeled essentially as dataflow analysis problems for which effective solutions are known and further show how these solutions can be exploited to serve as the basis for mechanical creation of analyzers for these conditions.

Index Terms—Dataflow analysis, finite state machines, sequencing, specification, static analysis.

I. Introduction

The importance of assuring high quality in software has been recognized for decades. In that time progress has been made toward developing software quality tools and techniques, but it is still very difficult to develop high quality software

[1] This work was supported in part by the National Science Foundation under Grant DCR-8403341, the U.S. Department of Energy under Grant DE-FG02-84ER13283, and the Defense Advanced Research Projects Agency under Grant DARPA-1537626.

Kurt M. Olender and Leon J. Osterweil, "Cecil: A Sequencing Constraint Language for Automatic Static Analysis Generation,"
IEEE Transactions on Software Engineering 16:3, March 1990. © 1990 IEEE

and to accurately determine the quality of developed software. We believe that the most fundamental techniques required in assuring software quality are the detection of the presence of errors (the goal of most testing activities) and the determination of the absence of errors (the goal of validation and verification). Errors can be present in any software object—ranging from specifications to design objects, code, and test cases. Further, errors can be of various kinds—functional errors, errors of omission, security errors, and so forth.

We believe, however, that all errors can be viewed as inconsistencies between a specification of intent and a specification of an approach to satisfying that intent with some solution vehicle. A design error can be seen to be a specification of a solution approach which, if implemented, would produce a system whose behavior is inconsistent with the intent embodied in the requirements specification that the design was intended to address. Similarly, code errors are inconsistencies between what the design stipulates must be done and what the code actually effects. Inadequate performance, robustness, or security can similarly be seen as execution-time characteristics that are inconsistent with the requirements or design specifications of these characteristics. Unfortunately, all too often these characteristics are not made explicit or rigorous and inconsistencies are identified only in the minds of users, customers, or managers. Often these unstated specifications differ among these individuals leading to differences of opinion as to whether errors or inadequacies exist at all.

The notion of error is a relative one. All errors are inconsistencies between specifications and solutions. An erroneous solution is only erroneous with respect to the specification that it purports to satisfy. For example, testing—the process of attempting to detect the presence of errors—cannot be a definitive process unless and until there exists a suitably definitive specification of intent against which to test. Similarly, validation and verification must be based upon the existence of both the software object to be evaluated and a software object which captures the intent which the object must satisfy. Moreover, the more rigorously these objects are expressed, the more rigorous and definitive that testing, validation, or verification process can be.

Historically, testing has most often been directed at code, because code is written in a programming language with syntax and semantics that are rigorously defined at least in terms of the observed actions of the machines on which compiled and loaded versions are executed. Even in the case of testing code, however, the results are usually not as rigorous and definitive as desired due to the lack of correspondingly well defined specifications of intent. The functional intent of programs has most often been captured in terms of first order predicate calculus assertions [9], [10], [18]. In some cases whole new assertion languages have been developed to facilitate capturing functional intent [24]. To the extent that specifications of functional intent can be made complete and consistent with the intent residing in the minds of all humans concerned with the software development project, these assertions then form a firm and undeniably useful basis for functional testing, validation, and verification activities. Much has been written about the difficulty of creating functional specifications that are complete and consistent with human intent [7].

It seems useful to create specifications of intent that do not necessarily capture the entire functional intent residing in human minds. Instead, we suggest that it is still useful, and often far easier, to express only some aspects of a program's behavior, especially when it is easy to determine that all humans clearly intend for the program to behave in this way. We suggest that it is easier to identify a consensus about more general and higher level properties and functions than to find a similar consensus about all the details and aspects of how a program must work.

In this paper we explore the use of event sequences as a formalism with which to express specifications of intent. We acknowledge that this specification formalism is inadequate for the expression of complete, detailed functional properties of software. One the other hand, we argue that this formalism is still quite useful, as it is effective in capturing a wide range of expressions of functional intent, and, as we shall see later, in describing some common situations that characterize such nonfunctional aspects of software as safety and reliability.

This point of view was advanced by Taylor and Osterweil, who argue that there are certain inescapably algorithmic aspects of all software and that these aspects virtually assure that there are some requirements on the sequencing of the events in that software [34]. We can obtain some idea of the significance of sequencing by studying errors due to omitted or superfluous code. Clearly these can be considered errors in sequencing, as the missing or extra code will cause missing or extra events when the code is executed, thereby causing violations of constraints on the sequences in which those events can occur. Hence this is a large and important class of errors. In addition, however, omitted and superfluous code errors comprise only a proper subset of all possible sequencing errors as they exclude errors due to the incorrect selection of operators or operands. In one study, Ostrand and Weyuker found that 55% of all errors in a set of programs were due to omitted or superfluous code [30].

We conclude that errors in sequencing form a significant, although not all-encompassing, class of faults. The ability to detect such errors seems to be important and useful. We believe that a powerful and comprehensive event sequence analysis tool would be a strong aid to the detection of sequencing errors once the diagnostician has identified the appropriate events and precisely specified the desired or required sequences of those events. Further, the consequent focus such a tool would place upon identification of key events and precise specification of how they should be sequenced is appropriate and useful in itself.

In studying early tools for analyzing program event sequences (e.g., DAVE [11], [29]), and early global compiler optimizers [1], [17], we found that they incorporated only rudimentary languages for specifying the event sequences they sought. These tools detect a surprisingly varied collection of different event sequences, but these sequences are generally "hard coded" into tools with consequently rather inflexible analytic capabilities. We found that it was often useful and important to be able to detect different (although often similar) event sequences. Thus, hypothesizing that a flexible sequence analysis tool was needed, we first sought to create a powerful and precise language for specifying event sequences. This proved to be far harder than we had anticipated as the range of types of sequences that are useful seems to be quite wide. Further, we sought a language which could form the basis for the efficient, automatic creation of static analyzers to check for adherence of programs to the sequencing specification.

This paper describes the results of this work. First we describe Cecil, a powerful language for specifying event sequences. Then we describe an algorithm to perform static analysis and evaluation of programs against Cecil specifications. Finally we describe some experience with Cecil and Cesar (the analysis system for Cecil) and some ideas for extending this work.

II. Previous Work

As noted above, the first event sequence analyzers were custom built to scan for predetermined event sequences. This work will be summarized first. Next, more recent work on specifying event sequences and creating programmable sequence analyzers will be described.

A. Data Flow Analyzers

Data flow analysis is a powerful static analysis technique that was first incorporated into the global optimizers of compilers more than 20 years ago [1]. Its goal is to eliminate unnecessary computations in algorithmic programs. This is done by first determining the presence of certain standard sequences of operations that cause redundant computation, and then generating object code with the redundancies eliminated.

Subsequently it was discovered that the algorithms used to detect these redundancies for global program optimization have broader applicability. Fosdick and Osterweil suggested that these algorithms can find evidence of certain kinds of commonly occurring programming errors [11]. They defined a data flow anomaly to be a sequence of the events reference (r), definition (d), and undefinition (u) of a variable in a program that is either erroneous in itself or is often symptomatic of an error. They claimed that all programs have an implicit specification that these data flow anomalies should not occur.

Their DAVE [29] system statically detected instances of the anomalous sequences $<u, r>$ (uninitialized variables), $<d, d>$ and $<d, u>$ (redundant definitions) in Fortran programs using variants of the data flow algorithms previously used in compiler optimization. The first sequence listed is clearly erroneous. One cannot use a value that has not yet been computed. The last two sequences are not erroneous in themselves, but the value stored by the first definition is never used and its computation wasted. This may indicate either missing code between the two operations or that one of the operations is unnecessary and may be removed.

Since then several other systems, e.g., Freudenberger's system for SETL programs [12], have used data flow algorithms to find these and other anomalous sequences of operations on variables. The SETL system, for example, can find a potentially nonterminating loop by detecting when no loop control variable is defined within the body of the loop.

B. User-Specifiable Sequences

The systems described in the previous section detect the occurrence of a fixed set of sequences that are considered errors or anomalies over a fixed set of operations. Some work has also been done on permitting user specification of both the sequences and the operations.

The programming language Path Pascal supports a facility to embed a specification of the correct sequencing of the procedures encapsulated in a monitor [5], [6]. This specification is then used to generate code to directly enforce the constraints. The notation is based on the path expressions of Habermann [14].

A mechanism similar to Path Pascal's path expressions was proposed by Kieburtz and Silberschatz [23] in their access right expressions. They also develop a set of proof rules to aid in the development of programs that satisfy the sequencing constraints.

Howden uses finite state machines to specify sets of correct event sequences and gives algorithms for the static detection of violations of this specification [21], [22]. Howden's algorithms determine if all event sequences generated by a finite state machine representation of the program are accepted by the specification machine. This work is close in spirit to that which we describe here.

Flow expressions [33], event expressions [31], and constrained expressions [3], [8] are also extensions of regular expressions developed to specify sequencing in concurrent software. The extensions permit the definition of recursively enumerable languages, and thus suffer from the fact that there can be no general procedure for automatically generating analyzers for arbitrary flow expressions [2]. Our own specification language is designed to serve as the basis for the rapid automatic derivation of analyzers for any specification expressed in our notation.

Guttag's axiomatic specifications implicitly define sequencing constraints by defining the effects of particular sequences of the operations of an abstract data type [13]. The effects of some sequences may be explicitly described as an error or may be seen to have no net effect, which can be used to indicate a potentially unnecessary computation. We believe that this work can be coupled with our own work to effect the automatic creation of analyzers for designs that use axiomatic specifications.

McLean [26] has developed a logic for the specification and formal analysis of the correctness of sequencing based on the work of Bartussek and Parnas [4]. This work seems to have goals similar to our own, but aims to use formal logic techniques to determine proper or incorrect sequencing, while our work is aimed at using the fast data flow algorithms arising out of global code optimization for automatic analysis.

Hoare uses sequences in the specification of processes in CSP and defines a formal system for verification of these specifications [19], [20]. Here too, the work is based on the use of formal logic to verify correct sequencing, while we seek to use data flow algorithms.

Luckham's Task Sequencing Language (TSL) uses sequence specifications for concurrent Ada programs and includes the capability to instrument a concurrent Ada program to determine if violations of the sequencing constraints expressed in TSL occur [25]. This work is aimed at the post hoc analysis of dynamically generated event sequences of concurrent programs. Our work is aimed at the static analysis of programs, and currently cannot handle concurrency, although this is an issue we intend to address in future work.

III. Sequencing Constraints

To summarize the motivation for this work, sequencing forms an important domain of potential failures in software in that a significant number of such failures can be characterized by sequences of operations performed during an execution of the software that either directly cause failures or are often symptomatic of the presence of a fault. The ability to specify such sequences and later analyze a piece of software for the presence of these sequences would be an effective aid to the software engineer.

There are two valid directions from which the problem of specifying sequencing and statically detecting anomalies can be attacked. We can define a very general formalism to specify all possible sequencing behavior. We know there will be no general method for statically analyzing an arbitrary specification of this sort, but we can search for methods that permit effective analysis of subsets of the specifications. This is the direction taken in the constrained expression work [3], [8].

The other direction is to define a specification formalism for which every expression can be analyzed by a known method and explore the range of potential failures that the formalism and analysis method permit us to detect. This is the direction taken by Howden with his interface analysis work [22].

We attack the problem in this second way. In this section, after some preliminary definitions, we will present a summary of the model most often used for sequencing analysis and show with some practical examples why that model is inadequate for the description of sequencing behavior oriented toward static analysis. We then present a series of extensions to this model that incrementally add descriptive power that appears to be useful in a static scenario. We will assume the existence of a static analysis method for each of these models. In a subsequent section, we will give such a method for our final model.

A. Definitions

In this paper, we denote the set of all subsets of a set S by $\mathbb{P}(S)$. The conventional symbols for the other set operations and constants are used.

We define a *sequence* as an ordered list of elements from some domain set and denote it by a comma-separated list of elements enclosed in angle brackets. The empty sequence is $<\,>$. Concatenation of sequences is indicated by juxtaposition. For a sequence $s=<s_1, ..., s_n>$, we define first(s) = s_1, last(s) = s_n, jth(s) = s_j, and the reverse of a sequence, $s^r = <s_n, ..., s_1>$. A restricted sequence of s, s_x, is defined to be the sequence s from which every element not in X is removed. Thus, for example, $<a, b, c, b, d>_{\{b,c\}} = <b, c, b>$. Concatenation, closure, restriction, and reverse are defined for sets of sequences in the expected way.

A *regular expression* is a formula that describes a set of sequences [15]. A somewhat nonstandard regular expression grammar is used here, since regular expressions will be used as part of the sequencing constraint notation to be developed later. Some of the symbols in the usual formulation of regular expressions are not on the standard computer keyboard and so would be awkward to include in the language. In the interest of remaining consistent, the same form will be used everywhere.

Let Σ be a finite set of symbols called the *alphabet*, σ be an arbitrary symbol in Σ, # be a symbol explicitly not in Σ, and α and β be arbitrary regular expressions. The set of sequences described by α over alphabet Σ is denoted $\mathcal{L}(\alpha, \Sigma)$. The syntax of regular expressions is defined with a BNF grammar and the semantics are defined by the function $\mathcal{L}$. These definitions are given in Fig. 7.1. We use BNF notation for all grammars. Terminals are enclosed in single quotes, brackets enclose optional symbols, and braces indicate 0 or more repetitions of the enclosed symbols. Some of the BNF meta-symbols (e.g., the brackets, parentheses, and braces) may be similar to some terminals. Each major alternative is placed on a separate line to avoid large numbers of meta-parentheses. The alphabet symbols are identifiers composed of strings of consecutive uppercase or lowercase letters, periods, underscores, or hyphens.

An edge-labeled single-exit flowgraph is a connected, directed, labeled graph given by the sextuple G = (V, E, s, t, ψ, L) where V is a set of vertices, $E \subseteq V \times V$ is a set of directed edges, $s \in V$ is the sole vertex with no predecessors (the *entry vertex*), $t \in V$ is the sole vertex with no successors (the *exit vertex*), ψ is an alphabet of labels, and $L: E \rightarrow \psi$ is a function that labels each edge with a label from ψ. The special label # $\in \psi$ is called the *null label*. Note that the symbol # in a regular expression denotes the empty sequence. The graph is *connected* when every $v \in V$

is on a path from s to t (as defined below). The term *flowgraph* will always indicate an edge-labeled single-exit flowgraph.

```
regexp   ::=  event
         |    '?'
         |    '#'
         |    '(' regexp ')'
         |    regexp ';' regexp
         |    regexp '|' regexp
         |    regexp '•'
         |    regexp '+'
         |    '~' regexp
event    ::=  evtchar {evtchar}
evtchar  ::=  letter | digit | '.' | '_' | ':'
```

$$
\begin{aligned}
\mathcal{L}(\#,\Sigma) &= \{\langle\rangle\} \\
\mathcal{L}(\sigma,\Sigma) &= \{\langle\sigma\rangle\} \\
\mathcal{L}(?,\Sigma) &= \bigcup_{\sigma\in\Sigma}\mathcal{L}(\sigma,\Sigma) \\
\mathcal{L}(\alpha;\beta,\Sigma) &= \mathcal{L}(\alpha,\Sigma)\mathcal{L}(\beta,\Sigma) \\
\mathcal{L}(\alpha\mid\beta,\Sigma) &= \mathcal{L}(\alpha,\Sigma)\cup\mathcal{L}(\beta,\Sigma) \\
\mathcal{L}(\alpha\bullet,\Sigma) &= \mathcal{L}(\alpha,\Sigma)^* \\
\mathcal{L}(\alpha+,\Sigma) &= \mathcal{L}(\alpha,\Sigma)^* - \{\langle\rangle\} \\
\mathcal{L}(\sim\alpha,\Sigma) &= \mathcal{L}(?^*) - \mathcal{L}(\alpha,\Sigma)
\end{aligned}
$$

Fig. 7.1. Regular expression syntax and semantics.

Let u, v, and w be vertices, and uv denote edge $(u,v) \in E$. Then u is the *source* and v is the *target* of edge uv, u is called an *immediate predecessor* of v, and v is an *immediate successor* of u. A path p is a connected sequence of edges, such that

$$p = <u_1v_1, ..., u_nv_n>,$$
$$\text{where } \forall j\colon 1 \le j \le n-1\colon v_j = u_{j+1}.$$

The source of a path is the source of the first edge in the path. The target of a path is the target of the last edge in the path, that is:

source(p) = source(first(p))

target(p) = target(last(p)).

We will say that a path *starts* at its source and *ends* at its target, and that a path that starts at u and ends at v is a path *from* u to v, or sometimes simply call it path uv. If path uv exists in G then u is a *predecessor* of v and v is a successor of u. An edge is *on* a path when it is an edge in the sequence. A vertex is *on* a path when it is either the source of target of any edge on the path, that is:

on(uv, p) = $\exists j\colon j$th(p) = uv

on(v, p) = $\exists u\colon$ on(uv, p) $\lor$ on(vu, p).

We define G', the reverse of flowgraph $G = (V, E, s, t, \psi, L)$ by exchanging the entry and exit vertices and reversing every edge, that is:

$$G^r = (V, E^r, t, s, \psi, L^r),$$
$$\text{where } uv \in E^r \Leftrightarrow vu \in E \land L^r(uv) = L(vu).$$

Define the labeling function L to be a homomorphism from paths (edge sequences) to label sequences in the usual way, except that null labels are erased. The set of label sequences *generated* by a flowgraph is denoted $\mathcal{L}(G)$ and is given by

$$\mathcal{L}(G) = \{L(p)\colon p \text{ is a path from } s \text{ to } t \text{ in } G\}.$$

A *subflowgraph* G_{uv}, of G is a flowgraph for which u is the entry, v is the exit, which includes all the vertices and edges on paths from u to v) in the original graph G, and which labels each such edge as it is labeled in G.

B. A First Model for Sequencing Analysis

We begin by establishing some terminology and a philosophical perspective. We believe that the structure and behavior of an object as complex as a program must be viewed on many levels of abstraction and from various perspectives if we hope to gain a significant understanding of it. We wish to permit a program analyst the widest latitude in fixing the view that will be taken of the program's structure and behavior and in changing that view as necessary. To support this capability, we propose to model the execution of a program as a sequence of *events* where the definition of what constitutes an event is left to the analyst. At one moment, an analyst might be interested in examining the sequences of references, definitions, and undefinitions of variables. At another time, that analyst might be more interested in the sequences of data type transformations occurring in the program. A third time, the interesting behavior might be sequences of program counter values during an execution of the program. In all these cases, we believe that the analyst must be free to define the events of interest. We denote the set of interesting events as $\Sigma = \{\sigma_i\}$.

Having defined the events, the analyst must now be supported in reasoning about particular sequences of them. We refer to the sequence of events in Σ occurring during a single program execution as a *trace*, $T_\Sigma = <\sigma_{i_1}, \sigma_{i_2}, ..., \sigma_{i_n}>$. Thus, given that a single execution of a program is characterized by a trace, the program itself can be characterized as $P_\Sigma = \{T_\Sigma\}$, the set of all possible traces. Given an arbitrary sequence of events in Σ, $S_\Sigma = <\sigma_{j_1}, \sigma_{j_2}, ..., \sigma_{j_m}>$, we say that S_Σ is executable with respect to the program if $S_\Sigma \in P_\Sigma$.

We now define a *sequencing constraint* over Σ to be any set of sequences over Σ, $C_\Sigma = \{S_\Sigma\}$ and say that a program P *satisfies* a sequencing constraint C_Σ if and only if every executable trace in P_Σ is in the sequencing constraint C_Σ. In other words, we define the satisfaction of a sequencing constraint by a program in terms of the notion of set containment. The sequencing constraint represents the *valid* sequences of operations, i.e., those sequences that are considered correct.

If there is an executable trace for a program that is not in the sequencing constraint, then the program does not satisfy the constraint. We will call any such trace a *violation* of that constraint and say that a program *violates* a constraint if its set of executable traces contains a violation.

We have translated the problem of determining if a program satisfies a sequencing constraint into the problem of determining if one language is contained in another. Unfortunately, this problem is in general only solvable when both languages are regular.

Since we wish to have a specification formalism for which there is a general method to statically evaluate the satisfaction of a sequencing constraint by a program, then both the sequencing constraint and set of executable traces must be regular. It is easy to have our constraint be a regular language. Regular expressions and finite state machines are two commonly used formalisms.

Unfortunately, however, behavior of the program in general will not be characterizable by a regular language. Thus to perform our static analysis, we must use an approximation of the set of executable traces for the program that is a regular language and contains the set of executable traces. We can then test whether the approximation is contained in the sequencing constraint and, by transitivity, whether the program will satisfy the constraint.

A useful regular superset of a program's set of executable traces can be obtained from a flowgraph G for the program. The edges in G represent statements in the program and the structure of their interconnection represents the possible control flow between the statements. This flowgraph can be constructed by a static examination of the program text. We label an edge of this flowgraph with the event that occurs when the statement corresponding to that edge is reached during an execution or with the null event # if no interesting event takes place at that edge. Obviously, to perform a static analysis, we must also statically determine the event or events to which the execution of a particular statement corresponds. For the purposes of this paper, we will assume that can be done without specifying how.

If we consider an arbitrary path from the entry vertex to the exit vertex in G, the sequence of edges along that path also defines a sequence of events which is the sequence of labels on those edges. In effect, the labeling function for that flowgraph is a homomorphism from paths (edge sequences) to traces (event sequences). The set of all control flow paths from the entry to the exit of a flowgraph is regular and we can use the homomorphic image of those paths as our approximation, since homomorphism preserves regularity. This approximation must contain the executable traces since every execution of the program must correspond to some path through the flowgraph.

We call the traces in our approximation *static* because they are obtained by enumerating the statically determined control flow paths in G and call *unexecutable* those static traces that are not executable by the program.

C. Limitations of the First Model

The dangers and problems in this regular language model are well known. The inability to distinguish and effectively compensate for the effects of unexecutable traces (corresponding to control flow paths that can never be taken) is a classical problem with this technique. We will show that we can alleviate these problems by increasing the expressive power of the sequencing specification formalism.

Suppose that an analyst discovers some static traces of a program that are violations of a sequencing constraint. The analyst knows that a static trace may not be executable and is left to wonder whether or not the violations discovered are executable. Unexecutable violations are of no concern, since they will never actually occur. On the other hand, if every static trace is a violation then every executable trace must also be a violation and the program definitely violates the constraint.

Thus, the ability to determine whether all, or only some, static traces are violations is important. In this second case, the analyst needs more information—especially in the (not unusual) case of a large program in which an analysis tool detects hundreds or thousands of static violations. In that case it is useful, for example, to know that every trace containing an event generated by one particular statement in the program is a violation. If the statement is known to be executable, the importance of these violations is correspondingly increased as there must be at least one executable trace that contains an event generated by that statement and the program cannot satisfy the constraint. In addition, having located the cause of the violation, the task of correcting it is aided. Some previous systems, such as DAVE, were sometimes able to make this distinction.

```
procedure NOWRITE is
begin
    OPEN;
    CLOSE;
end NOWRITE;
```

Fig. 7.2. An example program.

A number of these points can be elucidated with an example. Let us specify a regular language sequencing constraint as the language denoted by the regular expression C_*.

$$C_* = (open; write*; close)*$$

Now consider procedure **NOWRITE** in Fig. 7.2. This program might be intended to create an empty file, or it might also be missing one or several write statements. For this reason, an analyst might wish to consider the sequence <OPEN, CLOSE> as a violation and want such sequences to be detected and reported. Recall that violations need not be sequences that directly cause a failure but may simply be often symptomatic of a fault and demand closer examination.

Since procedure **NOWRITE** satisfies C_*, the analyst might rather use as a sequencing constraint the language denoted by regular expression C_+ that requires the existence of a write operation.

$$C_+ = (open; write+; close)*$$

The sequence <OPEN, CLOSE> is now a violation of the constraint.

Using C_+ as our constraint rather than C_* does not solve all problems however. Consider procedure **WRITELOOP** in Fig. 7.3. Assuming **Done** and **Compute** do not generate events in Σ, our selected event set, the executable traces of procedure **WRITELOOP** are given by the regular expression (open; write*; close). This program satisfies C_* and violates C_+, but that is unfortunate. The program in the second example is quite common, and generally unobjectionable, but violates C_+ just as the more objectionable procedure **NOWRITE** does.

```
procedure WRITELOOP is
begin
   OPEN;
   while not Done loop
      Compute;
      WRITE;
   end loop;
   CLOSE;
end WRITELOOP;
```

Fig. 7.3. A second example program.

Restricting ourselves to a specification that defines a sequencing constraint as a set and its satisfaction as set containment forces a choice between C_* and C_+ as our constraint. The use of C_* will allow some sequences that we may prefer to consider violations, while C_+ will mark as a violation a program construct that is considered correct.

The most conservative choice is to select C_+, and allow a large number of correct sequences to be mistakenly branded as invalid. This was one problem with the DAVE system. Many users were discouraged by having to search through large anomaly reports to find the important phenomena. In this paper, we seek a specification formalism powerful and flexible enough to permit diagnosticians to reduce the number of spurious violations detected.

D. A Second Model

We now gain increased analytic sharpness by enhancing our regular language containment model. We redefine a sequencing constraint to be a regular language and a relation, either set containment or nonempty intersection. The regular language gives a set of sequences as before, but now a program satisfies the constraint only if its set of static traces has the specified relation to the sequences in the constraint.

Important flexibility is gained by supporting the specification of both set containment and nonempty intersection. In our file example our new sequencing constraint is that the static traces are contained in C_* and have a nonempty intersection with C_+. Since satisfaction is a predicate, it is natural to combine constraints with boolean operators in this way.

E. Limitations of the Second Model

This enhancement is still not quite what we need. When an analysis tool detects a static trace that satisfies a constraint using the nonempty intersection relation, the analyst still must determine whether or not that trace is executable. If it is not, then the program itself does not satisfy the constraint although the static approximation does. Making the usually reasonable assumption that the set of static traces is not empty, then if it is also contained in the valid traces, the program will satisfy the constraint. As will be seen later, our algorithm makes evaluating this dual constraint simple. If that is not the case, then the analyst must examine those static traces further.

```
procedure IFWRITE is
begin
    OPEN;
    if Condition then
        while not Done loop
            Compute;
            WRITE;
        end loop;
        CLOSE;   -- 1
    else
        CLOSE;   -- 2
    end if;
end IFWRITE;
```

Fig. 7.4. A third example program.

A second problem can be seen by considering procedure **IFWRITE** in Fig. 7.4. We again assume that **Done**, **Compute**, and **Condition** do not generate any events in Σ, our designated event set. This gives us the same set of static traces as procedure **WRITELOOP**, so **IFWRITE** also satisfies the new sequencing constraint. In this example, however, there are two different **CLOSE** statements marked 1 and 2 following the **OPEN** statement. No trace containing a close event generated by statement 2 contains a write event. Thus, if we execute statement 2 we will never have previously executed a **WRITE** statement. This is just as suspicious here as it was in procedure **NOWRITE**, yet the use of our new constraint does not detect it.

While it is reasonable to assume that some static traces are unexecutable, it seems far less reasonable to assume that some statements are unexecutable. It seems particularly worth detecting the situation where every trace containing events generated by one particular statement is a violation. Thus, distinguishing between events generated by different statements gives us additional power to elucidate the proper sequencing of events.

F. A Third Model

Detecting the violation of a close event never preceded by a write event in procedure **IFWRITE** requires that sequencing constraints be applied to a subcomponent of the program. In this case, the subcomponent is that portion of the program on execution paths from the entry to statement 2. We can define that subcomponent as a subflowgraph.

A sequencing constraint will now restrict subtraces bounded by particular events, much as done in TSL [25]. Unlike TSL, the subtrace bounds, called *anchors*, are not arbitrary sequences, but single events. The new sequencing constraint is formed by adding to the regular language and relation a set of *start anchors* and a set of *end anchors*, respectively, marking the entry and exit of the appropriate subflowgraphs.

A sequencing constraint C is redefined as a quadruple (R, Q, A, B) consisting of a regular language R, relation Q, set of start anchor events A, and a set of end anchor events B. Let P be a program with flowgraph $G = (V, E, s, t, \Phi, L)$. The anchor sets define a set of subflowgraphs of G, $\Gamma_G(A, B)$, where

$$\Gamma_G(A, B) = \{G_{vw} : \exists uv, wx : L(uv) \in A \land L(wx) \in B\}.$$

These subflowgraphs have their entry at the target vertex of an edge labeled by some event from the start anchor set, their exit at the source vertex of some event from the end anchor set, and consist of all edges and vertices from G that are on paths from that entry to the exit. Note that this set is nonempty only when there is at least one edge uv labeled by an event from A, at least one edge wx labeled by an event from B, and there is at least one path from v to w. Also note that the edges labeled by the defining anchor events are not included in the subflowgraph, so the bounding events are not included in the subtraces to be constrained and are not required to be events in traces of R. The subgraph bounding events may be specified only to delineate the sets of subtraces to be constrained, and as such are irrelevant for the actual sequencing. On the other hand, the anchor events are not prohibited from the regular language alphabet. Anchor events not in the regular language alphabet that may occur in the static traces of a subflowgraph are ignored by restricting the traces to the events in the alphabet. The program satisfies the constraint if the set of static traces for all subflowgraphs (restricted to the events in the regular expression alphabet) has the desired relation to the constraint trace set. Obviously, if $\Gamma_G(A, B)$ is empty, the constraint is trivially satisfied.

Program P with flowgraph G satisfies sequencing constraint quadruple $C = (R, Q, A, B)$ if and only if $\forall G_{vw} \in \Gamma_G(A, B) : Q(\mathcal{L}(G_{vw})_\Sigma, R)$ where $R \subseteq \Sigma^*$. What might a sequencing constraint of this form be for the output file example? Let s be the event that occurs when execution of the program is started, and t be the event that occurs when the execution of the program is terminated. The names were chosen since these events correspond to entering the entry vertex and leaving the exit vertex of the flowgraph for the program. The events s and t will be in Roman font while the vertices will be italicized. Every static trace starts with s and ends with t.

If the set of events Σ is {open, write, close}, $\subseteq$ is set containment, and $\cap \emptyset$ is non-empty intersection, a new sequencing constraint for this example is:

$$(\mathcal{L}((\text{open}; \text{write} *; \text{close}) *, \Sigma), \subseteq, \{s\}, \{t\})$$
$$\wedge (\mathcal{L}(? +, \Sigma), \cap \emptyset, \{\text{open}\}, \{\text{close}\})$$

The first quadruple of this constraint is essentially C_s. It gives the specific requirements of the overall sequencing of the events in Σ over an entire trace (less the bounding s and t events). The second quadruple adds a constraint to detect the suspicious sequence <open, close>. That quadruple requires that there be at least one path with at least one (non-null) event between all open and close event pairs. Because of the sequencing requirements of the first quadruple, the first and last events on that path must be write events.

IV. Cecil: A Sequencing Constraint Language

A. Syntax and Semantics of Cecil

The definition of a language for sequencing constraints is simply a matter of defining a suitable syntax for the constraint quadruples and their boolean combinations.

An *anchored, quantified regular expression* (AQRE) represents a sequencing constraint quadruple. It consists of an alphabet, an optional start anchor set (enclosed in brackets), a quantifier keyword, a regular expression, and an optional end anchor set also enclosed in brackets. A full Cecil sequencing constraint will consist of some boolean combination of AQRE terms. The grammar for Cecil is given in Fig. 7.5. The *regexp* term is a regular expression as defined in Fig. 7.1. The *expr* nonterminal is provided for convenience. It is often the case that several AQRE terms will share the same alphabet. It is simpler to write the alphabet once.

The semantics of Cecil are defined by the mapping from Cecil AQRE terms to constraint quadruples in Fig. 7.5. Assume that ρ is some regular expression, *quant* is an arbitrary quantifier (either **forall** or **exists**), Q is the corresponding set predicate (either $\subseteq$ or $\cap \emptyset$, respectively) and Σ, X, and Y are arbitrary sets of events. The Cecil AQRE term of the form listed in the left-hand column represents the constraint quadruple given in the right-hand column.

Note that the grammar does not require either anchor set to be explicitly present. There are situations when only some initial or terminal subtrace is important in the sequencing and other events are irrelevant. For example, one sequencing constraint on the operations on a stack is that the first operation must be the one that initializes the stack. Only the first event in a trace is constrained. Such examples have been found to be common and the omission of anchor sets is used to denote them. Again let s and t represent respectively the start and termination events of a program. Omitting the end anchor indicates a constraint on the prefixes of traces of a subflowgraph. The end anchor is implicitly {t}, and ?* is appended to the regular expression, as seen in the third AQRE term definition of Fig. 7.5.

eventlist	::=	{event ','} event
anchor	::=	'[' eventlist ']'
quantifier	::=	'forall'	'exists'
aqre	::=	[anchor] quantifier regexp [anchor]
expr	::=	['not'] aqre
		expr 'or' expr
		expr 'and' expr
		'(' expr ')'
alphabet	::=	'{' eventlist '}'
spec	::=	alphabet expr
		spec 'or' spec
		spec 'and' spec
		'(' spec ')'

Cecil AQRE	Constraint Quadruple
$\{\Sigma\}$ $[X]$ **forall** ρ $[Y]$	$= (\mathcal{L}(\rho,\Sigma), \subseteq, \{X\}, \{Y\})$
$\{\Sigma\}$ $[X]$ **exists** ρ $[Y]$	$= (\mathcal{L}(\rho,\Sigma), \cap\emptyset, \{X\}, \{Y\})$
$\{\Sigma\}$ $quant$ ρ $[Y]$	$= (\mathcal{L}((?*;\rho),\Sigma), Q, \{s\}, \{Y\})$
$\{\Sigma\}$ $[X]$ $quant$ ρ	$= (\mathcal{L}((\rho;?*),\Sigma), Q, \{X\}, \{t\})$
$\{\Sigma\}$ $quant$ ρ	$= (\mathcal{L}((?*;\rho;?*),\Sigma), Q, \{s\}, \{t\})$

Fig. 7.5. Syntax and semantics of Cecil.

Omission of the start anchor is defined similarly. It defines a constraint on a suffix of a trace. The start anchor event is {s} and ?* is prepended to the regular expression, as shown in the fourth AQRE term definition in Fig. 7.5. Omission of both anchor sets has the combined effect.

The boolean operators **and**, **or**, and **not** have the conventional meaning. A conjunction of expressions is satisfied by a program if both subexpressions are satisfied, a disjunction when at least one is satisfied, and a negation is satisfied when the subexpression is not satisfied.

B. The File Example Revisited

Some examples of the use of Cecil to specify sequencing constraints are in order. The file module example of Section III-F will be the first. In that section, a specification consisting of the conjunction of two constraint quadruples was defined. The corresponding Cecil expression for that constraint is given in Fig. 7.6.

```
{open, close, write} (
    [s] forall (open; write*; close)* [t]
    and [open] exists ?+ [write] )
```

Fig. 7.6. A Cecil expression for the file example.

C. DAVE Revisited

The DAVE data flow analysis system performed sequencing evaluation for a fixed set of data flow anomalies which have been described earlier. Cecil can be used to specify those constraints. The events defining this view of the program behavior are the reference (r), definition (d), and undefinition (u) of variables.

The following Cecil expression defines the *undefined reference* anomaly, stating that the last event on every path into a reference event must be either a reference or a definition.

$\qquad$ **{r, d, u} forall (r | d) [r]**

In effect, this expression prohibits a reference that might possibly be undefined. To prohibit a reference that is guaranteed to be undefined, the quantifier can be changed to **exists**, obtaining:

$\qquad$ **{r, d, u} exists (r | d) [r]**

A program will satisfy this expression if every reference has a definition or reference immediately preceding it on at least one path. A violation occurs only when an undefinition precedes the reference on every path.

The *dead definition* anomaly requires a similarly simple Cecil expression. We must specify that every definition must always be immediately followed by a reference. The Cecil expressions for this is:

$\qquad$ **{r, d, u} [d] forall r**

As with the undefined reference expression, the quantifier can be changed to prohibit only definitions that are guaranteed to be dead by requiring that a definition be followed by a reference on only one execution path, as follows:

$\qquad$ **{r, d, u} [d] exists r**

By proceeding in this way, we see that it is a straightforward exercise to use Cecil to express all the anomalies—both errors and warnings—detected by DAVE.

V. An Algorithm for Sequencing Evaluation

The Cecil notation of Section IV is interesting but not extremely useful without a way to evaluate programs against the constraints it expresses. In this section, after some additional definitions, we define a method to statically evaluate Cecil constraints.

A. Additional Definitions

A *deterministic finite state machine* (DFSM) $M = (\Sigma, S, i, A, \delta)$ is an alphabet of events Σ, a finite nonempty set of *states S*, an *initial state* $i \in S$, a set of *accepting states* $A \subseteq S$, and a state transition function, $\delta: \Sigma \rightarrow (S \rightarrow S)$.

The domain of the state transition function can be extended to the set of traces by composing the functions for each individual event in the trace. Sequence α is accepted when $\delta(\alpha)(i) \in A$. The set of traces accepted by M is denoted by $\mathcal{L}(M)$. A DFSM may also have a nonaccepting state called the *crash* state, $c \in S$, which can never be left once entered.

$$c \notin A \wedge \forall \sigma \in \Sigma: \delta(\sigma)(c) = c$$

A *meet semilattice* $\Lambda = (X, \sqsubseteq, \sqcap)$ is a set X, a partial ordering $\sqsubseteq$, and an associative, commutative, idempotent meet operation, $\sqcap: S \times S \rightarrow S$. The set must contain a special bottom element $\bot$ that satisfies the property, $\forall x \in S: \bot \sqsubseteq x$. A meet semilattice may also contain a *top* element $\top$ that satisfies the property $\forall x \in X: x \sqsubseteq \top$, but its existence is not required.

The typical example of a meet semilattice is a set of sets, ordered by the subset relation, where the meet operation is set intersection and bottom is the empty set. In the interest of brevity, some details on these definitions are omitted from this paper. Those interested should consult [16].

A *dataflow analysis framework* $D = (\Lambda, F)$ is a meet semilattice and a set of unary functions F over Λ called an *operation space*. D is a characterization of a class of data flow problems over a flowgraph. Some information is desired at each vertex in a flowgraph of a program. The labels on the edges are assumed to alter this information when execution passes along that edge. The value at a vertex is a function of the values at its immediate predecessors as transformed by the labels on the incoming edges from those predecessors. This defines a system of simultaneous equations whose solution gives the values at each vertex. The meet semilattice defines the possible values and how they are combined at a vertex with more than one predecessor. The operation space defines the possible transformations that a label may perform. If F satisfies certain conditions (see [16]), and all functions in it are monotonic with respect to Λ, then D is called *monotone*. If all functions in F are also distributive over $\sqcap$, it is *distributive*.

An instance I of D consists of a pair (G, H) where G is a specific flowgraph and $H: E \rightarrow F$ is a mapping of edges to functions. This defines a specific set of equations to be solved.

If D is monotone, the *maximal fixed point* (MFP) of the equation system defined by I can be computed efficiently. If D is distributive, the solution obtained by an MFP algorithm is also the "best" solution (of a possibly infinite number) of the equation system defined by I. This solution is called the *meet over all paths* (MOP) solution.

For the purposes of this paper, it is sufficient to note that many MFP algorithms exist for data flow analysis frameworks ([16], [32], among others). Specific algorithms will not be discussed.

B. A Data Flow Analysis Framework for Sequencing Evaluation

Evaluating a Cecil expression (i.e., determining whether or not a submitted program satisfies the Cecil expression) requires that the set of traces generated by a flowgraph be compared to a regular language. Since this problem is defined using a flowgraph, an algorithm can be obtained if it can be cast into a data flow analysis framework. In establishing a particular framework, the meet semilattice and operation space are defined so as to be convenient for the problem at hand. It is advantageous if the framework defined is distributive as then the MOP solution can be extracted using any MFP algorithm.

For now, no assumptions are necessary about how the flowgraph or regular language are obtained as long as an algorithm to perform the necessary comparison can be obtained. We simply wish to find a data flow analysis framework that permits the comparison to be made. We will take up the problem of obtaining the flowgraph and the regular language later.

Let $G = (V, E, s, t, \psi, L)$ be some flowgraph and R be some regular language over alphabet $\Sigma \subseteq \Psi$. Also let $P = \mathcal{L}(G)_\Sigma$.

Assume that the required comparison is $P \subseteq R$ and consider a DFSM $M = (\Sigma, S, i, A, \delta)$ that accepts R. In other words, $R = \mathcal{L}(M)$. If every trace in P is accepted by M, P must be contained in R. P may be an infinite set, so its traces cannot be enumerated and individually checked with M. Let $\mathfrak{M}(v)$ be the set of states that M could be in after applying δ to the trace associated with any path from s to v in G.

$$\mathfrak{M}(v) = \{\delta\big(L(p)\big)(i) : p \text{ is a path from } s \text{ to } v \text{ in } G\}$$

Consider the set of states at the exit vertex of the flowgraph $\mathfrak{M}(t)$. If every state in $\mathfrak{M}(t)$ is accepting in M then every trace in P is accepted by M.

$$\mathfrak{M}(t) \subseteq A \Leftrightarrow P \subseteq R$$

Now suppose that the required comparison of P and R is $P \cap R \neq \emptyset$. This condition is satisfied if at least one trace in P is accepted by M. Again, not every trace can be individually checked, but if $\mathfrak{M}(t) \cap A \neq \emptyset$, there must be at least one path from s to t in G with a trace (by definition in P) that causes an accepting state in $\mathfrak{M}(t)$ and is therefore in R. P and R cannot be disjoint.

$$\mathfrak{M}(t) \cap A \neq \emptyset \Leftrightarrow P \cap R \neq \emptyset$$

Determining containment or nondisjointness is merely a matter of changing the comparison, given a value for $\mathfrak{M}$.

Howden takes a variant of this approach with his depth first search based algorithm [21]. While walking the flowgraph, his algorithm applies the appropriate state transitions from δ according to the events labeling the edges, but he takes advantage of the fact that the quantification is always universal with his DFSM specification notation to avoid computing $\mathfrak{M}$. Instead he computes only the state sets caused by a subset of the paths at any one time. When no valid state transition along some path is possible, the flowgraph language cannot be a subset of the language accepted by the DFSM. Computing $\mathfrak{M}$ explicitly for each vertex in the flowgraph enables the use of both sorts of quantification with essentially the same algorithm.

The task then is to find a data flow analysis framework to compute $\mathfrak{M}$. The values needed are sets of states from a DFSM. The meet operation reflects how values are combined when two (or more) paths come together. Since the desired value is the set of all possible states that the DFSM could be in, set union is chosen. This requires superset as the ordering relation and therefore bottom is the set of all states and top is the empty set. Given the DFSM M above, the meet semilattice is:

$$\Lambda = (\mathbb{p}(S), \supseteq, \cup).$$

The operation space F must also be defined. Let F contain all total unary functions over states extended to sets of states in the conventional way as the image of its argument. Note that if $X = \emptyset, f(X) = \emptyset$. Also let F contain the function $\emptyset$, which returns the empty set regardless of the argument.

The assignment of operation space functions to the edges must be defined for an instance I of D. Let $G' = (V', E', s', t, \psi', L')$ be a modified subflowgraph derived from G by adding a new label $\hat{\imath}$ to ψ, a new entry vertex s', and an edge from s' to s labeled with $\hat{\imath}$. Let $f_{\hat{\imath}}$ be the function that maps every state in S to the initial state $i, f_{\#}$ be the identity function, and f_{σ} for all $\sigma \in \Sigma$ be $\delta(\sigma)$, all extended to $\mathbb{p}(S)$. All these functions are in F. Then $H(uv) = f'_{L'(uv)}$ for every edge uv in E'. The instance I of D is (G', H). The extra vertex is added to ensure that the DFSM starts out in its initial state, in other words $\mathfrak{M}(s) = \{i\}$. The MOP solution defines the value at the entry vertex of the instance flowgraph (s') to be I.

Given these definitions, then $D = (\Lambda, F)$ is a distributive data flow analysis framework and the MOP solution of an instance of D defined above produces the set of states $\mathfrak{M}$. The proofs may be found in [27].

C. Intraprocedural Evaluation of an AQRE

Given this distributive data flow analysis framework, any MFP algorithm permits the computation of $\mathfrak{M}$, and consequently the determination of whether the language generated by a flowgraph is either contained in or nondisjoint from some regular language. The use of this capability to evaluate a Cecil expression consisting of a single AQRE is straightforward. The flowgraph is some subflowgraph determined by the anchor sets in the AQRE. The regular language is determined by the alphabet and regular expression. The comparison performed is determined by the quantifier.

As an example, suppose we wish to analyze procedure **IFWRITE** from Fig. 7.4 against the first AQRE term from Fig. 7.6.

　　{ open, close, write }
　　　[s] forall (open; write*; close)* [t]

We generate the flowgraph assuming that events open, close, and write are generated by the correspondingly named procedures and all other statements generate the null event #. The original entry vertex, s is 1, while s' is 0. The exit vertex t is 8. The vertices are each labeled with the appropriate value of $\mathfrak{M}$ based on the three state DFSM that accepts the language denoted by the regular expression in the AQRE term.

If we assume that $\Gamma_G(\{s\}, \{t\} = \{G_{1,8}\}$ (the entry and exit events are considered to occur, respectively, just before and after the entry and exit vertices of the flowgraph), then add S' to that flowgraph, we see that the program does satisfy the constraint because $\mathfrak{M}(8) = \{1\}$ which is exactly the set of accepting states A for the DFSM. In this particular case, Γ_G is a singleton set, so only one application of an MOP algorithm is required.

There is one apparent problem with this method. It seems that when Γ_G contains multiple subflowgraphs, we must execute our MOP algorithm multiple times. That could be expensive if there were a large number of edges labeled by the anchor events in the overall flowgraph. Suppose in our example that we want to analyze the program against the second AQRE term in our output file example.

　　{ open, close, write } [open] forall ? + [close]

This situation corresponds to the example of Fig. 7.8. Here $\Gamma_G(\{open\}, \{close\})$ is a doubleton since there are two distinct close statements in the program. It appears that we would have to execute our MOP algorithm twice. Fortunately, there is a way around that restriction.

Suppose that in the flowgraph, there is only one edge labeled by start anchor events, but many edges labeled by end anchor events. Then Γ_G is a set of subflowgraphs, $\{G_{xy}: y \in Y\}$, all with the same entry vertex x, each terminating at a distinct vertex y in Y. Also consider the subflowgraph G_x. Each vertex y is also in G_x, and the paths from x to v must be the same in G_x as in G_{xy}, so $\mathfrak{M}(v)$ is the same regardless of whether G_{xy} or G_x is used to compute it. The satisfaction of a program with multiple end anchor vertices can be determined by computing $\mathfrak{M}$ for G_x, and comparing to the set of accepting states A the results $\mathfrak{M}(y)$ for the appropriate vertices y.

If we execute the MOP algorithm to propagate DFSM states in subflowgraph $G_{2,8}$ of Fig. 7.8, we will obtain the same $\mathfrak{M}$ value at vertices 6 and 7 as if we had separately analyzed both $G_{2,6}$ and $G_{2,7}$. Note that the constraint is satisfied at vertex 6, but violated at vertex 7, since $\{0\}$ and $\{1\}$ are disjoint.

Thus, one execution of an MOP algorithm can handle every subflowgraph sharing the same entry vertex simultaneously, when followed by one comparison for each subflowgraph exit. From the standpoint of paths, the quantification is over the paths entering each y from the subflowgraph entry vertex.

Now consider the dual situation, when end anchor events start at a single vertex y and start anchor events are located at some set of vertices $\{X\}$. Unfortunately, when there are multiple start anchors, serious problems occur if we blindly follow the procedure for creating an instance of the data flow analysis framework given above. If $\mathfrak{M}(y) \subseteq A$ then every path between every x and y is in the AQRE regular language, exactly as desired for the universal quantifier. Unfortunately, if $\mathfrak{M}(y) \nsubseteq A$ the particular x at the head of the path causing the nonaccepting state cannot be distinguished. That information would almost certainly be required in a practical evaluation tool. Existential quantification gives an even more serious problem. $\mathfrak{M}(y) \cap A \neq \emptyset$ does not satisfy the semantics of Cecil. In this situation, nondisjointness of $\mathfrak{M}(y)$ and A only implies that there is at least one subflowgraph in Γ_G that has a trace in the constraint AQRE language. The semantics state this must hold for all subflowgraphs.

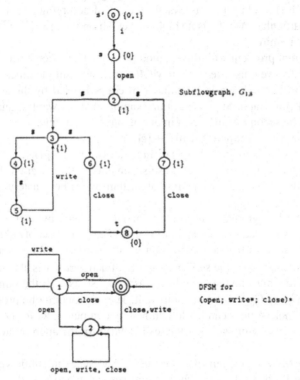

Fig. 7.7. Example of an analysis.

Both problems can be handled by analyzing the reverse of the flowgraph against the reverse of the AQRE. This should have no effect on the comparative sequencing since both the flowgraph and the constraint are reversed, but the multiple start anchor/single end anchor case is transformed into the solvable single start anchor/multiple end anchor situation. At the conclusion of the MFP algorithm, examine $\mathfrak{M}(x)$ for each x and perform the appropriate comparison. From a path perspective, when the reverse of the subflowgraph is used, the quantification is over the paths leaving each x (as opposed to entering) in the original flowgraph when $\mathfrak{M}(x)$ is examined.

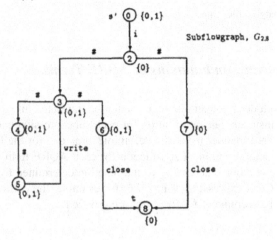

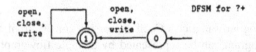

Fig. 7.8. Another analysis example.

If both multiple start and end anchor vertices are present, an evaluation that satisfies the semantics of Cecil cannot in general be performed in a single execution of the MOP algorithm. Reversing does not help; there are multiple start anchors in both orientations. Evaluating such a constraint requires one execution of the MOP algorithm for each set of subflowgraphs with the same entry vertex. Many of the subflowgraphs will be small, since not all vertices will be reachable from every subflowgraph entry, but even so, it will certainly greatly increase the computation resources required to perform an evaluation.

Fortunately, Cecil AQRE terms with multiple start and end anchors can often be rewritten as a combination of two or more AQRE terms using s or t as anchor events (since s and t are generally the only events guaranteed to exist in only one location) that adequately reflects the desired sequencing and requires only one application of an MFP algorithm per AQRE term. This may involve the use of s or t implicitly by omitting a start or end anchor. Fig. 7.9 gives an example of such a reformulation. In this case we specify that the first event after an open on at least one path must be a write event, and similarly for the last event immediately preceding a close event.

```
{open, close, write} (
   [s] forall (open; write*; close)* [t]
   and [open] exists write
   and exists write [close] )
```

Fig. 7.9. A more efficiently analyzed file sequencing constraint.

D. Evaluation of Boolean Combinations of AQRE Terms

A Cecil expression that includes boolean operators cannot be translated into a single data flow framework instance, but the solution for each subexpression can be combined in a straightforward manner using the definitions provided for the logical operations. Given the determination of satisfaction for each AQRE term as a predicate, those values are combined according to the function determined by the boolean operators. In the Cecil expression of Fig. 7.6, for example, the entire expression is satisfied when both conjunct AQRE terms are satisfied.

E. Pragmatic Considerations

Our algorithm determines if a program satisfies a Cecil expression consisting of a single AQRE term when the program can be represented by a single flowgraph and the events labeling the edges in that flowgraph are those in the Cecil constraint. Any real nontrivial program will not fit this model. Some statements will be calls to procedures and functions, which may contain statements that map to Cecil events or may be calls to still other routines. An evaluation of a real program against a Cecil constraint must take this into account.

Even when the algorithm is extended to handle interprocedural analysis, it does not quite permit the analysis of an actual program. Look closely again at **IFWRITE** in Fig. 7.4. There are **OPEN** and **CLOSE** statements, but what are those statements acting on? In **IFWRITE**, it is some unnamed file. Any real program will have variables and other data objects on which the statements act. A program that uses several files should satisfy any sequencing constraints on each file independently.

An event is really an *operation* acting on some *object*. A sequencing constraint restricts the sequence of operations on a single object, similarly to access right expressions [23]. A sequencing constraint in that context was applied to each instantiation of a class of objects independently. The definition of what constitutes an "object" is part of the view definition one performs by selecting the events. The data flow anomaly detection performed by DAVE considered every variable having the same lexical name, regardless of type, to be a single object. Freudenberger's SETL data flow anomaly system considered a single object (in the context of finding potentially nonterminating loops) to be the set of all variables referenced in the loop control predicate [12]. Constraining the sequencing of operations on some abstract data type, such as a file or stack, would require considering an object to be a variable of that type. In another situation, the object might be the state of the program as a whole. One might want to constrain the sequence of calls to a set of subprograms that affects that state as a whole. The definition of an object then is that collection of data affected by an operation in the current analysis view.

Our procedure also assumes that statements in a program can be associated with the Cecil events they generate. There are two approaches to solving this problem. One is to force the user to code the Cecil events into the appropriate parts of the program with special comments, which are detected by the flowgraph building part of the analysis system. Another, the approach used by our analysis system, Cesar, is to permit the definition of patterns, which when matched against the program text or some intermediate representation, are mapped to specific Cecil events.

Some details of the solutions for these problems are described in [27], [28].

VI. Summary and Conclusion

We have developed a notation capable of describing broad and diverse classes of sequencing problems that is also capable of driving the mechanical creation of efficient analyzers (based on global program optimization techniques) which can effectively solve these problems.

Our research has indicated that the precise definition of sequencing problems is more difficult than we had earlier supposed as a sequencing problem such as undefined reference from Fosdick and Osterweil is actually a family of related problems [29]. The precise specification of any particular member of this family requires some notational intricacy. The Cecil language developed here seems to be sufficiently precise and effective. Further research aimed at applying Cecil to the description of a variety of diagnostic problems is needed in order to confirm that the notation is effective.

Another important feature of Cecil is that it can be used as the basis for mechanical creation of effective analyzers. Here our work is based upon showing that sequencing problems are profitably viewed as dataflow analysis problems for which good algorithms already exist. Our research has shown how such algorithms can be adapted to solve specific sequencing problems expressed in our notational formalism, where the adaptation process is also guided by the formalism.

We have implemented a prototype system called Cesar for the evaluation of Fortran programs against Cecil constraints that does handle both procedures and objects. We are currently expanding this analyzer to programs written in C and Ada. We shall experiment with this system to further determine the practicality and effectiveness of our ideas.

Ultimately we see the most important application of these ideas as being in flexible, adaptable software environments. We believe that users of such environments will need to quickly and easily create powerful diagnostic aids to study program phenomena which may evolve dynamically and where the need to study such phenomena may arise suddenly. At such times, users may wish to use sequence analysis techniques to come to a better understanding of the structure of their programs. We believe that our formalism is the basis for the rapid, precise specification of such phenomena. We further believe that the mechanical analyzer generation method we have developed in Cesar will then be effective in quickly analyzing the user's program and returning valuable diagnostic information.

Accordingly, we proposed to embed Cecil and Cesar in an interactive software development environment in an attempt to evaluate these ideas and come to a better understanding of how they complement more classical dynamic testing techniques.

Acknowledgments We thank J. Buxton, R. Taylor, and M. Young for their helpful comments.

References

[1] F. E. Allen, "A basis for program optimization." in *Proc. 1971 IFIP Congr.* 1971.

[2] T. Araki and N. Tokura. "Flow languages equal recursively enumerable languages," *Acta Inform.*, vol. 15. pp. 209-218. 1981.

[3] G. S. Avrunin, L. K. Dillon, J. C. Wileden, and W. E. Riddle, "Constrained expressions: Adding analysis capabilities to design methods for concurrent software systems," *IEEE Trans. Software Eng.*, vol. SE-12, pp. 278-292. Feb. 1986.

[4] W. Bartussek and D. L. Parnas. "Using traces to write abstract specifications for software modules." Dep. Comput. Sci., Univ. North Carolina, Chapel Hill. Tech. Rep. 77-12, 1977.

[5] R. H. Campbell and R. B. Kolstad, "Path expressions in Pascal." In *Proc. 4th Int. Conf. Software Engineering*, Sept. 1979. pp. 212-219.

[6] —, "An overview of Path Pascal's design," *SIGPLAN Notices*, vol. 15. pp. 13-24. Sept. 1980.

[7] R. A. DeMillo. R. J. Lipton. and A. J. Perlis, "Social processes and proofs of theorems and programs," *Commun. ACM* vol. 22. pp. 271-280, May 1979.

[8] L. K. Dillon. G. S. Avrunin, and J. C. Wileden, "Constrained expressions: Toward broad applicability of analysis methods for distributed software systems," Dep. Comput. Inform. Sci., Univ. Massachusetts. Amherst, Tech. Rep. 86-15, May 1986.

[9] B. Elspas. K. N. Levitt, R. J. Waldinger. and A. Waksman. "An assessment of techniques for proving programs correct." *ACM Comput. Surveys*, June 1972.

[10] R. W. Floyd. "Assigning meaning to programs," in Proc. *19th Symp. Applied Mathematics*, 1969. pp. 19-32.

[11] L. D. Fosdick and L. J. Osterweil. "Data flow analysis in software reliability." *ACM Comput. Surveys*, vol. 8. pp. 305-330, Sept. 1976. (Reprinted as Chapter 5)

[12] S. M. Freudenberger. "On the use of global optimization algorithms for the detection of semantic programming errors." Ph.D. dissertation. Courant Inst., New York Univ., 1984.

[13] J. V. Guttag. E. Hornung. and D. R. Musser. "Abstract data types and software validation," *Commun. ACM*, vol. 21, pp. 1048-1064. Jan. 1979.

[14] A. N. Habermann, "Path expressions," Courant Inst., New York Univ., Tech. Rep., 1975.

[15] M. A. Harrison. *Introduction to Formal Language Theory*. Addison-Wesley, 1978.

[16] M. S. Hecht, *Flow Analysis of Computer Programs*. New York. North-Holland, 1977.

[17] M. S. Hecht and J. D. Ullman. "A simple algorithm for global data flow analysis." *SIAM J. Comput.*, vol. 4, pp. 519-532. Dec. 1977.

[18] C. A. R. Hoare, "An axiomatic basis for computer programming," *Commun. ACM*, vol. 12, pp. 576-583. Oct. 1969.

[19] —, "A model for communicating sequential processes." Oxford Univ., Tech. Rep., 1979.

[20] —, *Communicating Sequential Processes*. Englewood Cliffs, NJ: Prentice-Hall, 1985.

[21] W. E. Howden, "A general model for static analysis," in *Proc. 16th Hawaii Int. Conf. System Sciences*, pp. 163-169.

[22] —, *Functional Program Testing and Analysis*. New York: McGraw-Hill, 1987.

[23] R. B. Kieburtz and A. Silberschatz, "Access-right expressions." *ACM Trans. Program. Lang. Syst.*, vol. 5, pp. 78-96, Jan. 1983.

[24] D. C. Luckham. "An overview of Anna, a specification language for Ada," in *Proc. IEEE Ada Applications and Environments Conf.*, Oct. 1984. pp. 116-127.

[25] D. C. Luckham, D. P. Helmbold, S. Meldal. D. L. Bryan. and M. A. Haberler. "Task sequencing language for specifying distributed Ada systems (TSL-1)," Comput. Syst. Lab., Stanford Univ., Rep. CSL-TR-87-34, July 1987.

[26] J. McLean, "A formal method for the abstract specification of software," *J. ACM*, vol. 31, pp. 600-627. July 1984.

[27] K. M. Olender. "Cecil/Cesar: Specification and static evaluation of sequencing constraints." Ph.D. dissertation. Univ. Colorado, 1988.

[28] K. M. Olender and L. J. Osterweil. "Cesar: A static sequencing constraint analyzer," in *Proc. Third Testing Analysis, and Verification Symp.*, Dec. 1989.

[29] L. J. Osterweil and L. D. Fosdick, "DAVE-A validation, error detection and documentation system for FORTRAN programs." *Software—Practice and Experience.* vol. 6, 1976.

[30] T. J. Ostrand and E. J. Weyuker. "Collecting and categorizing software error data in an industrial environment," *J. Comput. Syst. Sci.*, vol. 4. pp. 289-300, 1984.

[31] W. E. Riddle. "An approach to software system modeling and analysis," *Comput. Languages*, vol. 49-66. 1979.

[32] B. G. Ryder and M. C. Paull, "Elimination algorithms for data flow analysis," *ACM Comput. Surveys*, vol. 18, pp. 277-316, Sept. 1986.

[33] A. C. Shaw. "Software descriptions with flow expressions." *IEEE Trans. Software Eng.*, vol. SE-4. pp. 242-254, May 1978.

[34] R. N. Taylor and L. J. Osterweil. "Analysis and testing based on sequencing specifications." in *Proc. 4th Jerusalem Conf. Information Technology*. May 1984, pp. 260-266.

Part II: The Software Lifecycle

Lifecycle Environments

A Retrospective View of the Contributions of Leon J. Osterweil

Lori A. Clarke

Department of Computer Science, University of Massachusetts, Amherst, MA USA 01003

clarke@cs.umass.edu

Abstract Throughout his career, Leon Osterweil has made significant contributions that have impacted the research and state-of-the-practice on development environments. Initially his focus was on programming environments, mostly addressing issues needed to support his work in program analysis. Later his focus expanded to software lifecycle issues, such as flexible component interaction models, efficient system regeneration, and the use of process definitions as the major coordination mechanism to orchestrate the interactions among collections of tools, hardware devices, and human agents. His current research continues to address environment issues, but now the emphasis is on supporting continuous process improvement by providing process languages, execution, simulation, and an assortment of analysis tools for evaluating the effectiveness, safety, and vulnerabilities of processes for a range of domains, from healthcare, to digital government, to scientific workflow.

1. From Program Analysis to Programming Environments

The early work on program analysis undertaken by Osterweil and Fosdick [21,37], Ryder [47], Balzer [5] and others initiated a new research direction, where analysis was used not only to assist with compilation but also to help find problems in the code. The early analysis work was primarily concerned with supporting FORTRAN, and Osterweil and Fosdick were working with the Numerical Analysis Group (NAG) in Oxford, England, which was trying to develop efficient and accurate numerical software packages [35] in close collaboration with Argonne National Labs, a major user of such libraries. As discussed in Part I of this book, program analysis has continued to grow as an important research area, as software

P.L. Tarr, A.L. Wolf (eds.), *Engineering of Software*,
DOI 10.1007/978-3-642-19823-6_8, © Springer-Verlag Berlin Heidelberg 2011

systems have grown in size and complexity while also becoming a driving force of much of our societal infrastructure.

Early work in program analysis, however, soon confronted inherent and difficult problems in implementing these approaches, first as isolated tools and even more so as collections of tools. These problems laid the foundation for a thread of work, undertaken by Osterweil and others, addressing the need for *environments* of tools that support the full lifecycle of software activities. The early work on Software Development Environments (SDEs), such as Interlisp [60] and Mesa [54], were extremely innovative but were focused on a single, central programming language. The Gandalf Project [23] and the Cornell Program Synthesizer Project [44,59] built upon and generalized these approaches by creating meta-programming environments that could be instantiated for different programming languages. For the most part, these environments were tightly integrated around a central repository and one focused goal, the development and execution of a program. The Toolpack project [33] took a somewhat broader view of environments and recognized that collections of tools would be needed to support the various software engineering activities. It argued that these tools should not be monolithic, but instead they should be decomposed into tool fragments that could be called upon in different ways to achieve support for the many varied activities associated with software development. In many regards, this was one of the first arguments for component-based software engineering, made at a time before the infrastructure was available to easily define the components or flexibly glue them together.

In addition to recognizing the importance of component-based development, the Toolpack project was grappling with how to deal with software evolution. At that time, the FORTRAN systems being developed were considered large and recompilation and reanalysis were expensive. If one piece of the system changed, then did all of the tools in the environment have to be reapplied? Building on the success of Make [20], which automatically assembles executables from various source files for Unix, Clemm and Osterweil developed Odin [14]. Odin would also automatically assemble the executables from various source files, but it would first analyze what had changed in the system and then, based on those results, determine which tool fragments needed to be reapplied and automatically initiate their execution. Moreover, Odin tried to determine when it should eagerly recompute and save intermediate results versus lazily delay and only recompute when a current version was needed.

2. Integrated Software Development Environments

Toolpack was one of the first attempts to recognize that software development was a complicated set of processes and would need to be supported by a collection of tools that interacted with each other. The US Department of Defense (DoD) was just starting to recognize the importance of software systems to their mission, and Defense Advanced Research Projects Agency (DARPA), which previously had primarily focused on networking and artificial intelligence, initiated research programs to support the development of large, complex systems. The DARPA-funded Arcadia Project was novel in that from the get-go it involved collaborations among researchers from different institutions. The academic ties to Osterweil were quite strong however. The major academic departments were the University of California, Irvine, the University of Colorado, Boulder, and the University of Massachusetts, Amherst, along with TRW and Incremental Systems, Inc. It is notable that the university efforts were all led by former students of Osterweil or their descendants.

Early SDEs, now called Integrated Development Environments (IDEs), focused on how to have a collection of tools work together to support the software development process. Based on the success of the programming environments for LISP and Mesa, interest developed for providing an environment for Ada, an emerging language at the time. Early Ada documents [6] outlined an agenda that went beyond just programming language support and included support for the full software lifecycle. Most of these efforts, however, assumed that these environments would be tightly integrated, in that there would be a single repository and a single user interface. Thus, any new tools would have to be developed with this common architectural view, which would no doubt limit extensibility. The Arcadia Project [26,57,58] broke from this view and argued for alternative integration models. These included using loose interaction models, object management, tool composition, and process models.

In their work on interaction models, Maybee, Heimbigner and Osterweil developed the Q system [28]. Q, like the Field system being developed about the same time by Reiss [42,43], supported loose interaction among distributed components and provided much more flexibility than commonly used RPC or message passing models. With respect to data interoperability, Q built upon the Module Interconnect Language [39,40] and IDL [27,52] work that was going on at that time to support data interoperability across languages. It is interesting to note that Q was the first open source and publicly available implementation of the CORBA 2.0 standard [32]. Subsequently, CORBA and other middleware systems built upon and extended many of the ideas that initially appeared in Q. A similar approach to loose interaction was also incorporated into the Chiron user interface system [66] that is now the standard architectural model for user interfaces.

The work on object management was an attempt to circumvent the restricted relational data base view of objects that assumed that there would be, at least conceptually, a single repository and associated data schema. APPL/A [53], PGraphite [56,62], Triton [24] and then Pleiades [55], Arcadia object management prototypes, included capabilities that allowed abstract data types to be defined, manipulated, and made persistent. The Arcadia object management work, as well as other efforts in this area (e.g., [3,31]), led to interesting interactions between the database community and the software engineering community and was the precursor of work on object-oriented data bases (e.g., [1,2]) and the impetus to incorporate persistence into programming languages [22].

Another contribution that arose from the Arcadia project was the importance of providing clean interfaces to various language-independent, intermediate results that arose from front-end compilation and analyzes. For example, language-independent interfaces to commonly used objects such as abstract-syntax trees, control flow graphs, dependency graphs, etc., facilitated the application of further analyses, one of the focal areas of the Arcadia Project [13,45,46]. This tool composition approach that was advocated in the Arcadia project has been subsequently widely adopted in environments such as Eclipse [18] and Visual Studio [61].

The research on interaction models, object management, and tool composition was, in some regards, focused on software architectural models, an important thread of much of the Arcadia project. This emphasis, directly or indirectly, led to some of the earliest work on software architecture, such as the PIC model for describing access control among components [63], the C2 interaction model [29], architectural classification work [30], and one of the earliest papers to introduce the concept of software architecture and associated concerns [38]. All of the Arcadia researchers engaged in long, and often heated, arguments about these topics and all benefited from these exchanges. The Taylor paper in Chapter 9 further elaborates on many of these issues and the ensuing research that built upon these early insights.

3. Process-driven Environments

One of the major insights that arose from the Arcadia project was Osterweil's realization that Make, Odin, and all of the existing scripting notations were inadequate to capture the complex interactions that were needed to describe how agents—that is, software components, hardware components, or human users—were to interrelate and interact in an IDE. Osterweil postulated that nothing short of a programming language would suffice in his seminal paper [34], "Software Processes are Software Too". In this paper, Osterweil argued that it was necessary to accurately represent all the desired interactions among agents required by all of the development phases (e.g., requirements, design, etc.) in order to support the careful planning required to develop a software system. Moreover, he argued that the many analysis tools in the Arcadia environment, as well as the infrastructure components, such as the middleware and object management components, had to be orchestrated by process definitions defined in a rich, process language with well-defined semantics so that it, too, could be the subject of analysis.

This work was the harbinger of a rich body of work on software processes, described in more detail in Part III. Osterweil, however, soon viewed this work on process definition as going far beyond software development, which he now viewed as just one domain of interest, albeit an important one. He saw processes everywhere and soon came to realize that having an articulate process language provided an important basis for developing an environment to support systematic process improvement in many different domains.

4. Environments for Continuous Process Improvements

Osterweil was strongly influenced by the work of Deming [16] and Shewhart [48] on the study of process improvement. He realized that the process language that he had developed, Little-JIL [7], could be used to capture complex processes in a number of domains. Building upon his earlier work on SDEs and his view that processes are software too, he argued that process definitions need to be as carefully developed and analyzed as any other software system. This led to work with Clarke and Avrunin on developing a Process Improvement Environment [4] that included a visual editor for the language, plus a set of analysis capabilities. Analysis techniques that were originally developed to capture requirements of software systems [15,51] and to verify these requirements [17] were enhanced to address the complexities of process definitions. In some cases, the strong control-oriented view of process definitions made them even more amenable to this type of analysis than more data-oriented software systems.

To evaluate the hypothesis that a process improvement environment could benefit a wide variety of domains, case studies were undertaken in the areas of healthcare [9,10,25], on-line dispute resolution [11], elections [49], scientific workflow [19,36] and other areas. Each domain illustrated the benefits of this approach and provided insights about possible enhancements to the process improvement environment itself. For example, the work on healthcare resulted in the development of hazard analysis techniques to detect vulnerabilities, such as single points of failure [8], and discrete event simulation capabilities [41] to evaluate the comparative effectiveness of alternative processes or resource assignments. Some of the issues that have arisen during this work are reminiscent of early research threads that emerged in the early SDE work. For example, maintaining coherence between process performers and executing processes extends the early work on GUI design and event based notification with more extensive mediation mechanisms [50] that now need to be extended even further to support on-line process-guidance. Modeling complex processes, such as emergency room patient flow, often requires not only object management, but also resource management so that contested items can be effectively allocated and utilized. This has led to research on defining and allocating very diverse types of resources, such as those found in challenging real-world domains [64,65].

Because the Little-JIL language was specifically designed to support the flexibility that human agents like to retain, this process improvement approach is seen as particularly applicable to *human-intensive systems*, that is systems where human decisions and participation are an integral part of a complex process [12]. Such human-intensive systems arise in a range of domains from healthcare, to emergency response, to command and control, and will probably continue to grow in importance as devices, software systems, and human ingenuity are brought together to solve complex problems. Cugola et al. describe their recent work on applying process programming to the human-intensive domain of service-oriented computing in Chapter 10. Osterweil's current work is focusing on environments for modeling, evaluating, and executing such systems, going beyond the application of static analysis techniques to detect errors and vulnerabilities to also include on-line process monitoring and guidance as well as process improvements based on post-execution assessment and probabilistic analysis.

5. References

[1] Andrews T, Harris C (1987) Combining Language and Database Advances in an Object-Oriented Development Environment. In: Object-Oriented Programming Systems Languages and Applications

[2] Atkinson M, Bancilhon F, DeWitt D, Dittch K, Maier D, Zdonik S (1989) The Object-Oriented Database System Manifesto. In: First International Conference on Deductive and Object-Oriented Databases

[3] Atkinson MP, Bailey PJ, Chisholm KJ, Cockshott WP, Morrison R (1983) An Approach to Persistent Programming. The Computer Journal 26(4):360-365

[4] Avrunin GS, Clarke LA, Osterweil LJ, Christov SC, Chen B, Henneman EA, Henneman PL, L. C, Mertens W (2010) Experience Modeling and Analyzing Medical Processes: UMass/Baystate Medical Safety Project Overview. In: First Intl. Health Informatics Symp.

[5] Balzer RM (1969) Exdams--Extendable Debugging and Monitoring System. In: 1919 Spring Joint Computer Conference

[6] Buxton J (1980) Requirements for Ada Programming Support Environments. Department of Defense

[7] Cass AG, Lerner BS, McCall EK, Osterweil LJ, Sutton Jr. SM, Wise A (2000) Little-JIL/Juliette: A Process Definition Language and Interpreter, demonstration paper. In: 22nd International Conference on Software Engineering

[8] Chen B, Avrunin GS, Clarke LA, Osterweil LJ (2006) Automatic Fault Tree Derivation from Little-JIL Process Definitions. In: Softw. Process Workshop and Process Sim. Workshop

[9] Chen B, Avrunin GS, Henneman EA, Clarke LA, Osterweil LJ, Henneman PL (2008) Analyzing Medical Processes. In: Thirtieth Intl. Conf. on Software Engineering (Reprinted as Chapter 21)

[10] Clarke LA, Avrunin GS, Osterweil LJ (2008) Using Software Engineering Technology to Improve the Quality of Medical Processes, Invited Keynote. In: Thirtieth Intl. Conf. on Software Engineering

[11] Clarke LA, Gaitenby A, Gyllstrom D, Katsh E, Marzilli M, Osterweil LJ, Sondheimer NK, Wing L, Wise A, Rainey D (2006) A Process-Driven Tool to Support Online Dispute Resolution. In: 2006 International Conference on Digital Government Research

[12] Clarke LA, Osterweil LJ, Avrunin GS (2010) Supporting Human-Intensive Systems. In: FSE/SDP Workshop on the Future of Software Engineering Research

[13] Clarke LA, Richardson DJ, Zeil SJ (1988) TEAM: A Support Environment for Testing Evaluation and Analysis. In: SIGSOFT '88: 3rd Symp. on Softw. Dev. Environments

[14] Clemm GM, Osterweil LJ (1990) A Mechanism for Environment Integration. ACM Transactions on Programming Languages and Systems 12 (1):1-25 (Reprinted as Chapter 12)

[15] Cobleigh RL, Avrunin GS, Clarke LA (2006) User Guidance for Creating Precise and Accessible Property Specifications. In: 14th Intl. Symp. on Foundations of Softw. Engineering

[16] Deming WE (1982) Out of the Crisis. MIT Press, Cambridge

[17] Dwyer MB, Clarke LA, Cobleigh JM, Naumovich G (2004) Flow Analysis for Verifying Properties of Concurrent Software Systems. ACM Trans. on Softw. Engineering and Methodology 13 (4):359-430

[18] Eclipse-an Open Development Platform (2007) http://www.eclipse.org/.

[19] Ellison AM, Osterweil LJ, Hadley JL, Wise A, Boose E, Clarke LA, Foster D, Hanson A, Jensen D, Kuzeja P, Riseman E, Schultz H (2006) Analytic Webs Support the Synthesis of Ecological Data Sets. Ecology 87 (6):1345-1358

[20] Feldman SI (1979) MAKE-A Program for Maintaining Computer Programs. Software - Practice and Experience 9 (4):255-265

[21] Fosdick LD, Osterweil LJ (1976) Data Flow Analysis in Software Reliability. ACM Computing Surveys 8 (3):305-330 (Reprinted as Chapter 5)

[22] Gosling J, Joy B, Steele GL (1996) The Java Language Specification. Addison-Wesley

[23] Habermann AN, Notkin D (1986) Gandalf: Software Development Environments. IEEE Transactions on Software Engineering SE-12 (12):1117-1127

[24] Heimbigner D (1992) Experiences with an Object-Manager for A Process-Centered Environment. In: Eighteenth International Conference on Very Large Data Bases

[25] Henneman EA, Avrunin GS, Clarke LA, Osterweil LJ, Andrzejewski CJ, Merrigan K, Cobleigh R, Frederick K, Katz-Basset E, Henneman PL (2007) Increasing Patient Safety and Efficiency in Transfusion Therapy Using Formal Process Definitions. Transfusion Medicine Reviews 21 (1):49-57

[26] Kadia R (1992) Issues Encountered in Building a Flexible Software Development Environment: Lessons from the Arcadia Project. In: 5th Symp. on Softw. Dev. Environments (Reprinted as Chapter 14)

[27] Lamb DA (1987) IDL: Sharing Intermediate Representations. ACM Transactions on Programming Languages and Systems 9 (3):297-318

[28] Maybee MJ, Heimbigner DM, Osterweil LJ (1996) Multilanguage Interoperability in Distributed Systems. In: 18th International Conference on Software Engineering

[29] Medvidovic N, Oreizy P, Robbins JE, Taylor RN (1996) Using Object-Oriented Typing to Support Architectural Design in the C2 Style. In: 4th Symposium on the Foundations of Software Engineering

[30] Medvidovic N, Taylor RN (2000) A Classification and Comparison Framework for Software Architecture Description Languages. IEEE Transactions on Software Engineering

[31] Morrison R, Dearle A, Bailey PJ, Brown AL, Atkinson MP (1985) The Persistent Store as an Enabling Technology for Project Support Environments. In: 8th Intl. Conf. on Software Engineering

[32] OMG (1995) CORBA 2.0/Interoperability, vol OMG TC Document 95.3.xx. Revised 1.8 edn. Object Management Group, Framingham, MA

[33] Osterweil LJ (1983) Toolpack-An Experimental Software Development Environment Research Project. IEEE Transactions on Software Engineering SE-9 (6):673-685 (Reprinted as Chapter 11)

[34] Osterweil LJ (1987) Software Processes are Software, Too. In: Ninth International Conference on Software Engineering (Reprinted as Chapter 17)

[35] Osterweil LJ (1997) Improving the Quality of Software Quality Determination Processes. In: The Quality of Numerical Software: IFIP TC2/WG2.5 Working Conference on the Quality of Numerical Software Assessment and Enhancement. Chapman & Hall London

[36] Osterweil LJ, Clarke LA, Ellison AM, Boose ER, Podorozhny R, Wise A (2010) Clear and Precise Specification of Scientific Processes. IEEE Transactions on Automation Science and Engineering 7 (1):189-195

[37] Osterweil LJ, Fosdick LD (1976) DAVE-A Validation Error Detection and Documentation System for Fortran Programs. Software Practice and Experience 6 (4):473-486

[38] Perry DE, Wolf AL (1992) Foundations for the Study of Software Architecture. ACM SIGSOFT Software Engineering Notes 17 (4):40–52

[39] Purtilo J (1985) Polylith: An Environment to Support Management of Tool Interfaces. In: SIGPLAN '85 Symposium on Language Issues in Programming Environments

[40] Purtilo JM (1994) The POLYLITH Software Bus. ACM Transactions on Programming Languages and Systems 16 (1):151–174

[41] Raunak MS, Osterweil LJ, Wise A, Clarke LA, Henneman PL (2009) Simulating Patient Flow through an Emergency Department Using Process-Driven Discrete Event Simulation. In: 31st Intl. Conf. on Software Engineering Worksh. on Softw. Engineering in Health Care

[42] Reiss SP (1985) PECAN: Program Development Systems that Support Multiple Views. IEEE Transactions on Software Engineering SE-11 (3):276-285

[43] Reiss SP (1990) Connecting Tools Using Message Passing in the FIELD Environment. IEEE Software 7 (4):57-67

[44] Reps TW, Teitelbaum T (1984)The Synthesizer Generator. In: SIGSOFT/SIGPLAN Software Engineering Symposium on Practical Software Development Environments

[45] Richardson DJ, Aha SL, Osterweil LJ (1989) Integrating Testing Techniques Through Process Programming. In: SIGSOFT 3rd Symp on Testing, Analysis, and Verification

[46] Richardson DJ, O'Malley TO, Moore CT, Aha SL (1992) Developing and Integrating Pro-DAG in the Arcadia Environment. In: 5th SIGSOFT Symp. on Softw. Dev. Environments

[47] Ryder BG (1974) The PFORT Verifier. Software - Practice and Experience 4:359-378

[48] Shewhart WA (1931) Economic Control of Quality of Manufactured Product.

[49] Simidchieva B, Engle SJ, Clifford M, Jones AC, Peisert S, Bishop M, Clarke LA, Osterweil LJ (2010) Modeling and Analyzing Faults to Improve Election Process Robustness. In: 2010 Electronic Voting Technology Workshop/Workshop on Trustworthy Elections

[50] Sliski TJ, Billmers MP, Clarke LA, Osterweil LJ (2001) An Architecture for Flexible, Evolvable Process-Driven User Guidance Environments. In: Joint 8th European Softw. Engineering Conf. and 9th ACM SIGSOFT Symp. on the Foundations of Software Engineering

[51] Smith RL, Avrunin GS, Clarke LA, Osterweil LJ (2002) PROPEL: An Approach Supporting Property Elucidation. In: 24th International Conference on Software Engineering

[52] Snodgrass RT (1989) The Interface Description Language: Definition and Use. Computer Science Press, Rockville, MD

[53] Sutton Jr. SM, Heimbigner D, Osterweil LJ (1995) APPL/A: A Language for Software-Process Programming. ACM Trans. on Software Engineering and Methodology 4(3):221-286

[54] Sweet RE (1985) The Mesa Programming Environment. In: SIGSOFT/SIGPLAN Symposium on Language Issues in Programming Environments

[55] Tarr PL, Clarke LA (1993) PLEIADES: An Object Management System for Software Engineering Environments. In: SIGSOFT Symposium on Foundations of Software Engineering

[56] Tarr PL, Wileden JC, Clarke LA (1990) Extending and Limiting PGraphite- style Persistence. In: Fourth International Workshop on Persistent Object Systems

[57] Taylor RN, Belz FC, Clarke LA, Osterweil LJ, Selby RW, Wileden JC, Wolf A, Young M (1998) Foundations for the Arcadia Environment Architecture. In: ACM SIGSOFT Software Engineering Symposium on Practical Software Development Environments (Reprinted as Chapter 13)

[58] Taylor RN, Clarke LA, Osterweil LJ, W. SR, Wileden JC, Wolf A, Young M (1986) Arcadia: A Software Development Environment Research Project. In: ACM/IEEE Symposium on Ada Tools and Environments

[59] Teitelbaum T, Reps TR (1981) The Cornell Program Synthesizer: A Syntax Directed Programming Environment. Communications of the ACM 24 (9):563-573

[60] Teitelman W, Masinter L (1981) The InterLisp Programming Environment. Computer 14 (4):25-33

[61] Visual Studio. (2010) http://www.microsoft.com/visualstudio/en-us/.

[62] Wileden JC, Wolf AL, Fisher CD, Tarr PL (1988) PGRAPHITE: An Experiment in Persistent Typed Object Management. In: Third ACM SIGPLAN/SIGSOFT Symposium on Practical Software Development Environments

[63] Wolf AL, Clarke LA, Wileden JC (1989) The AdaPIC Toolset: Supporting Interface Control and Analysis Throughout the Software Development Process. IEEE Transactions on Software Engineering 15 (3):250-263

[64] Xiao J, Osterweil LJ, Wang Q (2010) Dynamic Scheduling of Emergency Department Resources. In: First ACM International Health Informatics Symposium

[65] Xiao J, Osterweil LJ, Wang Q, Li M (2010) Dynamic Resource Scheduling in Disruption-Prone Software Development Environments. In: Fundamental Approaches to Software Engineering.

[66] Young M, Taylor RN, Troup DB (1988) Design Principles Behind Chiron: A UIMS for Software Environments. In: Tenth International Conference on Software Engineering

Software Architecture, (In)consistency, and Integration

Richard N. Taylor

Institute for Software Research
University of California, Irvine
Irvine, CA 92697-3455 U.S.A.
taylor@ics.uci.edu

Abstract As other chapters in this volume demonstrate, Leon Osterweil has made critical contributions to software analysis and testing. That stream of contributions began with his work in the DAVE project, which produced a static data flow analysis tool capable of analyzing FORTRAN programs. What I am sure Lee did not recognize at the time was that this work also launched him on a path to making critical contributions in environment architectures, inconsistency management, and integration technologies. These contributions arose from his work with Toolpack, Odin, the Arcadia project, and their recent successors. This chapter traces some of these key results, highlighting not only Lee's contributions, but places where they remain to be fully exploited.

1. Architecture

DAVE has a simple premise: examining data flow relationships in source code can identify potential problems [8]. Performing such examination requires a bit of work, however. The source code must be scanned, parsed, a flow graph constructed, annotations placed upon the graph designating actions on variables, flow analysis performed, and results, keyed to the source code, "pretty-printed" to the programmer. As an ensemble the DAVE tool performs its job and highlights errors and possible errors in the code. When viewed as a collection of "micro-tools," however, the potential for creating a variety of other tools becomes apparent. For instance, scanning, parsing, and pretty-printing functions could be combined with other functions that provide statement-by-statement execution frequency counts to enable a programmer to determine what portions of the source code could profitably be optimized. This insight led Osterweil to focus a central part of the follow-on Toolpack project on tool design and integration strategies, a step that ultimately produced a variety of environment, architecture, and integration results.

P.L. Tarr, A.L. Wolf (eds.), *Engineering of Software*,
DOI 10.1007/978-3-642-19823-6_9, © Springer-Verlag Berlin Heidelberg 2011

Toolpack [7] (reprinted in Chapter 12) was envisioned as ultimately supporting the mathematical software development community, which provided the impetus for its creation. A major impact, however, was in the environments community. The stated goal of the Toolpack project was "... to establish a positive feedback loop between environment developers and a broad and diverse base of environment users by supplying those users a sequence of environments that is increasingly responsive to the users' needs." The implication of change over time, involving the addition of new functionality and the possibility of changing existing functionality, meant that a premium had to be placed on the environment's architecture.

As with DAVE, the initial set of tool fragments in Toolpack focused on functions that would be useful in analyzing and testing mathematical software written in FORTRAN. These functions included compilation, editing, formatting, structuring, testing, debugging, static error detection, portability checking, documentation generation, and program transformation. Each of these functions involved the execution of a variety of sub-functions or tools, with substantial reuse of some of the tool fragments among the high-level services provided by the environment. Given the goal of having an extensible and growing environment, the key design question focused on how the tool fragments should be managed and combined.

Other contemporary or preceding environments had promoted the composition of tool fragments, such as Unix filters. Unix, and in particular the make program [4], also provided a means for the orchestration of multiple tool fragments to produce a programmer's desired result. Osterweil advanced from this work, adding a rich, type-based means for declaring the relationships between tool fragments, and a command interpreter, which focused on enabling the user to state what outcome was desired, without having to know the details of the potentially many tool fragments that would have to be invoked in order to accomplish the goal.

This work matured over several years, becoming led by Osterweil's student, Geoff Clemm, and ultimately yielded the Odin tool integration and management system [3] (reprinted in Chapter 12). Odin represented a major shift in software environments, for it convincingly shifted the focus from tool orientation to data orientation. Along with Unix, contemporary advanced programming environments such as Interlisp and Smalltalk were tool-focused: users employed often very powerful functions to achieve goals. But in these environments the focus is on giving commands—invoking tools or functions to achieve some purpose. Odin, however, changed that focus. As the Odin paper states, "The Odin project followed the suggestion ... that an environment must be data centered, rather than tool centered, and adopted the philosophy that Odin-integrated environments should be devices for using tools to manage repositories of software data in such a way as to expedite responses to interactive user commands."

Odin maintained a data structure known as the Odin Derivation Graph, which describes the type-based relationships between all the tool (fragments) resident in the environment. By having the user state the (type of) object wanted, and the system knowing what objects currently reside in the object repository, Odin could infer a sequence of tool invocations that would begin with some subset of the existing objects and ultimately produce the requested object. While the superficial similarity to **make** is clear, the underlying mechanisms were far more complex.

"Make automatically applies tools to assure that changes to some objects are reflected in other related objects. Odin supports this object management feature as well. With Make, however, for all but single-input/single-output tools, the user must explicitly name each individual object which is to be automatically updated and the exact sequences of tools to be used in doing so. Odin, on the other hand, enables users to define types of objects and to prescribe general procedures for automatically creating and updating instances of those types from corresponding instances of other types. ¶Thus, the Odin user may create a new object and then immediately request a derivation requiring the complex synthesis of many diverse tools and the creation of many intermediate objects. A Make user would have to set up directory structures naming all of these objects and would have to define the derivation process in detail. Odin automatically constructs storage structures as needed, in accordance with the derivation process that it creates from a more general specification of how tools interconnect." [3]

As mentioned, the Odin Derivation Graph (ODG) worked in conjunction with the object repository to produce the information requested by the developer. The object repository was managed through the use of a Derivation Forest, which maintained the set of atomic and derived objects that Odin managed. The objects in the repository were essentially files. For example, a FORTRAN source text file would be entered by the user as an atomic object; subsequently other objects could be derived from it, such as a parse tree or formatted source file.

In retrospect, the ODG and the Derivation Forest can be seen as *architectural models*. But whereas the architectural models that became popular in the mid-1990's modeled the structure of software *products*, the Odin models were models of the *environment*—the current palette of tools and the current object repository. (We will return to this observation below.)

Odin also comprised a command interpreter, designed to handle interactions with the user and to invoke the mechanisms that would use the ODG and the Derivation Forest to produce the desired result. This means that Odin essentially comprised an extensible part and a fixed part—extensibility primarily represented by the ODG and the fixed part by the tools that used it. This bipartite structure carried over into the next major project in which Osterweil was involved, Arcadia.

The Arcadia project started with a goal similar to Toolpack's: provide a comprehensive, extensible development environment. The explosion of software and hardware technologies in the 1980's and 90's meant, however, that greater demands were to be satisfied by environments, and environments should be expected to exploit advances in hardware, especially display and networking technologies. Arcadia was thus targeted at distributed, multi-person development and, not surprisingly, was itself a distributed, multi-person project. As such, one of the project's earliest needs was for a model of the target environment that would enable effective communication between the developers and that would serve to govern its development.

Two early models of Arcadia strongly reflected Osterweil's experience and contributions from the earlier projects. The earliest model, shown below, appeared in [12] (reprinted in Chapter 13).

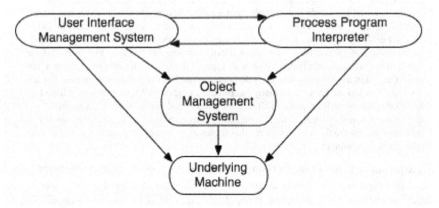

Fig. 9.1. Arcadia-1, the "fixed part"

"Figure [9.1] depicts the infrastructure or *fixed* part, of an environment and thus does not show any of the process programs, tools, and software objects that populate an environment." The fixed/variant distinction from Odin thus carried forward. The Arcadia "Object Management System" also reflected Odin (along with the experiences of others in the Arcadia Consortium). The "Process Program Interpreter", which was responsible for executing processes in the environment, carried forward the insights about computing environment results based upon dynamic models of the tools resident in the environment. Of course there is much more to the process program aspect of Arcadia; we will consider this in a moment.

The second early model of Arcadia appeared in [9] and is sketched in Figure 9.2 below. This model is explicitly a layered virtual machine of services, where the elements shown are the "fixed part." In this model a greater level of detail is found, reflecting the insights of the Arcadia developers in more precisely articulating the relationships between the main fixed elements.

The major innovation that Osterweil provided to Arcadia, however, was the broad notion of process programming. While Part III of this volume addresses Osterweil's process contributions more generally and broadly, a key initial focus of the process programming work was coordinating and applying tools in an environment. In other words, taking the tool orchestration concepts from Toolpack/Odin and making them yet richer and more powerful. As the initial Arcadia reference [12] (reprinted in Chapter 13) states, "A process program indicates how the various software tools and objects would be coordinated to support a process." That a process program was necessary for coordinating tools and objects reflected the growing understanding of just how complex software development is.

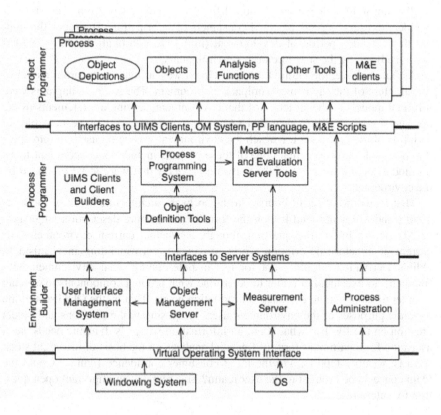

Fig. 9.2. Arcadia-1 Virtual Machines Diagram

More broadly, process programs, in the context of software development environments, began to address the issues of *why* software objects were created. Odin, after all, left the choice of what objects to display or create up to the user; there was no context into which the objects "fit". Process programming provided that context for Arcadia, by enabling specification of the processes within which various objects were needed. In the earliest explorations of process programming, the processes were focused on configuration management-related activities. Rather than just rebuilding an executable, for example, after a change to a source file, the Arcadia mechanisms, in the particular form of APPL/A [10] programs, contained relations and triggers which enabled the monitoring of conditions on objects and the subsequent application of tools upon detection of a trigger condition. Thus upon the event of a source file exceeding a specified size, for example, a program could be triggered to post a message, perform a checkpoint, rebuild the system, or invoke some other process.

The inclusion of APPL/A thus represented another step in the development of environment architectures towards better supporting the goals of the user. Osterweil's contributions have a common theme of moving away from users-as-tool-wielders to users as producers and consumers of information. The focus throughout this extended period of development (mid 1970's through the early 1990's) was on advancing the structure of the environments.

As noted above, the Odin Derivation Graph was an important partial model of the structure of the (dynamic) Toolpack environment. The Arcadia diagrams were informal models of the structure of that environment, serving as statements of the designers' goals. APPL/A provided a way of precise, powerful, and executable description of the processes for which the environment was being used. In retrospect it appears odd, however, that none of these projects included a concomitant focus on models of the structure of the software *products* that were to be produced by the environments.

That focus did arise, of course, in the software architecture work of the mid-1990's and following, and it took the form of architecture description languages, or ADLs[1]. An interesting question, though, is whether current environments, or current architecture description work, provides a corresponding mechanism to Odin's Derivation Graph —not for use in determining what environment tool fragments to execute, but rather to determine what product components to execute in order to satisfy some *end-user's* information needs. That is, the ODG served the dynamic purposes of the environment user, composing tool executions and object creation on the fly. But what about an information worker's dynamic needs, such as asking for a particular form of financial analysis on the basis of historical stock records, weather reports, and the latest consumer confidence figures? Could the Odin concepts be brought to the user realm? This remains an important open question for future research.

2. Consistency and Inconsistency

Software development has, from the outset, involved a struggle for consistency. A bug in a program is nothing more than an inconsistency between the operational effect of a program and its specification, whether that specification is simply the syntactic rules of the language, or the intent of those who procured the software for their use. Osterweil has always been clear on this matter, as I can attest from the earliest time I began working with him. The expression of intent, the specification against which behavior is compared for consistency, has played out in much of his work, including the use of assertions and units checking in programming, a practice he advocated while at Boeing [13].

---

[1] I think it is not a stretch to say that work on ADLs and a focus on the structure of and styles of software products arose in part because of the increasing complexity of the structure of software environments. The second Arcadia architecture diagram, above, is explicitly structural, and the paper in which it appeared [9] focused on its properties as a layered virtual machine.

As one develops a deeper understanding of software development, however, one begins to recognize how many kinds of consistency are potentially at issue, and more importantly, how it is nigh-impossible, and certainly undesirable, to maintain full consistency with all specifications at all times during development. Requirements specifications may themselves be internally inconsistent; cost-conscious development may entail explorations among several alternative solution paths to determine which yields a system "close enough" to the desired specification yet within an acceptable budget.

The role, therefore, of inconsistency during software development became more prominent and accepted in software development as understanding of all the issues deepened (see, e.g., [1]). Osterweil's approach, in work done jointly with Stan Sutton and Dennis Heimbigner, focused on the explicit management and control of (in)consistency. In particular, APPL/A provided a means for stating desired relations between software entities (i.e., the particular desired consistencies) and triggers that would monitor the relations to detect the presence of inconsistency, and, if so desired, effect some action in response to the inconsistency [11].

A very simple use case for this approach is in configuration management: when a source file is changed, it becomes inconsistent with a previously compiled executable. Detection of the existence of the changed file can trigger a recompilation and system rebuild. Of course, in a large system, such immediate recompilation and rebuild may be undesirable: a rebuild might, according to policy, also require execution of a regression test suite, and such action might take a week or more to perform. If many source files are to be changed as part of an upgrade, a more sensible strategy is to wait until some specified management condition, and at that time build and retest. Clearly, statement of all the conditions and considerations of when an action should be triggered can be complex. Hence Osterweil and his colleagues made the APPL/A relation and triggering mechanism quite powerful. "In accordance with our language design goals, the APPL/A consistency model is motivated by two ideas: that the criteria for consistency are evolving and relative and that inconsistency must be accommodated as a normal condition." [10]

The power and effectiveness of APPL/A's relations and predicates for the management of (in)consistency is still, regrettably, not fully explored. Given APPL/A's basis in Ada and concomitant needs for a powerful object management system underneath the language, not all aspects of the design have been explored in practice. Subsequently, Osterweil led exploration of lighter-weight process constructs with the Little-JIL language [2]. In Little-JIL the use of a flexible exception handling mechanism supplanted the richer notion of relations, predicates, and triggered actions. While reverting to the "exception" designation may seem like a step away from the normalization of inconsistency, the terminology is familiar to developers and in keeping with the goal of allowing process specifiers to maintain a primary focus on the desired course of events. Moreover, rather than a tacked-on notion of exception handling, Little-JIL's exceptions are a normal part of process development. It is the making of exceptions unexceptional that normalizes the management of inconsistency. An interesting question for the future is whether advances over the past few years in event-based middleware combined with contemporary software repositories could enable exploitation of all of APPL/A's relation and predicate trigger mechanisms.

3. Integration

In many respects the major technical focus of Osterweil's primary environment projects has been integration. As discussed above, the structures of Toolpack/Odin and Arcadia are structures designed for extension and the cooperative application of many tools or tool fragments in support of development processes. APPL/A provided a critical mechanism for integration beyond the tool dependency graph of Odin: a rich process language enabling the specification of complex, detailed development processes, themselves involving myriad objects and tools. The primary Arcadia reference, [5] (reprinted in Chapter 14)—written by that mysterious researcher, "R. Kadia"—devoted much of its attention to the several mechanisms exploited by the project. In addition to the mechanisms already described, Osterweil contributed to another notable innovation from Arcadia, Q.

Q [6] is a multilingual inter-process communication mechanism which predated (and yet surpassed) technologies such as CORBA. The problem that Q addressed was endemic to Arcadia: the environment was (deliberately) composed of elements written in a variety of programming languages (Ada, C++, C, Prolog, and Tcl, for instance), running in multiple concurrent processes, and often on multiple hardware platforms. Within the processes, depending on the programming language used, multiple threads were active. The need was to enable efficient, procedure-call style communication—integration—between the heterogeneous elements. It was clear that simple remote procedure call mechanisms were insufficient. RPC-focused mechanisms usually assume a client-server model, and such was not the case in Arcadia. While the need for argument marshalling and multi-lingual data exchange was shared with some other contemporaneous technologies, no other project at the time addressed the complex problems associated with accommodating the peer to peer communication patterns, and where peers themselves were multi-threaded.

Though twenty-plus years have passed since the initial version of Q, it is evident that Q provided services in the early 90's that are hard to realize even now. Most modern systems studiously avoid the issues of multi-lingual interoperability, which is a cornerstone of integration. Many systems still cling to a client-server model as well, where clients are often single-threaded. The more interesting comparison for Q is with event message services. Event-based integration mechanisms were common in Arcadia, and the technologies matured side-by-side. The wisdom now seems to be that for the tightest and fastest integration that (effectively) monolingual single-thread RPC is still the choice, whereas for any other type of integration event-based protocols dominate.

4. Conclusion

Leon Osterweil most clearly deserves the thanks and recognition of the community for the pioneering work he has done in the areas of environment architectures, consistency management, and software integration. His contributions in tool technology have always been grounded in technical detail, addressing the genuine problems of the software development community. As an unselfish collaborator he led, guided, suggested, prodded, critiqued, praised, and molded researchers as well as research projects. He provided vision, directions, and technical substance. As my advisor, mentor, and friend he has been instrumental in guiding me in my research path, for which I am very grateful.

References

[1] Balzer R (1991) Tolerating Inconsistency. In: 13th Intl. Conference on Software Engineering
[2] Cass AG, Lerner BS, Sutton Jr. SM, McCall EK, Wise A, Osterweil LJ (2000) Little-JIL/Juliette: a process definition language and interpreter. In: Proceedings of the 22nd international conference on Software engineering
[3] Clemm G, Osterweil L (1990) A Mechanism for Environment Integration. ACM Transactions on Programming Languages and Systems 12(1):1-25 (Reprinted as Chapter 12)
[4] Feldman S (1979) Make—a program for maintaining computer programs. Software: Practice and Experience 9(4):255-265
[5] Kadia R (1992) Issues Encountered in Building a Flexible Software Development Environment: Lessons from the Arcadia Project. In: Fifth ACM SIGSOFT Symposium on Software Development Environments (Reprinted as Chapter 14)
[6] Maybee MJ, Heimbigner DM, Osterweil LJ (1996) Multilanguage Interoperability in Distributed Systems. In: 18th International Conference on Software Engineering
[7] Osterweil LJ (1983) Toolpack—An Experimental Software Development Environment Research Project. IEEE Transactions on Software Engineering SE-9(6):673-685 (Reprinted as Chapter 11)
[8] Osterweil LJ, Fosdick LD (1976) DAVE—A validation error detection and documentation system for FORTRAN programs. Software: Practice and Experience 6(4):473-486
[9] Osterweil LJ, Taylor RN (1990) The Architecture of the Arcadia-1 Process Centered Software Environment. In: Sixth International Software Process Workshop
[10] Sutton Jr. SM, Heimbigner D, Osterweil LJ (1995) APPL/A: A Language for Software Process Programming. ACM Trans. on Software Engineering and Methodology 4(3):221-286
[11] Sutton Jr. SM, Heimbigner D, Osterweil LJ (1990) Language constructs for managing change in process-centered environments. In: Proceedings of the fourth ACM SIGSOFT symposium on Software development environments (Reprinted as Chapter 19)
[12] Taylor R, Belz F, Clarke L, Osterweil L, Selby R, Wileden J, Wolf A, Young M (1988) Foundations for the Arcadia Environment Architecture. In: Proc. ACM SIGSOFT/SIGPLAN Software Engineering Symp. on Practical software development environments (Reprinted as Chapter 13)
[13] Taylor RN (1983) An integrated verification and testing environment. Software: Practice and Experience 13(8):697-713

Process Programming in the Service Age: Old Problems and New Challenges

Gianpaolo Cugola, Carlo Ghezzi, and Leandro Sales Pinto

Dip. di Elettronica e Informazione, Politecnico di Milano, Italy, e-mail:
{cugola,ghezzi,pinto}@elet.polimi.it

Abstract Most modern software systems have a decentralized, modular, distributed, and dynamic structure. They are often composed of heterogeneous components and operate on heterogeneous infrastructures. They are increasingly built by composing *services*; that is, components owned (designed, deployed, maintained, and run) by remote and independent stakeholders. The quality of service perceived by the clients of such a composite application depends directly on the individual services that are integrated in it, but also on the way they are composed. At the same time, the world in which applications are situated (in particular, the remote services upon which they can rely) changes continuously. These requirements ask for an ability of applications to self-adapt to dynamic changes, especially when they need to run for a long time without interruption. This, in turn, has an impact on the way service compositions are defined using ad-hoc process languages that are defined to support compositions. This paper discusses how the service setting has revamped the field of process (workflow) programming: where old problems that were identified in the past still exist now, how we can learn from past work, and where and why new challenges instead require additional research.

1. Introduction and Historical Perspective

Software is the driving engine of modern society. Most human activities are either software enabled or entirely managed by software. Examples range from healthcare and transportation to commerce and manufacturing to entertainment and education. We are today in a stage where existing Web technology allows the data available in every node to be accessed from any other node, being it static or mobile, through the network fabric. We are moving to a stage where functionalities (services) may be openly accessed and integrated to provide new functionality and serve different users.

Although the terms *(software) service* and *service-oriented computing (SOC)* are becoming widely used, they should be made more precise to better understand

P.L. Tarr, A.L. Wolf (eds.), *Engineering of Software*,
DOI 10.1007/978-3-642-19823-6_10, © Springer-Verlag Berlin Heidelberg 2011

the nature of the problems we are currently facing. A service is a software component that provides some functionality of possible general use. Functionalities can be of different levels of complexity, generality, and granularity. Services and SOC differ with respect to *(software) components* and *component-based computing* in that services are owned (developed, deployed, run, and maintained) by independent stakeholders, who make them available for external use by multiple potential clients. Their use may be possible under certain *conditions* and may be subject to a *service-level agreement (SLA)*. The conditions and the SLA are part of a *contract* that binds service users and service providers. The conditions may include a price that the user has to pay for use. The SLA should state both the functional and nonfunctional properties that the service declares to offer. For example, it may indicate that the service offers a localization function having a given precision and that the average time to update the coordinates is 100 msec. In the current state of practice, contracts are often loose. Many research efforts are currently directed towards making them formal, and hence enforceable. The push to progressing in this direction has both economic and legal motivations.

Service-oriented computing has promise, but it also raises new problems. The promise is that in the future, one may expect a real service marketplace to become available, where even inexperienced users might be empowered by their ability to access a large variety of useful functionalities. The problem is, realizing this promise requires significant technological advances. For example, the way existing services may be discovered and the process languages or notations through which users may compose them are still quite primitive and hard to master. The hope that even non-technical users might become directly engaged is far from being real. A key obstacle is the openness and instability of the environment in which clients and services are immersed today. The environment changes continuously and unpredictably. Existing services may be discontinued or they may change in a way that violates their SLA and invalidates the client's expectations. They may change the conditions under which clients may use them. Clients may also change their expectations, or the context in which a service is requested may change, requiring a different service to be selected to address the new needs. New services may also become available, which might give better response to the clients' needs. How can this dynamic complexity be managed?

Defining and managing *service orchestrations* in an open and evolving environment is hard. It is especially hard if the proposed solution is based on traditional "programming" approaches adopted by current mainstream workflow languages. The "orchestration code" needs to take care of an intricate control flow in which one tries to capture all possible ways things can go wrong and react to exceptional conditions to continue to meet the requirements in the presence of anticipated and unanticipated changes.

This situation has very strong similarities to what was discovered in the late 1980s and in the 1990s in the research area on *software processes*. This area was mostly boosted by Osterweil's seminal work [17]. Osterweil recognized the need to formalize the software development process so that it could be analyzed, improved, and automated. This area was sometimes referred to using the term *process programming*, although the low-level term "programming" does not do justice to the real essence of Osterweil's proposal. Rather, the idea was that software processes were important conceptual entities to understand, model, and possibly automate. Indeed, the same concept was later applied to other human-intensive domains besides software development, where the term *workflow* instead of *process* became more commonly used[1].

One of the important findings of the work on (software) processes was that because of the active and creative role of humans in the process, *deviations* [8] were important to handle [20, 3]. The software process, in fact, supports humans and manual activities as well as automated tools. Unlike tools, humans cannot be seen as "subroutines" to invoke to get fully predictable results. Moreover, humans can tolerate inconsistencies, whereas tools seldom can. Finally, because processes are long-running entities, they need to evolve as the situation may change during the course of execution. Having recognized these distinctive features, the process work in the 1990s sought ways to model flexible processes through sophisticated mechanisms and studied how to manage deviations and inconsistencies arising in the process enactment. This past work can be classified in three main directions:

Process programming with exceptions. A number of approaches investigated how to adapt the exception handling constructs that are supported by standard programming languages for inclusion in languages intended for process definition and automation. The emphasis here is on using a process language, as in Osterweil's original proposal, to program the process. Perhaps the most completely developed approach is the APPL/A language [20], which is based on an imperative paradigm. The idea of using exceptions has the obvious advantage that the *normal* process flows are clearly distinguishable from the *exceptional* flows in the process description. This allows for a certain degree of separation of concerns and supports a cleaner programming style than handling exceptional conditions through conventional *if–then–else* constructs. The main drawback of this approach is that it requires all possible exceptional conditions to be identified before writing the process code. This can be quite restrictive in highly dynamic contexts in which new and unanticipated cases may arise.

Reflective mechanisms. Through reflection, languages support reasoning about, and possibly modification of, programs. Reflective features are often available in conventional programming languages. They have been also proposed and experimented within process languages. As an example, in our past work on the SPADE environment [4], we developed a fully reflective process modeling language (SLANG) based on Petri nets, which allows meta-programming. That is, in SLANG one can develop a process whose objective is to modify an existing process or even an existing process instance. The potential advantage of such an approach over the previous one is clear: the process model does not need to anticipate all possible exceptional situations, since it can include the (formal) descrip-

---

[1] In this paper, the terms *process* and *workflow* will be used interchangeably.

tion of how the process model itself can be modified at execution-time to cope with unexpected situations. The main drawback of this approach is that it may bring further rigidity into the approach: not only the process must be modeled (or "programmed") in all detail, but so also must the meta-process, i.e., the process of modifying the model itself.

Flexible approaches. Both previous cases are based on the assumption that a precise and enforceable process model is available and there is no way to violate the prescribed process. In other terms, there is no way to treat a deviation from the process within the formal system. Reflective languages support changes to the process, but all possible changes must follow a predefined change process, i.e., again there is no way to "escape" from a fully defined, prescriptive model. The key idea to overcome this limitation was to abandon the ambitious but unrealistic goal of modeling every aspect of the process in advance, following an imperative, prescriptive style, to focus on certain constraints that should be preserved by the process, without explicitly forcing a pre-defined course of actions. Any process that satisfies the constraints would thus be acceptable. This brings a great flexibility in process enactment, avoiding micro-management of every specific issue while focusing on the important properties that should be maintained. Usually, these approaches are coupled with advanced runtime systems that support the users in finding their way through the actual situations toward the process goals, while remaining within the boundaries determined by the process model. An early example of this approach is described in [7].

In the remainder of this paper, we describe our current work, which focuses on process programming for service compositions. We developed a language, called DSOL, which can be classified in the last category. We propose a *declarative* approach to model service orchestrations, i.e., workflows that compose existing services to build new ones. As a result, we obtain a language that is easier to use and results in more flexible and self-adapting orchestrations than the existing mainstream languages adopted in the area, like BPEL and BPMN. An ad-hoc engine, leveraging well-known planning techniques, interprets such models to support automatic dynamic service orchestration at run-time.

The rest of this contribution is organized as follows. Section 2 presents a deeper analysis of the deficiencies of current mainstream service composition languages. Section 3 looks back to identify similar issues that were recognized in the past and the solutions provided by research at the time. We also identify what is new in the current setting and how all this may drive the search for new solutions, like DSOL (Section 4). Section 5 draws some conclusions and discusses future work directions.

2. Limitations of Currently Available Orchestration Languages

Throughout the last two decades, different approaches were taken towards so-called *process programming* using workflow languages. Several programming and modeling languages were defined in an attempt to best define and automate different kinds of processes. More recently, the advent of SOC has attracted much research into the area of business processes, to provide foundations for formalization, automation, and support to business-to-business integration, where services provided by different organizations are combined to provide new added-value services that can be made available to end users.

Two languages emerged as the de-facto standards for modeling service orchestrations: BPEL [1] and BPMN [21]. Although the two have some differences [18], they share a number of commonalities that result in the same limitations in modeling complex processes. In particular, both adopt an imperative style, in which service orchestrations are modeled as monolithic programs that must capture the entire flow of execution. This requires service architects to address every detail in the flow among services—they must explicitly program all the sequences of activities and take care of all dependencies among them, consider all the different alternatives to accomplish the orchestration goal, and forecast and manage in advance every possible fault and exception that may occur at run-time.

To be more precise about this issue, consider the following example. Suppose we have to orchestrate some external services to buy tickets for a (night) event, and to arrange for transportation and accommodation for those participating in the event. Initially, a participant provides the name of the city where she lives, the event she wants to attend, the relevant payment information, and her desired transportation and accommodation types. The first action to perform is buying the ticket, followed by booking transportation, which can be arranged either by plane, train, or bus (the participant may express a preference). After booking the transportation, the accommodation (hotel or hostel, in this order of preference, unless explicitly chosen by the user) must be booked. In general, the preferred option is to book the transportation in such a way that the participant arrives at the event's location the day before the event and departs the day after, booking two nights at a nearby hotel/hostel, to allow for free time to visit the place. It is also acceptable to stay a single day (the day of the event) if this is the only way to successfully organize the trip.

To model this orchestration using BPEL (and the same is true for BPMN), we must explicitly code all possible action flows. Unfortunately, there are many. Indeed, even if we do not consider possible exceptions to the mainstream process, this requires addressing alternative actions (e.g., booking a train is not required if a plane has already been booked), actions that must be done in sequence (e.g., buying the ticket before finding transportation), and actions which depend on the result of other actions (e.g., the choice of transportation depends from the preference of the user). This is quite significant and complex.

```
...
<scope name="EventPlanning">
 <scope name="BookTransportation">
  <if>
   <condition>
    <!-- preferredTrans equals airplane or
         preferredTrans is null -->
   </condition>
   <scope name="BookFlight">
    <compensationHandler>
     <!-- Cancel flight reservation -->
    </compensationHandler>
    <invoke operation="bookFlight"
            inputVariable="transDetails"
            outputVariable="flightBooked" .../>
   </scope>
  </if>
  <if>
   <condition>
    <!-- preferredTrans equals train or
         (preferredTrans is null and not flightBooked) -->
   </condition>
   <scope name="BookTrain">
    <compensationHandler>
     <!-- Cancel train reservation -->
    </compensationHandler>
    <invoke operation="bookTrain"
            inputVariable="transDetails"
            outputVariable="trainBooked" ... />
   </scope>
  </if>
  <if>
   <condition>
    <!-- preferredTrans equals bus or (preferredTrans is null and
         not flightBooked and not trainBooked -->
   </condition>
   <scope name="BookTrain">
    <compensationHandler>
     <!-- Cancel bus reservation -->
    </compensationHandler>
    <invoke operation="bookBus"
            inputVariable="transDetails"
            outputVariable="busBooked" ... />
   </scope>
```

```
    </if>
    <if>
     <condition>
      <!-- not (trainBooked or flightBooked or busBooked) -->
     </condition>
     <throw faultName="TransNotBooked" />
    </if>
   </scope>
  </scope>
  ...
```

Fig. 10.1. Booking transportation in BPEL.

Fig. 10.1 shows a code snippet that expresses the alternatives for booking the transportation in BPEL. It is easy to observe how convoluted and hard to read it is, especially if we consider that this is just a small fragment of quite a simple case study and that we have not considered possible exceptions. Indeed, the situation becomes much more complex when run-time exceptions, such as a failure while invoking an external service, have to be considered. We need to be able to forecast these and add code to manage them, designing alternative paths and including code to undo actions that must be retracted when alternative paths are followed.

It is our belief that this is mainly a consequence of the imperative paradigm adopted by mainstream orchestration languages, which closely resemble (imperative) programming languages, forcing service architects to precisely and explicitly enumerate all possible flows of actions, with the additional drawback that the code for fault and compensation handling is mixed with the main process flow.

As we mentioned in the introduction, we believe that possible solutions to mitigate these problems can be found by examining research solutions in the past decade in the area of software process modeling. We survey the relevant part of this research in the next section, while in Section 4 we present a novel approach to service orchestration, which leverages our experience in that area [4, 7] to abandon the imperative way of modeling orchestrations in favor of a declarative style. The run-time system of the declarative language may use known planning techniques to automatically determine the exact order in which different steps can be performed and how to operate in case of both expected and unexpected faults.

3. Looking to the Past to Take Inspiration for the Future

Although service composition languages, like BPEL and BPMN, were born in a different environment from the one in which software process modeling languages were proposed, they share many commonalities. Indeed, both software processes and generic business processes are long-lived, complex, dynamic entities that must interact with an external environment that they usually cannot fully control. Such environments are inevitably subject to changes, which are hard to predict and almost impossible to prevent. Thus, changes often lead to unexpected situations that force the process to deviate from the originally intended course of actions.

This commonality suggests that current research on service composition languages could profit from taking inspiration from past research on software process modeling, in particular with respect to the mechanisms to model and handle exceptions and deviations.

The most common and often used solution to the problem of managing exceptional situations is by providing specific language constructs to describe them and to model the actions to manage them, as in languages like APPL/A [20] and, later, Little-JIL [15]. As we mentioned in Section 1, this approach, also used by mainstream business process languages like BPEL and BPMN, and by several Workflow Management Systems [19], is limited in that it can only handle expected exceptions, forcing the process modeler to forecast at design time all possible situations that may lead to a deviation from the standard course of actions. This limitation is exacerbated by the fact that languages which follow this approach usually adopt a normative paradigm of modeling and a rigid runtime system, which do not allow deviations from the model at process execution time if something unexpected happens.

Even if we ignore the difficulty of anticipating, at design-time, everything that could go wrong at run-time, just modeling the forecasted exceptions is a cumbersome and error-prone task. To address this problem, a number of exception handling patterns were proposed [16]. They help process designers to identify and reuse existing solutions, simplifying the development and maintenance of process models. These patterns could be reused easily in the domain of service compositions. However, the approach would still be based on an explicit enumeration of all expected exceptions and on explicitly programming how they can be handled.

Some software process execution environments—such as SPADE [4], OASIS [12], Endeavors [5], EPOS [11], and IPSE 2.5 [6]—adopted reflective languages, through which process models and even their running instances may be accessed as data items to be inspected and modified at process enactment time. This approach allows the *meta-process*, i.e., the process of changing the running instance of the model, to be also modeled, as a special step of the process itself. While this brings an unprecedented level of expressiveness to the language, it also requires a lot of effort from the process modeler, who is asked not only to model the software development process, but also the meta-process, in all detail. For this reason, reflection is considered an effective approach to manage major exceptional situations, which require a radical departure from the originally modeled process, and particularly those situations that are expected to occur again. For the other (minor but more frequent) cases, which happen sporadically and require quick responses, other approaches are required.

One example of such approaches in the area of software process modeling is a system we developed a few years ago: PROSYT [7]. Three intuitions guided the design of PROSYT:

- the need to abandon the normative approach to process modeling and, consequently, the imperative style that was typical of previous process languages;
- the need to add flexibility into the runtime system, to allow the users involved in a process to deviate readily from the expected course of actions if an unexpected situation arises; and
- the need to abandon the activity-oriented approach to modeling, which often results in focusing only and too early on those aspects of the process that are directly related to the specific course of actions that the process modeler had in mind. Conversely, we preferred an approach focusing on the general constraints that guide and govern the domain in which the process operates.

Moving from these ideas, we designed a language called PLAN–Prosyt LANguage–which adopts an *artifact-based* approach to modeling. PLAN allows process designers to focus on the artifacts produced during the process (together with the basic operations to handle them), rather than on the activities that fragment the process into elementary steps. This shift is similar to the transition from imperative programming languages to the object-oriented paradigm. Moreover, in PLAN the expected flow of actions is never stated explicitly. Instead, the constraints (i.e., pre-conditions) to invoke operations on each artifact type, and a set of invariants that have to hold for each artifact, are the basis for building a process model and for guiding the control flow.

At process enactment time, an advanced runtime support system interprets the PLAN model, allowing the users involved in the process to execute actions in the order they find more effective to pursue the process goals under the actual circumstances. When something unexpected happens, users are allowed to deviate from the modeled process temporarily, by violating some of the pre-conditions to invoke actions, as long as the overall invariants hold. This allows small deviations to be handled without the need to modify the process model. At the same time, PROSYT allows different consistency-checking and deviation-handling policies to be specified and changed at runtime on a per-user, per-artifact basis, to precisely control the level of deviation allowed. This brings great flexibility in process enactment and avoids micro-management of every specific issue of the process, while focusing on the fundamental properties that have to be guaranteed.

Other software process execution environments adopted approaches similar to those introduced in PROSYT. For example, SENTINEL [9] adopts an activity-based approach, in which software processes are modeled as a collection of state machines. State transitions are guarded by preconditions. To guarantee safe behaviors, transitions may legally occur when all the preconditions hold; however, state transitions can also be triggered by human interaction, and in this case, some preconditions can be explicitly violated, allowing minor deviations to the process model. The process is allowed to continue enactment as long as no invariant assertions — which define safe states — are violated. If violations occur, a reconciling process must be carried out to fix corrupted state variables, after which the process execution can resume in a safe way.

Provence [13] adopts a different approach, in which the process model is used to monitor the process, rather than automating it. Provence is based on an event-action system, called Yeast [14]. When relevant events occur in the actual process, Yeast notifies Provence. Provence matches those events with the process model to trigger actions and state changes. Although Provence does not have any specific support to handle unforeseen situations, its approach provides an interesting way to support detection of changes in the process state (which can become inconsistent with respect to the process model) as soon as they occur.

PEACE [2] and GRAPPLE [10] follow a goal-oriented approach, implemented using a logic-based formalism (in PEACE) and ad-hoc planning techniques (in GRAPPLE). In both systems, the process model is defined only through the objectives that must be satisfied, while at enactment time the runtime support system finds the best ordering of activities to accomplish the given goals. This approach increases the environment flexibility, reducing the need for deviations.

The lessons learned by looking at the systems above were at the core of our recent work in the area of service orchestration, which lead to the development of DSOL, the subject of the next section.

4. The DSOL Approach

Our main motivation in defining a new language for service orchestrations was the fact that none of the currently available languages designed for this purpose were able to cope efficiently with unforeseen exceptions, a feature we consider fundamental for a system that has to operate in an open, dynamic world.

After some initial research, looking also at past experience in process modeling, we realized that to achieve this goal, we have to rethink the way in which service orchestrations are defined: we need a paradigm shift. As we already noted, the imperative programming style adopted by most process languages seems to be inappropriate to supporting flexible orchestrations for several reasons: (i) processes are modeled in a normative and rigid form, making runtime adaptations hard to achieve; (ii) they must capture completely different aspects within a single monolithic model, from control flow to exception and compensation handlers; (iii) they require sophisticated programming skills, precluding SOP from reaching a key goal: empowering even non-technical users to build their own service orchestrations.

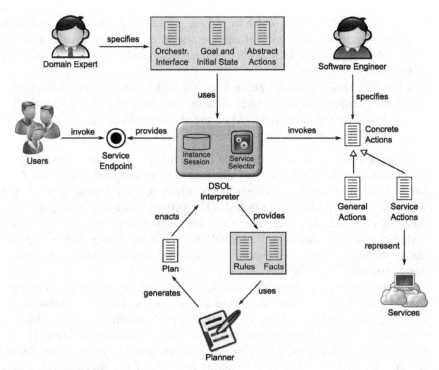

Fig. 10.2. The DSOL approach to service orchestration

The language DSOL—*Declarative Service Orchestration Language*—that we defined to support service orchestration and its runtime support system, adopts a radically different, *declarative* approach. With DSOL, we aim to achieve two different goals: (i) simplify the definition of complex service orchestrations, in order to empower even non-technical users, such as domain experts; and (ii) increase the possibility of runtime adaptations by letting orchestrations evolve when unforeseen situations happen, or when the orchestration's requirements change.

A service orchestration modeled in DSOL includes different aspects, which are defined separately using different idioms, possibly by different stakeholders who bring their own competencies. Specifically, as shown in Fig. 10.2, a service orchestration in DSOL includes the following elements:

- the definition of the *orchestration interface*, i.e., the signature of the service that represents the entry point to the orchestration;
- the *goal* of the orchestration, as a set of facts that are required to be true at the end of the orchestration. This is is usually expressed by a domain expert, who is not necessarily competent in software development;
- the *initial state*, which models the set of facts that one can assume to be true at orchestration invocation time (usually described by the same domain expert who formulates the goal);

- a set of *abstract actions*, which model the primitive operations that can be invoked to achieve a certain goal and are typical of a certain domain. They are described using a simple, logic-like language that can be mastered even by non-technical domain experts;
- a set of *concrete actions*, one or more for each abstract action, written by a software engineer to map abstract actions into the concrete steps required to implement the operation modeled by the abstract action, e.g., by invoking an external service or executing some code.

At orchestration invocation time, the *DSOL Interpreter* translates the goal, the initial state, and the abstract actions into a set of *rules* and *facts* used by the *Planner* to build an abstract plan of execution, which lists the logical steps through which the desired goal may be reached. The Interpreter then enacts the plan by associating each step (i.e., each *abstract action*) with a *concrete action* that is executed, possibly interacting with external services. If everything goes as expected and all the steps are executed successfully, the workflow terminates and control is transferred back to the client.

Unfortunately, as we have indicated, real world service orchestrations may encounter situations that prevent them from terminating normally. To tolerate exceptions to the standard flow of actions—both expected and unexpected—DSOL provides both specific language constructs and ad-hoc run-time facilities. For the former, it is possible to associate different concrete actions with the same abstract action. This gives the Interpreter the ability to try different options to realize each step of a plan. Indeed, when an abstract action A has to be executed, the Interpreter tries the first concrete action implementing A. If this fails (e.g., the service is unavailable), the Interpreter automatically captures the exception and tries the second concrete action, which invokes a different external service, which hopefully is available and executes correctly.

If, however, none of the available concrete actions can execute correctly, a second mechanism is available: the ability to build an *alternative plan* to execute when something bad happens at run-time. That is, if the Interpreter cannot realize a step (i.e., an abstract action invoked with specific parameters) of the current plan, it invokes the Planner again, forcing it to avoid the failed step. This causes a new plan to be computed that excludes the failed step. By comparing the old and new plans, considering the current state of execution, the Interpreter is able to calculate the set of actions that must be *compensated* (i.e., undone), as they have already been executed but are not part of the new plan.

In summary, by combining the ability to specify different implementations (i.e., concrete actions) for each step of a plan, plus the ability to rebuild failed plans in search of alternative courses of actions, possibly achieving different but still acceptable goals, our language and run-time system allow robust orchestrations to be built in a natural and easy way. Indeed, by combining these mechanisms, DSOL orchestrations are able to work around failures and any other form of unexpected situation automatically, by self-adapting to changes in the external environment.

This fundamental characteristic is also achieved thanks to the DSOL approach to modeling orchestrations, which focuses on the primitive actions typical of a given domain more than on the specific flow of a single orchestration. This approach is reminiscent of the solution we experimented with PROSYT [7], which decomposes processes in terms of the artifacts involved in it, leaving aside the traditional top down decomposition into activities. The goal is the same here: to maximize the chance that when something bad happens, even if not explicitly anticipated at modeling time, the actions that may overcome the current situation have been modeled and are available to the Planner and Interpreter (to the user, in the case of PROSYT).

This brief description shows the main advantages of the DSOL approach with respect to traditional ones:

1. It achieves a clear separation among the different aspects of an orchestration: from the more abstract ones, captured by goals, initial state, and abstract actions, to those closer to the implementation domain, captured by concrete actions.
2. It meets one of the original goals of service-oriented computing; i.e., it involves users who are not expert in software development into the cycle.
3. By focusing on the primitive actions available and letting the actual flow of execution be built automatically at run-time through the Planner, it allows orchestration designers to focus on those aspects that are typical of a certain domain and remain stable over time, ignoring the peculiarities of a specific orchestration, which may change when requirements change. This last property also holds the promise of increasing reusability, since the same abstract and concrete actions can be reused for different orchestrations within the same domain.
4. By separating abstract and concrete actions, with several concrete actions possibly mapped to a single abstract action, the DSOL Interpreter can find the best implementation for each orchestration step and try different routes if something goes wrong at run-time, in a fully automated way.
5. Because abstract actions only capture the general rules governing the ordering among primitive actions, the Interpreter, through a careful re-planning mechanism, can automatically overcome potentially disruptive and unexpected situations that occur at run-time.
6. The modularity and dynamism inherent in the DSOL approach allow the orchestration model to be changed easily at run-time, by adding new abstract/concrete actions when those available do not allow the orchestration's goal to be reached.

5. Conclusions

Service-oriented computing shows great promise. Through it, an open and dynamic world of services becomes accessible for humans, who can be empowered by useful application components that are developed by service providers and exposed for possible use. Service-oriented computing may also generate new business. For example, it supports service provision by brokers who can integrate third-party services and export new added-value services. Because services live in open platforms, the computational environment is continuously evolving. New services may be created, old services may be discontinued, and existing services may be evolved by their owners.

Service-oriented computing raises several important challenges that need to be addressed by research to become successful. In particular, how can the new systems we build by composing existing services be described? How can such descriptions accommodate the need for tolerating the continuous changes that occur in the computational environment?

Service compositions may be achieved through workflow languages. Workflows describe processes through which humans interact with software components and compose them to achieve their goals. The existing workflow languages that have been developed to support service compositions, unfortunately, are still very primitive. In this paper, we argued that much can be learned from the work developed in the past in the area of software processes and software process programming. This area was pioneered by the Osterweil's work and the key challenges were identified in the keynote he delivered at the International Conference on Software Engineering (ICSE) in 1987 [17]. Although seldom acknowledged, we believe that many of the findings reached by this research area may provide useful inspiration to tackle the problems arising in service-oriented computing.

The work we describe here traces back to the research in software processes that was originated by Osterweil and builds on (some of) the lessons learned at the time to propose a new approach to service composition that we have been recently exploring.

Acknowledgments This work was partially supported by the European Commission, Programme IDEAS-ERC, Project 227977-SMScom; and by the Italian Government under the projects FIRB INSYEME and PRIN D-ASAP.

References

[1] Alves A, Arkin A, Askary S, Bloch B, Curbera F, Goland Y, Kartha N, Liu CK, Konig D, Mehta V, Thatte S, van der Rijn D, Yendluri P, Yiu A, eds. (2006) Web Services Business Process Execution Language Version 2.0. Tech. rep., OASIS.
[2] Arbaoui S, Oquendo F (1994) PEACE: goal-oriented logic-based formalism for process modelling. Research Studies Press Ltd., Taunton, UK

[3] Balzer R (1991) Tolerating inconsistency. In: Proc. 13th int. conf. on Software engineering

[4] Bandinelli SC, Fuggetta A, Ghezzi C (1993) Software process model evolution in the spade environment. IEEE Trans. Softw. Eng. 19:1128-1144

[5] Bolcer G, Taylor R (1996) Endeavors: a process system integration infrastructure. In: Proc. Fourth International Conference on the Software Process

[6] Bruynooghe R, Parker J, Rowles J (1991) Pss: A system for process enactment. In: Proc. 1st International Conference on the Software Process

[7] Cugola G (1998) Tolerating deviations in process support systems via flexible enactment of process models. IEEE Trans. Software Eng. 24(11):982-1001

[8] Cugola G, Di Nitto E, Fuggetta A, Ghezzi C (1996) A framework for formalizing inconsistencies in human-centered systems. ACM Trans. Softw. Engineering and Methodology 5(3)

[9] Cugola G, Di Nitto E, Ghezzi C, Mantione M (1995) How to deal with deviations during process model enactment. In: Proc. 17th international conference on Software engineering

[10] Huff KE (1990) Grapple example: processes as plans. In: Proc. 5th international software process workshop on Experience with software process models, ISPW

[11] Jaccheri L, Larsen J, Conradi R (1992) Software process modeling and evolution in epos. In: Proc. 4th International Conference on Software Engineering and Knowledge Engineering

[12] Jamart P, van Lamsweerde A (1994) A reflective approach to process model customization, enactment and evolution. In: 'Applying the Software Process', Proc. 3rd International Conference on the Software Process

[13] Krishnamurthy B, Barghouti NS (1993) Provence: A process visualisation and enactment environment. In: Proc. 4th European Software Engineering Conference

[14] Krishnamurthy B, Rosenblum DS (1995) Yeast: A general purpose event-action system. IEEE Trans. on Software Engineering 21:845-857

[15] Lerner BS, McCall EK, Wise A, Cass AG, Osterweil LJ, Sutton Jr. SM (2000) Using little-jil to coordinate agents in software engineering. In: Proc. 15th International Conf. on Automated Software Engineering

[16] Lerner BS, Christov S, Osterweil LJ, Bendraou R, Kannengiesser U, Wise A (2010) Exception handling patterns for process modeling. IEEE Trans. on Software Engineering 99(RapidPosts):162-183

[17] Osterweil L (1987) Software processes are software too. In: ICSE '87: Proc. 9th international conference on Software Engineering (Reprinted as Chapter 17)

[18] Ouyang C, Dumas M, Aalst WMPVD, Hofstede AHMT, Mendling J (2009) From business process models to process-oriented software systems. ACM Trans. Softw. Eng. Methodol. 19(2)

[19] Russell N, van der Aalst W, ter Hofstede A (2006) Workflow Exception Patterns. In: Advanced Information Systems Engineering.

[20] Sutton Jr. SM, Heimbigner D, Osterweil LJ (1990) Language constructs for managing change in process-centered environments. Proc. fourth ACM SIGSOFT symposium on Software development environments (Reprinted as Chapter 19)

[21] White SA (2008) Business Process Modeling Notation, V1.1. Tech. rep., OMG (2008)

Toolpack—An Experimental Software Development Environment Research Project[1]

Leon J. Osterweil

Department of Computer Science, University of Colorado, Boulder, CO 80309.

Abstract   This paper discusses the goals and methods of the Toolpack project and in this context discusses the architecture and design of the software system being produced as the focus of the project. Toolpack is presented as an experimental activity in which a large software tool environment is being created for the purpose of general distribution and then careful study and analysis. The paper begins by explaining the motivation for building integrated tool sets. It then proceeds to explain the basic requirements that an integrated system of tools must satisfy in order to be successful and to remain useful both in practice and as an experimental object. The paper then summarizes the tool capabilities that will be incorporated into the environment. It then goes on to present a careful description of the actual architecture of the Toolpack integrated tool system. Finally the Toolpack project experimental plan is presented, and future plans and directions are summarized.

I. Introduction

This paper describes Toolpack,[2] a project in progress to build and evaluate a prototype software development environment. The purpose of the Toolpack project is to gain insight into some of the central questions confronting the would-be builder of a software environment by creating and studying an experimental prototype.

It is becoming generally agreed that if software tools are to be effectively exploited they must be amalgamated into well integrated collections. It also seems agreed that these collections should be broad in scope, easy to use, and highly efficient in actual operation. Such a well integrated tool collection has come to be

---

[1] This work supported by the National Science Foundation under Grant MSC8000017, the Department of Energy under Grant DE-AC02-80ER10718, and the U.S. Army Research Office under Contract DAAG 29-80-C-0094.

[2] Toolpack is a research project involving cooperation among researchers from Argonne National Laboratory, Bell Telephone Laboratories, Jet Propulsion Laboratory, Numerical Algorithms Group Ltd., Purdue University, University of Arizona, and University of Colorado at Boulder.

Leon J. Osterweil, "Toolpack—An Experimental Software
Development Environment Research Project,"
IEEE Transactions on Software Engineering, November 1983. © 1983 IEEE

called an environment. To be more specific, in an earlier paper [1] it was proposed that an environment was a collection of software tools which had the following five properties.

1) *Breadth of Scope*: Capabilities spanning the entire range of activities to be performed in order to accomplish a complete specific software job.

2) *User Friendliness*: Input language and diagnostic capabilities which would neither intimidate nor harass the user, as well as sufficient adaptability to assure that the tools would remain useful and supportive as the user's work procedures and style underwent reasonable changes.

3) *Tight Integration*: Tools which are sufficiently aware of each other's capabilities to avoid the semblance of overlapping capabilities as well as the possibility of incompatibility.

4) *Internal Reusability*: An architecture and design which encourages the reuse of simple modular capabilities in furnishing the various fundamental capabilities of the environment.

5) *Use of a Central Database*: An architecture and design in which the various functional tools draw their inputs from, and place their outputs back into, a central repository of information. This repository is to be considered the focus of all knowledge about the software project.

Although much of this seems clear and well agreed to, it is far less clear how to go about building such an environment. In particular it is unclear how to achieve each of the five characteristics just described with a single software system. There is even considerable question about whether the five are consistent and compatible with each other.

For example, it has been suggested [1] that tight integration and internal reusability might be inconsistent objectives. It appears, at least on the surface, that tools which are keenly aware of each other might be difficult or impossible to construct from standard self-contained modules.

The need to center the environment around a database containing all project information also poses a problem. Clearly, a given software development project generates an enormous amount of information. If the database is to contain all information spanning all aspects and phases of the project, then it would have to contain all of this information and reflect all of the myriad relations which characterize the project and its status. It is not clear that this can be done in an efficient, cost-effective way. Thus there arises the question of whether a central database can be created in a manner which is consistent with the need for efficiency and breadth of scope.

In considering how such an environment might be built it is reasonable to look to the paradigm of the software development life cycle as a model, and to simply follow accepted software development life cycle procedure. Thus, conventional wisdom suggests that one should start construction of a software development environment by carrying out a careful analysis of the requirements. In the process of doing so one should obtain the answers to the questions raised above. For example, careful requirements analysis should make clear the specific actual needs for the various pieces of information and relations which must be in the central database. Similarly, the requirements analysis process should make clear the performance requirements (e.g., access speeds) necessary in order for the environment to be acceptably fast and inexpensive.

Here the circular nature of this problem starts to become apparent. In order to pinpoint the requirements for an effective software development environment sufficiently to definitively obtain answers to the above questions, it is essential to be able to interview a wide variety of software developers who are knowledgeable and experienced in such matters. Specifically, it is essential to get definitive answers about experiences and judgments concerning specific tool capabilities and the items of information which they utilize and create. It is unfortunately the case that this sort of knowledge and experience is very rare, because of the lack of widespread use of a variety of software development tools. In fact, it is the lack of widespread effective utilization of superior tools that has led us to believe that environments must be created. Hence, there seems to be a paradox in that the knowledge needed to form the basis for an environment building effort is not available for precisely the same reasons that are prompting the effort in the first place.

Further, there seems to be agreement that access to superior software development environments will rapidly cause developers to change the manner in which they do their work. Thus any guesses about what might be needed in the way of tool capabilities and configurations would probably change as experience with environments grew. Thus it seems that here, as in the case of other software projects which are designed to address a new and evolving problem, it is naive to expect that we will be able to definitively establish a firm baseline set of requirements.

Instead what must be done is to evolve a strategy for studying the requirements for a software development environment which assures that there is steady progress towards the goal of sufficient knowledge and confidence to justify embarking upon a full scale environment development activity. One way of doing this is to embark on a program of constructing a series of increasingly ambitious experimental prototype environments. If each prototype is designed to be the object of study and the sequence is arranged in such a way that the most critical requirements and design issues can be elucidated or resolved by the early prototypes, then there would seem to be good reason to expect that an effective environment would emerge as an end-product of this process.

It is in this spirit that the Toolpack project has embarked upon a plan for producing a sequence of at least three successive releases of an environment for software production.

II. Goals of the Toolpack Prototype Development Effort

The main goal of the Toolpack project is to establish a positive feedback loop between environment developers and a broad and diverse base of environment users by supplying those users a sequence of environments that is increasingly responsive to the users' needs. The purpose of this feedback process is twofold. One purpose is to create and promulgate a vehicle for the more effective development and maintenance of software. The other is to obtain reliable, detailed, quantitative answers to many of the central questions confronting software development environment builders. Specifically, it is expected that at least the following issues will be elucidated or resolved.

1) What is an acceptably broad and complete suite of tool capabilities for supporting some specific software development jobs?

2) How important are various data items and relations and how accessible must they be to various sorts of environment users?

3) Is there a set of modular "tool fragments" which is sufficiently powerful yet flexible to provide the basis for a broad yet tightly integrated set of tool capabilities?

4) What are the general characteristics of a user interface language which is sufficiently powerful, yet acceptably "friendly"? In order to get reliable insights into these questions it is important to construct prototypes in such a way that a large and diverse community of users will become active users of the environment. Thus the Toolpack project has taken great pains to assure that its prototype environments will be of great interest and assistance to a large and significant community of users.

The target community for the Toolpack prototype is the community of mathematical software developers. This community is in many ways a nearly ideal target community. The mathematical software community is among the oldest software production communities, tracing its origins to the small group of scientists who conceived of the stored program computer in the 1940's. Thus it is a coherent group that has well agreed upon goals and procedures. Among the accepted procedures of this community is the utilization of tools (e.g., see [2], [3]). In addition, the community has consciously and innovatively striven toward quality for perhaps a longer period of time than any other software community. This has manifested itself, for example, in the notable "PACK" projects of the 1970's [4].

This community is perhaps unique in that it has long held that portability is a necessary characteristic of high quality software. Thus the community is accustomed to receiving and evaluating new software items as a community, regardless of differences in the hardware/software configurations being used by different members of the community. Of course, it is essential that such new software items be presented in portable form.

There are other characteristics of the mathematical software community that cause it to be very desirable for our purposes. It has long ago established a single programming language (Fortran) as its, more or less uniform, standard. Thus a suite of support tools of interest and value to the entire community can be made source language specific. This greatly simplifies the problem of writing generally useful and acceptable tools.

The software produced by this community is ordinarily rather modest in size, usually aggregating less than 10 000 lines of source code. This also simplifies the problem of writing acceptably efficient tools.

In addition, the mathematical software community generally follows a software life cycle model which is far simpler than the life cycle models which are widely espoused by and for many other software development communities. Mathematical software development rarely, if ever, begins with *formal* requirements analysis. Similarly, there is rarely a *formal* preliminary (or architectural) design phase. This appears at first glance to be paradoxical, especially in view of the high quality and good acceptance of mathematical software over the past decades. The explanation appears to be that mathematical software requirements and preliminary design specifications have been derived over a period of decades (if not centuries) by mathematicians and numerical analysts. These specifications appear as mathematical formulas in books and technical reports. Thus the process of producing mathematical software appears to start on this base and proceed immediately with what other communities would label detailed (or algorithmic) design. These designs are often expressed directly in the form of code for a higher level pseudolanguage such as SFTRAN [5], Ratfor [6] or EFL [7], but perhaps more routinely they are coded directly in a relatively portable Fortran dialect. There then follows a familiar pattern of testing, documentation, and the upgrading and adjustment that is most often referred to as "maintenance."

It is doubtlessly true that mathematical software began encountering, and grappling with, the sorts of data manipulation problems whose solution would benefit from the more formal requirements and preliminary design techniques prevalent in other communities today. It might be interesting to conjecture about why these contemporary techniques have never been adopted by the mathematical software community, but such conjecture would digress from the issue at hand. The issue is that this community currently does not generally perceive the need for these techniques and associated tools. Thus their absence from Toolpack should not endanger community acceptance. This acceptance can be based only on solid support for the life cycle as it is practiced, rather than as it might or should be practiced.

This prevailing life cycle model is particularly fortunate for the Toolpack project because it suggests that a tool support set can be relatively modest, addressing the creation, testing, analysis, documentation, and transportation of only code (and perhaps some algorithmic design) and still be considered to be a complete tool set by this community. More fortunately still, most if not all of these tool capabilities have already been produced and evaluated to some extent by some members of the community. Thus a comprehensive tool set will not be totally unfamiliar to the community. Further, the preexistence of such tools means that the environment production activity can focus more on the issues of integration, user interface, and database contents, and will not need to be preoccupied with more mundane matters such as the recreation of tool capabilities whose reproduction will contribute less to the accumulation of new knowledge about environments.

With these factors in mind, the Toolpack project has set out to build a portable environment capable of extending comprehensive support to the community of people who are engaged in producing, testing, transporting, and analyzing mathematical software written in Fortran. Toolpack project environments will be made available through a series of releases, each of which is designed to improve upon its predecessors as a consequence of experience and evaluation obtained through extensive and diverse utilization of those predecessors.

The specific approach to the architecture and design of the family of Toolpack environments will now be summarized.

A more complete summary can be found in [8]. It should be stressed that this approach has been arrived at only after extensive discussions and consultations designed to determine the preferences and predispositions of the mathematical software community so as to assure, as well as feasible, widespread acceptance of the Toolpack project environment releases. The approach has also been designed so as to assure that the qualitative and quantitative observations of user experiences will make substantial contributions towards resolution of the critical environment design issues enumerated above.

III. Requirements and Functional Capabilities of the Toolpack Environment

The purpose of Toolpack is to provide strong, comprehensive tool support to programmers who are producing, testing, transporting, or analyzing moderate size mathematical software written in Fortran 77.

A. Overall Requirements

The following are taken to be the basic assumptions upon which the Toolpack environment architecture and design are based.

1) The mathematical software whose production, testing, transportation, and analysis is to be supported by Toolpack systems shall be written in a dialect of Fortran 77. This dialect shall be carefully chosen to span the needs of as broad and numerous a user community as is practical.

2) Toolpack software and systems are to be designed to provide cost effective support for the production by up to 3 programmers of programs whose length is up to 5000 lines of source text. They may be less effective in supporting larger projects.

3) Toolpack software and systems are to be designed to provide cost effective support for the analysis and transporting of programs whose length is up to 10 000 lines of source text. They may be less effective in supporting larger projects.

4) Toolpack software and systems will support users working in either batch or interactive mode, but may offer stronger more flexible support to interactive users.

5) Toolpack software and systems will be highly portable, making only weak assumptions about their operating environment. They will be designed, however, to make effective use of large amounts of primary and secondary memory, whenever these resources can be made available.

B. Toolpack Tools

The Toolpack group is in agreement that the following tool capabilities constitute a sound basis for a programming support system for the production of high quality Fortran programs: 0) a compiling/loading system; 1) a Fortran-intelligent editor; 2) a formatter; 3) a structure; 4) a dynamic testing and validation aid; 5) a dynamic debugging aid; 6) a static error detection and validation aid; 7) a static portability checking aid; 8) a documentation generation aid; 9) a program transformer.

A compiling/loading capability is generally available on host operating systems. Thus no tool development effort in this area has been undertaken. Tools are to be developed and experimented with in all of the nine other areas, however. In fact, significant tool capabilities have already been developed in some of these areas, as shall be described subsequently.

1) *Fortran-Intelligent Editor:* A powerful editor [9] is included in Toolpack to assist the programmer in producing Fortran source code. This editor offers a range of general text manipulation facilities, including the usual capabilities for inserting, deleting, locating, and transforming arbitrary strings of characters. In addition, the editor will be incrementally upgraded to provide the following facilities for constructing and modifying Fortran programs.

- The user will be able to abbreviate Fortran keywords; these abbreviations will be automatically expanded by the editor.
- The editor will assure that various fields of Fortran statements are placed in the proper columns.
- As with the Cornell Program Synthesizer [10] and the Mentor [11] system, the Toolpack editor will prompt the user for anticipated constructs. Moreover, the subsequent incoming statement will be checked for syntactic correctness and certain kinds of semantic consistency, e.g., the usage of a variable against declarations of the variable.
- The user will be able to search for occurrences of specified variables and labels. The editor will be able to distinguish those occurrence from occurrences of the same string of characters in other contexts, e.g., comments.

It will be possible to confine searching and replacement operations to fixed domains of a program, such as a particular DO loop or a particular subroutine. For example, it will be possible to change all occurrences of a given variable (say X) to another variable (say Y) within a specified subroutine.

2) *Formatter*: The Toolpack project provides a tool to put Fortran programs into a canonical form. In particular, the formatting tool, called Polish-X [12] has the following capabilities.

- Variables and operators are set off by exactly one space on either side, except in certain cases, e.g., subscripts.
- DO loop bodies and IF statement alternatives are indented.
- Statement labels can optionally be put in regular increasing order.
- It is possible to optionally align the left- and right-hand margins of statements.
- It will be possible to insert ON and OFF markers to indicate that Polish-X is to leave certain sections of the program unaltered.

3) *Structure*: The ability to infer and emphasize the underlying looping structure of a program is useful. The failure of Fortran 77 to supply suitable constructs for doing so has left a significant void in the language. Hence a tool is being provided that will recast Fortran 77 program loops as, for example, DO WHILE loops, either simulated in Fortran 77 by canonical constructs or realized explicitly, according to the rules of Ratfor [6], EFL [7] or SFTRAN [5]. This tool will, moreover, be able to automatically upgrade many Fortran 66 GO TO'S to Fortran 77 IF-THEN-ELSE constructs. Such structuring often improves readability and comprehensibility, and serves as valuable documentation. The structuring capability in Toolpack will be closely patterned after the UNIX[3] struct command [13].

4) *Dynamic Testing and Validation Aid*: The Toolpack project provides a facility for automatically inserting instrumentation probes into Fortran 77 programs and for creating useful intermediate output from these probes at run time. This facility enables the user to capture and view a variety of trace and summary information. It is possible, for example, to capture a program's statement execution sequence or to generate a histogram of the relative frequencies of execution of the various statements. Similarly, it is possible to capture and study subroutine execution sequences and histograms, or variable evolution histories.

It is possible for the user to implant in the subject program monitors for certain kinds of errors. For example, the user is able to specify that either all or certain specified arrays are to be monitored to be sure that the subscripts by which they are referenced stay within declared bounds.

This facility also incorporates a capability for checking the outcome of an execution against specifications of intent fashioned by the user. The specifications of intent are to be embodied in assertions, stated in comments and expressed in a flexible assertion language. These assertions are expanded into executable code by the Toolpack dynamic testing facility. Once an assertion violation is detected, relevant information about the program status at the time of the violation is automatically saved.

---

[3] UNIX is a registered trademark of Bell Laboratories.

A system, called Newton [14] (see Fig. 11.1), is being developed in experimentally guided increments to provide the functional capabilities just outlined.

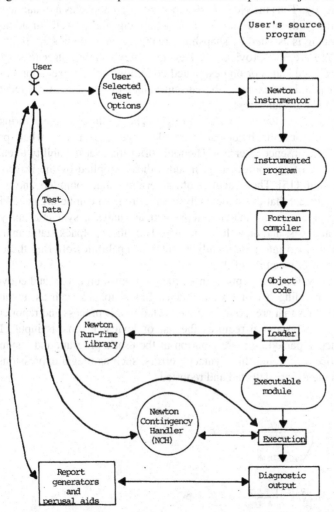

Fig. 11.1. Organization of the Newton dynamic analysis system.

The dynamic testing capability has already been found to make it all too easy to produce very large amounts of output. Tool support should be provided to aid the process of inferring useful diagnostic and documentation information from this raw output. This support would treat the output from the dynamic execution as a database of information, and would consist of database management aids and report generators to organize and format the diagnostic output for ease of understanding. There are currently no firm plans to construct such a tool.

5) *Dynamic Debugging Aid*: Debugging is facilitated by the ability to scrutinize, to arbitrary levels of detail, the progress of the execution of a program that is behaving incorrectly. Thus the Newton system, classified above as a dynamic testing and validation aid, can be viewed as a debugging aid as well. In addition, however, debugging is assisted by snapshot, breakpoint and single-step-execution capabilities. These are also provided by Newton. They enable a user to suspend execution at designated sites or on designated conditions. While execution is suspended the user is able to examine the current values of variables, the execution history to date, and the source text.

6) *Static Error Detection and Validation Aid*: The Toolpack project furnishes flexible capabilities for statically detecting a wide range of errors and, where possible, for proving the absence of errors. The tools offer the user the ability to easily select from a range of capabilities that includes those supplied by the Dave data flow analysis system [15]. The structures of modern modular compilers and of the Dave II system suggest that the static analysis of a program can be organized into the following progression of analytic steps: lexical analysis, syntactic analysis, static semantic analysis, and data flow analysis. Thus the Toolpack static analysis capability is subdivided into individually selectable capabilities offering these levels of analytic power (see Fig. 11.2).

The lexical analysis step accepts as input the program source text, and converts it into the corresponding list of lexical tokens. Illegal tokens such as unknown keywords or variables that are too long, are detected in this process and reported.

The syntactic analysis step requires the list of lexical tokens as input. This process constructs a parse tree representation of the user's program and a symbol table. In the process of doing this, syntactic errors, such as illegal expressions or malformed statements, are detected and reported.

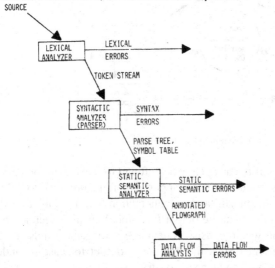

Fig. 11.2. Organization of the Toolpack static analysis system.

The static semantic analysis step builds upon the output of the first two static analyzers and produces a number of structures designed to represent and elucidate the functioning of the program. These structures facilitate the checking and cross-checking that can detect such errors as mismatched argument and parameter lists, unreachable code segments, inconsistencies between variable declaration and usage, and improper DO loop nesting and specification.

The data flow analysis step rests upon the semantic information and flowgraph structures built by the other three analyzers, and produces reports about the references and definitions effected by each statement and subprogram of the user's program. These reports are then the basis for analytic scans of all possible program execution sequences. These scans produce reports about whether there is any possibility of referencing a program variable before it has been defined, or defining a program variable and then never referencing it.

A tool is needed for centralizing and coordinating error reporting from these four static analysis tools. Such a tool would be similar in purpose to the error reporting tool discussed in Section III-B4). Here too, there is currently no firm plan to build such a tool.

7) *Static Portability Checking Aid*: The Toolpack project will furnish a capability for statically determining whether or not a given Fortran 77 program is written in such a dialect and style as to facilitate transporting the program. This capability will be modeled after the PFORT Verifier [16], a very successful and useful tool for checking the portability of Fortran 66 programs. Such portability obstacles as use of statement types not defined in the language standard (e.g., NAMELIST), assumptions about word lengths (e.g., packing of multiple characters in a word without use of the CHARACTER data type), and use of nonportable machine constants will be detected and reported.

Certain interprocedural checks not done by the PFORT Verifier, but supported by Dave, will be incorporated into the Toolpack portability checker. For example, Fortran programs sometimes rely for correct execution upon assumptions about the parameter passing mechanism of the compiler on which the programs were developed. Data flow analysis determines the treatment of every parameter and COMMON variable by every subprogram with sufficient precision that nonportable parameter passing practices can be detected. The functional capabilities needed to create this portability aid are quite similar to those needed by the static error detection and validation aid just described. A primary difference is that this tool, as opposed to most other Toolpack tools, will need to analyze and support a restricted Fortran 77 dialect, as opposed to a liberalized, extended dialect.

8) *Documentation Generation Aid*: The Toolpack group recognizes the importance of high quality program documentation and the desirability of tool support for the process of creating it. The group believes that the static and dynamic analysis capabilities already described create items of information that are useful program documentation. A documentation tool will be designed to draw upon this information and facilitate its availability. In addition, the documentation aid will assist the preparation of user-generated documentation. This capability is expected

to evolve, guided by experience with the dynamic and static analysis tools and report generators.

9) *Program Transformer*: There is general agreement among Toolpack group members that it is highly desirable to produce a program transformation tool as part of the Toolpack project. It is agreed that the tool should offer such capabilities as assistance in translating one dialect of Fortran to another, assistance in altering a program to perform its computations at a different level of precision, and facilities for creating special-purpose control or data structures.

There is currently little agreement, however, about the tradeoffs this tool should make between power, rigor, efficiency, and usability. Three specific tools have been proposed—a template processor system, a macroprocessor system, and a correctness-preserving transformation system.

The template processor [17] is designed to enable the user to define Fortran language extensions by establishing data structure "templates." These templates can be named in the body of a Fortran program along with program data objects. The program data objects are then taken as arguments to be imbedded in the template description. The effect of this is that the user can employ and manipulate complex data structures in a source program without having to define those data structures within the program. This also leaves open the possibility that an expert could establish these complex data structure templates for users who lack the expertise to create the structures, but who, nevertheless, have a need for them. The template processor is designed to be extremely easy to use, but does little to guarantee that the Fortran statements it generates are correct or efficient.

The macroprocessor, adapted from the software tools collection, is similar in operation to the template processor. It enables users to define macros (code skeletons) which can then be expanded into actual bodies of code with the incorporation of parameters supplied to the macro at an invocation site in a user's program. Here too, the macros can be written by an expert and made available to casual users, much like a subprogram library. Macros are more complicated and difficult to write than templates, but have the advantage of assisting the writer in preparing efficient and correct Fortran programs.

The correctness-preserving transformation system, called TAMPR [18], is the most powerful and sophisticated of the three proposed transformation systems. TAMPR constructs a parse-tree representation of the subject Fortran program, enables the user to analyze and transform the tree, and finally translates the transformed tree back to equivalent Fortran source code. TAMPR scrutinizes the transformation rules to be sure that the transformations that they specify do not alter the functionality of the subject program. This aspect of TAMPR makes it the safest of the three transformation systems. In addition, because the user is completely free to analyze and transform as much of the tree as desired, TAMPR has virtually limitless transformation power. The main drawbacks to this system are that, at least in prototype form, it appears to be very expensive to use and requires that the user be highly skilled and conversant with mathematical formalism.

In order to assist the Toolpack group and the mathematical software community in evaluating these three alternatives, all will be made available as part of Toolpack so that a large and diverse user community can compare and evaluate them in a variety of usage contexts.

10) *Additional Capabilities*: Support from individual Toolpack group members has been expressed for eventual inclusion of a preprocessor for Ratfor [6], EPL [7], or SFTRAN [5], for a document preparation aid like ROFF, for a source text version control facility, and for a tape archiving program. Decisions about inclusion of such capabilities in Toolpack will hinge upon experience gained with early releases.

IV. Tool Integration Strategy

The tool objectives described in Section III are to be achieved by a software system, currently implemented in prototype form, called the Integrated System of Tools (IST). A primary motivating goal of the architecture and design of the IST is that user support be supplied in as direct and painless a fashion as is feasible. In particular, the IST attempts to relieve the user of having to understand the natures and idiosyncrasies of individual Toolpack tools. It also relieves the user of the burden of having to combine or coordinate these tools. Instead the IST encourages the user to express needs in terms of the requirements of the actual software job. The IST is designed to then ascertain which tools are necessary, properly configure those tools, and present the results of using the tools to the user in a convenient form.

The architecture and design encourage the user to think of the IST as an energetic, reasonably bright assistant, capable of answering questions, performing menial but onerous tasks and storing and retrieving important bodies of data.

In order to reach this view, the user should think of IST as a vehicle for establishing and maintaining a file system containing all information important to the user, and using that file system to both furnish input to needed tools and capture the output of those tools. Clearly, such a file system is potentially quite large and is to contain a diversity of stored entities. Source code modules certainly reside in the file system, but so do such more arcane entities as token lists, and flowgraph annotations. In order to keep IST's user image as straightforward as possible its design assures that most file system management be done automatically and internally to the IST, out of the sight and sphere of responsibility of the user. The user, in addition is encouraged to have access to only a relatively small number of files—only those such as source code modules and test data sets which are of direct concern. The user may create, delete, alter, and rename these entities. More important, however, the user may manipulate these entities with a set of commands which selectively and automatically configure and actuate the Toolpack tool ensemble. The commands are designed to be easy to understand and use.

They borrow heavily on the terminology used by a programmer in creating and testing code, and conceal the sometimes considerable tool mechanisms needed to effect the results desired by the user.

A. *User Visible IST File System Entities*

In order to encourage and facilitate the preceding view, IST supports the naming, storage, retrieval, editing, and manipulation of the following classes of entities, which should be considered to be the basic objects of IST.

1) *Program Units*: An IST program unit (PU) is the same as a Fortran program unit, except that IST requires a number of representations of the program unit other than the source code (e.g., the corresponding token list and parse tree). The identity, significance, and utilization of these other representations are to be made transparent to the casual user. They are managed automatically by IST. On the other hand, they are accessible and usable by more expert users through published standard naming conventions and accessing functions.

2) *Program Unit Groups*: Any set of IST program units which the user chooses to designate, can be grouped into an IST program unit group (PUG). Other PUG's may also be named as constituents of a PUG, as long as no circularity is implied by such definitions. Ordinarily, it is expected that a PUG will be a body of code which is to be tested as part of the incremental construction process. Hence a PUG might be a set of newly coded program units and a test harness. It is, however, not unreasonable (and indeed potentially quite useful) to consider a subprogram library to be a PUG as well. Here, too, an IST PUG will consist of more than just source text, but the user will not need to be aware of the existence of any such additional entities.

3) *Test Data Collections*: An IST test data collection (TDC) is a collection of test data sets to be used in exercising one or more IST execution units. A test data collection may consist of one or more sets of the complete input data needed to drive the execution of some complete executable program. Each test input data set may also have associated with it a specification of the output which is expected in response to processing of the specified input.

4) *Options Packets*: An IST tool options packet (OP) is a set of directives specifying which of the many anticipated options are to be in force for a particular invocation of one of the Toolpack tools integrated into IST. We see, for example, the need for test option packets (TOP's) to specify dynamic testing probe insertion options and formatter option packets (FOP's) to specify program source text formatting options, among others. Standard options packets will be created initially by the individual toolmakers and automatically incorporated as part of a newly installed IST. These standard options packets will undoubtedly be altered to meet the needs of individual users and installations. In addition, entirely new option packets will probably be built to satisfy individual needs. It should be stressed,

however, that tool options will also be specifiable directly as part of a tool invocation command. Options so specified may either replace or supplement an option packet specification.

5) *Procedures*: An IST procedure is a sequence of IST commands—which can be directed to the command interpreter simply by specifying the procedure name. IST procedures are expected to be command sequences for accomplishing generally useful standard jobs. Thus writing a procedure enables the user to save the effort of respecifying a standard sequence of commands whenever a standard job must be done. This capability is supplied as a convenience and is intended to supplement, not replace, the one-at-a-time command invocation capability.

It is expected that Toolpack project software will facilitate the process of capturing and analyzing the procedures which users define and utilize. This will thereby provide an experimental basis for gaining insight into the development procedures which users actually follow, as well as insight into how these procedures change with the availability of effective tools.

B. The File System

Clearly the primary feature of the IST is the central file system of information about the subject program. The user is encouraged to think and plan work in terms of it, and the functional tools all draw their input from it and place their output into it. A schematic diagram of this architectural feature is shown in Fig. 11.3.

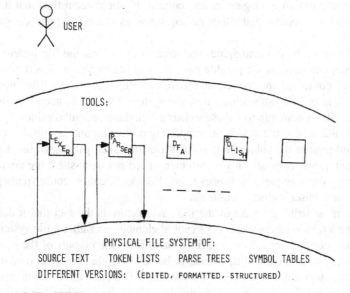

Fig. 11.3. The IST file system.

IST itself manages the file system primarily by means of a tree structured directory system and a modular set of file accessing and updating primitives. IST files do not correspond directly to host machine files, but will rather be mapped onto segments of one or more large host system files. The IST file accessing and updating capabilities effect this segmentation and operate directly upon these large host system files. The objectives of this approach are to reduce the overhead of dealing directly with, and depending too heavily upon, host file systems and to increase the portability of IST. An implementation of such a set of I/O capabilities (called PIOS), has been written in portable Fortran [19]. A tree structured file directory system (PDS) has also been written in portable Fortran [19]. They have, moreover, been integrated into a portable file directory and accessing mechanism. This tandem has been used in implementing the IST file system.

It is expected that an IST file system would be initialized with the start of a programming project and remain and grow throughout the lifetime of the project. There is no reason why several users might not all access this file system although PIOS requires that the file system be accessed by one user at a time, or by more than one user only in noninterfering ways.

This pragmatic restriction appears to be a workable one for this prototype effort. In the long run, however, it threatens to be a severe one. A full-fledged multiuser file system offering file protection and permission capabilities will be needed if the Toolpack concepts are to be broadened to support wider needs and communities.

In contemplating these needs and appropriate solutions, one is lead, it seems inescapably, to the conclusion that such a file system must be viewed as the basis for effective configuration management and control. It would seem thus that it is only through this perspective that adequate requirements and consequent designs can be evolved.

The architecture of the IST anticipates the need for this in that the file system is designed and implemented as a separable module. The file system is directly used only by the IST command interpreter, and there only through standard functions and subroutines. In order to substitute a new file system it would be necessary only to have that file system support these existing functions and subroutines. It is true, of course, that a new file system incorporating protection and permission capabilities would require the submission of identification, such as passwords, with each file system access request. This requirement, need not necessitate the alteration of existing calling sequences, however, as this identification could (perhaps should) reside in the user's global data areas.

Perhaps the most striking aspect of the IST architecture is the fact that it does not hypothesize a relational database as its central element but rather a file system. As noted earlier, certain elements of the file system (e.g., the outputs of the static and dynamic analysis tool capabilities) seem to be best thought of as relational databases. It is less clear that it is essential for the entire Toolpack information repository to be relational. It is important that this hypothesis be tested and evaluated because the operational costs of large relational database systems appear to be quite high, possibly undermining their practical utility.

Toolpack will test the important hypothesis that a software development environment can be successful even when relational database technology is applied only to smaller, more localized bodies of data.

In order for these objectives to be achieved there must be an underlying agreement about the naming of file system entities. As stated earlier, each of the file system entities created by the user (see Section IV-A) has a unique name which the user assigns. Different views, versions, or aspects of the entity have distinct names which are arrived at by attaching qualifiers as dictated by published naming conventions to the user name. In some modes of use, the user will not need to be aware of these qualified names in order to get useful work done. This is because IST has considerable power to infer the names of needed views and versions from the context of the IST commands issued by the user. More advanced users seeking to carry out the more powerful and sophisticated functions of the IST will find it important to know these naming and qualification conventions, however. In order to best understand this the IST command language will be presented next.

C. The IST Command Language

The form of an IST command is as follows:

        command_name list_of_pu's options_specification

where the command_name must be chosen from the list of available tool capabilities, list_of_pu's is a list of PU's and/or PUG's which the user specifies, and options_specification is either the name of an options packet for the tool specified, or an explicit list of options specifications, or both.

Command names have been defined as two letter sequences because it is believed that users prefer to avoid verbosity. Thus in order to invoke the formatting tool, the user would input the sequence "fm." In order to invoke the static analysis capability, the user would input the sequence "an," and so forth. Actual user experience with these choices and user reactions to them will dictate whether or not a more verbose form of these command names will eventually be adopted, perhaps as an option.

The list_of_pu's which follows the command name is the list of PU's to which the specified command is to be applied. Thus if the user wishes to format dozens or even hundreds of PU's, this can be accomplished readily by grouping the PU's into one or more PUG's and then specifying the PUG's after the command name. This ability to group PU's in flexible ways and then have tools process them as conceptual units is seen as one very important feature of the IST.

It should be noted that there is no prohibition against placing a single PU in several different PUG's. The user may wish to group a subroutine library together as a PUG because the library is a conceptual unit to the user. The user may wish to group the subroutine library with several different test drivers. This can be done by creating several different PUG's which differ from each other only in that they incorporate the different test drivers. This is permitted by the IST. Furthermore, there are no diseconomies in doing so.

If, for example, the user directs that one of two overlapping PUG's be formatted and then directs that another overlapping PUG be formatted next, the IST recognizes that the subroutine library shared by both has been formatted after having formatted the first PUG, and does not then repeat the formatting of the subroutine library in formatting the second PUG. The mechanism for effecting this efficiency will be described shortly.

The options_specification is optional. If the name of an options packet is included here, then the options specified in that packet will be used to configure the tool named in the command in processing the list of PU's. If no options packet is specified here, then the IST will access and employ a default options packet which is stored in the file system.

It is also possible for the user to specify options explicitly directly on the command line. In this case the explicitly named options are used to either augment or override the options listed in the options packet.

It is important to observe that, although the invocation of a tool through the IST may involve a great deal of work, the user is informed of the disposition of the command only by a very terse message. The purpose of this message is merely to advise the user of whether or not the command has been executed successfully, and where further information about the execution can be found. Invariably the further information will be found in a set of files, whose names are made available to the user. Usually these files are report files which the user may list out by using file listing commands. As observed earlier, however, it is expected that the more sophisticated analytic tools will produce report files which will be best absorbed by the user with the aid of special browsing or perusal tools. These tools will accept report files as their input and digest and format the files in response to user commands for certain types of information.

The various IST tools create and access the various versions and views of the PU's in order to get their work done. The user is able to access these versions and views, but is shielded from the necessity to do so. The static data flow analysis capability, for example, will need access to a parse tree, symbol table and flow graph of all PU's of the PUG's it is directed to analyze. The user need not know any of this, however, and need only specify the name of the PUG to be analyzed. The IST command language is obliged to understand that these other files are necessary and is empowered to create them by invoking entire complex sequences of lower level tools about which the end user need know nothing. Furthermore, once these lower level tools have created these versions and views, the IST command language interpreter may choose to store them for future reuse. Thus, if the user subsequently asks to have the analyzed program formatted, the IST will recognize that some of the work needed in order to do the formatting has already been done in the process of doing earlier analysis. The IST command interpreter is equipped with sufficient logic to recognize which internal files contain this useful information and to reuse it in formatting. It is expected that these capabilities should enable the IST to effect significant efficiencies in actual use. More details about how this is accomplished will be presented shortly. In order to do so, however, is important to first understand the virtual file system concept.

D. The Virtual File System

A stated design objective for IST is that it run effectively on a wide range of machines, effectively utilizing larger amounts of storage when and if they can be made available. One way in which large amounts of storage can be effectively utilized is to store all derived and intermediate entities for possible future reuse. Storage economies can be gained by refusing to store those entities and instead regenerating them as needed. The strategy for retaining or regenerating these entities must be adjustable and transparent. It is highly desirable that both the end user and the tool ensemble always be safe in assuming that any needed named entities and derived images will always be available. Thus it is necessary that the IST file management system assume the responsibility for either retrieving these items directly or having them created or regenerated (in case storage exigencies precipitated their deletion by IST). A conceptual diagram of the virtual file system architecture is shown in Fig. 11.4.

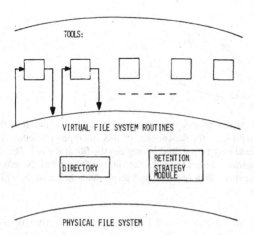

Fig. 11.4. The IST virtual file system concept.

For example, suppose a functional tool needs the parse tree of a particular PU, call it SUBR.

It is the job of the IST command interpreter to assure that the file exists and is up-to-date before allowing the tool to begin execution. The command interpreter assures this by querying the IST directory see whether the file is either absent or obsolete. If so, the command interpreter sees that the file is created. Guidance for this process comes from an internal directed acyclic graph (DAG) which specifies how the various IST file system images are derived from each other. This is done by having each node represent a file system entity type, and each edge represent the tool needed to produce the entity at its tail from the entity at its head. Of course, some tools may require and/or produce more than one file type. An example of a very simple DAG is shown in Fig. 11.5. Using this DAG the command interpreter produces an ordered list of the steps needed to create missing files, translates this list into tool invocations, and effects their executions before allowing the original requesting tool to begin execution.

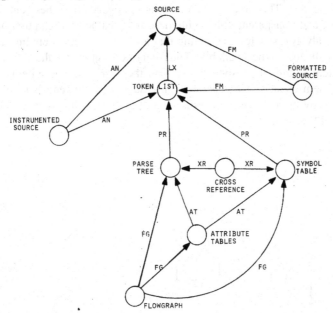

Fig. 11.5. A sample dependency DAG. Each node represents a type of file to be found in the Toolpack/IST file system. Each edge represents the dependency of this file type on another file type. Specifically, the file type at the head may be required in creating the file at the tail. The label on the edge represents the tool fragment needed to create the file type at the tail. Note that some tool fragments (e.g., FM) require more than one file type to produce their output, while others (PR) produce more than one file type.

In the example, the command interpreter would first determine whether or not current version of "SUBR/TRE" already exists. If so the invoked tool would be allowed to execute. If not the command interpreter would look up "TRE" in the dependency DAG, and see that a parse tree is derived from a token list by a parser and a token list is derived from source text by a lexical analyzer. The command interpreter would then check for the existence of the token list for SUBR. If it were present IST would cause the parser to produce the required parse tree. If the token list were absent, the command interpreter would issue commands to invoke the lexical analyzer first and the parser next. If the source text were not in the field system, an error message would be passed to the user.

This virtual strategy is also employed to enable source text versions such as formattings and instrumentations and entire static analysis and dynamic testing databases to be purged to save space and to be recreated only on demand. This flexibility should prove useful in hosting the IST on smaller machines. Here it may be necessary to permanently store only source text. Under these circumstances all derived images and intermediate entities will be routinely purged, and always recreated on demand. This extra computation seems a reasonable trade for lack of storage.

There appears to be little experience in devising strategies for deciding which entities to delete and when to delete them for the various machines and architectures on which IST will have to be hosted. Hence a lengthy period of experimentation and adjustment will be necessary. The replacement/retention strategy will be encapsulated in a module to facilitate this.

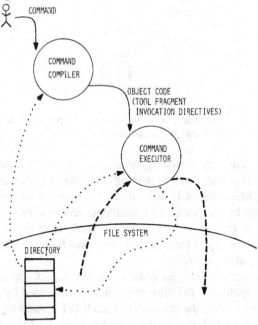

Fig. 11.6. Overview of the IST command interpreter showing two main phases—compilation and execution. Dotted lines show flow of information into and out of the file system directory. Dashed lines indicate data flow through the file system itself.

E. The Command Interpreter

The IST command interpreter processor consists of two phases—compilation and sequential tool invocation (see Fig. 11.6). Compilation, in turn, consists of three subphases: command syntactic analysis, semantic analysis, and object code generation (see Fig. 11.7).

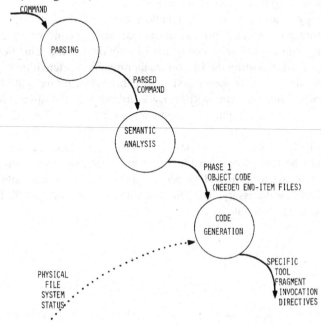

Fig. 11.7. Breakdown of the command compilation process into its three subphases. Note that only code generation requires information about current file system status.

Syntactic analysis is accomplished by a parser generated by a parser generator. The command language is small and uncluttered making it comfortably describable by parser-generator input. Moreover, it is recognized that users' reactions to IST may be strongly influenced by the perceived friendliness and ease of use of the command language itself. It thus seems important to enable changes in the language when and if experience indicates they are desirable. This is clearly facilitated by the parser-generator-created parser.

The second compilation phase, semantic analysis, is more complex entailing the selection of the standard template of IST files and functions indicated by the command (see Fig. 11.8). In particular, the semantics of each IST command are defined by a standard sequence of IST file system types-namely the file types which contain the information and data objects directly needed to satisfy the user's command.

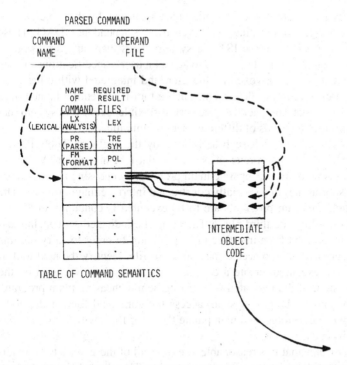

Fig. 11.8. Diagram showing operation of the semantic analysis phase of command compilation. The incoming parsed command has two parts, the command name and a list of subject files-the files which the user wants processed by the given command (in this example no options are specified). In this phase, the command name is used as an index into the table of command semantics which associates with the command name, the names of one or more file types which contain the information which the user is requesting in invoking the state command. Intermediate object code is formed by pairing off all combinations of such file types and stated operand files.

Because IST employs the virtual file strategy just described, it cannot be expected that all of the files of the types which the semantic analysis phase indicates are needed will be physically present. Thus it is the job of the code generation subphase of compilation to infer from the list of needed files and the physical file system status an ordered list of intermediate files to be created and the tool fragments needed to create them.

The end product of this phase is a sequential file of IST code describing in detail all steps to be carried out by IST tool fragments in order to effect the specified command in the exact context of the current state of the IST file system. As such this phase might well be viewed as a pseudocompilation into a machine independent intermediate code.

In closing this description of the compilation phase, it seems important to observe that the structure of the command compiler makes it amenable to dynamic alteration so as to accept command language extensions. This is due to the fact that each of the three compilation phases is essentially table driven. The parsing phase is driven by parse tables; the semantic phase is, driven by the table of templates; and the code generation phase is driven by the dependency DAG. These three tables are to be stored in the IST file system. Thus there appears to be no reason that a user tool might not be written to accept a user's specifications of how a new tool fragment is to be invoked by the user, and integrated with other fragments and file types within the file system. Such a tool is currently planned, it is expected that it will make Toolpack/IST the sort of flexible, extensible system that will grow and adapt to the needs of different user communities.

A program chaining approach such as is used by the Software Tools Project [20] is used in the second interpreter phase-sequential tool invocation. With this strategy each tool is made into a separate main program by encasing the tool function (which is a subroutine) in a specially constructed interface main program. The sequence in which the main programs are to be executed is contained in the sequential file produced by the third phase. Effecting the indicated sequencing and error branching is the job of the interface main program. In order to carry out this job the main program is able to access the command file, identify the next tool or tool fragment to be executed, create a command directing the invocation by the host operating system of the indicated tool or fragment's encasing main program, present the command to the host system, access the command file for the arguments needed by encased tools, and manipulate the error flags with which it communicates with its encased tools.

Experience indicates that it is reasonable to expect all of these tasks to be readily achievable on a wide spectrum of current systems. Thus this chaining strategy seems to offer an ideal combination of flexibility and portability potential.

V. Summary

The foregoing sections have described the design and implementation strategy for the early releases of the Toolpack IST. In these sections there have also been discussions of the ways in which these releases will be used as experimental vehicles for obtaining answers to the four basic questions outlined in Section II. Specifically, we have the following.

1) The Toolpack tool suite will be evaluated to see whether it is adequate to cover the needs of mathematical software developers.

2) The Toolpack file system and diagnostic databases will be instrumented and monitored to help ascertain the precise data needs of mathematical software developers as they perform their jobs.

3) The specific tool fragments from which the Toolpack tool capabilities are constructed will be evaluated to determine how readily and flexibly they form the basis for these capabilities. Alterations to this set of fragments may be necessitated.

4) Reactions to the proposed command language (which borrows concepts taken from Lisp, the UNIX shell, and the Make processor [21]) will be monitored, and attempts will be made to determine underlying basic requirements for such languages. Perhaps more important, the adaptability of the Toolpack tool fragments and the ability to readily contrive new tools in response to changing user needs will be carefully observed. The combined efficacy of the flexible command language and the adaptable tool fragments will be studied to determine whether they effect an acceptably friendly user interface.

VI. Future Directions and Plans

It is anticipated that the early releases of the Toolpack IST will provide definitive enough information that it will be reasonable to design with some assurance a variety of other environments which should be broader in scope.

One clear direction in which these techniques should be readily extended is towards newer and more interesting languages. A frequent criticism of this work is that it is too centered on Fortran, a language which is becoming increasingly out of step with the most modern thoughts about high level languages. It seems inappropriate to debate the relative merits of Fortran here, especially since this paper should, by now, have made it clear that Fortran was chosen primarily because it offers an excellent experimental vehicle. A critical mass of Fortran tools is already in existence and a receptive, perceptive community of users of both the language and tools is also in existence.

Of greater importance, however, is that the IST design concepts and actual software have been designed in such a way as to facilitate their conversion to support other languages. Lexical analysis, syntactic analysis and semantic analysis have all been modularized in separate tool fragments. Other tool fragments operate on abstract representations of source programs, and are thus well insulated from the source language and its peculiarities. It seems that the IST could offer similarly strong support for other languages if the lexical, syntactic, and semantic analysis tool fragments were replaced by tool fragments for analyzing some other language. Moreover, the lexical and syntactic analyzers are currently automatically produced from analyzer generators. Some research is underway to investigate the practicality of using attribute grammars to specify and drive the creation of semantic analyzers as well. Thus it appears that there is hope that these three language dependent front-end tool fragments might one day be automatically generated from a language specification.

This seems to be a good plan for the future, and there is honest optimism that it is an achievable goal. This optimism must, however, be tempered by the suspicion that many of the back-end tool fragments incorporate implicit assumptions about the semantics of Fortran which will only be ferreted out and concentrated in the semantic analysis module after considerable experimentation, observation, and adjustment.

It would seem that the best way to work in this direction is to promptly begin design of an IST-like capability for a more modern, sophisticated and challenging language. Ada[4] seems to be a very logical choice. One reason for this choice is that, here too, there is a community that is sensitive to the importance of tools. The Ada community has in fact already gone to the trouble of producing a preliminary specification for a tools environment [22]. Prototype environments for Ada are already under construction. They are not based upon the notions of reusable tool fragments and a virtual database, and thus should serve as illuminating comparison bases with an environment which is based upon these notions.

Ada also seems a good choice because of the ways in which it encourages and supports the concept of modularity. There are language facilities for writing higher level code which assumes the existence of support modules whose code may not be visible. What is visible to the writer of this higher level code is a summary view of the interface which this support code presents. Clearly, this summary view is a very logical candidate for inclusion in a file system supporting the construction of the higher level code. The Ada language itself does not go beyond the point of mandating that a rudimentary view of this interface be furnished by the creator of the support modules. It is clear, however, that such a rudimentary view is minimal, but far less than desirable. For example it would be preferable to have this view contain enough information to enable the sort of thorough data flow analysis that is suggested in [23] and [24]. The writer should not be burdened with having to provide such a large amount of information, however. With an architecture such as this paper suggests, however, the information could be created by analytic tool fragments and stored in the file system for future use. A large body of diverse information about support modules could be accumulated incrementally over a long period of time and either stored over a period of time (or regenerated on demand according to the dictates of local economies) for the benefit of users who wish to be guided to the proper use of these modules.

It is worthwhile to observe in closing this discussion of application to other languages that the language in which tool fragments is coded should not be a concern of the end user. In particular, there is no apparent reason that the language in which tool fragments are coded be the same as the language in which the code being analyzed is written. Toolpack/IST tool fragments are currently written primarily in languages such as Ratfor which are converted by preprocessors into Fortran 66. This was done because Fortran 66 was perceived as being the most reliable portability vehicle, and one of the requirements of the Toolpack project is that Toolpack software be portable. Other languages are becoming sufficiently standardized that they can no longer be overlooked as portability vehicles. Other environments, moreover, may not need to be as highly portable. Under these new and changing circumstances it would be reasonable to code tool fragments in other

---

[4] Ada is a trademark of the U.S. Department of Defense Ada Joint Program Office.

languages. These tool fragments could coexist quite nicely with older tool fragments written in Fortran derivative languages if that were to prove to be expedient.

Another important issue that will be addressed as an outgrowth of this work is the issue of how best to distribute this sort of environment across a range of newer hardware, such as personal work stations. This issue clearly comes up as a consequence of viewing the central file system as being multiuser accessible. If the various users are considered to be working at their own work stations, then the central file system is already distributed. A whole range of contingent issues then become important.

Finally, there is the issue of going beyond the current user interface language with its tool orientation to a language which is knowledge based and oriented towards being a query system. It appears that current and contemplated user interfaces are tool oriented, requiring users to be at least somewhat expert in the capabilities of individual tools. It would be far preferable if the user interface was designed so as to give users the impression of the existence of a knowledge base. Thus the development environment's user interface would take on more the appearance of a query system to support program development than an imperative language for invoking tools. The Toolpack architecture leans in this direction because of the virtual strategy adopted for the file system. Needed files are automatically materialized in indirect response to tool invocations. It is only an extension of this notion to consider that tools themselves might be automatically invoked as well in indirect response to requests for key program development information. The experimental results gotten from early releases should indicate how far this inclination should be continued, as well as the ramifications of such a continuation for the internal architecture.

Acknowledgments The design of the Toolpack IST is the product of a great deal of collaborative work and discussions with individuals inside and out of the project. In particular, some early design concepts of the command language were contributed by S. I. Feldman of Bell Laboratories. The concepts underlying his Make processor were, obviously, also quite influential in the design of IST. Most of the design work and development of the command interpreter and IST file system were done by G. Clemm. The implementation work has been ably led by A. L. Shafton. The design and implementation of key command interpreter tool fragments was led by G. Clemm, B. Welch, and M. Maybee.

References

[1] L. J. Osterweil, "Software environment research directions for the next five years," *IEEE Computer*, vol. 14, pp. 35-43, Apr. 1981.

[2] *Proc. Conf Programming Environment for Developing Numerical Software*, Jet Propulsion Laboratory, Pasadena, CA, Oct. 18-20, 1978.

[3] *Proc. Conf. Comput. Environment for Math. Software*, Jet Propulsion Laboratory, Pasadena, CA, July 15, 1981.

[4] W. R. Cowell and L. D. Fosdick, "Mathematical software production," in Mathematical Software III. New York: Academic, 1977, pp. 195-224.

[5] SFTRAN III, Programmer Reference Manual, JPL Internal Document, 1846-98, Pasadena, CA, Apr. 1981.

[6] B. W. Kernighan, "Ratfor-A preprocessor for a rational Fortran," Bell Labs. Comput. Sci. Tech. Rep. 55.

[7] S. I. Feldman, "The programming language EFL," Bell Labs. Comput. Sci. Tech. Rep. 78, Murray Hill, NJ, June 1979.

[8] L. J. Osterweil, "Draft Toolpack architectural design," Dep. Comput. Sci., Univ. Colorado, Boulder, Nov. 1, 1981.

[9] S. J. Hague, "The provision of editors for the manipulation of Fortran," Toolpack Document SJH 11112, Nov. 1981; available from Appl. Math. Div., Argonne Nat. Lab., Argonne, IL, 60439.

[10] T. Teitelbaum and T. Reps, "The Cornell program synthesizer: A syntax-directed programming environment," *Commun. Ass. Comput. Mach.* vol. 24, pp. 563-573, Sept. 1981.

[11] V. Donzeau-Gouge, G. Huet, G. Kahn, and B. Lang, "Programming environments based on structed editors: The mentor experience," INRIA Res. Rep. 26, Rocquencourt, France, 1980.

[12] L. D. Fosdick, "POLISH-X transformations," Dep. Comput. Sci., Univ. Colorado, Tech. Rep. CU-CS-203-81, May 1981.

[13] B. S. Baker, "An algorithm for structuring flowgraphs," *J. Ass. Comput. Mach.*, vol. 24, pp. 98-120, Jan. 1977.

[14] J. Feiber, R. N. Taylor, and L. J. Osterweil, "Newton-A dynamic program analysis tool capabilities specification," Dep. Comput. Sci., Univ. Colorado, Boulder, Tech. Rep. CU-CS-200-81, Mar. 1981.

[15] L. J. Osterweil and L. D. Fosdick, "DAVE—A validation, error detection, and documentation system for FORTRAN programs," *Software—Practice and Experience*, vol. 6, pp. 473-486, Sept. 1976.

[16] B. G. Ryder, "The PFORT verifier," *Software—Practice and Experience*, vol. 4, pp. 359-377, 1974.

[17] W. Ward and J. Rice, "A simple macro processor," Toolpack Document WW/JR 10921, Sept. 1981; available from Appl. Math. Div., Argonne Nat. Lab., Argonne, IL 60439.

[18] J. M. Boyle and K. Matz, "Automating multiple program realizations," in *MRI Conf. Rec. XXIV Symp. Comput. Software.* Brooklyn, NY: Polytechnic Press, 1976, pp.421-456.

[19] D. R. Hanson, "The portable I/O system PIOS," Dep. Comput. Sci., Univ. Arizona, Tech. Rep. 80-6a, Apr. 1980, revised Dec. 1980.

[20] D. Scherrer, "COOKBOOK-Instructions for implementing the LBL software tools package," Lawrence Berkeley Lab., Univ. California, Berkeley, Internal Rep. LBID098, 1978.

[21] S. I. Feldman, "Make—A program for maintaining computer programs," *Software—Practice and Experience*, vol. 9, pp. 255-265, Apr. 1979.

[22] J. N. Buxton, and V. Stenning, "Requirements for Ada programming support environments," *Stoneman*, Dep. Defense, Feb. 1980.

[23] R. N. Taylor and L. J. Osterweil, "Anomaly detection in concurrent software by static data flow analysis," *IEEE Trans. Software Eng.*, vol. SE-6, pp. 265-278, May 1980. (Reprinted as Chapter 6)

[24] R. N. Taylor, "Static analysis of the synchronization structure of concurrent programs," Ph.D. dissertation, Dep. Comput. Sci., Univ. Colorado, Boulder, 1980.

A Mechanism for Environment Integration[1]

Geoffrey Clemm and Leon Osterweil

University of Colorado at Boulder

Abstract This paper describes research associated with the development and evaluation of Odin—an environment integration system based on the idea that tools should be integrated around a centralized store of persistent software objects. The paper describes this idea in detail and then presents the Odin architecture, which features such notions as the typing of software objects, composing tools out of modular tool fragments, optimizing the storage and rederivation of software objects, and isolating tool interconnectivity information in a single centralized object. The paper then describes some projects that have used Odin to integrate tools on a large scale. Finally, it discusses the significance of this work and the conclusions that can be drawn about superior software environment architectures.

1. BACKGROUND

A primary goal of software environment research is to devise superior development and maintenance processes and effectively integrate software tools to support them. The development of a large software system can easily cost between $50 and $400 per line [l], yet the quality of the end product is often disturbingly low. The cost of maintaining such systems over their lifetime usually far exceeds original development costs. Further, software costs have been steadily increasing over the past decade. Most observers blame the twin problems of high cost and low quality on the lack of orderly, systematic processes for developing software and the lack of software tools that effectively exploit computing power to support them. Accordingly, there has been much work on software tools and processes during the past decade. There have been some proposed software processes that stress extensive documentation of software products. Often these are not widely used because they are onerous without significant tool support. Many tools are not used because they do not support specific processes, or are not well integrated with each other.

---

[1] This work was supported by U.S. Department of Energy grants DE-FG0264ER13283 and DE-ACOP-80ER10718 and National Science Foundation grants MCS-8000017 and DCR-8403341.

Geoffrey Clemm and Leon J. Osterweil, "A Mechanism for Environment Integration,"
ACM Transactions on Programming Languages and Systems (TOPLAS) 11:1, January 1990.

Thus, software is usually developed in a manual, ad hoc way. Even where effective software processes are defined, they are rarely adequately supported by tools, making it difficult to experimentally determine just how effective they are and whether they should be promulgated more widely. Similarly, it is difficult to definitively evaluate individual tools, as they often do not clearly support tasks within popular processes, and are thus not comparable to manual efforts or other tools. We believe that the emergence of software environments is catalyzing improvements in processes and tools by providing a common evaluative framework. This paper describes a research software system called Odin [3, 4], which facilitates the rapid and effective integration of software tools, thereby aiding experimentation and evaluation.

We believe Odin is a language and interpretation system for what DeRemer and Kron have called "programming in the large" [5]. Odin was first used to integrate a family of FORTRAN development, testing, and maintenance tools in the Toolpack project [16]. It was subsequently used to integrate tools to support software development in C [8], and then to integrate tools to support the creation of attribute grammars. Currently, Odin is being used to support a variety of large-scale tool integration applications, including a data flow analyzer generator project [14]. The Odin architecture, our experiences in exploiting it, conclusions about the Odin architecture, and principles to which these experiences have led us, are the subjects of this paper.

In Section 2 we describe the philosophical basis upon which Odin rests, Section 3 describes related work; Section 4 describes the details of Odin's design and some implementation issues; Section 5 the language used to specify the way in which tools are to be integrated; Section 6 the language that users employ to actually use tools; Section 7 our experiences in using Odin; and Section 8 suggests likely future research directions.

2. THE ODIN TOOL INTEGRATION PHILOSOPHY

Odin was originally designed as part of the Toolpack project [16], whose aim was to integrate both existing and proposed tools for supporting the development, testing, and maintenance of FORTRAN code. Flexibility and extensibility were also key Toolpack goals. At the time (1979) there was considerable interest in software environments, but very few had been built, and there were virtually no successful environment architectural paradigms to guide our work. Thus, the design and evaluation of an innovative environment integration paradigm became another major goal of the Toolpack project.

The Odin project followed the suggestion (e.g., [2,15,17]) that an environment must be data centered, rather than tool centered, and adopted the philosophy that Odin-integrated environments should be devices for using tools to manage repositories of software data in such a way as to expedite responses to interactive user commands.

Accordingly, a primary design issue was determination of the contents and structure of the repository. In Odin-integrated environments, the repository consists exactly of those software objects that are the inputs to, and outputs from, the various tools to be integrated. Thus, for example, such code-related objects as source code, object code, parse trees, symbol tables, and flow graphs populate the repository, but so do such non-code-related objects as documentation, test data, test results, and program structure representations.

Odin manages these large-grained objects by coordinating and managing the application of correspondingly large grained tools such as parsers, instrumenters, prettyprinters, and data flow analyzers. Odin views each software object as an operand, and the tools that manipulate the objects as operators that manage these objects and their relations to each other. Odin facilitates the synthesis of these tools into larger tools, while relieving users of the burden of figuring out the details of how to do this synthesis. Odin enables users to create objects that may be derivable only by a complex process involving many tools, simply by specifying the object in a precise yet terse way. The object may have been created earlier, it may have been built out of objects that have subsequently been changed, or it may never have been created before at all. In all of these cases, Odin creates an efficient derivation process for building or rebuilding the desired object and executes that process. Often, Odin makes considerable use of existing objects to speed creation of the newly requested object.

Odin can be thought of as an interpreter for a high-level command language whose operands are the various software objects in the data repository and whose operators are tool fragments. Later, we show how these operands can be aggregated into structures, that the operands are best thought of as being typed, that the set of types is extensible, and that the tool operators enforce a strong typing discipline upon the user.

3. RELATED WORK

Odin's approach to tool and object management has some unique features, but also builds upon concepts found in other systems.

Odin builds upon the UNIX[TM][2] view of tools, in that is aimed at the easy concatenation of loosely coupled tool fragments into larger tools. UNIX, however, only supports simple-minded tool concatenation comfortably. UNIX tool fragments are easily combined by connecting consecutive tool fragments by a single data stream, called a pipe. Effective software development and maintenance, however, require complex tools with multiple connections. Thus Odin supports the synthesis of

---

[2] UNIX is a trademark of AT&T Laboratories.

complex tools out of tool fragments that communicate with each other through multiple data streams.

Odin also builds upon the Make [6] model of software object management. Make automatically applies tools to assure that changes to some objects are reflected in other related objects. Odin supports this object management feature as well. With Make, however, for all but single-input/single-output tools, the user must explicitly name each individual object which is to be automatically updated and the exact sequences of tools to be used in doing so. Odin, on the other hand, enables users to define types of objects and to prescribe general procedures for automatically creating and updating instances of those types from corresponding instances of other types.

Thus, the Odin user may create a new object and then immediately request a derivation requiring the complex synthesis of many diverse tools and the creation of many intermediate objects. A Make user would have to set up directory structures naming all of these objects and would have to define the derivation process in detail. Odin automatically constructs storage structures as needed, in accordance with the derivation process that it creates from a more general specification of how tools interconnect.

The key construct in doing this is the Odin Derivation Graph, which models the way in which tools can be synthesized. The edges in this graph correspond to the tools that Odin integrates. The nodes correspond to types of objects. User requests are treated as requests for named objects, which are considered to be instances of types contained in the Derivation Graph. Graph traversal is used to determine which tools must be used to create which specific instances of which intermediate types in order to eventually satisfy the dataflow needs of the tools that produce the requested objects. Objects that have been requested before are likely to have been retained to expedite response to subsequent user requests. As with Make, however, Odin does not return retained objects to the user if the objects from which they have been built have changed. Instead, Odin automatically rederives the requested object from its changed predecessors. The Derivation Graph is a key and complex feature of Odin, and is described in considerable detail in Section 5.

Arbitrarily complex new tools (and object types) are integrated by editing models of their interactions with existing tools into the Derivation Graph. This represents a great improvement over the way in which Make exploits new tools. In Make, except when adding simple UNIX pipe-style tools, every object that is to be either directly or indirectly built using the new tool must have its Makefile altered to show precisely how the new tool is to be used.

The System Modeler [9,10,18], developed at Xerox for the Cedar programming environment, and Apollo's DSEE (Domain Software Engineering Environment) [11-13] both incorporate a more explicit tool and object model than does Make. For example, System Modeler explicitly captures the object flows between the Cedar editor and the Mesa compiler/linker. Both DSEE and Cedar are examples of very tightly integrated environments in which both the tools and integration mechanisms have direct knowledge of each other. Users enjoy important benefits from such tightly coupled toolsets. Such tight coupling, however, makes it correspondingly difficult to expand and alter the toolsets. In addition, it means that these tool integration mechanisms are tied to the particular tools and environments for which they have been developed. Make and Odin, on the other hand, are more general and reusable. They are not tied to any particular host environment.

The modeling capabilities of DSEE and System Modeler, moreover, seem to us to be inadequate. They, like Make, fail to successfully separate declarative information about the objects from algorithmic information about the tools that manipulate the objects. Instead, this information is combined into a single text object. Their analog of the Make system's "Makefile" is called the "System Model" in both. As a result, as in the case of Make, information about a particular tool must often be specified repeatedly in new System Models, a significant burden for complex tools. Further, it requires the individual updating of all of these System Models when the interface to a tool is modified or when a new tool is to be incorporated into a project. In Odin, objects and tools are described separately. This enables a single tool expert to precisely specify the behavior and use of a given tool, saving each potential user the trouble of reproducing that specification every time the tool is to be used.

Odin's modeling language is also more powerful than those of the systems just described in its support for command parameters. When users specify parameters in their commands, Odin can tap the considerable flexibility built into underlying tools, yet analyze such parameterized commands accurately enough to correctly identify intermediate results of earlier parameterized commands for reuse.

Some of Odin's superior default capabilities have already been described. Although both Make and DSEE contain mechanisms for providing "default" rules for tool activation and object creation, the semantics of these rules are too simple to allow for the specification of complex tool interactions. In environments such as Toolpack, which must integrate a complex and fluctuating toolset, the need for more powerful modeling languages and default rules is critical.

Odin's object-modeling capabilities also support the specification of object aggregates—such as arrays and structures. One result is that Odin can manage the integration of tools, such as source text splitters, which produce an unpredictable number of objects as outputs. Earlier systems such as Make are unable to model such tools. Odin can also adjust its object-management strategy dynamically, depending on the outcomes of tool executions. For example, in order to integrate "include processing," objects which "include" other objects must be processed by tools as if the text of included objects was part of the including object. In earlier systems such as Make, include processing requires the creation and explicit invocation of metatools. Odin integrates a special tool fragment that generates the list of objects included by an object, and the output of this tool determines the input dependencies of the object.

4. THE DESIGN OF ODIN

As noted above, Odin facilitates tool and object management by grouping objects into types and then specifying tool interactions in terms of the way the tools use and create instances of these types. Thus, the Odin design centers around two structures: the Derivation Graph, which specifies type and tool interconnections, and the Derivative Forest, which specifies how actual objects (instances of the types) are related to each other. This section describes these two structures, how they are used, and the languages that specify them.

4.1 Object Management in Odin

Odin encourages users to directly request needed software objects, without worrying about how the object might be created, whether it has been built before, or whether something similar might be used as a suitable starting point. Odin's job is to expedite the process of furnishing such requested objects.

Odin carefully names each object in its store so that the name accurately reflects the way the object either has been, or could be, derived from elementary objects in the store by a sequence of tool fragments. This fully elaborated name then guides an efficient search of the object store. If the requested object is already there, the search terminates with a pointer to it. If it is not, the search terminates at an object or objects representing some progress from the store's most elementary objects toward what has been requested. Odin then uses the fully elaborated name to prescribe the sequence of tool fragments that can take the already existing object(s) and derive them into what has been requested.

For example, if the user wants a pretty-printed version of source text "joe", which had previously been prepared for a debugging session by an instrumentation tool, then the user would request the object:

joe : ins : fmt

namely, the object that results from starting with joe, then producing an instrumented (ins) version of it, and then producing from it a formatted (fmt) version. Although the user may view this as the sequential execution of two tools—an instrumenter and a formatter—each of these two is achieved by the sequential execution of several smaller tool fragments. Thus, in Toolpack/IST, the Toolpack toolset integrated under Odin, instrumentation is accomplished by the sequence: lexical analysis, parsing, semantic analysis, and then finally instrumentation. Formatting is accomplished by the sequence: lexical analysis, parsing, and then formatting. Thus the object requested by the user is built by at least half a dozen tool fragments, most of which need not be understood by the user.

Odin builds this tool fragment execution sequence by first creating the internal name of the requested object and then searching for an expedited sequence of tool executions for building the object from what is currently in the store. The organization of the store expedites such searches. If the requested object is present, it is immediately returned to the user. If joe is present, but none of its derivatives are, then Odin constructs a procedure for deriving the requested object from joe. Along the way, the following objects (and a number of others) are also built:

joe : lex	(joe's token list)
joe : prs	(joe's parse tree)
joe : nag	(joe's semantic attribute table)
joe : ins	(instrumented version of joe)
joe : ins : lex	(token list for instrumented version of joe)

All are stored for possible future reuse. If "joe: ins" is present in the store (e.g., the user may have previously requested the instrumented version of "joe"), Odin would use it as the basis for a simpler and faster derivation procedure, namely, executing only the lexical analyzer and formatter using joe : ins as input.

The Odin Derivative Forest is key to understanding this derivation process.

4.1.1 The Odin Derivative Forest.

Odin's object store is structured into a forest—the Derivative Forest—which indicates how objects have been produced from each other. The object store contains two classes of objects—atomic and derived. Atomic objects are those that Odin cannot reproduce on its own. They have entered the store by text insertion or explicit importation from the host file system. Derived objects have been created by the action of Odin-integrated tool fragments. Each atomic object is the root of a tree in the derivative forest, where the tree consists of all objects derived, directly or indirectly, from the root by Odin-integrated tool fragments.

Fig. 12.1 shows such a derivative forest, in which "sam", "joe", and "bob" are all atomic objects of type "source code". The tree rooted by "sam" has two subtrees—one represents "sam"'s parse tree and the other represents an instrumented version of "sam". The tree rooted by "bob" has one subtree whose root represents a formatted version of "bob". It is, in turn, the root of a subtree that represents the parse tree and the instrumented version of the formatted version of the original "bob" source code.

The tree rooted at "joe" illustrates the use of parameterized object descriptions. The "ins" subtree of "joe" has two subsubtrees, each rooted at a different instrumented derivative of "joe". Sometimes, additional information can be associated with an object to affect the derivatives produced from that object. In Odin, this additional information is captured as a "parameter" of that object, and is specified by appending a '+' and the parameter. For example a "debug" parameter could cause the compilation derivative to contain runtime checks; a "library" parameter could cause the load derivative to have undefined externals satisfied from a nondefault library; and a "format" parameter could cause all printable derivatives to be generated in line-printer format. Fig. 12.1 specifies default parameterization for one in-

strumented version of "joe", and the explicit parameterization "no-comments" for
the other, as follows:

    joe +no_comments : ins

Values can be assigned to parameters, and these values may be other Odin objects.

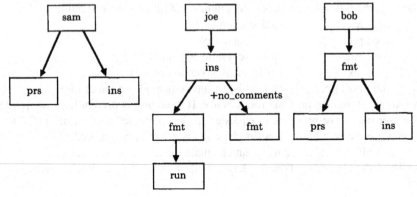

Fig. 12.1. An illustration of an example Odin Derivative Forest, showing both atomic and derived objects.

4.1.2 Alteration of Objects.

The need to change stored objects (e.g., by editing them) complicates the management of derived objects. When an atomic object (e.g., source text) is modified, Odin considers the result to be a new object, namely a new version of the original object. If the user specifies a name for this new object, it becomes the root of a (temporarily descendantless) derivative tree. If not, the new object automatically replaces the original object. In this case, it is not safe to assume that objects derived from the original are correct derivatives of the new object.

Odin assigns a date and timestamp to each object in its store. Whenever a derived object is older than any of the ancestors in its derivative tree, it is treated with suspicion. For example, if the user requests "sam : ins" and Odin finds that "sam : ins" already exists, Odin first compares the time and datestamps of "sam" and "sam : ins". If "sam" is newer than "sam : ins", a rederivation process is begun.

It is tempting to suggest that this comparison process be avoided by always deleting all derivatives of an atomic object that has been edited. Odin does not do this because some editing procedures create only superficial changes that do not alter many of the object's derivatives. Odin incorporates difference analyzers to make this determination and to avoid costly and unnecessary rederivations.

In the example just given, for instance, editing "sam" may only alter comments. If so, the previous scan table, parse tree, symbol table, and instrumentation are still correct derivatives of the edited version of "sam". Odin detects this and saves most of the work of rederivation. Once Odin recognizes that the present version of "sam" is new, it rederives the scn_cmt and scn_tab derivatives, compares the new derivatives to the old ones, and finds that the new scn_cmt object is different, but the new scn_tab object is not. Odin then replaces the old scn_cmt object with the new version, but merely updates the time and datestamp on the old scn_tab object, indicating that it is a correct derivative of the new "sam" object. Derivatives of "sam : scn_tab", such as the prs-sym and pm-nod objects, are also correct derivatives of "sam", and need not be rederived. Odin recognizes that "sam : ins" is also a correct derivative and updates its time and datestamp without rederiving it. Thus only the scanner has been rerun in response to this superficial editing of "Sam". Even this relatively minor rederivation, moreover, is carried out only in response to a user request for that derived object, or one of its descendants.

4.1.2.1 Trustworthiness and Validity of Objects.

Odin attaches to each object a status-level attribute indicating how much confidence the object should be accorded. The status level is an enumerated type whose values are OK, WARNING, ERROR, NOREAD, NOFILE, and ABORT. Odin assigns an ordering to these values, with OK being the highest and ABORT the lowest. The status level of an atomic object is always OK. The status level of a derived object is the least of the status levels of the objects derived by the tool fragments used to produce the object. An object's status level is indicated whenever it is requested, unless the status level is OK. The actual warning or error messages that were produced are considered to be objects in the Odin object store. These objects are specified by appending the ": warn" and ": err" derivations, respectively, to specifications of the objects to which they apply. Thus, if the request for the object

> joe : run

indicated that abort status was set for that object, the errors that caused the abort status are the contents of the object

> joe : run : err

When key objects have been changed and now have reduced status levels, Odin broadcasts this news to derived objects to which such changes are expected to be particularly significant. Such derivatives are said to be related to such key higher level objects by a "sentinel" relation. The existence of a sentinel relation between pairs of objects effects the automatic rederivation of derived objects and the automatic reporting of sufficiently low status level of any such rederivations. Sentinel relations create a network of constraints among the objects in Odin's store, as the store is being built up. This network facilitates the early, effective, and effortless detection of changes to higher level objects which cause errors in key derivatives of those objects. For example, suppose

> thesis.txt : spell
>
> prog.c +input=(thesis.txt) :run

are two Odin objects each of which is derived from the object "thesis.txt". If these two objects are marked as being "sentinels," then every modification to "thesis.txt" will effect an automatic rederivation of both. If either rederivation causes an error or warning, the user will be notified. Assume that the ":spell" object is a list of spelling errors and has status ERROR if the list is nonempty, and assume the ":run" object creates an executable and has status ERROR if any error messages are generated in attempting to compile and run. If "thesis.txt" is modified, Odin will automatically rederive those objects, automatically checking that the "thesis.txt" object is spelled correctly and that it is acceptable to the "prog.c" program. Thus Odin enables the user to specify automatic checking to determine when certain changes have undesirable effects.

4.1.3 Compound Objects.

Odin objects may be either simple or compound. Simple objects have no internal fine structure visible to Odin. Compound objects are lists or structures of Odin objects, and they arise in two ways—through the action of tools or through explicit construction by users.

4.1.3.1 Tool-Generated Compound Objects.

A source text object consisting of more than one compilation unit is a compound object. It may arise as output from another tool, from editing, or it may be input from the host environment. Odin must initially treat such objects as simple objects, but can treat them as compound objects after the user invokes a special tool (e.g., a "splitter") to detect the fine structure. These tools associate a key with each component of the compound object to enable users to extract the components.

For example, suppose "joe : output" is generated by executing "joe", and is compound because joe's execution creates multiple output streams. The tool that derives ": output" objects is expected to associate with each output stream a meaningful key, such as the filename associated with the stream, to enable users to access these component objects.

Users specify the components of a compound object by appending an at-sign ('@') and the key. For example, if "joe : output" consists of three components whose keys are "DATA", "source.list", and "source.errors", then they are specified as

     joe : output @DATA
     joe : output @source.list
     joe : output @source.errors

4.1.3.2 User-Created Compound Objects.

Users create compound objects directly by using pointers—Odin objects of type "ref". For example, in Fig. 12.2, "sally" and "jane" are "ref" objects, where "sally" consists of pointers to the three objects: "sam", "joe", and "bob", and "jane" consists of pointers to "bob" and "tim".

A compound object can be an input to a tool, in which case the output is usually the compound object that is the composition of the objects produced by applying the tool to each of the components of the input object. For example, if the user requests

> sally : ins

Odin produces a compound object consisting of pointers to

> sam : ins   joe : ins   bob : ins

To do this, Odin assures that the "scn_tab", "prs_sym", and "prs_nod" objects are created for each of "sam", "joe", and "bob". These are all stored as descendants of the "sam", "joe", and "bob" "f77" atomic objects. The object "sally : ins" is itself stored as a descendant in the derivative tree of "sally". It consists of pointers to

> sam : ins   joe : ins   bob : ins

which reside in their respective derivative trees. Odin recognizes if any or all of these individual "ins" objects had been created previously, and does not rederive them. Similarly, these derived objects are available for reuse in satisfying subsequent user requests made indirectly through other "ref" files. In the example shown in Fig. 12.2, if the user requests the object "jane : ins" after requesting "sally : ins", Odin simply sets a pointer to "bob : ins", but will derive the "tim : ins" to satisfy the request. Thus, Odin manages overlapping aggregate objects without needless inefficient repetition of work.

Odin "ref" objects are also used to define object hierarchies. This enables the modeling of programs as hierarchies of procedures. At lower levels, procedures must be modeled as overlapping sets of support procedures and libraries. In constructing this hierarchy, the user need not be concerned with assuring that the constituent objects are mutually disjoint, as no inefficiencies in tool application result from this. Instead, the hierarchical structure is free to reflect the program's logical structure.

Applying tools to such structures is easy and natural, as the user simply applies needed tools to the highest level "ref" object. Odin is often able to quickly satisfy such requests, because very few objects need be recreated. For example, when a program is being maintained, many of the objects which the user indirectly requests have probably recently been created and need not be rederived. In the usual maintenance scenario, determining which objects need to be recreated is painstaking and perilous. Most users avoid it and its risks by doing massive rederivations, often needlessly duplicating considerable previous work. Odin assures that only necessary rederivations will occur. Users simply issue one terse command at an appropriately high conceptual level.

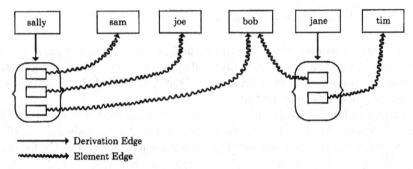

Fig. 12.2. An illustration of an example Compound Object, showing both derivation edges and element edges.

As the pointers in a compound object may point to objects of different types (even other compound objects), this construct may be used to build arbitrary graphs of objects.

5. THE ODIN SPECIFICATION LANGUAGE AND DERIVATION GRAPH

Odin also incorporates a specification language that enables tool integrators to specify how the various tool fragments and object types relate to each other. The language is designed to facilitate the integration of existing tools or sets of tools under the Odin System, with no modification to the tools themselves. This is critical when a tool only exists in the form of executable binary, as is often the case for host-system provided tools.

For example, a host-system compiler can be incorporated into an Odin-integrated environment by describing the input/output behavior of the compiler using the Odin specification language, but without having to alter the compiler. Odin itself provides a variety of internal tools to make this possible. For example, one Odin internal tool interprets an object containing a list of object names as a "collection of objects," so that this collection of objects can be treated as a single object by a user of Odin. Odin ensures that a request to run a tool on this collection invokes the tool on each of the elements in the collection.

Another internal tool builds the Odin Derivation Graph. This tool uses the specifications of all tools and object types that are expressed in the Odin specification language to construct a single graph representing all of the relations among these tools and types.

Details of the Odin specification language are provided in [4]. A brief summary of salient features of this language is provided here.

All specifications of tools written in the Odin specification language consist of the name of the tool and a description of its input/output behavior. For example, a simple formatter is described as follows:

    fmt "formatted version of C code":

       USER pol_c.cmd

        :c

where "fmt" is the type of the result of applying a C code formatter, "formatted version of C code" describes this object, "pol_c.cmd" is the name of the formatting tool, and "c" names the type of object suitable as input to the formatter. Note that this tool specification also serves as a specification of the types with which the tool deals. Thus the totality of all tool specifications is also a specification of all of the types of objects integrated by Odin.

The input/output behavior of a tool can be far more complex than this simple example, but this basic model of naming the output of a tool, naming the procedure that invokes the tool, and describing the input to the tool, is always followed.

5.1 Object Types

Every type of object that is to be made available for editing directly by the user is given a unique "atomic object type." Every type of object that is produced by some computer program or tool is given a unique "derived object type." A description of a derived object type consists of a description of the structure of the derived object followed by a description of the tool that produces the derived object and a description of the inputs needed by the tool.

5.1.1 Derived Object Structure.

Due to the great variety in the output behavior of tools, it is necessary to provide a flexible language for describing the various possible kinds of derived object types. Examples of different kinds of outputs that a tool might generate are a single data object, a single object that refers to another object, a fixed number of different kinds of output objects, or an arbitrary number of similar output objects.

5.1.1.1 Simple Derived Object.

Some common simple object types are assembler code generated from a higher level language, executable binary, crossreference listings, and error reports. A simple object type is analogous to a basic variable type in a programming language, such as Boolean, character, or integer. Odin allows a user to introduce an arbitrary number of such basic types.

An example of a simple type declaration for a linking loader is
  exe "executable binary":
     USER ld.cmd
        :c.o
In this example, the type "exe" is declared as a simple type, produced by the tool
"ld.cmd" from input of type "c.o".

5.1.1.2 Compound Derived Object.

An object that is of type "compound derived object" consists of a set of objects,
each of which is of the same object type, called the "element object type" or is
another compound derived object of the given type. A compound object that contains only objects of the element object type is called a "flat compound object"—
one that also contains other compound objects is called a "nested compound object." A flat compound object is analogous to an array in a programming language—a nested compound object is analogous to a tree.

A tool must be specified as producing a compound object type when it produces an arbitrary number of objects of the same type, or when it produces references
to an arbitrary number of objects.

An example of a compound type declaration is given by this specification for a
tool that scans a C source code file for included files:
     c-ref(h) "included files":
        USER c_ref.cmd
           :c
In this example, "c_ref" is declared as a compound type whose elements are of
type "h".

5.1.1.3 Composite Derived Object.

An object whose type is a "composite" derived object consists of a fixed number
of objects whose types may be different. This is analogous to a record or structure
type in a programming language. Odin considers most tools that produce multiple
outputs to be tools that produce a single composite object as output. The members
of a composite object type can be compound or simple object types.

An example of this is the following composite type declaration for a C compiler:
     cc <
        c.o "object code produced by the C compiler"
        c.list "listing produced by the C compiler"
     > "C compiler output":
     USER cc.cmd
        :c

        : c_ref
In this example, the compiler produces two outputs: the object code and a listing
file.

5.1.2 Inputs.

More than one input object is often needed by a tool in order to produce its output.
These input objects are specified as a list of object types, each preceded by a colon. These object types can be atomic object types, derived object types, or parameter object types.

   Normally, when a derived object is being produced, the actual inputs to a tool
are determined automatically by Odin, based on the specified input objects. Often,
a user wishes to pass additional information to certain of the tools. This can be
done by appending a list of parameters to the description of the derived object. A
parameter consists of a parameter type followed by the information that is to be
placed in the input object corresponding to that parameter object type. Normally, a
tool will allow a parameter to be omitted, in which case a default value will be assumed.

   An example of a tool that allows such parameters as inputs is one that checks
out a particular revision of a file from a file that contains a tree of revisions in a
compact form. A possible Odin specification for such a tool is
        c "checked out version of a C file":
            USER co.cmd
                : c,v
                : PARAMETERS (date revision who state)
In this example, "c,v" is the type of file expected as input, "date", "revision",
"who", and "state" are the optional parameter types, and "c" is the type of file
produced as output.

5.2 Casting

We consider the objects that Odin manages to be instances of types, and the tool
fragments that Odin invokes to be operators on the type instances. Odin assures
that tool fragment operands are always objects of the proper types. This involves
casting inappropriately typed objects where necessary and advising the user when
casting is impossible.

   The focus of this typing and casting mechanism is the Odin Derivation
Graph—the structure that, as noted earlier, is built from the tool specifications in
order to record which tool fragments are currently incorporated, which types of
objects they produce and require, and the way in which these various tool fragments can be synthesized and concatenated. The nodes of the Derivation Graph

represent the types of the objects in the object store, and the edges represent ways in which new objects can be created from existing objects. New objects can be created either by casting or derivation, each of which is represented by a different type of Derivation Graph edge.

Casting is done when Odin determines that an existing object is the needed input to a particular tool fragment, but that the object is not of the type required by the tool fragment. If the nodes representing these types are connected in the Derivation Graph by a "cast" edge, then Odin will retype the object to enable the needed tool fragment to use it. This does not alter the contents of the object. For example, in Toolpack/IST, inputs to the scanner must be of type "source text." The outputs of the formatter (fmt) and the instrumenter (ins) are both source text, but are typed "fmt" and "ins", so that these different objects can be distinguished. Objects of type "fmt" and "ins" are made legal inputs to the scanner by casting their types to "source text." The Derivation Graph reflects this by including two cast arcs, one to "source text" from "fmt" and one to "source text" from "ins."

The Derivation Graph also contains derivation arcs to represent how tools can derive new objects from existing ones. Each derivation arc represents a tool fragment which Odin can invoke to derive an object of the type indicated by its head node. The tail of a derivation arc represents the type of the object needed as input to this tool fragment. Several derivation arcs may be needed in order to completely characterize the behavior of a single tool fragment.

Fig. 12.3 shows a part of the Derivation Graph that represents the tool fragments and object types managed by Odin to form Toolpack/IST. Cast relations are shown as dotted arcs and derivation relations are represented by solid arcs. We now use this figure to show how Odin creates the formatted version of the instrumented version of source text object "joe". If the middle tree of the Derivative Forest of Fig. 12.1 initially consists of the root only, namely atomic object "joe", then when the user gives the command, Odin first examines the Derivative Tree to see if "joe : ins : fmt" has already been created. As "joe" has no descendants at all, Odin next determines that "joe: ins: fmt" cannot be built until "joe : ins" is built, and tries to construct "joe : ins". Odin consults the Derivation Graph and sees that an object of type "ins" (such as "joe : ins") is derived from an object of type "f77", an object of type "prs_sym" (parser symbol table), and an object of type "prs_nod" (parse tree). The Derivation Graph indicates that the parser produces both parser symbol tables and parse trees.

Odin next determines that the parser requires an object of type "scn_tab" (scanner table) as input. This object is not present either, and thus "joe : scn_tab" must also be built. The Derivation Graph shows that the scanner table is built by the lexical analysis (scanner) tool fragment using an "f77" source text object as input. Thus Odin infers that the scanner must be invoked before the parser. Odin sees that "joe" is an object of type "f77", and now has determined that "joe:ins" can be built from existing objects by first invoking the scanner using "joe" as input, then invoking the parser using "joe : scn_tab" as input, and finally invoking the instrumenter using "joe", "joe : prs_sym", and "joe : prs_nod" as inputs.

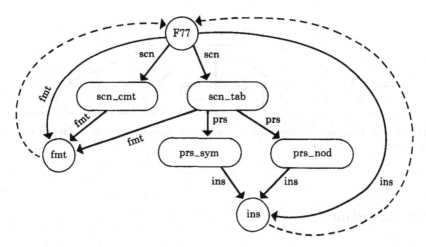

Fig. 12.3. An illustration of a portion of a typical Odin Dependency Graph, used to represent the relations between tool fragments and object types. This illustration is taken from the Dependency Graph used in integrating Toolpack/IST, and shows the use of both Derivation Edges and Cast Edges.

Now Odin must create "joe : ins : fmt", assuming that "joe : ins" and various intermediate objects are already created. Odin assumes that the Derivative Tree rooted at "joe" will appear as shown in Fig. 12.4, and that the following objects will all be direct descendants of "joe":

joe : scn_cmt (comments embedded in joe source text)

joe : scn_tab (joe's scanner table, sometimes referred to as the token list)

joe : prs_sym (joe's symbol table)

joe : prs_nod (joe's parse tree)

joe : ins (instrumented version of joe)

Odin must determine how the desired object, "joe : ins : fmt", is to be created as a node of a subtree rooted at "joe : ins". Odin examines the Derivation Graph and finds that an object of type "fmt" can be derived from an object of type "f77", an object of type "scn_cmt" and an object of type "scn_tab" by using the formatting tool fragment. As "joe : ins" is not of any of these types, Odin must do some intermediate work. Odin determines that "joe : ins" is of type "ins" and that objects of type "ins" can be cast to objects of type "f77". Thus Odin determines that the scanner can in fact be applied directly to a cast of "joe : ins", to create "joe : ins : scn_tab" and "joe : ins : scn : cmt." Those objects, along with "joe : ins" (cast to type "f77"), are sufficient inputs to enable the formatter to execute and produce the final object, "joe : ins : fmt".

This process would be significantly expedited if "joe : ins" were already in the object store at the time the user requested "joe : ins : fmt". In this case, "joe : ins" would be a direct descendant of "joe", and Odin would have invoked only the scanner and formatter to build the requested object.

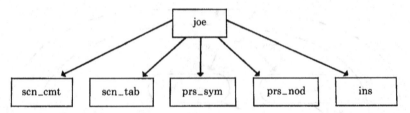

Fig. 12.4. An illustration of a typical Derivative Tree, showing derived objects of potential utility in further object derivation.

5.3 Extensibility

The Derivation Graph is the basis for the extensibility of Odin-integrated toolsets. The Derivation Graph is accessed and maintained by the Odin command interpreter and is not accessible to the various tool fragments themselves. Tool fragments have no knowledge of the sequence in which they may be called. They never directly invoke each other. Odin invokes them assuring correct flows of needed objects between tool fragments. As a result, a tool fragment can always be replaced by another, provided that the replacement produces objects of the same types and draws upon objects of the same types created by the other tool fragments in the toolset. This enables considerable flexibility in replacing tool fragments, and makes it straightforward to integrate new tool fragments. New tool fragments are characterized by their input and output object types. Input object types must all already exist, but output types may be either partially or totally new. New output types must be represented by new nodes in the Derivation Graph. Once edges connecting the input types to the output types—new and old—have been inserted into the Derivation Graph, Odin has complete knowledge of when to invoke the new tool fragment and how to optimize the creation of objects that it produces.

Tool and object type specifications can be altered by use of a simple text editor. Thus altering or extending an Odin-integrated toolset entails making alterations to the Derivation Graph through text-editing changes made to specifications written in the Specification Language, running the Derivation Graph generator, and placing the new tool fragment(s) in an appropriately public location.

In cases where new or altered tools create new types of output objects, it is also desirable that complete accessing function clusters for the new types be made available. When types are defined in this way, their implementation structures are more effectively hidden from using tools, and can therefore be modified transparently to those tools. Tool writers can treat objects of these new types as abstractions, leading to the flexibility needed in developing and migrating a prototype integrated toolset. Thus, new tool fragments that create new data types should be supplied not simply as a single executable capable of generating instances of that type, but rather in the form of a collection of executables for manipulating the instances of the type, while hiding its internal implementation. Ideally, Odin should take a positive role in enforcing the use of accessing primitives by all tools and tool fragments. Presently, this enforcement is carried out informally in the Odin-integrated toolsets that have been constructed to date.

5.4 Experiences with the Odin Specification Language

Although the Odin System has been in use for several years, both in research projects and in classroom assignments, during that time only a half dozen or so people have participated in the development of an Odin Derivation Graph. The reason for this is that, unlike other weaker system-modeling languages that require changes to the system model when the objects in the system change, an Odin Derivation Graph requires modification only when the tools change. Thus, only the tool builders become involved with the specification language.

After polling the small community of Odin tool builders, the predominant criticism is that the beginning tool builder needs more help from the Derivation Graph compiler (better error messages with hints as to how to proceed). On the positive side, once the first Derivation Graph is written, it is comparatively easy to modify. In addition, the flexibility and efficiency of the Odin interpreter provides important support for the production of a unified software environment from a disjoint set of software tools.

Our experience to date indicates that Odin is indeed a vehicle for readily extending and modifying integrated toolsets. We have succeeded in incrementally incorporating dozens of tools and tool fragments into Toolpack/IST—some of which we produced ourselves and some of which were captured from host environments. The current Toolpack/IST Derivation Graph contains over 60 user tools and tool fragments and 50 instances of Odin internal tools. New tool fragments have been incorporated into Toolpack/IST in as little as a few minutes. We have attempted to treat object types as data abstractions, but this has been largely voluntary, because many important Toolpack tools were captured from host environments and could not be altered to sharpen the boundaries between abstract data type accessing functions and functional tool capabilities. Toolpack/IST was used to maintain itself. This was a considerable job, as Toolpack/IST consists of 150,000 lines of source code, with 15 megabytes of derived data.

6. THE ODIN REQUEST LANGUAGE

The Odin Request Language is imperative and object oriented. It contains two basic commands, Display and Transfer, and a variety of utility commands. The utility commands support such capabilities as command scripts, history maintenance, and system parameter manipulation. They are described fully in [4], but are not discussed here.

6.1 The Display Command

The display command prints an Odin object to the current standard output device, normally a terminal screen, and is implicitly invoked whenever an Odin object is requested. An object is requested by naming the root of its derivative tree and then appending the names of derivative tree nodes needed to unambiguously specify a path to the requested object. The appended nodes are separated from each other and the root by a colon (:).

For example, if "joe" is a root source text object, and the user requests

    joe

Odin will print the source text object "joe". If the user requests

    joe : fmt

    joe : ins

Odin will print the objects derived from "joe" by the "fmt" tool and the "ins" tool (in Toolpack/IST these are the formatter and instrumenter, respectively). Further, the user can specify

    joe : ins : fmt

in which case Odin will print the object derived by first instrumenting "joe" and then formatting the instrumenter output. The user can specify arbitrarily many successive derivations by Odin-integrated tool fragments in this way.

Clearly, these derivatives are created only after the Odin interpreter had previously built lexical analyses and parses of the various versions of "joe". The user can also view these intermediate objects by specifying the keywords used to describe their types. For example, to see the token list produced by lexically analyzing "joe", the user specifies

    joe : scn_tab

Some very complex derivation processes are concealed behind the Odin command language. For example, if joe were an executable main program, then the user could specify

    joe : rin

The keyword "rin" is the name of a tool fragment that executes "joe", accepting input interactively from the user and displaying output interactively as well. Thus, "rin" indirectly effects the compilation, loading, and interactive execution of the program represented by the "joe" source text.

As described earlier, objects are parameterized by appending a plus sign (+) and parameters after the name of the object. Parameters can be names of atomic objects, or names of compound objects, such as a "ref" objects. Thus, supposing "sally" is a "ref" object pointing to "sam", "joe", and "bob", then sally : fmt

would specify the object pointing to the objects derived from "sam", "joe", and "bob" by the formatter, and

     sally +newtopts : ins

would specify the object pointing to the objects derived from "sam", "joe", and "bob" by the instrumenter according to the specifications in "newtopts". In this regard, it should be noted that sally is the specification of the "ref" object. Simply specifying it would not return the concatenation of the source text of "sam", "joe" and "bob", but rather the ref file itself:

     sam

     joe

     bob

To obtain the concatenated source texts for these files, the user would have to request the object created by the "cmpd" tool, an Odin unary operator defined on "ref" objects.

6.2 Basic Commands—The Transfer Command

The transfer command copies the contents of one Odin object into a second Odin object, which must be atomic. This is specified by appending to the name of the first object a right-angle-bracket ('>') and the name of the second object. For example,

     joe > tom

copies the contents of "joe" into "tom".

     joe : run : err > joe.err

puts into "joe.err" a copy of the list of errors generated in attempting to run " joe".

    Odin objects can be given as input to host-system editing tools by appending to the object a right-angle-bracket ('>') and a colon (':'), and then specifying the host system command. For example,

     joe > :vi

invokes the host system editor "vi" on the Odin object "joe".

     joe : run : err > : more

uses the "more" processor to display the errors obtained in running "joe". In case the colon and host-system command name is omitted, a default host-system editor is invoked.

7. EXPERIENCES WITH ODIN

Odin has been used in a number of tool integration projects. In this section we describe two that seem exemplary.

7.1 The Toolpack Project

As noted earlier, much of the impetus for creating Odin came from the need to create a flexible, extensible tool-integration system for the Toolpack project.

Odin was successfully used to integrate tools ranging from simple text manipulators to complex data flow analyzers. The tools integrated were produced both at the University of Colorado and elsewhere. Some were provided as source code, others only in executable form. Some had very simple structure and interaction with the rest of the toolset, while others interfaced with a variety of other tools. Some tools were highly interactive, while others were batch oriented.

Toolpack/IST is a prototype not currently supported or distributed widely. Its architecture and set of initial tool fragments have formed the basis of the Toolpack/l system, currently distributed by NAG Ltd., Oxford, England. The development paths of these two systems have diverged. In this section we describe experiences with, and inferences drawn from, Toolpack/IST.

Toolpack/IST was originally designed and implemented as an environment supporting the backend phases of development and maintenance of FORTRAN programs. It has emerged as an environment capable of supporting other languages and development phases as well. In fact, its earliest use was in integrating host-system C tools in support of its own development. As FORTRAN tools were integrated by Odin, it incrementally became an environment for supporting C and FORTRAN backend development and maintenance. Frontend tools have not been integrated, but no obstacle to doing so appears to exist.

Much of the perceived power of Odin-integrated toolsets seems to arise from its object orientation. Odin orients users of even modest collections of tools toward identifying key object types, some of which may only be produced as the result of long and complex tool applications. Users seem to readily embrace the central importance of such key types, once they have vehicles for efficiently creating and studying instances of the types. For example, source-text modules are instances of one such key type, but the objects containing all errors arising from compiling and loading collections of procedures into an executable are instances of another key type—an error report type. Once all of a program's source code is assembled into a single Odin structure, users are able to readily make and evaluate changes through a small iterative loop, entailing the creation of instances of error-report type objects (through Odin's integration of the compiler and loader) and the use of a text editor to make changes to source-text type objects. After source text edits are made, Odin determines which source code procedures to recompile, invokes the loader (only if the new compilations change any object code), and assembles all error messages from both the compiler and loader into a single error-report object to present to the user. The net effect is a feeling of being able to operate easily and efficiently on objects of just the right conceptual level.

Odin executes as a subsystem of the host operating system. Thus, running under UNIX, the user enters Odin and carries out work by invoking Odin commands.

Odin gets the user's work done by invoking functional tools, some of which may be UNIX tools. The difference between using Odin and using an ordinary UNIX system with Make is that Odin has the effect of creating a powerful conceptual layer. By staying within Odin, the user can create new objects simply by naming them as instances of key types. By virtue of their being typed, these objects have useful attributes and fit into definable places in potentially complex object structures. The other objects in these structures are automatically created as well. The consistency of these objects and structures is automatically maintained in a very efficient manner. The net effect is a feeling of being able to program efficiently in a very high-level typed language. Operating systems command languages such as the UNIX shell also attempt to support this sort of "programming in the large." Perhaps the single most salient programming capability that Odin supports, but operating systems languages fail to support (and which Make does not support either), is a satisfactory notion of object typing. Our experience with Toolpack/IST suggests that this is a very useful and powerful capability.

7.2 The Integration of the GAG Toolset

Odin was also used to integrate the GAG attribute grammar system [7], which had previously been integrated with command-language scripts. GAG takes an attribute grammar specification and an associated lexical analyzer, and produces the specified semantic analyzer. GAG was implemented as a large set of tools coordinated through operating system procedure files for management, control, inter-tool communication, and error reporting. As Odin contains facilities for supporting just these sorts of needs, the conversion to integrate GAG under Odin was not too difficult. The result was a version of GAG that ran under Odin, but that offered few execution-speed or space efficiencies. The Derivation Graph did not offer a clear model of the GAG toolset, although the user interface did seem cleaner as a consequence.

In a second phase of this experiment we scrutinized the GAG system structure to detect ways in which Odin's philosophy and approaches might be applied to integrating GAG more efficiently without changing the existing GAG tool fragments.

The three basic approaches to improving efficiency via Odin object management are abstraction, partitioning, and parameterization. Abstraction (producing intermediate abstractions of source objects) and partitioning (splitting source objects into disjoint pieces) require extensive modification to the internal structure of a tool system, and thus were not appropriate to the GAG experiment. The third approach, parameterization, requires identifying which system parameters affect which tool fragments. Frequently, there are intermediate objects that are not affected by the specified parameters, and therefore can be reused in several different parameterized queries.

In the GAG system, flags and options are used to modify tool behavior. Odin allows each flag or option to be a distinct parameter type, and each tool to specify which parameters are of interest. In the original GAG system, all options to all tools were stored in a single file. This file was preprocessed to produce a "control file," which was then passed to each succeeding tool fragment, which extracted option values of interest. Splitting the single control file into a set of individual parameters allows Odin to determine which derivatives are affected by a parameter change. Since many GAG options only affect later tool fragments, the specification of each option as a separate parameter type in the derivation graph provided significant increases in reuse of objects. For example, if a user makes several requests that differ only in the options passed to the cross-reference tool, the Odin system reuses all analyses and simply reruns the cross-reference tool with the differing parameters. This parameterization provided the most significant benefits that were observed.

This experience with GAG helped to strengthen our opinion that it is useful and natural for software objects to be labeled by the activities that created them. Clearly, this labeling should include a specification of the tools that created them, but it should also reflect any adaptations made to these tool functions.

The effects of the optimization described above varied considerably—in some cases little speed improvement was noticed, but in other cases speedups of a factor of ten were measured. Savings of storage space are far harder to evaluate. Odin automatically rederives requested objects and automatically purges objects when it has no more cache storage. Thus the size of Odin's storage area can be specified by the user. Less storage obliges more recomputation and longer running times. Thus there can be no absolute claim for reduction in the amount of storage needed. Certainly, any amount of storage sufficient to support an Odin-integrated GAG procedure can also be made sufficient to support execution of the same GAG procedure not using Odin. This, on the other hand, would generally require lengthy, painstaking, and error-prone alteration of the GAG procedure file. Odin's ability to automatically support effective tool execution in varying amounts of space is probably its greatest contribution to storage efficiency. This enables users to make time versus space trade-off decisions and have them effectively supported by Odin.

7.3 Evaluations

These experiments have helped us evaluate various principles for integrating software tools into effective environments. Most directly, the Odin project was a vehicle for studying the use of an object-management system to integrate tools. Within that context, we chose to integrate smaller tool fragments, but to manage relatively large-grained objects. We chose to manage objects by organizing them using two relations-hierarchy and derivation. We chose to optimize for tool flexibility and extensibility by materializing the underlying structure of object types and tool fragments, making this structure essentially an object itself. In the following subsections we evaluate each of these architectural choices.

7.3.1 Object Orientation.

Our experiences have shown that centering an environment around an object store is a very effective way to integrate an environment. In Toolpack/IST it made the functional capabilities of a wide variety of tools more easily and economically accessible to users. We found a number of situations where it was natural and easy to name a desired object that could only be constructed by a complex chain of tool applications. In GAG, we found that identifying the underlying objects to be managed led to more efficiency in applying tools. At the very least, this work has indicated that other systems that make tools the center of attention err in not giving at least equal attention to the objects managed by those tools.

7.3.2 Tool Granularity.

In studying the object structure of environments, we realized that most tools manipulate a surprising variety of data objects. Considering the lifecycle of these objects led to a better understanding of the internal structure of many common tools and the idea that tools should be viewed as aggregates of tool fragments. In retrospect, this simply asserts that tools should be synthesized from commonly used modules. There should be no need to further justify this architectural decision.

7.3.3 Object Granularity.

Odin manages objects that may be either large or small. This paper describes our experiments using Odin to manage large objects. We experimented briefly with Odin as a manager of integers using tool fragments that were simply arithmetic operators. The result was an amusing, though inefficient, computational system which did, however, underscore the high overhead costs that Odin incurs in order to manage objects. Thus, it seems most effective to use Odin to manage larger data objects that may be aggregates of smaller objects. Thus, for example, Toolpack/IST manages entire lexical strings rather than tokens, and entire symbol tables rather than individual symbols. This enables users to access the large-grained objects easily, but requires special-purpose tools to access the smaller objects. These tools present a nonuniform appearance to users and hide the relations among the smaller-grained objects. We believe that an object-management system to efficiently and effectively manage a broad spectrum of sizes of objects is needed. Odin is capable of doing this, but in its current implementation is unacceptably inefficient.

7.3.4 Organization of the Object Score.

We developed an organizational structure for objects that was adequate to represent the relations we encountered among our objects, but not so complex as to pose serious efficiency problems. We rejected the idea of using a full relational database to manage our software objects, because the relational model is ill-suited to represent needed relations such as hierarchy. Further, we feared that this would invite modeling more relations than necessary, and would require excessive effort in propagating the effects of changes in objects.

Instead, we chose to use only hierarchy and derivation to organize the objects in our store. These two relations effectively supported the integration of the toolsets described in this paper. We believe that both are essential organizing agents in any environment object store. Hierarchy enables us to effectively manipulate and reason about complex software objects. Derivation is essential in keeping track of which objects can and cannot be spooled and purged, and which must be altered or updated in response to changes in others. We believe that these two relations are a minimal subset of those needed in an environment object store. Others may be useful, especially in managing a store of objects of diverse sizes.

7.3.5 Flexibility and Extensibility.

The Odin architecture effectively supports the need to alter and extend the functionality of an environment. The key to doing this is the isolation in a single structure—the Derivation Graph—of all information about how objects of various types are created from each other by tools. Tool fragments have no knowledge of how they relate to each other, thereby avoiding the need to modify existing tools, to add new tools, or alter other existing tools.

The Odin Derivation Graph is best considered to be an object—namely, the object used to schedule the coordination of tool interaction and to modify an environment's tool and type structure. Odin facilitates these processes by providing a language with which to describe the Derivation Graph and tools to support its compilation, viewing, and alteration.

Our experiences with Odin strongly indicate the importance of materializing the type and tool interaction structure of an environment as an object.

8. FUTURE RESEARCH DIRECTIONS

We believe that the basic ideas underlying Odin are a sound basis for the integration of software environments. Having completed this work, however, we see ways in which these basic ideas can and should be extended.

8.1 Varying Grain Sizes

We believe that an environment must effectively manage objects whose sizes range from very large to very small. The problem of efficient management of the very large collection of very diverse objects in a software project is one which has not yet been effectively addressed. Further, the problem of developing a uniform interface that effectively furnishes access to these objects needs to be better addressed.

8.2 User Interface

This project has sharpened our appreciation of the problems of providing users suitable access to the resources managed by an environment. Our primary focus was on managing large-grained objects. We provided a clean and uniform command language to access these objects. We found, however, that most users spent most of their time dealing with the smaller objects contained in the larger objects. Access to these smaller objects was provided through viewer tools created for each of the various object types. These viewers were custom built and not standardized. As a result, users were confronted with a nonuniform interface to the smaller objects, with which they spent most of their time.

Clearly, viewer tools must be treated in the same way as other tools in a well-designed environment. They must be composed of smaller, modular tool fragments. We must identify a set of modular viewing tool fragments and demonstrate that they can be effectively composed into special-purpose viewers for the requisite wide range of environment objects.

In addition, it is clear that viewers must assist users in understanding the environment command-execution process itself. The help facilities provided by Odin are a primitive start in helping users understand what Odin does and how it works. Structures such as the Derivative Forest and the Derivation Graph are as central to the user's understanding of the software objects being created and managed as they are to Odin's ability to manage them effectively. A key part of an environment's user interface must be a facility for depicting the object store and showing users how it is being changed by command executions.

Acknowledgments The work described here has been strongly influenced by Stuart I. Feldman, formerly of Bell Telephone Laboratories, now of Bell Communications Research. Feldman's Make processor served as an important starting point for our own work. Numerous conversations with Feldman served to sharpen our insights and to mold this work. In addition, our research colleagues at the University of Colorado, Boulder, were a constant source of challenging and important feedback and comment.

REFERENCES

1. Boehm, B. W., and Standish, T. Software technology in the 1990s: Using an evolutionary paradigm. *Computer 26*, 11 (Nov. 1983).
2. Buxton, J. N., and Stenning, V. Requirements for Ada programming support environments. Stoneman, DOD, Feb. 1980.
3. Clemm, G. M. Odin-An extensible software environment. Univ. of Colorado, Dept. of Computer Science Tech. Rep. CU-CS-262-84, 1984.
4. Clemm, G. M. The Odin system-An object manager for extensible software environments. Ph.D. dissertation, Dept. of Computer Science, Univ. of Colorado at Boulder, CU-CS-314-86, 1986.
5. Deremer, F., and Kron, H. Programming-in-the-large versus programming-in-the-small. *IEEE Trans. Softw. Eng.* SE-2, 2 (June 1976), 80-86.
6. Feldman, S. I. Make—A program for maintaining computer programs. *Softw. Pract. Exper.* 9 (1979), 255-265.
7. Kastens, U., Hutt, B., and Zimmerman, E. *GAG: A Practical Compiler Generator.* Springer Verlag, New York, 1982.
8. Kernighan, B. W., and Ritchie, D. M. *The C Programming Language.* Prentice Hall, Englewood Cliffs, N.J., 1978.
9. Lampson, B., and Schmidt, E. Practical use of a polymorphic applicative language. *In Proceedings of the 10th POPL Conference*, 1983.
10. Lapson, B., and Schmidt, E. Organizing software in a distributed environment. *SIGPLAN Not. 18* (June 1983).
11. Leblang, D. B., and Chase, R. P. Computer aided software engineering in a distributed workstation environment. In SIGPLAN/*SIGSOFT Symposium on Practical Software Development Environments* (Pittsburgh, Pa., April 1984). ACM, New York, 1984.
12. Leblang, D. B., and McLean, G. D. Configuration management for large scale software development efforts. In *Proceedings of the Workshop on Software Engineering for Programming-in-the-Large* (Harwichport, Mass., June 1985).
13. Leblang, D. B., Chase, R. P., and McLean, G. D. The DOMAIN software engineering environment for large scale software development efforts. In *Proceedings of the IEEE Conference on Workstations* (San Jose, Calif., Nov. 1985). IEEE, New York, 1985.
14. Olender, K., and Osterweil, L. J. Specification and static evaluation of sequencing constraints in software. In *Workshop on Software Testing* (Banff, Canada, July 1986), pp. 14-22, and Univ. of Colorado Dept. of Computer Science Tech. Rep. CU-CS-334-86.
15. Osterweil, L.J. Software environment research directions for the next five years. *Computer 14* (April 1981), 35-43.
16. Osterweil, L.J. Toolpack-An experimental software development environment research project. *IEEE Trans. Softw. Eng.* SE-9 (Nov. 1983), 673-685. (Reprinted as Chapter 11)
17. Riddle, W.E. The evolutionary approach to building the Joseph software development environment. In *Proc. IEEE Softfair-Softw. Devel. Tools, Techniques, and Alternatives,* 1983.
18. Schmidt, E.E. Controlling large software development in a distributed environment. Ph.D. dissertation, Computer Science Div., EECS Dept., Univ. of California, Berkeley, 1982.

Foundations for the Arcadia Environment Architecture

Richard N. Taylor, Frank C. Belz, Lori A. Clarke, Leon Osterweil, Richard W. Selby, Jack C. Wileden, Alexander L. Wolf, and Michal Young

Richard N. Taylor, Richard W. Selby, and Michal Young are at Department of Information and Computer Science, University of California, Irvine[1]

Lori A. Clarke and Jack C. Wileden are at Department of Computer and Information Science, University of Massachusetts, Amherst[2]

Leon J. Osterweil is at Department of Computer Science, University of Colorado, Boulder[3]

Frank C. Belz is at TRW, Redondo Beach, California[4]

Alexander L. Wolf is at AT&T Bell Laboratories, 600 Mountain Avenue, Murray Hill, NJ

Abstract Early software environments have supported a narrow range of activities (*programming* environments) or else been restricted to a single "hard-wired" software development process. The Arcadia research project is investigating the construction of software environments that are tightly integrated, yet flexible and extensible enough to support experimentation with alternative software processes and tools. This has led us to view an environment as being composed of two distinct, cooperating parts. One is the *variant* part, consisting of process programs

[1] This work was supported in part by the National Science Foundation under grant CCR-8704311, with cooperation from the Defense Advanced Research Projects Agency (ARPA Order 6108, Program Code 7T10), by the National Science Foundation under grants CCR-8451421 and CCR-8521398, Hughes Aircraft (PYI program), and TRW (PYI program).

[2] This work was supported in part by the National Science Foundation under grant CCR-87-04478, with cooperation from the Defense Advanced Research Projects Agency (ARPA Order 6104), and by the National Science Foundation under grants DCR-8404217 and DCR-8408143.

[3] This work was supported in part by the National Science Foundation under grant CCR-8705162, with cooperation from the Defense Advanced Research Projects Agency (ARPA Order 6100, Program Code 7E20), by the National Science Foundation under grant DCR-0403341, and by the U.S. Department of Energy under grant DEFG02-84ER13283.

[4] This work was sponsored in part by TRW and by the Defense Advanced Research Projects Agency/Information Systems Technology Office, ARPA Order 9152, issued by the Space and Naval Warfare Systems Command under contract N00039-88-C-0047.

and the tools and objects used and defined by those programs. The other is the fixed part, or *infrastructure*, supporting creation, execution, and change to the constituents of the variant part. The major components of the infrastructure are a process programming language and interpreter, object management system, and user interface management system. Process programming facilitates precise definition and automated support of software development and maintenance activities. The object management system provides typing, relationships, persistence, distribution and concurrency control capabilities. The user interface management system mediates communication between human users and executing processes, providing pleasant and uniform access to all facilities of the environment. Research in each of these areas and the interaction among them is described.

1. Introduction

The purpose of a software environment is to support users in their software development and maintenance activities. Past attempts to do this have indicated the vast scope and complexity of this problem. The Arcadia project is a consortium research effort aimed at addressing an unusually broad range of software environment issues. In particular, the Arcadia project is concerned with simultaneously investigating and developing prototype demonstrations of:

- environment architectures for organizing large collections of tools and facilitating their interactions with users as well as with each other,
- tools to facilitate the testing and analysis of concurrent and sequential software, and
- frameworks for environment and tool evaluation.

This paper describes the research rationale and approach being taken by Arcadia researchers in investigating environment architecture issues. Although details concerning the tool suite and the evaluation framework are outside the scope of this paper, attempting to assemble these components into a coherent environment will provide a non-trivial test case for experimentally evaluating this architecture.

The remainder of this section presents a high-level overview of our proposed environment architecture. The major components of the architecture are described. Each of these represents a major research subarea being investigated as part of this project. The ensuing sections describe the major goals and rationale for each of these subareas. Although each subarea is an interesting research project in its own right, the most challenging questions are often raised by the interactions among subareas. Indeed, it is the importance and complexity of these interactions that requires research in the subareas be pursued cooperatively. One of the novel features of the Arcadia project is that it is synergistically exploring many of these issues.

1.1 Arcadia Environment Architecture Goals

Osterweil observed [40] that a software environment must be broad in scope, highly flexible and extensible, and very well integrated. Subsequent research has underscored how essential those characteristics are in a software environment, but has also indicated that there are some fundamental tensions among them. Most strikingly, it seems that a well-integrated environment is easiest to achieve if the environment is limited in scope and static in its content and organization. Conversely, broad and dynamic environments are typically loosely coupled and poorly integrated. Unfortunately, poorly integrated environments impose excessive burdens upon users, and small static environments are quickly outgrown. Thus, it is necessary to conduct research on environment flexibility/extensibility techniques, on environment integration techniques, and on understanding the tensions between these two often-conflicting goals. This is precisely the intent of the Arcadia research project, which is developing a prototype environment architecture directed toward maximizing both flexibility/extensibility and integration and toward understanding the tradeoffs between them.

The requirement that an environment be flexible and extensible springs from a variety of sources. First, users are different and perceive their needs differently. In addition, projects are different and have different support requirements. Further, as projects progress, their needs change and workers' perceptions of these needs also change. These factors all dictate that environments must be flexible enough to change the nature of their support for users as painlessly as possible. In addition, as new tools and technologies appear, a software environment must readily incorporate them. Otherwise the environment will become increasingly inefficient and obsolescent.

Arcadia research on environment flexibility/extensibility focuses on supporting the notion of process programming [39,41]. The basic idea is that process programs, written in a process programming language (PPL), will describe the diverse software processes that users want to employ in developing and maintaining software. The tools available to support software activities will be operators or functions in this language and the operands will be the various objects created by tools or users. Because of the complexity of software processes, a PPL will need to have at least the power of a general-purpose programming language, extended to satisfy the requirements of process programming.

With this environment model, flexibility is obtained by supporting alterations to process programs. Extensibility is achieved by writing new process programs or by modifying existing process programs to incorporate new tools, subprocesses, types or objects. For example, a new tool is incorporated into the environment by writing a new process program, or modifying an existing process program, that explicitly indicates the way this tool will interact with other tools in the environment and the types of objects this tool will use and create.

To assure that the flexibility/extensibility gained through process programming does not come at the expense of integration, Arcadia researchers are also investigating integration techniques. The requirement for tight integration has a variety of manifestations. Users should interact with the environment in a uniform way, instead of accommodating themselves to each tool's idiosyncratic interface. In addition, environment tools should share information among themselves, assuring that users are not pestered to supply the same information multiple times nor needlessly paying for recomputation of available information. Environment components should be shared whenever possible as well, to keep the size of the environment down and to prevent performance penalties due to excessive paging and thrashing. Integration issues such as these seem to divide neatly into internal and external integration issues.

In the Arcadia project, internal integration research focuses on the investigation of environment object management issues. In recent years it has become increasingly clear that environments require powerful object management mechanisms. The earliest software environments were little more than intelligent editors [28], whose object management needs were modest, in keeping with their modest functionality and scope. As environment power and scope have grown, however, effective object management has become a daunting task. Object managers must be capable of effectively storing and retrieving software objects for a broad spectrum of tools. Software objects may be internal data structures, such as parse trees, symbol tables, and abstract syntax graphs, or external products, such as source code, test plans, and designs. Software objects may vary in size from a single byte to millions of bytes, may persist in the object store for seconds or years, may be manipulated by transactions that are brief or last for months, and may be self contained or intricately interrelated to other objects. Further, if the environment is to be flexible and extensible, the object manager must be capable of reacting effectively to a wide variety of changes.

External integration research in the Arcadia project focuses on investigation of user interface management issues. The user's interactions with all of the tools and facilities of an environment must be as uniform and comfortable as possible. Because software tools are so varied, environments must support the effective use of a gamut of user interface technologies, ranging from simple textual interfaces to direct manipulation of complex graphical displays. Moreover, independent evolution of both the tool base and user interface technology must be accommodated. In addition, environments must support multiple users acting in various roles. An environment user interface management system must also be able to project multiple views of a software object and to maintain consistency among these views.

Several other research projects are exploring approaches for providing strong integration mechanisms, external or internal, or powerful flexibility and extensibility mechanisms. For the most part these issues are being investigated in isolation, and the results often appear to be inconsistent with each other. For example, there are object management systems (e.g., most classical databases) that seem to offer acceptable support for modest, relatively inflexible environments, but their support is inadequate for more complex, flexible, and extensible environments [4]. Similarly, some excellent user interfaces have been developed, but often these are closely tailored to fixed tool configurations. Environments that are more flexible seem to undermine the power of such user interfaces.

Arcadia researchers are simultaneously investigating environment integration and environment flexibility/extensibility to study the tensions and interactions between them. To experimentally evaluate our approach, we are developing a prototype environment. The architecture of this environment is designed to foster research in each of the major subareas and accelerate understanding of the interplay among them. The Arcadia project will yield research insights in each of the major subareas as well as an environment prototype that effectively synthesizes and demonstrates these research findings.

1.2 Architecture Overview

The high-level architecture of the Arcadia prototype environment, called Arcadia-1, is depicted in Fig. 13.1. The Process Program Interpreter (PPI) component is responsible for carrying out the instructions of the process programs. This component communicates with users through the User Interface Management System (UIMS) and accesses software objects via the Object Manager. All three of these components must interact with an underlying virtual machine for basic operating system support. In our early work we are assuming this machine to be the Berkeley UNIX[5] version 4.3 operating system running on a network of Sun workstations.

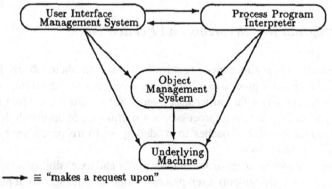

⟶ ≡ "makes a request upon"

Fig. 13.1. Invariant Components of the Arcadia-1 Environment.

The architecture is designed so that the capabilities of each important subarea can be defined separately, through carefully specified interfaces that provide the appropriate functionality while hiding implementation details. This separation of

---

[5] UNIX is a registered trademark of AT&T

concerns, captured by the system modularity, facilitates orderly evolution based on continuing research activity in each subarea. Clearly each key component must still interact with other key architectural components in supporting the overall architecture. For example, research into using process programming to achieve flexibility and extensibility is constrained by and coordinated with parallel research into using object managers and user interface management systems to achieve tight internal and external integration.

Fig. 13.1 depicts the infrastructure, or *fixed* part, of an environment and thus does not show any of the process programs, tools, and software objects that populate an environment. It is anticipated that these components will change frequently, so they are referred to as the *variant* part of the architecture. The Arcadia architecture encourages change to the variant part, and discourages change to the fixed part. Of course, there are bound to be circumstances under which the fixed part will require change as well, but presumably such changes should occur infrequently.

One of the contributions of the Arcadia project is the recognition of the need to separate the fixed and variant parts of an architecture. We intend to experimentally explore where the boundary between these two parts lies and the ramifications of this distinction.

2. Software Process Programs

2.1 Process Program Requirements and Related Work

Software development and maintenance organizations carry out their jobs by following carefully thought out processes. Difficulties arise because specifying and modifying these processes is a far harder task than expected and is therefore not done effectively. Modelling software processes is a useful way to approach these difficulties, and a number of approaches to modelling software processes have been proposed [47,73,20,57,6,44].

As the previous discussion on environment flexibility and extensibility reveals, environments must not only support user processes but they must also support change to those processes. Different users employ different processes. At different times a user may wish to change processes, perhaps because a better way of doing work suggests itself, because the overall project process has changed, or because the user may wish to begin using a new tool. In all of these cases, the needed changes seem to be accurately viewed as changes to the model describing the user's process. In effect we are suggesting that environment flexibility and extensibility are to be achieved by carrying out maintenance changes to process programs.

Process programming differs from earlier work in that it hypothesizes the need for a full programming language. At a minimum, process programming languages need to provide powerful typing mechanisms and a variety of powerful flow of control mechanisms such as concurrency, exception handling, and complex looping constructs. An important part of our research involves determining the necessary characteristics of such languages and defining at least one such language and developing an interpreter for it.

A process program indicates how the various software tools and objects would be coordinated to support a process. It would also be used to indicate to a process program interpreter which operators are to be carried out by humans, rather than tools or hardware. These operations would appear as subprocesses, which would not be further elaborated, but would be bound to human execution agents. The Arcadia research project is providing a framework for investigation of this premise.

Operating system control languages have attempted to support the specification of software processes, and we believe that these are primitive antecedents of process programming. In this context, system utilities are process programming language operators and the files managed by the operating system's file system are their operands. Command files or scripts are primitive process programs, using the operating system command language as a process programming language. These languages, however, do not usually enable users to assign types to data objects, specify complex control sequences, access operands smaller than files, or invoke operators smaller than executable programs and tools.

The lack of a rich type system in these languages is a serious deficiency. Key software objects, such as parse trees, requirements specifications, testcases, and bug reports, should be viewed as instances of types. These types seem readily definable using typing mechanisms in modern programming languages. Object typing is a powerful vehicle for organizing the objects managed in a software project, and for defining and organizing the operators—both human and machine executable—to be employed by the project.[6] Object typing is discussed further in Section 3.

Another deficiency is the lack of sufficiently powerful flow of control capabilities. Many operating system command languages incorporate some flow of control operators, but these are usually quite primitive, often consisting only of basic looping and alternation constructs (*csh* is an exception here). These restrictions are unacceptably constraining in trying to program real software processes, as some early work has shown. Perhaps the most notable of this early work was the diagrammatic software lifecycle modelling, such as the "Waterfall Model" [53]. In this work, principal software processes were represented by boxes, and the only flow of control that was shown was that which could be represented using arrows.

---

[6] In either case, the semantics of operations can be formally defined using, for example, pre- and post- conditions.

These models were attacked as being incomplete and naive. Their weak flow of control capabilities made it impossible, for example, to depict concurrent activities, which are essential to any real, large-scale software activity.

Another deficiency in operating system command languages is their inability to show relations such as data flow and process hierarchy. Software process models have attempted to represent key relations among a variety of types of software objects. For these models notations have been developed in which, for example, data objects are differentiated from process objects by using different shaped boxes. Different relations are usually indicated by differently shaped lines and arrowheads and by different colors. Some examples of advanced techniques and notations for diagrammatic representations of processes are ETVX boxes [48], SADT diagrams [51] and Software Development Graphs [5]. These notations and representations are limited because there are so many valid relations among the software objects in a real software project, and different users may at different times wish to study various combinations of them. Creating a single diagram showing all of these relations is hardly a solution, as such a diagram is so complicated as to confound all understanding. Creating a single internal representation capturing all the relations among the objects and subprocesses of a software process, and then using tools to draw specific diagrams ("views") upon request, is a more promising approach. The PMDB project moved in this direction by proposing a model of the life-cycle process [44] in terms of its objects and relationship types and by performing a prototyping exercise exploring views based on user roles [43]. It did not, however, model explicitly the activities that produce such objects and relationships.

Some earlier software environments can be viewed as providing process programming support for limited software development activities. For instance, systems such as *PAISLey* [76], *RSL/REVS* [3], *SARA* [21], Data Flow Diagram Designs [70], Jackson System Development [12], and *USE* [71], support the creation of certain fixed types of specifications and designs. Code development is supported by programming environments, such as *Interlisp* [65], *Arcturus* [58], and *Cedar* [64], which incorporate tools for editing, parsing, debugging, and documentation. Similarly, intelligent editors such as the *Cornell Program Synthesizer* [63], *Integral-C* [52], *Gandalf* [24], and *Mentor* [19] effectively integrate user activities around a parsed representation of code. As long as the user's activities fall within the domain of these environments, they provide strong support. If the user seeks to model software products and processes outside this domain, support from these environments falters.

Support for limited, pre-determined processes has taught us a great deal about those processes but has also demonstrated how quickly users want to stray beyond those boundaries. Products and processes must be expected to vary from user to user, from location to location, and from time to time. Thus no fixed predetermined process will be adequate for a wide range of software activities, or even for a single software activity over a period of time. Thus it seems imperative that the full power of a general purpose programming language be available to users attempting to express the full range of processes to be supported.

We believe that progress towards understanding what constitutes adequate products and effective processes can only follow from experimentation with alternatives. The best way to facilitate such experimentation seems to be to enable users to describe software products and processes in ways that are convenient and effective and to support the rapid interpretation of processes in terms of software tools and procedures. This seems tantamount to creating environments in which the product specifications, process descriptions, and set of operators is specifiable by the user, and in which the environment exploits this specification to fashion its support.

2.2 Arcadia Process Programming Research

Arcadia research in this area involves two interrelated activities, process research and process programming research. The first has as its goal to gain a better understanding of the process of developing software, and the second to develop means of representing the process in terms of a process programming language and its execution support.

We are starting to understand the requirements for a process programming language. Unfortunately, the specification of such a language depends upon the accumulation of experience in writing process programs. Thus there is a "research deadlock" between the need for a process programming language and the need to write process programs. We are breaking this deadlock through some prototyping projects. These projects are aimed at studying specific language features that seem important to process programming by adding those features to existing general purpose languages and then using these enhanced languages to write process programs. These process programs then serve as vehicles for studying the suitability of the new features. By proceeding in this way we avoid the cost of creating a language from scratch while enabling the evaluation of the new feature.

One such prototyping activity involves a language called *Appl/A* [27], and the writing of process programs making use of *Appl/A*. *Appl/A* is a superset of Ada that enables the definition of relations among software objects. Ada was chosen as the base language for *Appl/A* because it seems to be sufficiently powerful to support many sorts of capabilities needed in process programming and also because it is the language targeted for support by the early versions of Arcadia. Thus we hope that Arcadia may be useful at an early date in providing support for the maintenance of some of its own critical modules. We chose to enhance Ada with a relation capability because we believe that contemporary languages have failed to provide appropriate mechanisms to represent explicitly interconnections among complex objects, a capability that seems to underlie most realistic software processes.

In *Appl/A* we are experimenting with a relation management capability in an attempt to see just what features that capability should offer. *Appl/A* supports the definition of relations as sets of arbitrary tuples of software objects. It enables users to specify just how the various components of these tuples should be related to each other, and how the consistency of these components can be verified and maintained. As such, we believe that *Appl/A* provides a very basic capability that is needed in any process programming language.

The primary vehicle for studying process programming and for the evaluation of process programming language features, such as those supported by *Appl/A*, has been the development of realistic process programs. In one such experiment we are using process programming to describe process models such as Boehm's spiral model [6,7]. In another experiment, the PMDB+ project, we are extending the PMDB model to include process descriptions emphasizing selected aspects of the life-cycle process, such as change control, configuration management and project management and control. In this project, we will focus on typing issues, mechanisms in support of change, and architectural interface concerns.

In the Bopeep (But One Prototype End-to-End Process) project we are developing process programs covering key software development and maintenance phases such as requirements specification, design, testing, and maintenance. For example, in this project we have written a series of requirements specification process programs that treat requirement development as an activity aimed at creating a directed graph of requirements elements, where each element is viewed as essentially a template. The fields of the template specify such types of requirements as functionality, robustness, efficiency, and accuracy. It is the job of the requirements analyst to specify which elements contain which fields and then to put values into the appropriate fields. The requirements analyst must also indicate any relationships among the various requirements elements and between requirements elements and other software objects.

For the design phase, we are writing process programs that attempt to codify such design methodologies as Object Oriented Design [8] and Parnas' Rational Design Methodology [42]. Not surprisingly, we are finding that many of the structures and mechanisms used in developing the requirements processes are also helpful in developing the design process programs.

Our experimentation is leading to the creation of a library of prototype process programs that are helping us understand these processes. It also helps us to evaluate the features incorporated into *Appl/A* as well as understand what other process programming language features are needed. Although *Appl/A* has proven to be quite useful, our experiments have indicated that there are important process programming features that are not supplied by *Appl/A*, nor indeed by any language built atop Ada. One obvious feature is a type hierarchy. While different nodes of a requirement element may be of different types, it is clear that they must all share some common features (e.g., author, date, parent, and children attributes), and that they are probably beneficially modelled as being subtypes of a common parent type.

It is also clear that certain types of dynamism are important. For example, often it is useful to be able to design a new requirements element "on the fly," as the need for a somewhat different requirements element description becomes apparent. To do this, a new element type must be created dynamically, then instantiated, and then filled with attribute values. In fact, the way in which a new type is filled with values might also be expected to vary with the type, indicating that subprocesses should also be dynamically defined and instantiated. Test planning provides another example of the need for dynamism. During test planning, the test plan is created as a software object. This may entail such subactivities as development of test cases, encoding of algorithmic strategies for the systematic execution of the test cases, and development of procedures for capturing test results. Much later in the development process, after code has been developed, this test plan object must be executed. This entails treating the test plan object as a process, rather than as an operand. We believe that such dynamic capabilities are important to a wide range of software processes. The passive/active nature of some software processes points to the desirability of a language in which code and data can be freely interchanged. (Lisp is an example of a language having this property.) Thus we are investigating how this property might be blended with other desirable process programming language features.

It should also be noted that this work is leading to the impression that a strictly imperative, algorithmic language is not likely to be suitable as a process programming language. Although many aspects of many kinds of software process seem to be inherently procedural and algorithmic, there are other software activities that seem best described with a declarative or rule based paradigm. The processing that systems such as Make [22] and Odin [17] carry out is guided by rules that specify how software objects should be kept consistent with each other. In our prototyping we have found a number of applications for this sort of capability. We have found, for example, that it is far easier to specify that certain attributes of certain requirements elements must satisfy a certain logical relation to each other and that there are certain well-defined activities (such as the invocation of a tool) that need to be carried out to restore needed consistency. These sorts of specifications are far easier to make than imbedding active code to restore needed consistency in a variety of places distributed throughout the algorithmic part of process programs.

On a more ambitious level, we believe that design creation processes might also be easier to code if it were possible to specify certain parts of the process by means of rules. In design creation the goal is to create a design specification. Often (e.g., in the case of the Software Cost Reduction methodology [42]), it is quite possible to specify the goal object—namely a complex structure of carefully prescribed design elements—but it is not clear how to give complete procedural details on how to construct it. In such cases it is often reasonable to create rules that guide and constrain activities, such as the selection of good candidates for design elaboration, or that can intelligently raise issues about apparent inconsistencies among design elements. Thus some aspects of design seem to be rule-based. Other

aspects, such as the orderly elaboration of details of design elements and their correlation with each other, are more procedural. This suggests that a process programming language might ideally be a language that combines procedural and
rule-based paradigms. *Appl/A* takes a cautious step in that direction by enabling
the specification of certain fields of relations—e.g., consistency conditions among
software objects—as rules. This ability to mix procedural coding with rule coding
has proven useful.

The process programs we have built to date have been pieces of software of
significant size and complexity. The code for these processes has spanned dozens
of pages, and in many cases, lowest level details have still not been specified.
Thus these process programs still leave a great deal of initiative and creativity to
humans. We expect that lower levels of detail will be inserted over time, thereby
making the process programs more complete and more highly dependent upon
tools. It is interesting to note that, although our original intent was to simply produce code, we found that it was necessary to develop requirements specifications
and designs first. In retrospect, this is totally appropriate as process programs are
complex software, and we have been trained to approach the development of
complex software by starting with the creation of precode artifacts. In particular
the design has proven to be more useful in understanding the nature of the
processes we have written than the code itself.

We expect that firm understandings of the requirements for a process programming language and of the key software development and maintenance
processes will continue to develop in parallel over a period of years.

3. Object Management

3.1 Object Management Requirements and Related Work

An environment user's primary objective is to create and/or maintain a *software
product*. No matter what process program might be used in creating and maintaining it, a software product typically will be a very complex and highly interrelated
collection of objects. Those objects will be of widely different kinds, ranging from
source code and executable modules to documentation and test plans. Each kind of
object will have an associated set of applicable operations, but operations applicable to one kind of object will generally not be appropriate for use with other kinds.
This suggests that an environment's infrastructure should provide support for
managing typed objects and a rich set of relationships among them.

Most environment builders have had to rely on a traditional file or database
system for managing the objects associated with their environment. It is now

widely believed, however, that a much richer set of capabilities for controlling object creation, access, and organization is essential to a software environment. In particular, a suitably powerful object management system will enhance the environment's support for change, integration, software reuse, and cooperative work by multiple developers.

As Fig. 13.1 indicates, the object management system will be a major component of the Arcadia environment infrastructure. It will be responsible for managing two distinct categories of objects: the *components* of the software products being produced by users of the environment, and the *tools and information structures* that constitute the environment itself. From the process programming perspective, the former can be viewed as the (input and output) data manipulated by a process program while the latter are the operators and internal data structures of the process program.

Thus, the object management system will provide the underlying mechanism upon which the data management capabilities of a process programming language can be implemented by its interpreter. A particular process programming language might present its users exactly the same object management capabilities that the environment's object management system provides, as an assembly language presents its users exactly the same data types provided by the underlying machine. It seems likely, however, that a process programming language might offer a different view of objects than that provided by the environment's object manager. In either case, the properties of the object management system will influence the data management aspects of an environment's process programming languages.

Work on environments during the last decade has elucidated some of the important requirements for an object management system. In particular it seems clear that an object management system for a software environment should provide support for:

- types,
- relationships,
- persistence, and
- concurrency and distribution.

Each requirement poses interesting problems. The capabilities sought for each of these areas and the problems we foresee are discussed below.

Type systems. We view a type system as the primary mechanism for describing and maintaining objects. The object manager should be able to enforce the type system, hiding the internal structure of typed objects behind well-defined interfaces and strictly controlling the operations that can be performed on those objects. If all objects are instances of abstract data types, it is easier to share objects or to change their implementations. Thus, basing the object management system on a typing system that fully supports data abstraction will contribute to environment flexibility and software reuse.

Current approaches to object management in environments fall far short of providing full support for typed objects. Typically, the components of a product are treated simply as files and tools are viewed as operators applicable to the contents of those files. Usually in such systems, only a predetermined and limited number of different kinds of components (e.g., source file, object file) and operations (e.g., compiler, linker) are available. *Make* and to an even greater extent *Odin* [17] improved on this simple view by using file name extensions as a weak form of typing mechanism for files. It also allowed users to define which tools could operate on or produce files of various types. The *System Modeller*, developed as part of the *Cedar* system [32] used the term "object" for referring to the files containing product components, but did not treat the objects as instances of abstract data types. The Common APSE Interface Set (CAIS) [10] defines a system model with three kinds of nodes-file, structural, and process but does not treat those nodes as typed objects. Recent revisions to the CAIS model [11] add a rich form of typing that specifically addresses the issue of tool evolution and environment interoperability. *Gandalf*'s SVCE mechanism [25] employs strong type checking to determine consistency of syntactic units during version control. While clearly improving on the simple use of files, all of these systems provide only partial support for typed objects. Meanwhile, work on support for typed objects within the traditional database community [61,13,77], while encouraging, is still in its primitive stages and far from providing the flexibility and power needed for object management in a software environment [4]. Recent work on rich type systems, particularly in the context of object-oriented languages, is also encouraging, but also still in its infancy. No consensus has yet emerged on a desirable and appropriate set of features for such a type system.

Thus, the kind of type system needed to describe the objects populating a software environment is one of the major object management research issues. The type system needs to be flexible and powerful enough to capture the relevant properties of environment objects. Tools, processes, and perhaps even types themselves need to be treated as typed objects. Once the capabilities of the type system are clearly delineated, suitable mechanisms for realizing those capabilities must be found. While there are many intriguing proposals for type mechanisms, it is not clear which of these (e.g., single vs. multiple inheritance, specification vs. representation inheritance, generics, static vs. dynamic binding) form a compatible set providing the capabilities needed for environments.

Relationship systems. Closely related to the ability to precisely define and maintain the typed objects in the environment is the ability to capture and maintain the relationships among those objects. Much environment work in the last ten years has focused on mechanisms for describing, reasoning about, or exploiting relationships among objects. Examples of relationships include those connecting various versions of a module, or those between the modules constituting a configuration, or those between a module and all the others that it calls, or those joining activities in a work breakdown structure. Examples of tools that reason about or exploit relationships among objects include version control systems [67,46], automated system building tools [22], call graph analyzers, and work activity management systems [23]. Explicitly indicating the relationships among an environment's tools and information structures should make it easier to modify the environment since the effect of changes can be determined. Moreover, capabilities that rely on relationships, such as inference and derivation, will enhance environment integration by allowing users to interact with the environment at a high level, leaving the intermediate steps to be automatically determined. Generic relationship capabilities will also enhance integration by providing a uniform set of capabilities across different kinds of relationships.

A weakness in previous work is that there has been no systematic treatment of the numerous and complex relationships that exist among environment objects. The CAIS notions of primary and secondary relationships (also found in the node structure of the *ALS* [66]), *Odin*'s derivation graphs, and the system models of Cedar represent important starting points. The concept of configuration threads found in *DSEE* [33] and the relationship capabilities for module interconnection languages provided by *Intercol* [68], *Inscape* [45], and *PIC* [74] are additional examples of partial treatments specialized to one class of relationships.

Thus, determining suitable primitives and constructors for defining the relationships needed in environments is another important object management research issue. It is not clear whether the diverse relationships needed in software development and maintenance can be captured in a single model or not. Moreover, how should the relationship structure and the type system interact? Associated with the relationship system is a set of capabilities, such as consistency checking, derivation tracking, and inferencing. Work needs to be done on identifying these capabilities and in exploring how generic such capabilities can be. For example, can generic consistency checking tools applicable to the relationship structure subsume the specialized consistency analyses associated with interface control or configuration management? Another important concern is when and how such capabilities are initiated. Some must be requested by the environment user, either directly or via an executing process. Others can be more effective if triggered by resulting events. Thus, support for "active" objects or daemons that are triggered by process or user-specified events in the environment is needed.

Persistence. The object manager must be able to preserve the components of software products and the constituents of software environments for arbitrary periods of time. Moreover, it should preserve both the structure and the restrictions imposed by the type system on how these objects can be manipulated. Under such a scheme, the traditional distinction between primary and secondary storage representations of objects is hidden within the typed object abstraction. This can free both environment users and environment builders from concern about distinctions between internal and external representations of objects and conversions between those representations. Thus, the object manager should support *persistence*, enabling objects to continue to exist beyond the lifetime of any of the tools or process programs that manipulate them and preserving the integrity of their types and relationships to other objects.

Current approaches to persistence, based on files or databases, require explicit action by the tools. Using a file system, a tool must take responsibility for converting the internal form of an object to an acceptable (e.g., linear) external form and, when needed, converting it back. There are few restrictions to assure that the type of an object is not violated (e.g., that its contents are not altered using an editor while it resides in the file) or changed (e.g., that a stack is not read back as an array). Using a database system, the tool must make calls on the database to explicitly store and retrieve information. Current databases provide support for only a limited number of types, so once again the tool must provide the conversion algorithms and there is no guarantee of type integrity. There has been some interesting work on merging database support into programming languages [2,18,38], although implemented prototypes have been very restrictive about the supported types [2] or the underlying program model [18].

Thus, providing persistence for arbitrarily complex, typed objects is an important research issue. To permit maximum flexibility in the creation of objects and their relationships, the persistence of an object should be a property orthogonal to all other object properties. It is not clear how persistence should be recognized in a program (e.g., declared as part of the type or explicitly requested with the instantiation of an object) or how invisible persistence can be (e.g., no need to explicitly "commit" or "linearize" objects). Supporting a rich type system and providing an invisible line between memory and secondary storage raise challenging problems.

Concurrency and distribution. To allow multiple users to work conveniently on the same software development project requires support for concurrent and distributed object management. Assuming a network of workstations, different members of a development project may simultaneously invoke the same or different tools to operate on one or more of the same objects. Thus, the object manager must be able to mediate concurrent use of objects and to maintain consistency of both the objects and their relationships. Ideally, the object manager should make the distributed nature of the object base and the concurrent access to its objects invisible to users and tools in the environment.

A variety of approaches for handling distribution and concurrency have emerged from programming language [1,29,34] and file system and database research [26,69,54]. Unfortunately, no single model for dealing with these issues is universally accepted within one of these domains, let alone for objects that move between them. Moreover, some of the more popular approaches are ill-suited for use in an environment object management system. Locking schemes, for example, typically apply to entire objects and do not permit concurrent access to disjoint subsets of an object's components, which may be a frequent occurrence in an environment. Transaction schemes generally presuppose relatively short duration transactions, while a software developer's transactions may last for days or weeks. The rollback approach to conflict resolution is also of questionable value in an environment, where a rollback could discard considerable human effort.

Thus, determining appropriate constructs for expressing distribution and concurrency constraints and the underlying mechanisms needed to support these constraints is yet another major object management research issue. It is not clear what storage management primitives need to be provided to adequately capture the distribution and concurrency needs of an environment. As with types, relationships, and support for persistence, the appropriate descriptive notations must be developed as well. Also, where should the desired concurrent/distributed behavior be described—in the tools that create the actual instances of the objects, in the abstract data types that define the objects, or in the process programs that describe how the objects are to co-exist within the environment?

3.2 Arcadia Object Management Research

As indicated above, much work has previously been done on problems related to object management. That work, however, has generally been directed toward solving individual problems, leading in some cases to incompatible solutions, and has not yet resulted in consensus on the appropriateness of those solutions. Moreover, much of the work has been oriented toward domains with needs other than those of software development and maintenance.

The approach to developing an object management system that is being taken in the Arcadia project is therefore one of synthesis and extension. In particular, we are initially looking to programming language technology for guidance in the design of a type system and the expression of distribution and concurrency constraints and initially looking to database technology for guidance in the design of mechanisms for persistence, relationships, and distribution.

It is clear that some new solutions are required to satisfy the special needs of software environments. To sharpen our understanding of those needs, in addition to examining process programs for a wide variety of activities, we are also examining a wide variety of tools that would make use of the object management system, and reflecting on our experience building *Odin*, *Keystone* [16], and *Graphite* [15], which can be viewed as primitive object management systems. We are also developing formal models for describing and evaluating the various capabilities intended for inclusion into the object management system. Finally, we are building a number of prototypes that allow us to gain direct experience with proposed capabilities.

Our conceptual view of the object management system is that it consists of three basic levels. At the top level are descriptive capabilities for specifying the types of objects, the relationships among objects, and the persistence characteristics of objects. At the middle level are capabilities for managing actual object instances and relationships, such as those to guarantee type consistency and to automatically trigger inferencing over relationships. The bottom level provides facilities for such things as storage management, concurrency control, and transaction management. We are using the models and prototypes to perform experiments within and across these levels.

Oros [50] is one model that we have developed as part of our investigation of the typing and relationship issues at the top level. It is being used to describe and evaluate the type system that we believe is appropriate for object management. *Oros* has a number of innovative characteristics. One is that objects, relationships, and operations are all treated as having co-equal importance, which reflects situations that we have encountered in trying to describe actual environment data types. Such equality is not found, for example, in the type systems of so-called object-oriented languages, where operations are unavoidably subservient to objects and relationships are not dealt with at all. Another characteristic of *Oros* is that relationships can be used as integral parts of a type definition. In other words, *Oros* allows the definition of types in terms of how their instances are related to instances of other types, not just the usual description in terms of the operations appropriate to instances of the type. As a simple example of the utility of this, consider the definition of a type for source-code modules. In a traditional definition, the fact that the instances of this type are related to instances of another type for target-code modules (thus the use of the terms "source" and "target") is only expressible implicitly. *Oros* permits this implicit aspect of the definition to be made explicit. A third characteristic of *Oros* is that it allows a distinction to be made between operations and relationships that are truly *definitional* of a type and those that are merely *auxiliary*. For example, if we view the translation of a source to a target as an operation, then that translation is to a great extent a definitional operation of the source (and, indeed, target) type. On the other hand, a pretty-printer viewed as an operation of the source type might be more appropriately considered auxiliary. We have found this distinction useful in a number of ways, but especially so in helping us address the problem of changing types in an environment, where a change to an auxiliary operation or relationship can be made to have a different impact than a change to a definitional operation or relationship.

Appl/A, which was mentioned in Section 2, and *PGraphite* [72] are two prototypes also at the top level of our conceptual layering of the object management system. *Appl/A* is exercising our ideas concerning relationships. It is intended as a vehicle for exploring the suitability of various automated constraint-satisfaction and inferencing techniques in the domain of process programming. Specifically, it provides a general framework for specifying goals in terms of "active" relationships over objects and provides mechanisms, such as backward and forward inferencing, for satisfying those goals. *PGraphite* is helping us to explore the interaction between typing and persistence, and thus complements the work on *Appl/A*. It concentrates on one kind of object, the directed graph, which is an extremely common data structure in environments. *PGraphite* provides a mechanism for the specification of types for directed graphs and automates the generation of implementations for those types in Ada. It also provides a means to indicate the persistence of particular objects as an orthogonal property of those objects. Finally, *PGraphite* provides a mechanism for specifying transactions against a persistent store as a "hook" for utilizing lower-level concurrency control and transaction management systems (see below).

Cactis [30] is a prototype at the middle level of our conceptual layering. It is a manager of object instances and relationships cognizant of the fact that the values contained in some objects and the relationships among those objects may depend upon the values in other objects and the relationships among those other objects. *Cactis* emphasizes efficient, automatic updating of values and relationships in response to changes to the values and relationships upon which they depend. One early client of *Cactis*'s services is *Appl/A*, which uses *Cactis* to manage relationships.

In addition to its role as a top-level prototype, *PGraphite* is providing insights at the middle level into the kinds of information about an object's type that must be available at run time to realize a general persistence mechanism. A version of *Appl/A* built upon *PGraphite*, where *PGraphite* would manage the persistence of *Appl/A* relationships, is planned for the near future.

Much work has already been done by others on the storage management, concurrency control, and transaction management capabilities of the bottom level of our conceptual layering [55,4,56,13] and we plan to make as much use of those results as possible. The problem we face is how to connect to those varied and evolving systems in such a way that we can easily experiment with the higher-level capabilities. Thus, our primary challenge at this level is to develop an appropriate interface mechanism. Our prototype of that mechanism is called Mneme [36]. Mneme offers a simple and efficient abstraction of low-level objects, supporting flexibility in three ways: the high-end languages/systems that can map down to that abstraction, the low-end managers/servers that can help implement that abstraction, and the specific management policies (such as clustering of objects to optimize access) that can be specified by the Mneme user. A version of *PGraphite* is being built on top of Mneme so that we can experiment with a variety of realizations for *PGraphite*'s mechanism of persistent-store transactions.

4. User Interface Management

4.1 User Interface Management Requirements and Related Work

The third major component of the environment infrastructure provides the human user pleasant and efficient access to the functions supported by both the fixed and variant parts of the environment. Broad consensus exists on the qualities that distinguish good user interfaces for software environments. *Uniformity* (or *consistency*) reduces the difficulty of learning new activities and moving between activities. The direct manipulation interaction paradigm, using graphics and pointing devices, increases the communication bandwidth between tool and user. *Permissive* (or *non-preemptive*) interfaces allow the user to interleave activities in a natural way.

Uniformity reduces the number of details a human user must remember, and increases skill transfer between activities. A uniform interface makes the same set of operations available everywhere they make sense, and allows the user to specify an operation in the same manner wherever it is available. Interpreter-based programming environments made significant early progress toward uniformity by unifying the command language and programming language of the environment. More recently, editor-based programming environments have provided a uniform set of commands for manipulating program source code, blurring the distinction between editing, compiling, and debugging. Limited progress has been made in providing a uniform interface across a wider variety of activities. This progress has been made, for the most part, by imposing informal standards (like the Macintosh user interface guidelines [31]) and providing libraries of reusable components (scrollbars, menus, and the like).

Uniformity becomes both more important and harder to maintain as the scope of an environment grows. A flexible, extensible environment will contain tools contributed by a diverse community of developers and users. Moreover, both the toolset and interaction techniques can be expected to evolve during the lifetime of the environment.

A critical problem, then, is decoupling the human interface from tools so that each may evolve independently. Providing a set of reusable components is helpful, but may not be enough by itself. The *SunView* facilities [62], for instance, encourage similar visual appearance across tools, but they are not much help in establishing consistent interpretations of mouse and keyboard actions within windows managed by tools. The X Toolkit translation manager [35] goes further, allowing input translation to be decoupled from individual components by providing a uniform input translation scheme for new "widgets" as well as for those supplied with the basic library. These graphical toolkits can effectively encapsulate application-independent interaction, but they fall short of decoupling the human interface from the functionality within particular application domains.

The interface between interaction and tool functionality (in the application domain) is the most troublesome interface in modularizing interactive graphics programs. Because graphics toolkits deal entirely with the graphical domain, they do not help clean up this interface. The problem of the interface between interaction and application domain functionality becomes apparent when one notes that other tools, as well as human users, may use a tool component. As many have noted, a good human-tool interface is generally not a good tool-tool interface. It is as difficult for a tool to make use of the text manipulation facilities of a screen-oriented editor or the calculation capabilities of a spreadsheet as it would be for the human user to directly access a library of text and formula manipulation procedures. An all-purpose interface, like UNIX character streams, is unlikely to be satisfactory in either role. In current UNIX-based systems, the set of tool-usable tools is quite disjoint from the set of interactive tools.

Direct manipulation, or more precisely the illusion of directly manipulating a set of objects, requires a rich visual representation of state. This visual representation unburdens the users' short-term memory, replacing recall tasks with easier recognition tasks. (Menus serve a similar purpose with respect to remembering commands.) Objects are referred to with a pointing device and through implicit pointing (e.g., cursor position.) Changes in the representation provide immediate confirmation of user actions. The basic principles of direct manipulation are applicable to character displays, but modern bitmapped workstations are capable of richer visual representations of state. Pioneering work in the application of graphics to programming and software engineering include the *Incense* debugging system [37], the *Balsa* algorithm animation system [9], and the *Pecan* programming environment [49].

Permissiveness is an essential aspect of direct manipulation, too seldom achieved in current systems. A permissive interface allows the user to choose the next action, arbitrarily interleaving interactions with each object depicted on the screen. The converse of permissiveness is preemption. A preemptive interface imposes an order on user actions. The prompt/input paradigm of gathering input is a classic example of preemption. Window systems are primarily a means of limiting preemption. Windows grafted onto a conventional system in the form of multiple virtual terminals provide a minimal degree of permissiveness, sufficient for the user to temporarily escape from the control of a single application. The multiple views of *Pecan* [49] and the *Pi* debugger [14] hint at the richer interaction possible when each tool may coordinate several threads of control.

4.2 Arcadia User Interface Management Research

User interface management is an active area of research, outside the context of software environments research as well as within it. In the Arcadia project, the *Chiron* system [75] is being developed as a prototype UIMS component to demonstrate our research approach. *Chiron* adapts and extends some key ideas from current UIMS research to address the particular demands of flexible, extensible software environments.

This subsection discusses our approaches to separating application functionality from interaction facilities, managing the display, and establishing a uniform interface to all the functions supported by an environment.

Separating functionality and interaction. Several current approaches to direct manipulation interfaces carefully separate the application domain (or model) from the presentation domain (or view). This separation is especially appropriate in software environments, since few software objects are inherently graphical. Even in the case of diagrams (e.g., structure charts, data flow diagrams, SADT diagrams), the meaning of the diagram can be distinguished from its representations in terms of boxes, lines, and text. In the Arcadia-1 prototype environment, tool components that manipulate model objects can be largely freed of concern with view objects. The *Chiron* system is used to build encapsulated tool components that maintain consistency between objects in the model and view domains, so that view objects accurately reflect the state of model objects and model objects properly respond to direct manipulation of view objects.

In "editor" environments supporting a narrow set of objects and functions, a central tool component typically maps the application data structure (usually a parse tree) to a visual representation. Separation of concerns between application domain and presentation domain is achieved, but at the cost of requiring all environment facilities to operate on a single shared data structure rather than a variety of data structures suited to different applications. Environments of wide scope require a more flexible scheme.

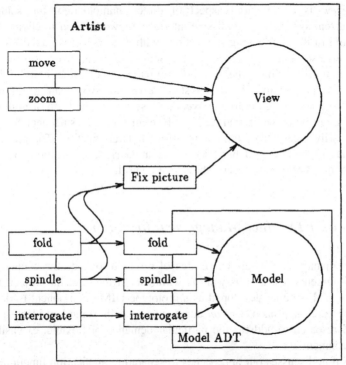

Fig. 13.2. An artist is logically "wrapped around" an abstract data type.

In the Arcadia-1 prototype environment, each abstract data type in an application domain may have an associated artist for maintaining a corresponding view object. An artist encapsulates decisions about how each particular data type is depicted; there is no requirement for all tools to share a single data type or data model, beyond the requirement that objects be cleanly encapsulated as abstract data types.

Artists for data structures were introduced by Myers [37] in the *Incense* symbolic debugging system. *Loops* [59,60] binds the equivalent of artists to objects using a specialized form of inheritance called *annotation. Chiron* adopts a more formal version of annotation for binding artists to abstract data types. An annotation on an abstract data type may add new operations, add local state (*instance variables*, in the nomenclature of object-oriented programming), and extend existing operations. New operations and extensions to existing operations may modify only new state.[7] An artist adds new state to keep track of the depiction of an object, and extends existing operations to update the depiction when the object is modified (Fig. 13.2).

The essential characteristic of annotation as a mechanism for binding artists to abstract data types is that neither the semantics nor the syntax (signatures of operations) of an object are changed. A tool component need not be modified just because the object it is manipulating is depicted on the screen; the interface to tools is not corrupted by the interface to human users.

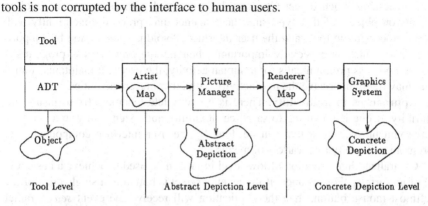

Fig. 13.3. Artists manipulate an abstract description of the display, and a rendering agent maps the abstract depiction to bitmap images.

Managing the display. The view objects created by artists could be actual bitmaps, but it is generally better to interpose an intermediate level of representation between application objects and their concrete depiction on the screen. *Chiron* provides a diagram-oriented 2½D hierarchical structure for describing displays, including nested and overlapping windows. Artists manipulate this *abstract depiction*. A separate rendering agent maps it into actual bitmap images (Fig. 13.3).

Operating on the abstract depiction has several advantages over purely procedural abstractions for operating on bitmaps. An artist may modify a display by making small changes to the abstract depiction, without concern for the extent of changes to the bitmap image (e.g., if moving a circle causes a previously obscured rectangle to become visible). More importantly, an abstract depiction can be used as a basis for input correlation, relating an input action (e.g., mouse click) with a particular application object. Whereas window systems typically provide input

---

[7] Most current implementations of annotation-like mechanisms do not enforce this restriction, but it is essential for reasoning about annotated abstract data types. The property we desire is that proofs involving a type T remain valid when an annotation T' is substituted for T.

correlation only down to the level of individual windows, *Chiron* provides correlation to the level of individual polygons, lines, and so forth.

Input model. Approaches to processing user input can be classified according to whether input routines appear as subroutines to the application (called the *prompting* or *internal control* model), or the application appears as a subroutine(s) to the input processor (*dispatching* or *external control* model), or the input routines and application are logically concurrent, cooperating processes. The prompting model is inferior from the user's point of view, because it is highly preemptive—the user has too little control over the program. The dispatch model, on the other hand, distorts the natural logic of some applications by forcing the programmer to "flatten" control structures. *Chiron* supports a concurrent model of input processing. Each object type may be associated with an agent for handling events on objects of that type, and these agents may proceed concurrently with other processing in tools and the user interface. Avoiding preemption by supporting concurrency is especially important when interpreting process programs— when a process program calls for a human activity, the user still maintains control and may freely interleave the new activity with other current activities.

Approaches to uniformity. There is no complete technical fix to insure uniformity, if one is unwilling to sacrifice flexibility and extensibility in a software environment. The most that can be done by the user interface component is to promote uniformity by a variety of means.

Centralized interpretation of low-level input can be used to achieve a basic level of uniformity. For instance, if the lexeme *select* is bound to a single click of the leftmost mouse button, then the application will receive the event *select*, rather than a raw key click, when the button is pressed. Binding of lexemes to raw events should always be under control of the user, rather than the tool builder. Techniques adequate for administering this level of interpretation are well known (e.g., the TIP tables of *Cedar*).

Central administration can also guarantee consistent interpretation of a small set of "global" commands, for instance, terminating a tool. Anyone who has attempted to kill an unfamiliar program in the UNIX system with keyboard incantations will appreciate the importance of such guarantees.

Reusable components are a complementary approach to promoting uniformity. Application-independent components, such as scrollbars, are already in common use. In the Arcadia-1 prototype environment, clean encapsulation of interaction facilities makes it feasible to provide reusable components for data abstractions in a particular application domain (e.g., Petri nets), as well. Since artists in an Arcadia environment are associated with abstract data types, the path of least resistance for tool developers is to reuse an artist for all interactive tools dealing with a particular data abstraction.

5. Conclusion

The Arcadia consortium has been formed to explore a number of issues in software environments. We are attempting to make major strides in the development of fundamental technologies, develop prototypes, conduct careful empirical studies, and move the technology to industrial practice.

This paper presents the approach being pursued by Arcadia researchers investigating software environment architectures. This project is exploring an architecture to support flexibility and extensibility as well as tight internal and external integration. We feel these issues, while often in conflict with each other, are necessary ingredients for environments to fulfill their potential of assisting users in software development and maintenance activities. Our research approach involves simultaneously investigating several challenging research areas and synergistically striving to develop compatible solutions in each.

The environment architecture that we have proposed has separated the basic components of the infrastructure, or fixed part, from the process programs, tools, and objects that constitute the variant part. The overriding job of the fixed part is to facilitate tight integration over the flexible/extensible variant part. This clear separation of concerns has helped to modularize the problem and to identify some important open questions and promising research directions.

Our approach is based on the process programming paradigm, where software processes are formally captured by programs, which are then executed by the process program interpreter. Formal descriptions of software processes, presented in an expressive language along with tools for creating and modifying such programs, provide a basis for flexibility and extensibility. The user interface management system supports external integration by providing a uniform method of communication between humans and executing software processes. The object management system supports internal integration by providing typing, relationships, persistence, distribution, and concurrency capabilities upon which process programs can be interpreted. We believe that among the most important results of the Arcadia effort will be understanding the tradeoffs that are possible and desirable in achieving effective user interface and software object management support in the face of the high degree of flexibility and extensibility afforded by process programming.

The Arcadia project has just completed its first year of funding, and results are still very preliminary. Arcadia researchers realize that to be convincing and to gain as much insight as possible, realistic prototypes must be subjected to well-designed empirical evaluation. The Arcadia researchers are currently implementing prototypes of all the major components of the environment infrastructure. Analysis tools are also being developed as part of this project and their insertion into the variant part, along with suitable process programs, will provide a challenging test for the architecture. In addition, an evaluation framework is being developed to enable meaningful empirical studies to be undertaken. Finally, technology transfer activities are being explored so that realistic industrial feedback can be obtained. These combined activities should lead to valuable research results, significantly advancing our knowledge and capabilities in software environments.

Acknowledgments Arcadia has benefited from the ongoing encouragement of William L. Scherlis and Stephen L. Squires. We gratefully acknowledge the contributions of participants from each institution of the consortium, who have been instrumental in shaping virtually every aspect of Arcadia. During the past two years key contributions have come from D. Baker, B. Boehm, A. Brindle, D. Fisher, D. Heimbigner, C. LeDoux, M. Penedo, D. Richardson, I. Shy, S. Sykes, W. Tracz, and S. Zeil. Additional contributions have been made by R. Adrion, G. Barbanis, G. Clemm, R. Cowan, J. Durand, E. Epp, S. Gamalel-Din, S. Graham, G. James, C. Kelly, S. Krane, R. King, D. Luckham, T. Nguyen, K. Nies, A. Porter, W. Rosenblatt, R. Schmalz, C. Snider, S. Sutton, P. Tarr, and D. Troup.

References

[1] *Military Standard Ada Programming Language* (ANSI/MIL-STD-1815A-1983). American National Standards Institute, Jan. 1983.

[2] M. Atkinson, P. Bailey, K. Chisholm, P. Cockshott, and R. Morrison. An approach to persistent programming. *The Computer Journal*, 26(4):360-365, 1983.

[3] T. E. Bell, D. C. Bixler, and M. E. Dyer. An extendable approach to computer-aided software requirements engineering. *IEEE Trans. on Software Engineering*, SE3(1):49-60, Feb. 1977.

[4] P. A. Bernstein. Database system support for software engineering. In *Proceedings of the Ninth International Conference on Software Engineering*, pages 166-178, IEEE Computer Society Press, Monterey, California, March 1987.

[5] D. Bjorner. On the use of formal methods in software development. In *Proceedings of the Ninth International Conference on Software Engineering*, pages 17-29, IEEE Computer Society Press, Monterey, California, March 1987.

[6] B. Boehm. A spiral model of software development and enhancement. *Computer*, May 1983.

[7] B. Boehm and F. Belz. Applying process programming to the spiral model. In *Proceedings of the Fourth International Software Process Workshop*, pages 1-11, Moretonhampstead, Devon, United Kingdom, May 1988.

[8] G. Booch. Object-oriented development. *IEEE Trans. on Software Engineering*, SE-12(2):211-221, Feb. 1986.

[9] M. H. Brown and R. Sedgewick. A system for algorithm animation. *Computer Graphics*, 18(3):177-186, July 1984.

[10] *DOD-STD-18.98, Common Ada Programming Support Environment (APSE) Interface Set (CAIS)*. Department of Defense, Oct. 1986.

[11] *Common Ada Programming Support Environment (APSE) Interface Set (CAIS), Proposed Military Standard DOD-STD-1838A (Revision A)*. Department of Defense, May 1988.

[12] J. R. Cameron. An overview of JSD. *IEEE Trans. on Software Engineering*, SE-12(2):222-240, Feb. 1986.

[13] M. J. Carey, D. J. Dewitt, D. Frank, G. Graefe, J. E. Richardson, E. J. Shekita, and M. Muralikrishna. *The Architecture of the EXODUS Extensible DBMS: A Preliminary Report*. Technical Report CS-644, Computer Sciences Department, University of Wisconsin - Madison, May 1986.

[14] T. A. Cargill. The feel of Pi. In *Winter 1986 USENIX Technical Conference*, pages 62-71, USENIX Association, Denver, Colorado, Jan. 1986.

[15] L. A. Clarke, J. C. Wileden, and A. L. Wolf. Graphite: A meta-tool for Ada environment development. In *Proceedings of the IEEE Computer Society Second International Conference on Ada Applications and Environments*, pages 81-90, IEEE Computer Society Press, Miami Beach, Florida, Apr. 1986.

[16] G. M. Clemm, D. Heimbigner, L. Osterweil, and L. G. Williams. Keystone: a federated software environment. In *Proceedings of the Workshop on Software Engineering Environments for Programming-in-the-Large*, pages 80-88, June 1985.

[17] G. M. Clemm and L. J. Osterweil. A *Mechanism for Environment Integration*. Technical Report CU-CS-323-86, University of Colorado, Boulder, Jan. 1986.

[18] *CLF Overview*. USC Information Sciences Institute, Marina del Rey, California, March 1986. Informal Report.

[19] V. Donzeau-Gouge, G. Huet, G. Kahn, and B. Lang. Programming environments based on structured editors: the Mentor experience. In *Interactive Programming Environments*, pages 128-140, McGraw-Hill Book Co., New York, 1984.

[20] M. Dowson, editor. *Proceedings of the 3rd International Software Process Workshop*, IEEE Computer Society Press, Breckenridge, Colorado, Nov. 1986.

[21] G. Estrin, R. S. Fenchel, R. R. Razouk, and M. K. Vernon. SARA (System ARchitects Apprentice): modeling, analysis, and simulation support for design of concurrent systems. *IEEE Trans. on Software Engineering*, SE-12(2):293-313, Feb. 1986.

[22] S. I. Feldman. Make—a program for maintaining computer programs. *Software–Practice & Experience*, 9(4):255-265, Apr. 1979.

[23] C. Green, D. Luckham, R. Balzer, T. Cheatham, and C. Rich. *Report on a Knowledge-Based Software Assistant*. Technical Report, Kestrel Institute, June 1983.

[24] A. N. Kabermann and D. Notkin. Gandalf: software development environments. *IEEE Trans. on Software Engineering*, SE-12(12):1117-1127, Dec. 1986.

[25] A. N. Habermann and D. E. Perry. System composition and version control for ada. In H. Huenke, editor, *Software Engineering Environments*, pages 331-343, North-Holland, 1981.

[26] D. Heimbigner and D. McLeod. A federated architecture for information management. *ACM Transactions on Office Information Systems*, 3(3):253-278, July 1985.

[27] D. Heimbigner, L. Osterweil, and S. Sutton. *APPL/A: A Language for Managing Relations Among Software Objects and Processes*. Technical Report CU-CS-374-87, University of Colorado, Department of Computer Science, Boulder, Colorado, 1987.

[28] P. Henderson, editor. *Proceedings of the A CM SIGSOFT/SIGPLAN Software Engineering Symposium on Practical Software Development Environments*, ACM SIGPLAN, Pittsburgh, Pennsylvania, Apr. 1984. (Appeared as SIGPLAN Notices, 19(51), May 1984.)

[29] C. A. R. Hoare. Communicating sequential processes. *Communications of the ACM*, 21(8):666-677, 1978.

[30] S. Hudson and R. King. The *Cactis* project: database support for software environments. *IEEE Trans. on Software Engineering*, June 1988. (to appear).

[31] *Inside Macintosh*. Apple Computer, Inc., Cupertino, California, promotional edition, March 1985.

[32] B. W. Lampson and E. E. Schmidt. Organizing software in a distributed environment. In *Proceedings of the ACM SIGPLAN '89 Symposium on Programming Language Issues in Software Systems*, pages 1-13, June 1983.

[33] D. B. Leblang and J. Robert P. Chase. Computer-aided software engineering in a distributed workstation environment. *SIGPLAN Notices*, 19(5):104-112, May 1984. (Proceedings of the First ACM SIGSOFT/SIGPLAN Symposium on Practical Software Development Environments).

[34] B. Liskov and R. Scheifler. Guardians and actions: linguistic support for robust, distributed programs. *ACM Transactions on Programming Languages and Systems*, 5(3):381-404, July 1983.

[35] J. McCormack. *X Toolkit Intrinsics - C Language X Interface*. Technical Report Review Version 2.1, Western Software Laboratory, Digital Equipment Corporation, Feb. 1988.

[36] J. Moss and S. Sinofsky. *Managing Persistent Data with Mneme: Issues and Applications of a Reliable, Shared Object Interface*. Technical Report 88-30, COINS, University of Massachusetts, Amherst, MA, Apr. 1988.

[37] B. A. Myers. Incense: A system for displaying data structures. *Computer Graphics*, 17(3):115-125, July 1983.

[38] J. A. Orenstein, S. K. Sarin, and U. Dayal. *Managing Persistent Objects in Ada*. Technical Report CCA-86-03, Computer Corporation of America, Cambridge, Massachusetts, May 1986.

[39] L. J. Osterweil. *A Process-Object Centered View of Software Environment Architecture*. Technical Report CU-CS-332-86, University of Colorado, Boulder, May 1986.

[40] L. J. Osterweil. Software environment research: Directions for the next five years. *Computer*, 14(4):35-43, 1981.

[41] L. J. Osterweil. Software processes are software too. In *Proceedings of the Ninth International Conference on Software Engineering*, pages 2-13, Monterey, CA, March 1987. (Reprinted as Chapter 17)

[42] D. L. Parnas and P. C. Clements. A rational design process: how and why to fake it. *IEEE Trans. on Software Engineering*, SE-12(2):251-257, Feb. 1986.

[43] M. H. Penedo. Prototyping a project master data base for software engineering environments. In *Proceedings of the First ACM SIGSOFT/SIGPLAN Software Engineering Symposium on Practical Development Environments*, Palo Alto, California, Dec. 1986.

[44] M. H. Penedo and E. D. Stuckle. PMDB - A project master database for software engineering environments. In *Proceedings of the 8th International Conference on Software Engineering*, pages 150-157, London, England, Aug. 1985.

[45] D. E. Perry. Software interconnection models. In *Proceedings of the Ninth International Conference on Software Engineering*, pages 61-69, March 1987.

[46] D. E. Perry. Version control in the Inscape environment. In *Proceedings of the Ninth International Conference on Software Engineering*, pages 142-149, March 1987.

[47] C. Potts, editor. *Proceedings of Software Process Workshop*, IEEE Computer Society Press, Egham, Surrey, United Kingdom, Feb. 1984.

[48] R. A. Radice, N. K. Roth, A. C. 0. Jr., and W. A. Ciarfella. A programming process architecture. *IBM Systems Journal*, 24(2):79-90, 1985.

[49] S. P. Reiss. PECAN: program development systems that support multiple views. *IEEE Trans. on Software Engineering*, SE-11(3):276-285, 1985.

[50] W. Rosenblatt, J. Wileden, and A. Wolf. *Preliminary Report on the OROS Type Model*. Technical Report 88-70, COINS, University of Massachusetts, Amherst, MA, Aug. 1988.

[51] D. T. Ross and K. E. S. Jr. Structured analysis for requirements definition. *IEEE Trans. on Software Engineering*, SE-3(1):6-15, Feb. 1977.

[52] G. Ross. Integral C - A practical environment for c programming. In *Proceedings of the Second ACM SIGSOFT/SIGPLAN Symposium on Practical Software Development Environments*, pages 42-48, Dec. 1986.

[53] W. W. Royce. Managing the development of large software systems. In *Proceedings, IEEE WESCON*, pages 1-9, IEEE, Aug. 1970. Also reprinted in Proceedings 9th International Conference on Software Engineering, pp. 328-338.

[54] M. Satyanarayanan, J. II. Howard, D. A. Nichols, R. N. Sidebotham, A. Z. Spector, and M. J. West. The ITC distributed file system: principles and design. *Operating Systems Review*, 19(5):35-50, 1985.

[55] A. H. Skarra, S. B. Zdonik, and S. P. Reiss. An object server for an object-oriented database system. In *Proceedings of the Object-Oriented Database Systems Workshop*, pages 196-204, IEEE Computer Society Press, Sep. 1986.

[56] A. Z. Spector. *Distributed Transaction Processing in the Camelot System*. Technical Report CMU-CS-87-100, Computer Science Department, Carnegie-Mellon University, Pittsburgh, Pennsylvania, Jan. 1987.

[57] *Proceedings of 4th International Software Process Workshop*, Moretonhampstead, Devon, United Kingdom, May 1988.

[58] T. A. Standish and R. N. Taylor. Arcturus: A prototype advanced Ada programming environment. *Software Engineering Notes*, 9(3):57-64, May 1984. (Proceedings of the ACM SIGSOFT/SIGPLAN Software Engineering Symposium on Practical Software Development Environments)

[59] M. Stefik and D. Bobrow. Object-oriented programming: Themes and variations. *AI Magazine*, 6(4):40-62, Winter 1986.

[60] M. J. Stefik, D. G. Bobrow, and K. M. Kahn. Integrating access-oriented programming into a multiparadigm environment. *IEEE Software*, 3(1):10-18, Jan. 1986.

[61] M. Stonebraker and L. A. Rowe. The design of POSTGRES. In *Proceedings of the ACM SIGMOD '86 International Conference on Management of Data*, pages 340-355, June 1986.

[62] *SunView Programmer's Guide*. Sun Microsystems, Inc., Mountain View, California, Feb. 1986.

[63] T. Teitelbaum and T. Reps. The Cornell Program Synthesizer: A syntax directed programming environment. *Communications of the ACM*, 24(9):563-573, Sep. 1981.

[64] W. Teitelman. A tour through Cedar. *IEEE Trans. on Software Engineering*, SE-11(3):285-302, 1985.

[65] W. Teitelman and L. Masinter. The Interlisp programming environment. *Computer*, 14(4):25-33, Apr. 1981.

[66] R. M. Thall. The KAPSE for the Ada Language System. In *Proceedings of the AdaTEC Conference on Ada*, pages 31-47, ACM, Oct. 1982.

[67] W. F. Tichy. Design, implementation, and evaluation of a revision control system. In *Proceedings of the Sixth International Conference on Software Engineering*, pages 58-67, Tokyo, Japan, Sep. 1982.

[68] W. F. Tichy. Software development control based on module interconnection. In *Proceedings of the Fourth International Conference on Software Engineering*, pages 29-41, IEEE Computer Society Press, Munich, West Germany; Sep. 1979.

[69] B. Walker, G. Popek, R. English, C. Kline, and G. Thiel. The LOCUS distributed operating system. *Operating Systems Review*, 17(5):49-70, 1983.

[70] P. T. Ward. The transformation schema: an extension of the data flow diagram to represent control and timing. *IEEE Trans. on Software Engineering*, SE12(2):198-210, Feb. 1986.

[71] A. I. Wasserman, P. A. Pircher, D. T. Shewmake, and M. L. Kersten. Developing interactive information systems with the user software engineering methodology. *IEEE Trans. on Software Engineering*, SE12(2):326-345, Feb. 1986.

[72] J. Wileden, A. Wolf, C. Fisher, and P. Tarr. PGraphite: an experiment in persistent typed object management. In *Proceedings SIGSOFT '88: Third Symposium on Software Development Environments*, Dec. 1988.

[73] J. C. Wileden and M. Dowson, editors. *Proceedings of the International Workshop on the Software Process and Software Environments*, ACM SIGSOFT, Coto de Caza, Trabuco Canyon, California, March 1985. (Appeared in ACM Software Engineering Notes, Vol.11, No.4, Aug. 1986).

[74] A. Wolf, L. Clarke, and J. Wileden. The AdaPIC toolset: supporting interface control and analysis throughout the software development process. *IEEE Transactions on Software Engineering*, 1988. (To appear).

[75] M. Young, R. N. Taylor, and D. B. Troup. Software environment architectures and user interface facilities. *IEEE Trans. on Software Engineering*, June 1988.

[76] P. Zave and W. Schell. Salient features of an executable specification language and its environment. *IEEE Trans. on Software Engineering*, SE-12(2):312-325, Feb. 1986.

[77] S. B. Zdonik and P. Wegner. Language and methodology for object-oriented database environments. In *Proceedings of the Nineteenth Annual Hawaii International Conference on System Sciences*, pages 378-387, Jan. 1986.

Issues Encountered in Building a Flexible Software Development Environment[1]

Lessons from the Arcadia Project

R. Kadia

Abstract This paper presents some of the more significant technical lessons that the Arcadia project has learned about developing effective software development environments. The principal components of the Arcadia-1 architecture are capabilities for process definition and execution, object management, user interface development and management, measurement and evaluation, language processing, and analysis and testing. In simultaneously and cooperatively developing solutions in these areas we learned several key lessons. Among them: the need to combine and apply heterogeneous componentry, multiple techniques for developing components, the pervasive need for rich type models, the need for supporting dynamism (and at what granularity), the role and value of concurrency, and the role and various forms of event-based control integration mechanisms. These lessons are explored in the paper.

1. Introduction

The Arcadia project goal has been to carry out validated research on software development environments. This research has stressed development of advanced prototypes to demonstrate concept feasibility and to demonstrate integration of these capabilities into an operational whole. Integrating the various Arcadia components has been an important forcing function, compelling consideration of how environment architecture issues and usage contexts impact the various individual components.

This paper presents some of the insights we have gained while building and experimenting with these components. We begin by briefly describing our goals and

[1] This material is based upon work sponsored by the Defense Advanced Research Projects Agency under Grants MDA972-91-J-1009, MDA972-91-J-1010 and MDA972-91-J-1012. The content does not necessarily reflect the position or the policy of the U.S. Government, and no official endorsement should be inferred.

R. Kadia, "Issues encountered in building a flexible software development environment: lessons from the Arcadia project," Proceedings of the fifth ACM SIGSOFT symposium on Software development environments, 1992.
DOI: 10.1145/142868.143768, © 1992 ACM, Inc. Reprinted with permission

the principal components of Arcadia. In Sections 4 through 8 we discuss several key lessons that seem to have general applicability to a wide range of environment efforts. Many of these lessons were learned by repeatedly encountering similar problems and devising similar solutions in diverse technical areas. Finally, we summarize our lessons.

2. Arcadia Overview

Arcadia believes an effective software development environment (SDE) is a collection of capabilities effectively integrated to support software developers and managers. For us, to be *effective* an SDE must be: extensible, incrementally improvable, flexible, fast, and efficient. Its components must be interoperable, it must be able to support multiple users and user classes, it must be easy to use, able to support effective product and process visibility, able to support effective management control, and it should be pro-active.

Through the years, Arcadia has evolved an architecture that addresses these objectives simultaneously. We have learned, however, that these various design objectives are not orthogonal and often conflict. Much of the most challenging work of Arcadia has been concerned with understanding the various tensions between these diverse desiderata and devising strategies for supporting adjustable compromises between conflicting SDE objectives. The focus of this paper is on the tensions that arose and the lessons we learned in our attempts to alleviate these tensions.

Arcadia's architecture is the result of our efforts to simultaneously achieve all of the above objectives in the presence of the various tensions. Several of the devices used to mediate these tensions are described later in this paper. In this section we briefly describe the principal components that form the basis for our architecture and indicate why we believe they are important to the structure of any SDE that attempts to meet the above-enumerated objectives.

2.1 Process Definition and Execution

The needs for flexibility, extensibility, and visibility into project and product status are addressed by Arcadia's capability for developing software development processes in an explicit form and for supporting their execution. Process models show how people, tools, and software systems are used to address process requirements, and process code then implements these models. Various Arcadia environment components support development and execution of the code. The need to flexibly meet changing requirements is met by Arcadia's ability to support change to process models and code.

2.2 Object Management

Arcadia generally treats software objects as instances of abstract data types. Objects can be used locally by an individual process or shared by processes. Object management facilities must provide for persistence, type integrity, interoperability, constraint maintenance, and multi-access mediation. These capabilities facilitate visibility into project and product status and provide support for multiple users and for efficient use of computer resources.

2.3 User Interface Development

To support multiple, coordinated depictions of objects and to provide flexibility in meeting changing user needs, Arcadia supports the development of custom tailored user interfaces. Graphical presentations and effective interaction mechanisms are essential. Moreover, they must be readily alterable. Accordingly, Arcadia provides a user interface development system (UIDS) designed for the rapid alteration and enhancement of user interfaces.

2.4 Measurement and Evaluation

Continuous improvement of product and process qualities is a primary underlying objective of Arcadia. Demonstrable improvement requires quantifiable measures of these qualities. Thus, Arcadia incorporates a system for taking static and dynamic measurements of software processes and the products that they build. As software process measurement and evaluation is still a young discipline, there is little agreement on metrics for guiding improvement. Thus Arcadia's measurement and evaluation system is flexible and adaptable to changes in measurement and evaluation requirements and approaches.

2.5 Language Processing

Software products and processes contain many components, expressed in a variety of languages. An environment must recognize, analyze, and support these languages. This is most effectively done through general, tailorable language processing capabilities. In addition, uniform, language-independent representations of each language facilitate processing and analysis of these languages.

2.6 Analysis and Testing

The need to assure high quality software products and processes requires Arcadia to provide facilities for analysis and testing. Arcadia takes a broad view of what constitutes a software product, construing products to consist of a wide variety of types of artifacts. Also, Arcadia does not believe that quality is a monolithic notion, but rather that superiority with respect to a variety of quality attributes is desirable. Thus a correspondingly diverse set of testing and analysis tools is provided.

2.7 Component Composition

Our work indicates that there is a fundamental tension in environment design between the need for effective interoperability and the need for flexibility and extensibility. Tools must communicate about details of their activities, yet the suite of such tools must change. Arcadia incorporates component composition mechanisms to help strike compromises between these needs. Arcadia is exploring interprocess communication capabilities that enable the synthesis of higher level tools and processes out of lower level components implemented as separately executing programs, possibly written in different languages and/or executing on different platforms.

2.8 Summary

We believe all of the above capabilities are desirable in a contemporary environment, but we also acknowledge that different environment projects may weight the desirability of these capabilities differently. Thus, the previously enumerated seven capabilities should be selectable and combinable arbitrarily. It is important to note, however, that any nontrivial subset of these seven capabilities cannot be expected to be smoothly integrated into an environment unless plans to do so have been made in advance, and unless the basic supports for these capabilities are firmly rooted in environment infrastructure elements. In our efforts to investigate these seven capabilities and their integration, we have gained insight into their requirements, limitations, benefits, and their interactions. Some lessons have involved general observations about environments and issues that arise in implementing environments. While some of these issues may not seem surprising, the extent of their impact sometimes was. In the remainder of this paper, we describe the cross-cutting issues that arose, not from the development of one capability or one project, but from our collective experience.

3. Heterogeneity

Our early concept of an Arcadia environment implicitly assumed relatively homogeneous approaches and infrastructure components. We rapidly discovered, however, that the range of issues faced by environment builders is so diverse that it exceeds the capabilities of available or expectable infrastructure components. Accordingly, Arcadia has been designed to facilitate the synergistic application of heterogeneous componentry. This heterogeneity is found across a surprising variety of infrastructure components, ranging from user capabilities such as artist-based visualizations to object management regimes. The following paragraphs briefly outline three areas in which the need for accommodating heterogeneity is apparent. Our techniques for accomplishing this are discussed in subsequent sections.

3.1 Multiple Prototypes

In order to simultaneously address open issues within the technical areas defined in Section 2, the Arcadia project has produced a wide spectrum of tools and infrastructure components for environment support. The diversity of issues addressed in each of these areas has necessitated the development of multiple prototypes embodying different solution approaches. In some cases a set of infrastructure components may be designed to provide a similar category of services, such as object management, but may have different interfaces due to fundamental differences in solution approaches or underlying models.

3.2 Multiple Languages

Software environments need to provide support for heterogeneity in programming and process languages. A software environment has a fundamental multilingual nature. It supports multiple process languages and multiple application development languages and incorporates components and infrastructure implemented in multiple languages. Environments also need to address software development-in-the-large issues that require execution and coordination across distributed platforms.

Initially the Arcadia project attempted to support a single product language and use a single implementation language (viz. Ada) exclusively so that the analysis tools developed could also be used on the environment itself. However, intrinsic shortcomings of Ada coupled with diverse needs for process and product representation and analysis resulted in our abandoning the single language approach and supporting a spectrum of language processing and communication requirements.

In order to investigate process programming issues, Arcadia has developed three primary process programming languages: APPL/A [20] (with TRITON [8]), Ada/PGRAPHITE/R&R [24] [22], and TEAMWARE [26], which each address different problem areas of process representation and analysis. The implementation languages of the infrastructure components are primarily Ada and C++, with a small amount of Lisp.

3.3 Diverse Objects

Software environments also support and manage a wide spectrum of objects that vary in terms of type, persistence, granularity, etc. In Arcadia, the range of objects includes composite software products as well as their constituent parts, from requirement specifications and implementations to test cases, measurement data, and bitmaps. The operations on these objects vary in length and complexity as well as require manipulation of fine- and coarse-grain objects. Infrastructure support for this heterogeneity in objects and their operations is substantially different from the support required for queries on sets of large numbers of homogeneous objects such as is required in other problem domains.

4. Component Technology

To accommodate these demands for heterogeneity, as well as to address many other objectives, the Arcadia project has exploited a variety of techniques under the general heading of component technology. Component technology goes far beyond the recognition and definition of major components and their interfaces. It includes "wrapping" techniques, language independence, the pervasive use of generics, and meta-descriptions and translators. Our objective is to provide considerable flexibility so that environment builders, and in some cases software developers, can tailor the environment and tools to meet their specific needs.

4.1 Abstract Interfaces

A central research principle in the development of these prototypes has been the use of abstract interfaces. When possible, these interface definitions have been standardized. Interface standardization enables researchers to investigate heterogeneous solutions to similar problems, to interchange component implementations, and to facilitate environment reconfiguration.

As one example use of standardized interfaces in Arcadia, the CHIRON UIDS [10] provides a standard interface to two different look-and-feel presentations: XView and Motif. Another example is the SMI storage manager interface, which provides a standard interface to various underlying storage managers, including Exodus [5], Mneme [15], and Ada's "direct I/O" files. On the other hand our experience has shown that creating standard interfaces is not always achievable, particularly when the underlying architectures are substantially different. A variety of other techniques, discussed below and in other sections, were developed to mitigate these situations.

4.2 Wrapping

The use of "wrapping" techniques has been useful to encapsulate unavoidable inconsistencies in interfaces. The CHIRON UIDS provides dispatchers that wrap arbitrary object ADT-interfaces. One key purpose of the dispatcher is to provide a common structure and interface to the ADTs for artists (which create visual depictions of the ADTs) to use. The AMADEUS measurement system [19] provides a script specification language for wrapping data collection tools and defining their conditions for execution. The script language provides the event monitoring subsystem of Amadeus with a consistent notation for describing these tools, which may have varied interfaces. Both the Chiron and Amadeus wrappers use event-based notification techniques, a topic which is considered more fully in Section 8.

4.3 Language Independent Common Representations

Analysis techniques have typically been applied to a small number of well recognized internal representations, such as abstract syntax graphs, control flow graphs, and call graphs. In the Arcadia project we have long recognized the need to agree on the interfaces to such abstractions so that, once created, these objects can be shared by many different analysis tools. Arcadia had the additional requirement that the representations be language-independent, so that the tools would be applicable to multiple, although somewhat related, languages. Our choice of an abstract syntax graph reflects this requirement.

We chose an IRIS-based abstract syntax graph [2] and negotiated an interface to the abstraction that supported creating and accessing the nodes, traversing the graph, and making graph instances persistent. The IRIS representation had several advantages. It is a language-independent representation where some aspects of the static semantics of the language are captured by a language description. This language description is also represented as an IRIS structure. Once a source program is translated into IRIS there is no distinction between a user-defined operator (e.g., pop) and a language-defined operator (e.g., +). This makes it easy to define new languages or extend or modify existing languages. Also, if tools judiciously use the description of the language instead of hardcoding any information about the language, they too will be language independent.[2]

The control flow graph, call graph, family of program dependence graphs, and task interaction graph [12] are other examples of shared internal representations with negotiated interfaces.

4.4 Generics

Another way that reusability and flexibility have been achieved is by the use of generics to instantiate general purpose components with specific types. The Control Flow Graph Generator, for example, is a language-independent tool that takes a description of the language and associated instructions about how to build a control flow graph for that language and generates an abstract data type that is used to instantiate a generic control flow graph build procedure. The same generic can be instantiated to build a control flow graph or a call graph for a language, just by altering the instructions on how to treat different operators of the language. The PRoDAGI program dependence graph generator [14] is a tool that constructs several packages of generic instantiation for a given dependence relation and associated build procedure; the instantiated packages provide an interface to manipulate and maintain the dependence relation.

4.5 Translators

Perhaps one of the most prevalent technologies employed in the Arcadia project is the use of translators, such as preprocessors and generators, that are often driven by specialized meta-languages. As described in section 5, we have extended the type model and functionality of Ada, our primary implementation language. These extensions have usually been accomplished via the use of syntactic language extensions that are preprocessed into Ada. Examples include APPL/A, a process programming language that adds extended relational data base capabilities to Ada; PIC [25], which adds module interconnection commands; PGRAPHITE, R&R, and REPOMANGEN, which together add graph, relation, and relationship types and persistence to the language. CHIRON extensively employs preprocessor technology to generate artist templates, client managers, and dispatchers, among other things.

---

[2] Cedar [21] earlier recognized the need to be able to ask the same kinds of questions about predefine operators as user-defined operators. The Cedar abstract machine provided such a capability.

Development of these processors has been supported by several translator building tools, which have made this approach viable for us.

4.6 Component Composition

Language heterogeneity, the advantages of a distributed systems architecture, reuse considerations, and other reasons have required development of mechanisms to support component composition. Three kinds of mechanisms have played important roles in Arcadia: (a) interprocess communication providing representation-level interoperability between processes, (b) multiple language bindings to services, and (c) automated development of interfaces providing type translation between programs in different languages.

An interprocess communication mechanism, called Q [13], has been developed based on Sun RPC/XDR and has been used to connect Ada and C programs. Distributed process execution is enabled through the Q IPC mechanism as well as through direct use of Unix IPC mechanisms such as RPC and sockets. Q is a generic that is instantiated with information about the representation of types and how they are to be encoded and decoded before and after transmission. Many components provide a layer of language bindings to support inter-language component composition. CHIRON provides a language extension to Ada whose translation enables (remote) use of a library of C++ gadgets. The TRITON OMS provides an Ada binding to the underlying Exodus storage manager written in a C++ extension. The AMADEUS measurement system provides Ada, C, and Unix shell script language bindings to its underlying measurement capabilities.

The Specification Level Interoperability (SLI) mechanism [23] attempts to automate the translation from one type model to another at a higher level of abstraction than is usually employed. In this approach, type declarations from programs written in different languages are translated into a common representation, called a unifying type model (UTM). In the current SLI prototype, this common representation is based on the OROS type model [18]. When a program in one language needs to make use of a type defined in another language, an interface to the defined type in the requested programming language can sometimes be automatically generated based on the representation in the common representation. For example, if an Ada program needed to call an existing C abstraction, the interoperability mechanism would use the common internal representation, first to help find the compatible type and then to create an Ada module implemented using the C abstraction.

5. Type Models

Our work in Arcadia has repeatedly revealed the need for rich type models to support software engineering. Features of such type models include expressive type definitions for the most frequently used software engineering abstractions, uniform treatment of entities as first-class objects, polymorphism and inheritance, and appropriate support to manage persistence, consistency, and concurrency.

To satisfy these needs, Arcadia has looked to both database systems and programming languages, but has found the type models typically provided in these disciplinary area to be lacking. The database community has recently acknowledged many of the deficiencies of database models [3, 27, 1] for software engineering. In particular, the type models of database systems tend to be too simplistic. For example, traditional database systems fail to provide the basic building blocks to support graph objects, a pervasive type in software engineering, and the typical navigational operations needed on such structures. There has been recent work on enhancing database type models so that they provide a richer set of base types and some support for inheritance, but these initial attempts, although promising, are still too restrictive.

Programming languages tend to offer richer type models than database systems in terms of constructors and primitive types, but fail to support relationship and relation types. Moreover, programming languages offer only limited support for persistence, consistency, and concurrency control, all of which tend to be supported by database systems. Some recent languages have attempted to provide support for polymorphism and multiple inheritance, but this support has been limited. Finally, neither database nor programming language type models treat most higher-level entities, such as types and operations, as first-class citizens. The remainder of this section describes the kind of support we found that we needed and some of our efforts to address these needs.

5.1 Type Model Extensions

Many of the objects manipulated by software engineering environments are graphs, such as abstract syntax graphs/trees, control flow graphs, or call graphs. Relationships (n-ary tuples) and relations (collections of relationships) are also ubiquitous types in environments. For example, software developers might want to maintain relationships between abstract syntax trees and their corresponding control flow graphs. In addition, software developers might want to ask questions about these relationships. For example, one might want to know which nodes in an abstract syntax graph actually describe the invocations that are captured in the call graph representation. It is clearly more convenient, reliable, and efficient to have built-in support for these abstractions than to have individual programmers developing their own models and implementations. Thus, as part of the Arcadia project we have extended Ada's type model to support graphs, relations, and relationships as though they were primitive types of the language. In the GRAPHITE system [6], and its successor PGRAPHITE, a model of directed graphs is provided that is a natural extension to the Ada type model. The graph abstraction includes operations for creating and manipulating nodes of the graph, as well as graph operations such as various forms of traversal. As an indication of the pervasiveness of graph objects in software development environments, GRAPHITE and PGRAPHITE have been used in over a dozen tools within Arcadia. APPL/A has extended the Ada type model to support relations and provides operations for creating and manipulating those relations. The R&R system was modeled after APPL/A but moved farther away from the traditional database model of relations by allowing relationships to be first class objects. This means that a relationship can be shared by more than one relation, a concept that has proven very useful to the analysis tools.

Both APPL/A and R&R provide some support for simple queries. Neither of these systems provides the type of support for complex and ad hoc queries that we feel is truly needed. Moreover, there needs to be better support for both navigation and queries over an object, including the ability to access the same object through both types of operations when appropriate.

5.2 First Class Citizenship

In our work on Arcadia we have frequently been frustrated by our inability to treat key programming language entities, such as types, tasks, and operations, as first class citizens. The inability to manipulate these objects, as we would any other object in a language, limits the flexibility of the components we are developing. For example, we would like to be able to pass operations and tasks as parameters. Without such support we have had to use preprocessors to generate low level code to get around these limitations. In CHIRON, for instance, when an operation of a depicted abstract data type is called, the corresponding artist operation must be called for each active artist associated with the object. Maintaining a list of active artists and then passing each package and operation that must be invoked would be a straightforward way to handle this. Unfortunately, as in most programming languages, packages and tasks are not first class citizens in Ada; thus, this cannot be done. There are numerous examples in Arcadia where such flexibility would be beneficial.

5.3 Polymorphism and Multiple Inheritance

A type model that supports polymorphism and inheritance is also desirable. Such a typing model clearly reduces the burden on the programmer when designing and coding complex systems. For example, Ada's polymorphism mechanism (generics) is not sufficiently powerful to support specification of a variable number of generic formal parameters. We have mimicked these facilities through the use of generator/preprocessor technology instead, e.g. in CHIRON and TRITON.

5.4 Consistency

Being able to control consistency is important when dealing with many different abstractions that may be related in complex ways. It can be argued that exception handling mechanisms provide a limited form of consistency control, depending on their recovery model. A more general model of consistency is desired where programmers can define arbitrary constraints that will cause an operation to be triggered if the constraint is violated. We have also found that it is desirable to allow programs to dynamically control constraint enforcement.

Although not currently implemented, APPL/A's definition supports the definition of constraints over relations. If a constraint is violated, a system defined exception is raised. The R&R system also defines a constraint mechanism. Currently R&R constraints can only be defined over relations and relationships but the intent is to extend the applicability to objects of any type. When a constraint is violated, a user defined operation is triggered. If no such operation is provided, a system defined default is triggered instead. Both APPL/A's and R&R's constraint constructs are programming language-level representations for the underlying event-based control integration mechanisms described in Section 8.

Constraints and triggers provide a powerful mechanism for achieving interoperability between abstractions that were not originally designed to coordinate their activities. This was our experience in implementing a demonstration that involved tools originally designed independently of each other. It can be a dangerous programming style, however, if not judiciously applied since it relies on side effects that can lead to circular dependencies.

6. Dynamic Definition and Access

Various forms of dynamism are essential in enabling the evolution of the Arcadia environment while it is in operation and being used for productive work. As with heterogeneity, Arcadia has struggled with the issue of dynamic definition and access with regard to a variety of objects in the environment. Of course, any interesting environment supports large classes of dynamically defined objects, along with some means for accessing those objects. But there is also a significant portion of any environment that is not easily evolvable. This induces a qualitative measure of "granularity" for dynamism. The degree of granularity is a measure of the effort needed to make a change that is visible to the environment.

Our initial emphasis on using Ada caused us to choose program recompilation as our unit of granularity. That is, many changes were not visible until dependent program units were re-compiled and re-instantiated in the environment. Over time, we have come to recognize that this level of granularity is not sufficient; in some situations, it is undesirable to recompile some collection of programs in order to effect changes. Rather, we are pursuing more interpretive approaches where changes can be immediately exported into the environment. This section addresses two main issues: identifying the objects that can change dynamically and defining the granularity of dynamic changes.

6.1 Sources of Dynamism in Arcadia

Object management is one obvious source of dynamic change in any environment. By definition, an object manager allows for the dynamic creation and manipulation of a variety of objects: application objects and indices, for example. Here, and subject to transaction semantics, changes to objects can quickly be made visible. A surprising number of object managers do not allow immediate changes to the schema, including even the addition of new types, without significant delays. For example, one of our initial object management systems, CACTIS [9], used recompilation in order to implement dynamic changes to schemas.

Our current object management systems, which are PGRAPHITE and TRITON, both provide substantial improvements in dynamic schema management. We recognize the difficulties around general schema changes [11], and in both PGRAPHITE and TRITON we have chosen to provide a level of support for dynamic schema changes that is useful without being comprehensive.

PGRAPHITE supports a structural object-oriented model in which the structure of objects is embedded into the accessing programs but provides a level of interpretation in accessing fields to these objects. As a result, one can extend objects to include new fields without having to re-compile accessing programs. Of course, deletion of fields or changes in the semantics of existing fields require tracking and re-compiling programs that depend on the modified fields.

TRITON provides a behavioral object-oriented model derived from the E [17] type model. TRITON embeds this model in a client-server architecture that supports certain kinds of immediate augmentation for recorded schemas. Specifically, it allows for the dynamic definition of functions, methods, classes, and triggers and deletion of the same. Changes require deletion followed by (re-)definition.

Dynamic procedure definition is provided by a facility for dynamically loading the code for methods and triggers, and by providing mechanisms by which clients of TRITON can invoke those newly defined methods with relatively low overhead. Addition of new structural fields, something that is easy in PGRAPHITE, is difficult in TRITON since that information is encoded into the compiled method code. TRITON also provides for the deletion of schema elements, although we are not sure that we have the appropriate deletion semantics. In order to address dynamism in the presence of multiple models, we have developed the A LA CARTE heterogeneous data management system [7]. A LA CARTE presents tools for incrementally integrating multiple object managers at various levels of processing, such as physical object management, transaction management, and data modeling.

We recognize that there are dependencies between the TRITON schema and the client programs that use it. So some schema changes will require (at least) recompiling dependent clients. It is possible to write clients that obtain sufficient schema information at execution time to react to changes. Type and instance browser programs are often written in this fashion.

User interface is another area where dynamic operation is desirable, and the CHIRON UIDS has evolved in the direction of increasing dynamism. In its first version (CHIRON-0), artist procedures had to be compiled into the application code and there was a limit of one artist per abstract data type (ADT). In CHIRON-1.0, the artists still had to be compiled with the application, but the single artist restriction was removed by the use of an event dispatcher per ADT. Multiple artists may register interest in the same ADT. Very recent changes in CHIRON have opened up the possibility (as yet unexploited) for adding and deleting artists on-the-fly without the need for recompilation.

Evaluation (in the form of AMADEUS) is both a producer and consumer of dynamism in Arcadia. As a consumer, it requires an ability to dynamically insert measurement probes into various processed in the environment without disrupting those processes. As a producer, AMADEUS uses its event mechanism to dynamically define and activate scripts that can process collected measurements.

6.2 Mechanisms Supporting Dynamism

Arcadia provides a variety of mechanisms supporting dynamism at a level of granularity requiring recompilation. Without being exhaustive, we can single out three mechanisms that directly support more rapid dynamic changes in Arcadia: events, dynamic loading, and client-server architectures.

As described in Section 8, the various event dispatchers in Arcadia allow for dynamic specification of procedures (or scripts or triggers) to be invoked whenever certain events occur. In effect, we have an anonymous invocation mechanism in which the recipients to be invoked can be defined and changed in a highly dynamic fashion.

TRITON supports dynamic loading of code into the TRITON server along with simple mechanisms for invoking that dynamically loaded code. This is currently only usable for object methods and for triggers, but the basic mechanism has potential applications in other components such as the CHIRON server where it could be used to extend its functionality on-the-fly.

The whole client-server apparatus in Arcadia (Q) provides a significant degree of dynamism. It allows a client program to invoke an (almost) arbitrary server program and to decide, on-the-fly, the particular server and operation within the service in which it is interested, CHIRON currently exploits this capability. This gives a rather different flavor to Arcadia compared to, for example, Cedar [21], which had the mixed blessing of a single address space where it was possible to dynamically bind code, but in so doing, inter-component dependencies were lost that made it difficult to unbind components.

6.3 Costs

We are aware that the use of dynamism, especially structural dynamism, does not come free. Often it is difficult to type-check with a compiler, or analyze with various tools. This introduces the possibility of run-time errors, which are the most expensive ones to find. When errors occur, they may be time or context-dependent, and the programmer may not even be able to capture the context. These difficulties should not be read as arguments against dynamism so much as they are arguments for using caution when it is introduced and for providing appropriate support to make its use as safe as possible.

7. Concurrency

There are a wide variety of reasons for supporting concurrency in a software development environment. For example, Arcadia has found that all too many SDEs are implicitly developed for single users. Our goal of providing a pro-active, heterogeneous environment for multiple users and multiple classes of users demanded that we use languages and system programming mechanisms that effectively support concurrency. Some of the many demands for concurrency in Arcadia are as follows. With regard to user interfaces we recognize that both users and tools may be simultaneously active and in need of periodic communication with each other. Consequently the UIDS must not preordain one or the other to be "in charge" and must therefore exhibit a concurrent control model. CHIRON is designed to support multiple users working cooperatively, such as through multi-view editing sessions. Similarly, the process programming mechanisms in Arcadia are designed to orchestrate the actions of multiple, concurrent users, cooperating on tasks such as creating a requirements specification. These process mechanisms must enable specification and enaction of cooperating concurrent activities. This objective has further consequences, requiring, for example, support for concurrency controls on shared data. We have also found that many process components are effectively expressed as reactive control units, which can best be described logically using formalisms involving concurrency. Effectively supporting flexible measurement and evaluation of processes also demands concurrency: monitoring and analysis activities should, in many cases, take place transparently, unobtrusively, and simultaneously with the monitored process. Concurrent mechanisms in the AMADEUS system support this non-interference approach. It is also clear, in all the above situations as well as others, that performance benefits can be achieved through the programming of concurrent activities.

Though not as obvious and stringent a demand for concurrency, the heterogeneous systems approach exhibited by the Arcadia environment is also perhaps best supported by distributed computation. For example, use of some tool may require execution on a particular hardware platform, distinct from the primary platform of the environment. Integration of that tool into a process would likely require distributed systems support, and would bring the potential for concurrency along at the same time.

There are three practical consequences of the needs for concurrency in Arcadia.

First, environment components supporting requirements wherein concurrency is a key part benefit from being programmed in a language which has effective constructs for using and controlling concurrency. This reduces the burden on the developer (as compared to simulating the concurrency in a sequential language) and keeps the implementation cleaner. On the other hand, for various reasons one does not always have this capability and therefore a fall-back strategy must be provided. Use of operating system capabilities from a sequential language is a natural resort. (This often leads to the creation of heavyweight processes with separate address spaces, which has other advantages discussed below.)

Second, the presence of concurrency presents many well-known challenges to developers: developing bug-free concurrent code is notoriously difficult. As a result, we found that our development benefited substantially from the use of good formal analysis. For example, the CHIRON system, consisting of approximately twenty Ada tasks in two Unix processes, was analyzed by the CATS analyzer (which performs a type of reachability analysis and temporal logic checking). Two race conditions and a deadlock possibility were thus identified and subsequently removed.

Third, because many tools do not anticipate working in a concurrent world, it is often necessary to adopt a defensive implementation strategy that protects tools from each other. For example, one version of the CHIRON system makes use of the XView user interface toolkit and processor. Since XView assumes a sequential control model, while CHIRON is concurrent, it was necessary to place them in separate address spaces, since the XView notifier destroyed the Unix signals used by the Ada (tasking) run-time system. More generally, the basic solution is to guarantee separate resources for each run-time system, including signals, file-descriptors, and possible heap memory. Heap memory does imply separate address spaces, while technically signals and descriptors do not (though on Unix they do.)

The use of separate address spaces also contributes, in an incidental fashion, to addressing several other issues, including strongly controlled interfaces and multi-language issues. Multi-language issues should be clear from the preceding paragraph. The issue with strongly-controlled interfaces is that, in the absence of effective language constructs and analyzers that guarantee that design-level interface rules are not violated, placing service providers and service requesters in separate address spaces yields an effective operational way of ensuring conformance to the interface rules. That is, "thin-wire" communication helps enforce the abstractions.

8. Event-based Control Integration Mechanisms

To facilitate the sorts of highly flexible control flow necessary in the face of rapid change in the structure and componentry of an environment, we found event-based control integration mechanisms to be broadly useful. For example, event-based control has been used from statistics gathering, to enforcing constraints, to maintaining consistency between multiple simultaneous graphical views of objects. In this section, we will first describe the various purposes served by the event-based mechanisms. The details of the mechanisms will then be contrasted.

The common objective of all the mechanisms discussed is the combination ("integration") of separate components to perform desired services. Such mechanisms are necessary when no single component suffices to perform the service and the necessary compositions of components are unpredictable. Moreover, an extensible mechanism is needed, so that new components can be added in a convenient, and often dynamic, manner. "Components" in the systems above include, for example, artists (CHIRON), data analysis agents (AMADEUS), and data-constraint maintenance programs (APPL/A and R&R).

In CHIRON, dispatcher events are accesses to the interface functions of abstract data type (ADT) instances (Ada packages, in the primary implementation). These events and the supporting mechanism are used to provide dynamic, non-invasive coordination of tools and artists, where artists are code units that provide customized graphical depictions of the state of the ADT instance. Among the functionality provided is simultaneous updates of all views of an object, regardless of which views are used as editing interfaces. In AMADEUS, an event is a fundamental abstraction on which process or product measurement and evaluation is based. (Events may be aggregated and analyzed to yield insight into products or processes.) The purpose of AMADEUS' event-based integration mechanism is to detect events and enter them into the measurement and evaluation framework, possibly resulting in changes to components in the environment.

Events in APPL/A are operations on relations. Their purpose is to allow automatic, reactive response to operations on relations. Response to a change to a file, for example, might be to issue a warning message that a configuration was out of date and to initiate recompilation of other components to bring the configuration back into a consistent state.

In TRITON, events are invocations of methods or functions stored in the TRITON server. Functions can be triggered upon such invocations, and may be used to support, e.g., unobtrusive monitoring, to provide forward and backward inferencing, and to export database events to the rest of the environment.

Events in NEXUS, the event-based control mechanism underlying R&R's constraint facilities, are similar to those in CHIRON in that NEXUS events are accesses to the interface operations of ADT instances. NEXUS events are used to support consistency maintenance over shared objects (e.g., R&R relations and relationships, and graphical depictions) where changes in the state of an object might be of interest to other entities in the environment.

It should be clear that the various Arcadia event-based integration mechanisms exist and operate at different levels of abstraction for the different purposes described above. Nevertheless, a common set of design issues can be used to highlight both similarities and differences. We first consider the notion of event types, then present several issues that arise in the context of event recognition and processing. Cross-cutting issues of dynamism and concurrency are then considered.

8.1 Event Types

Three types of events that are explicitly identified in AMADEUS cover all the event types in the Arcadia mechanisms: changes in data values, time-based events, and messages. Messages may represent (name, value) pairs or procedure/function calls (which includes operations on relations or relationships). The information content of messages, including the notion of the type system to which they belong, varies, and is discussed below. It is not clear that there is any intrinsic difference between event types; each may be modeled (and represented) different ways. An obvious but important observation is that the definition of an event is tied to a particular set of abstractions (e.g. what constitutes an event for Chiron's user interface purposes may not be an event for Nexus' constraint-management purposes, and vice versa).

8.2 Event Occurrence and Processing

Registration. Prior to event occurrence, event emitters may register descriptions of the kinds of events they may produce. Components interested in receiving events may register their interest in certain types (or values) of messages. Filtering, or transformation, protocols may also be registered. These items may be registered several places. There may be a single central authority for handling registrations or there may be many registration agents.

Event generation. Events may be "naturally occurring" or be seeded, either manually or automatically. Events are naturally occurring in CHIRON, APPL/A-TRITON, NEXUS, and in some AMADEUS components, in that the events occur as an ordinary part of achieving some other functionality, e.g., accessing an ADT instance's access function or operating upon a relation. Events in AMADEUS may be seeded. For example, a process program may have event generation code inserted to yield the raw data needed by AMADEUS; other events monitored by AMADEUS may be natural, such as watching for a file to be edited.

Recognition. Once an event occurs it must be recognized and thereby entered into the event-processing mechanism(s). This may happen by, e.g., the event-generating component, a database mechanism, or a "watcher" — a specific tool designed for that purpose. CHIRON events are recognized and initially handled by dispatchers, which are located in the application's address space. In TRITON, trigger detection and invocation is performed as part of the TRITON interface operations that invoke methods in the server. The NEXUS server is a component separate from object management services and is capable of operation on types not described via OM technology. AMADEUS events are recognized by specialized components (AMADEUS event servers), each having its own address space.

Representation and meaning. Events may be represented with strong or weak typing, and may convey their semantics either within the message or with respect to an external (to the message) definition. CHIRON messages are strongly typed, with their type system being the type system of the application. The message consists of the name of the operation performed, the value of all arguments to the operation, and the value of any return parameters. The meaning of the message is confined to the address space in which the event occurs. Both APPL/A and TRITON messages are similar. NEXUS messages are strongly typed, where the NEXUS type system is derived from the UTM, AMADEUS messages are weakly typed, being essentially (name, value) pairs encoded as ASCII strings, the interpretation of which is conventionalized by AMADEUS.

Processing. In general, event processing may involve collection and aggregation, filtering according to registered protocols, and propagation. Propagation may occur via a single distributor per environment, per event type, per object type, or per object. Distribution may be cascaded. Notions of transactions and rollback may be present. Propagation may be either synchronous or asynchronous, and whether it is synchronous or asynchronous may depend on the level of granularity considered. CHIRON events are processed by dispatchers, where there is one dispatcher per object. Some asynchrony of processing is possible but the primary notification activity is synchronous (involving the originator of the operation on the ADT, the dispatcher, and the listening artists). AMADEUS events are filtered and distributed by event servers under the control of scripts which define the desired processing in terms of which actions to take, such as which tools or processes should be executed. There may be multiple servers per AMADEUS application, and scripts are explicitly declared to have synchronous or asynchronous processing. In NEXUS, collection and propagation are performed by the NEXUS server, where there is one server per namespace. Synchronization in NEXUS is listener-controlled; the informer specifies a maximum level of synchronization that can be supported, and the listener specifies the minimum level that is desired.

Post-processing. Subsequent to processing of events, various activities may occur, such as sending of acknowledgments, modification of filtering policies, or generation of new events. CHIRON's dispatcher synchronization/transaction policy ensures one dispatch is complete before another can begin. AMADEUS events may cause further events to be generated and propagated which may cause additional scripts to be interpreted. Event generation may be turned off (or on) depending on the actions associated with event processing. TRITON triggers are invoked with a pre-defined interface that includes the arguments to the function or the result of the function. The trigger may perform arbitrary manipulations on that information and may even abort the actual invocation of the target method. NEXUS listeners may control the receipt of events by dynamically registering and unregistering with the server.

Cross-cutting Issues. Cutting across all the above are issues of dynamism and concurrency. Dynamism is the degree to which changes can be made to any of the definitions or mechanisms after their initial construction. Concurrency is the degree to which parts of the mechanisms may operate simultaneously. Some aspects of dynamism have already been identified. AMADEUS is the most dynamic of all the current mechanisms, as new event kinds may be generated while an Arcadia process is executing and new event servers to receive and dispatch events may be activated. Such dynamism goes hand-in-hand with AMADEUS' weakly typed message structure. The other mechanisms, more strongly typed, are less dynamic.

8.3 The Point

Though serving a wide range of purposes and though developed independently, a high degree of commonality of structure is present in the above subsystems. Tradeoffs among specific design choices are apparent. We conclude that this type of mechanism is widely adaptable and useful in the software environment context, well beyond the typical uses of early systems such as Field [16] and Softbench [4], which have been largely confined to infrequent control integration of large, monolithic (from the perspective of Field/Softbench) tools.

9. Conclusion

If we were pressed to summarize our lessons, we would have to say that Arcadia is about abstraction and flexibility in the face of the multiple tensions created by a broad set of goals and a wide variety of component technologies.

We remain convinced that appropriate use of abstraction remains a key to effective large-scale system development. All environment capabilities and artifacts (e.g., processes, operands, etc.) should be captured through disciplined used of abstraction. Further, we believe that these abstractions must not only capture functionality, but also support viewability, measurability, and persistence.

There do seem to us to be certain risks, however, in premature codification of abstractions. In the absence of a fixed structure, it is important to favor flexibility in the structuring of abstractions. That being the case, we found that it was preferable to define smaller and more general abstractions rather than larger and more specific abstractions.

As illustrated by our experience with abstractions, flexibility is the other hallmark of Arcadia. Many of the lessons we have learned involve our attempts to move in the direction of increasing flexibility. Heterogeneity, meta-languages, dynamism, events, concurrency, and powerful type systems are all driven by a requirement for flexibility.

In sum, we believe that the Arcadia project shows that it is possible to provide a system that begins to match the ambitious goals that we established for ourselves. In the process of producing such an environment, we have learned a number of lessons that, while specific to our own diverse research efforts, seem likely to be of interest and value to many environment projects outside Arcadia.

Acknowledgments This paper represents the opinions of the principal investigators of the current university Arcadia grants: University of Massachusetts: Lori A. Clarke, Jack C. Wileden; University of California at Irvine: Leon J. Osterweil, Debra J. Richardson, Richard W. Selby, Richard N. Taylor; University of Colorado: Dennis M. Heimbigner, Roger King. The work upon which this paper is based was the result of efforts of many people, including the following whom we would particularly like to acknowledge: Stephanie Leif Aha, Jennifer Anderson, Ken Anderson, Deborah Baker, Robert Balzer, Douglas Bell, Frank Belz, Jim Berney, Navdip Bhachech, Barry Boehm, Greg Bolter, Billie Bozarth, Debra Brodbeck, Mary Burdick, Mary Cameron, Yldong Chen, Satish Chittamuru, Pamela Drew, Jose Duarte, Matthew Dwyer, Stuart Feldman, Joseph Fialli, Charles Fisher, David Fisher, Kari Forester, Susan Graham, Thomas Huynh, Greg James, Rajesh Jha, Takuya Katayama, Alan Kaplan, Ruedi Keller, Walter R. Kopp, Peter Lee, Barbara Lerner, David Levine, Chyun Lin, Doug Long, Dave Luckham, Craig MacFarlane, Kent Madsen, Mark Maybee, Erik Mettala, Cynthia Tittle Moore, Elliot Moss, Kurt Olender, Owen O'Malley, Lolo Penedo, Adam Porter, Ron Reimer, William Rosenblatt, Wilhelm Schafer, Bill Scherlis, John Self, Izhar Shy, Xiping Song, Craig Snider, Tom Souksamlane, Stephen Squires, Stan Sutton, Peri Tarr, Kojii Tori, Dennis Troup, Sandy Wise, Alex Wolf, Harry Yessayan, Michal Young, Patrick Young, Steven Zeil, Hadar Ziv.

References

[1] M. Atkinson, F. Bancilhon, D. DeWitt, K. Dittrich, D. Maier, and S. Zdonik. The Object-Oriented Database System Manifesto. In *Proceedings of the First International Conference on Deductive and Object-Oriented Databases*, 1989.

[2] D. A. Baker, D. A. Fisher, and J. C. Shultis. The gardens of IRIS. Technical Report Arcadia-IncSys-88-03, Incremental Systems Corporation, August 1988. Draft.

[3] P. A. Bernstein. Database system support for software engineering. In *Proceedings of the Ninth International Conference on Software Engineering*, pages 166-178, 1987

[4] M. R. Cagan. The HP SoftBench environment: An architecture for a new generation of software tools. *Hewlett-Packard Journal*, 41(3):36–47, June 1990.

[5] M. J. Carey, D. H. DeWitt, D. Frank, G. Graefe, M. Muralikrishna, J. E. Richardson, and E. Shekita. The architecture of the EXODUS extensible DBMS. *In International Workshop on Object-Oriented Database Systems, pages 52-65, 1986.*

[6] L. A. Clarke, J. C. Wileden, and A. L. Wolf. Graphite: A meta-tool for Ada environment development. In *Proceedings of the IEEE Computer Society Second International Conference on Ada Applications and Environments*, pages 81–90, Miami Beach, Florida, April 1986. IEEE Computer Society Press.

[7] P. Drew, R. King, and D. Heimbigner. A toolkit for the incremental implementation of heterogeneous database management systems. *Very Large Database Journal*, 1(2), 1992.

[8] D. Heimbigner. Triton Reference Manual, 1 July 1990.

[9] S. E. Hudson and R. King. The Cactis project: Database support for software environments. *IEEE Transactions on Software Engineering*, 14(6):709-719, June 1988.

[10] R. K. Keller, M. Cameron, R. N. Taylor, and D. B. Troup. User interface development and software environments: The Chiron-1 system. In *Proceedings of the Thirteenth International Conference on Software Engineering*, pages 208–218, Austin, TX, May 1991.

[11] B. S. Lerner and A. N. Habermann. Beyond Schema Evolution to Database Reorganization. In *Proceedings of the Joint ACM OOPSLA/ECOOP '90 Conference on Object-Oriented Programming: Systems, Languages, and Applications*, Ottawa, Canada, October 1990.

[12] D. L. Long and L. A. Clarke. Task interaction graphs for concurrency analysis. In *Proceedings of the Eleventh International Conference on Software Engineering*, pages 44–52, 1989.

[13] M. Maybee, L. J. Osterweil, and S. D. Sykes. Q: A multi-lingual interprocess communications system for software environment implementation. Technical Report CU-CS-476-90, University of Colorado, Boulder, June 1990.

[14] C. T. Moore, T. O. O'Malley, D. J. Richardson, S. H. L. Aha, and D. A. Brodbeck. ProDAG: A program dependence graph system. Technical Report UCI-91-25, Department of Information and Computer Science, University of California, 1991.

[15] J. E. B. Moss. Implementing persistence for an object oriented language. In *Proceedings of the Workshop on Persistent Object Systems: Their Design, Implementation, and Use*, 1987.

[16] S. P. Reiss. Connecting tools using message passing in the field environment. *IEEE Software*, 7(4):57–66, July 1990.

[17] J. E. Richardson and M. J. Carey. Programming constructs for database system implementation in EXODUS. In *Proc. ACM SIGMOD Conf.*, pages 208-219, 1987.

[18] W. Rosenblatt, J. Wileden, and A. Wolf. OROS: Toward A Type Model for Software Development Environments. In *OOPSLA Conference Proceedings*, pages 297–304, 1989.

[19] R. W. Selby, A. A. Porter, D. C. Schmidt, and J. Berney. Metric-driven analysis and feedback systems for enabling empirically guided software development. In *Proceedings of the Thirteenth International Conference on Software Engineering*, Austin, TX, May 1991.

[20] S. M. Sutton, Jr., D. Heimbigner, and L. J. Osterweil. Language constructs for managing change in process-centered environments. In *Proceedings of ACM SIGSOFT '90: Fourth Symposium on Software Development Environments*, pages 206–217, December 1990. (Reprinted as Chapter 19)

[21] D. Swinehart, P. Zellweger, R. Beach, and R. Hagmann. A structural view of the Cedar programming environment. *ACM Transactions on Programming Languages and Systems*, 8(4):419–490, October 1986.

[22] P. Tarr, J. Wileden, and L. Clarke. Extending and Limiting PGRAPHITE-style Persistence. In *Proceedings of the 4th International Workshop on Persistent Object Systems*, Martha's Vineyard, MA, pages 74-86, August 1990.

[23] J. Wileden, A. Wolf, W. Rosenblatt, and P. Tarr. Specification Level Interoperability. *Communications of the ACM*, 34(5):73-87, May 1991.

[24] J. C. Wileden, A, L. Wolf, C. D. Fisher, and P. L. Tarr. PGRAPHITE: An experiment in persistent typed object management. In *Proceedings of ACM SIGSOFT '88: Third Symposium on Software Development Environments*, pages 130–142, Boston, November 1988.

[25] A. Wolf, L. Clarke, and J. Wileden. The AdaPIC toolset: Supporting interface control and analysis throughout the software development process. *IEEE Transactions on Software Engineering*, 15(3):250-263, March 1989.

[26] P. S. Young and R. N. Taylor. Team-oriented process programming. Technical Report UCI-91-68, Department of Information and Computer Science, University of California, 1991.

[27] S. Zdonik and D. Maier. Fundamentals of Object-Oriented Databases. In S. Zdonik and D. Maier, editors, *Readings in Object-Oriented Data Systems*, pages 1–32. Morgan Kaufman, San Mateo, California, 1990.

Part III: Software Process

From Process Programming to Process Engineering

Stanley M. Sutton Jr.

IBM T. J. Watson Research Center, P. O. Box 704, Yorktown Heights, NY 10598, USA
suttons@us.ibm.com

Abstract Osterweil proposed the idea of processes as a kind of software in 1986. It arose from prior work on software tools, tool integration, and development environments, and from a desire to improve the specification and control of software development activities. The vision of process programming was an inspiring one, directly leading to ideas about process languages, process environments, process science (both pure and applied), and to opportunities for process analysis and simulation. Osterweil, his colleagues, and a thriving community of researchers worldwide have worked on these and related ideas for 25 years now, with many significant results. Additionally, as Osterweil and others have shown, ideas and approaches that originated in the context of software process are applicable in other domains, such as science, government, and medicine. In light of this, the future of process programming looks as exciting and compelling as ever.

1. Introduction

Over the past 25 years or so there has been a torrent of research into software process—a flood that shows no signs of abating. There were (and remain) many currents in this work; among the most prominent and persistent have been process improvement, process maturity, and processes and methods themselves. One of the most significant has been idea of treating processes as a kind of software, that is, that "Software Processes are Software, Too" [67].

The idea that software processes are software, although initially somewhat controversial, has been recognized as one of the most influential in software engineering [68]. Its influence derives, in large measure, from the fact that it suggests many lines of research. These lines of research have been followed vigorously by Osterweil, his students and colleagues, and a large community of researchers. The purpose of this paper is to set the context of this idea and to review the work that has followed from it or been related to it. The main focus will be on topics related

P.L. Tarr, A.L. Wolf (eds.), *Engineering of Software*,
DOI 10.1007/978-3-642-19823-6_15, © Springer-Verlag Berlin Heidelberg 2011

to process programming. Topics pertaining to process-centered software environments are treated in Part II.

2. Background

Prior to the insight that processes represent a kind of software, Osterweil and his group had been working on static analysis tools (see Part I), derivation and dependency management, and integrated tool sets as a basis for software development environments (see Part II). This work included a cluster of ideas that pertain significantly to the view of processes as software and to the programming of software processes. These include: the application of tools to software artifacts to produce other artifacts; the formal specification of the dependencies between tools and artifact types; the machine interpretation of these formal specifications to automate the execution of tools and the derivation of artifacts; notions of dependency and consistency management; and the integration of all these elements into development environments.

The first detailed treatment of processes as software is a technical report by Osterweil titled "Software Process Interpretation and Software Environments" [65]. From the abstract of that report:

> This paper suggests and explores the idea that software engineering processes should be specified by means of rigorous algorithmic descriptions. The paper suggests that rigorous encodings of such processes as development and maintenance can serve both as guides to better understanding of the processes and as superior architectures for integrating software tools into environments.
>
> ... leads to deeper understandings of processes, better appreciation of the relations of processes to each other and to a truer understanding of such software engineering notions as reuse, metrics, and modularity.
>
> This paper also suggests that software process encodings should themselves be viewed as items of software which have been created as products of development processes...
>
> This paper also addresses the question of what sort of language might be needed in order to do an effective job of supporting the expression of software process programs.

The most essential ideas of processes as software and of process programming—indeed, the basis for an entire research program—are represented here: Processes should be given algorithmic encodings as programs—*process programming*. Process encoding should be represented in suitable formalisms—*process-programming languages*. Process encodings should be created as part of development processes—*process engineering*. Doing so should enable us to gain insight about fundamental software engineering notions—*process science*—and a better understanding of software processes—*applied process science*. And processes can serve as the basis for environment integration—*process-centered environments*.

This vision was sufficiently compelling to spur the emergence of a large and vibrant research community, which continues strong today, more than two decades later. The remainder of this essay provides an overview of some of the general issues around process programming, a broad review of process languages, and a brief discussion of software environments in relation to process languages. Finally, it discusses applications of process programming, particularly in areas in which Osterweil has contributed.

3. Process Programming

What does it mean to say that software processes are software? Essentially, it means that software processes can be given software-like representations [65,66], and that many of the same principles, techniques, and methodologies surrounding the development of software also apply to such representations of software processes. Many other ideas follow directly from this insight: process modeling and programming languages, process software engineering, process environments, etc. We refer to this overall vision of processes-as-software by the term that has been most commonly used, "process programming," where "programming" is intended to connote the range of software engineering, not simply coding.

Osterweil clearly stated from the outset that software processes should be given algorithmic descriptions [67]. The emphasis on "algorithmic" was important in the original context for several reasons. First, algorithmic descriptions should be rigorous. Second, algorithmic descriptions should be formal, and many of the benefits, such as the analyzability and executability of process descriptions, would derive from their formality. Finally, an algorithmic approach would address a problem that was prevalent at the time: process descriptions that were incomplete, inconsistent, and otherwise problematic.

There was immediate controversy over whether it was possible to program software processes meaningfully or usefully. The crux of this issue is that programs tend to be algorithmic, whereas software processes do not. For example, software development entails creative aspects that are inherently non-algorithmic. Moreover, processes are subject to significant, unanticipated irregularities that would cause algorithmic descriptions to be violated.

In retrospect, however, the *algorithmic* quality of process definitions was probably overemphasized. Many conventional software applications are not strictly algorithmic, and, as it has evolved, neither are most of the software processes that have been programmed. Instead, the benefits of process programming, such as analyzability and executability, have arisen mainly from the formality of process descriptions, and the utility of process programming has arisen in part from the possibility of describing many kinds of processes, algorithmic or not.

Osterweil also recognized many of the issues that might complicate an "algorithmic" approach to process programming from the beginning. He and others stated early that they expected humans to be a part of most processes. How to accommodate people and other agents has been a recurrent theme in his research [66,98,117,20]. Complicating factors such as exceptions and inconsistency management have also been a subject for research essentially from the outset of process programming [26,3,99,4].

Taking a practical approach, Osterweil proposed to demonstrate the feasibility of process programming directly, by writing process programs. Still in the very early days, even before there were any firm ideas about suitable process languages, he proposed the idea of BOPEEP: But One Plausible End-to-End Process (Program) [106]. This was intended to be a lifecycle-wide proof of the process-programming concept. At that time, with no experience to indicate otherwise, Osterweil thought that his research group might be able to write a simple but plausible, end-to-end process in a few months. This didn't happen, in part because the effort proved to be more challenging than initially expected, and in part because he came to realize that the issues involved warranted more detailed investigation.

Another early hurdle was the problem that Osterweil called "research deadlock" [106] between process programming languages and process programs, each being needed to some extent to investigate and validate the other. Somewhat later, Madhavji noted a similar interdependency between process understanding and process technology [59]. Thus, in the early years of process programming, many researchers spent considerable effort in bootstrapping to achieve an effective balance of language, processes, and supporting technologies.

Despite these challenges, in a few years there were a number of detailed or demonstrable process programs developed by Osterweil's group [31,93,103,92,107], and numerous other modeling systems had realized some degree of experimental or practical use (see the next section). As early as the sixth and seventh International Software Process Workshops [49,108], the major question was no longer *whether* processes could be programmed, but *how* they could best be programmed.

A final concern in the practicability of process programming is whether process programs are useful. That question is addressed in later sections of this essay.

4. Process Languages

When Osterweil first proposed the idea of processes as software, he suggested that support for sequential algorithmic logic, parallelism, and the ability to represent structured and typed objects were important language capabilities [65]. However, he also explicitly noted that different language paradigms might be useful for different purposes, and he considered process-control, functional, object-oriented, and database languages [66]. He also noted that humans would carry out parts of the process. Topics for future work included the language paradigm, compiler, and runtime support.

The topic of appropriate forms and features for process languages was pursued vigorously by the community for several years. Many existing languages were applied directly or extended, and some new languages were defined. Some existing configuration management and software specification systems were also applied directly or extended, and some new systems, mainly process-centered software environments, were developed. Some examples include: AP5 [22], an extended Lisp-based environment for executable specifications; HFSP [48], a new functional process language; MARVEL [46], a software environment kernel operating by rules; Melmac [33], a system supporting the execution of FUNSOFT nets (a form of Petri-net); StateMate [35], a system for specifying reactive systems; LOTOS [84], a language for temporal logic specifications; Hakoniwa [42], a process monitor and navigation system based on an activity sequence model; SLANG [6], the extended Petri-net language of the object-oriented SPADE process environment; PROCESS WEAVER [30], which supplemented UNIX with workflow; MERLIN [45], a knowledge-based environment using rules; Adele-TEMPO [7], a configuration-management system extended with rules for process; ALF [13], a framework for building process-centered environments; and EPOS [23], an object-oriented system for cooperative process modeling. Many others could be cited.

Osterweil's research group also spent some time experimenting with impromptu, ad-hoc languages to discover natural forms of expression for processes in a variety of domains, including software, cooking [26], specifying driving directions, and other everyday processes. Cooking was of interest because recipes represent a form of process description for heavily people-centric processes, while travel directions posed interesting challenges for conditional execution and exception handling. These efforts led to some new process language features.

Languages that came from Osterweil's group and across the Arcadia consortium included APPL/A (Ada with relations, triggers, transactions, and consistency rules) [99,100], P4 (rule-based inferencing) [36], Meteor (a framework for defining maintenance processes) [31], and Teamware [121] (a graphical workflow language for team processes).

These languages and frameworks, from Osterweil's group and the broader community, included a wide variety of features intended to address a range of process concerns. Most process languages include some form of imperative control, while many (often additionally) included some form of triggers, consistency rules, and transactions. Many languages also included support for data flow (if not also data definition) and aspects of resource management. It was recognized early on that process languages benefited from supporting multiple control paradigms [25,52], and a multi-paradigm approach was a de facto, if not featured, aspect of many process languages. Many languages had textual representations like traditional programming or specification languages, although a large group had graphical representations.

Some topics that received special attention in particular languages or systems included support for accommodating inconsistency (e.g., APPL/A [100], AP5 [22,4]); support for process change (e.g., SLANG [5], Teamware [120]), support for humans in the process (e.g., PROCESS WEAVER [30], Interact/Intermediate [77], Teamware [120]), and simplified means of expressing process control flow in textual languages (e.g., "a bi-level language" [47], ALF [13]).

After several years of process-language research, a number of broad issues and observations emerged. Some of the principal ones are as follows:

- **Broad applicability of languages and features**: All of the different kinds of languages, and many language features, were shown to have some applicability to process programming, including multiple different control and data-modeling paradigms [49,108].
- **Suitability to purpose**: The suitability of a language for process programming depends strongly on the purposes for which the language was used (for example, [80]). The diversity of purposes meant that most languages were good for something, and that no language would be good for everything.
- **Idiosyncrasies of approach**: The choices of language, language paradigm, and problems addressed were often based on the personal predilections of researchers. In the early days, especially, this was a good thing, since it promoted a broad range of lessons and experience. However, it left open the question of whether practitioners might insist on a wide variety of approaches or be content with a small number of common standards.
- **Technical versus "manageable" languages**: Consistent with the idea of process programming as a kind of software development, most of the earlier process languages were "technical" languages (programming languages, formal modeling languages, etc.). These languages could address many control or data issues that might apply to software processes. However, using them effectively required technical expertise. This made them less suitable for use by people whose backgrounds were mainly in areas such as management, business, etc.
- **Broad versus focused languages**: Another differentiator among process languages was the language features supported. Consider two of the earliest languages specifically developed for process programming: HFSP [48] and APPL/A [100]. HFSP was a small language that allowed a process to be defined according to a hierarchy of functions and represented the data flow between functions. It was limited in what it could express, but it could express that simply and elegantly. In contrast, APPL/A was defined by taking a large language (Ada 83 [2]) and adding features to it. It included two kinds of control flow (imperative, reactive) and several features targeted toward object management, including relations, transactions, and predicates. Many things can be expressed directly in APPL/A, but it had an elaborate programming model and tended to give rise to large programs that addressed many concerns.

The experiences with APPL/A were definitive for Osterweil's group in several respects. They validated the idea of process programming. They showed that a wide range of processes were programmable by a general-purpose programming language. They demonstrated the importance of reactive control and exception handling and the applicability of novel features for consistency and transaction management. They illustrated the diversity of concerns that might be relevant in programming a software process. But experience with APPL/A also made clear the limitations of large, general-purpose languages for process programming: the variety of features complicated learning and use, the programs were not concise, and the lack of process-oriented abstractions hindered process expression, understanding, and analysis. Additionally, APPL/A was a strictly textual language, and many process programmers or modelers preferred to take a graphical approach.

Moving beyond APPL/A, Sutton and Osterweil proposed a next-generation process language, JIL[1] [102]. JIL aimed to resolve some of the conflicting perspectives from previous process research in being able to support both high-level and low-level programming, to be a broad language that could be used in focused ways, and to allow programmers to program in a paradigm with which they felt most comfortable. It would have high-level, process-oriented abstractions. It would support general purpose programming constructs but also allow process steps to be orchestrated according to simple path expressions [12]. It would be a *factored language*: it would have a wide range of features (tasks, agents, triggers, consistency, transactions, data modeling, etc.) but allow programs to be written using selected subsets of features, according to application needs. And it would support multiple control paradigms, which could be used according to programmer preferences. The language would support both textual and graphical forms.

Osterweil's group realized that implementing the whole JIL vision would take considerable time and effort. They decided that a more practical strategy would be to develop a small and simple language first, one that could be designed and implemented in short order and leveraged immediately to investigate process issues. Thus was born Little-JIL.

Little-JIL [115,116] focuses on features related to the coordination of process agents. In JIL terms, it addresses the coordination factor of process languages. Little-JIL represents processes in terms of steps connected into graphs. Each step has an associated agent. Little-JIL programs interact with agents through an agenda management system [60]. Agents may be automated or human—Little-JIL does not distinguish. Agents are also managed as resources, along with data objects and other sorts of resources, and at runtime the Little-JIL interpreter interacts with a resource management system (where resource management is another factor in process representation) [78]. Control, agents, data, other resources, and events flow into and out from steps along the edges. Steps that are leaf nodes represent work that is accomplished by the associated agent outside the process' control. Steps that are interior nodes serve to control the execution of their substeps. Any control decisions are made by the associated agent. Within a step, control flow is divided into three parts: proactive, reactive, and exceptional. The proactive control is represented by one of four simple, path-expression-like operators. Reactions are steps that are triggered by the receipt of messages. Exception handlers conform to

---

[1] "JIL" stands for Julia Input Language. Julia was the envisioned process interpretation engine. It was named after Julia Child. JIL programs would be a form of process recipe.

a small number of simple patterns. Little-JIL has a novel, graphical syntax. In contrast with most visual process-modeling languages, which emphasize flow between steps at the same level of a process, Little-JIL emphasizes flow between steps at different levels of a process.

Little-JIL has been very successful in providing a platform for investigating coordination-related process issues (see Section 6.3). Little-JIL has also been an excellent language for programming processes that can be subject to static analysis (see Section 6.5). Conversely, as expected, Little-JIL has proven less useful in exploring issues relating to other process issues (e.g., transactions, artifact modeling). Despite its graphical syntax, high-level of abstraction, and semantic focus of the language, Little-JIL has not proven to be as intuitive to users as originally hoped. However, the language is tractable enough that knowledgeable Little-JIL programmers have been able to work effectively with non-programmer subject-matter experts in many fields to define significant Little-JIL programs in their respective domains (see Section 7).

After a number of years of intense exploration, research into process languages has declined in recent years as the community has shifted to taking advantage of the diversity of languages available. In the 2010 International Conference on Software Process [63], specifically dedicated to the theme "New Modeling Concepts for Today's Software Processes," only two papers really addressed this topic [8,56]. In other recent process conferences [58,110,111,112,113], interest in process languages has been similarly low.

Many other areas of process research are very active. It is a testament to the vigor of earlier research on process languages that attention has so fruitfully shifted from the languages in which processes are described to the processes themselves. Additionally, there is also a growing appreciation that commercially available process languages and support systems have advanced to the point where they may substantially address many of the needs of process researchers [70].

This is not to say that work on process languages has ceased entirely. It remains true that, if your work requires a process program or model, then the language you use will affect what you can do and how well you can do it. In Osterweil's group, there has been an ongoing effort to refine the features of Little-JIL to address the representation of process aspects other than coordination, such as resources [78], and to model process families [89]. Given the creativity shown by process-language researchers in the past and the new challenges the future holds, it will not be surprising if process languages again become an active area of research.

5. Process Environments

Part II provides a detailed treatment of process environments, but a few statements about the relationship of process-language research to that on process environments are in order. The body of research in process environments is comparable in size to that in process languages. This is no coincidence—often, the language and environment are two inseparable aspects of an integrated effort (e.g., MARVEL [46]; Hakoniwa [42], SLANG/SPADE [6], Adele-TEMPO [7], ALF [13], EPOS [23], and Merlin [45]). This close association is not absolutely necessary, but is natural because the environment can host not only language-specific interpretation and runtime capabilities but also specialized infrastructure it might require, such as for object management, communication, process-state management, process monitoring, and user-interfaces.

In the work of Osterweil and his associates, the relationship of languages to environments has been quite varied. APPL/A [100] is largely independent of the environment. Teamware [121] was supported by a dedicated environment. The Process Wall [37] is a process-state server that was independent of any process language. Meteor [31] is a language for specifying both maintenance processes and the integration of tools in an environment that supports those processes. In the Meteor approach, the environment itself is adapted to better represent and support a specific process. Little-JIL [115,14] also has a dedicated interpreter and editor, but the language and its tooling have been designed to allow a clean separation of environment components that do not support integral parts of the language. The execution of Little-JIL programs thus generally depends on providing these other services, such as agenda management, resource management, and artifact management. Additionally, agents (human or automated) must be provided to execute the work associated with process steps.

As with process languages alone, it does not seem that any single kind of relationship between process languages and process environments is ideal in all cases. As each of these arrangements may have its advantages and limitations, it seems that this relationship may be as important as the intrinsic properties of a language when selecting a language for some purpose.

6. Process-Programming Applications

In the early work on process programming [65,66,67], Osterweil suggested that treating process as an application domain could have many benefits. Some of these are reviewed below.

6.1 Process Understanding

Process understanding is perhaps the most direct benefit of process programming, and possibly the simplest to obtain. This understanding arises from the act of programming itself, from the need to examine the process and to capture it in a formal language with certain semantic specifications. If a process has not previously been defined, or if it has been defined only informally, then the attention required to create a programmatic representation may expose incompleteness, inconsistency, incorrectness, ambiguity, and other flaws. This was demonstrated with responses to the ISPW6 example process [53]. Not only did the example test the various languages, but the languages, in effect, also tested the example process [97]. This effect has also been observed with commercial development processes [29]. Even when a process is well understood, codifying it formally may make explicit some process aspects that were only implicit before, and it may aid learning and communication [55,8]. Additionally, the programming of processes may facilitate their comparison [94]. These types of process programming benefits are not restricted to software processes but have been observed in other sorts of processes [39].

Processes can be programmed or otherwise modeled without necessarily relying on any particular supporting technology. The understanding that arises from programming a process can be complemented by other means of investigation, such as static analysis, dynamic simulation, and monitoring.

6.2 Process Execution Support

Support for process execution is perhaps the most obvious benefit to seek from process programming but, because it requires extensive technological support, it may also be one of the most costly and challenging to obtain. Support for process execution is one of the principal goals of process research, particularly that which is sponsored or conducted by industry or government (e.g., [1,114,85,109]). There is a large commercial market for the automation of business processes and computer-aided design and manufacturing systems.

In practice, automated support for process execution has been applied in various ways for different purposes. These include, for example, electronic process guidance in support of process change [43], systems for process planning, information, and guidance [34], and the automation of processes such as testing [19].

Process execution has also been a topic of research within Osterweil's group. Process structure has been investigated as a specific influence on process executability [90]. An executable requirements process was developed and used for research purposes [103]. Practical software processes were developed to guide software designers [92] and to help novices with software design [15]. Additionally, a non-software process has been implemented for online dispute resolution [51].

6.3 Process Issues

Early on, Osterweil hypothesized that by representing processes as software, we might arrive at "a truer understanding of such software engineering notions as reuse, metrics, and modularity" [65]. Process programming has, indeed, been a vehicle for exploring many issues in software process and software engineering more generally.

Osterweil and his colleagues have used process programming to investigate consistency and inconsistency management [96], change propagation [99], transaction modeling [100,105], resource-based activity coordination and scheduling [78], the nature of rework [16], patterns of exception handling [57], and process families [101,89]. These are in addition to issues in process languages, process environments, specific software-process domains, process execution, and process analysis, as well as domain-related issues for processes outside of software engineering, that are addressed in other sections.

The larger process community also investigated a number of important issues through process programming or modeling. These include inconsistency management [3,4], rework [104], process change [5,62], process families [54], management and planning [52], and roles [11], among others.

The individual findings of these studies cannot be elaborated here, But they include clarifications of long-standing process concerns (e.g., rework and exception handling), new ways of thinking about software development (e.g., tolerating inconsistency), and approaches for practical applications in software engineering (e.g., management, planning, and roles). The overall significance is that process programming is indeed a useful tool for research. This is not surprising, as process programming and modeling introduce clarity in the expression of ideas and approaches, and they enable static analysis, dynamic simulation, and experimental evaluation to be used in answering questions and evaluating hypotheses.

6.4 Process Simulation

Simulation is one of the most widely used means of investigating software processes. It is especially well suited for this because processes can be difficult to test and to experiment with when in "live" use. A recent International Conference on the Software Process contained papers reporting the use of simulation to investigate late life-cycle manpower increases [10], custom projects in a multi-project environment [64], and incremental process modeling based on stakeholder concerns [119]. [122] provides an extended review of process simulation modeling.

Osterweil's work has focused much more on static analysis than on dynamic simulation, but he has addressed simulation of some processes outside of software engineering, including auctions [82] and hospital processes [83].

6.5 Process Analysis

In the broader software process community, process analysis has mainly meant the analysis of ongoing process executions or of records of process executions. There is a long history of this sort of work, for example [40,118,24,86,123,87]. Typical goals of such analyses are to correct or refine a process or to measure a process's fidelity to a process model.

More recently, as large repositories of process-related information have become more available, there have been efforts to analyze this information for process implications. For instance, [95] look at patterns of changes in a process repository, and [32] analyzes issue-management processes.

The work of Osterweil and his colleagues has emphasized the static analysis of process programs [72]. One technique they used is finite-state verification, which can find some process defects, errors in process definitions, and errors in property specifications [18]. Another technique is fault-tree analysis, which can help verify that the high-level goals of a process are satisfied and its rationale is fulfilled [39].

Static analysis has been used to identify significant properties in a wide range of processes, including threats to the robustness of a Scrum development process [74], race conditions in an auction process [21], points of failure in a blood-transfusion process [17], and the potential for fraudulent behavior in an election process [81]. Static analysis has also been proposed as an approach to process comparison [79], supplementing the technique of manual inspection [94].

7. Process Engineering

As Osterweil has written about "ubiquitous process engineering" [69]

> Software engineering has learned a great deal about how to create clear and precise process definitions, and how to use them to improve final software products. ... this knowledge can also be applied to good effect in many other domains where effective application of process technology can lead to superior products and outcomes.

Although this particular statement is relatively recent, the idea that other domains could inform process programming and vice versa is as old as the idea of process programming itself (e.g., [26]). Moreover, while Osterweil's earlier work on process programming emphasized aspects of processes that were particularly related to software (e.g., data modeling, transactions, and consistency management in APPL/A [100]), his later work has emphasized aspects of processes that are largely domain independent (e.g., coordination, agents, resources in Little-JIL [117]). This has enabled many of the techniques of software engineering, including requirements specification, coding, static analysis, and dynamic simulation, to be applied to processes in a wide variety of domains. Chapter 16 presents one such application, to the mechatronic domain.

In the field of ecology, with implications for science more broadly, process programming and related techniques have been applied to the specification and implementation of an analytic web [75]. This web coordinates the activities of scientists in distributed locations and automates aspects of the production of scientific data sets, helping to assure the provenance of data and the significance and reproducibility of scientific results [9,73,27]. The analytic web has also useful in the teaching of young scientists. This work has been published outside the field of software engineering [28,27] where it has been cited in scientific journals, government technical reports, and dissertations.

In the field of medicine, process programming has been applied to processes including blood transfusion [38,39], chemotherapy ordering and delivery [61], and emergency-room patient flow [83]. Static analysis and dynamic simulation have been used to evaluate the safety, efficiency, and overall quality of these processes [38,39,71,18]. As with the work on ecology, some work on medical processes has been published outside of the field of software engineering (e.g., [38,39,61]) and is cited in the medical literature and by government authorities [76].

Osterweil and his colleagues have applied process programming and process analysis to several processes related to government, including license renewal [91], elections [81,88], and online dispute resolution [51,50]. Still other fields treated in this way include business [124], knowledge discovery [44], and auctions [82]. Process programming clearly applies in all these areas, with benefits including automated support and improvements to qualities such as correctness, safety, and robustness. There is every reason to believe that these benefits can be extended to many other domains.

8. Conclusions

The work of Osterweil, his colleagues, and the broader software process community has demonstrated that process programming was a farsighted and fruitful vision. Osterweil's own contributions in this area, beyond the initial conception, have addressed process languages, process environments, process analysis and simulation, and the definition and study of processes and process issues.

In 2005, Humphrey set out global goals for process research [41]. He identified four critical areas of questions: designing processes, using processes, analyzing processes, and supporting processes. Osterweil and his colleagues have been contributing to each of these areas for more than two decades. That work, and the work of the larger community, still has momentum six years after Humphrey's call. Process research, development, and application are now truly global undertakings [58]. Work is still needed in the area of software engineering, but the potential for applications and benefits in other domains is firmly established. Fortunately, both despite and because of all of the work that has come before, there is still much to do.

References

[1] Abiteboul S, Adiba M, Arlow J, et. al. (1994) The GOODSTEP project: General object-oriented database for software engineering processes. Proc. 1st Asian Pacific Software Engineering Conference

[2] Ada LRM (1983) Ada '83 Language Reference Manual. ANSI/MIL-STD-1815A-1983

[3] Balzer R (1989) Tolerating inconsistency. Proc 5th Int Software Process Workshop

[4] Balzer R (1991) Tolerating inconsistency. Proc 13th Int Conf on Software Engineering

[5] Bandinelli S, Fuggetta A (1993) Computational reflection in software process modeling: the SLANG approach, Proc 15th Int Conf on Software Engineering (ICSE 1993). IEEE CS/ACM, 1993:144-154

[6] Bandinelli S, Fuggetta A, Grigolli S. (1993) Process modeling in-the-large with SLANG. Proc 2nd Int Conf on the Software Process

[7] Belkhatir N, Estublier J, Melo W (1994) Adele-Tempo: an environment to support process modelling and enaction, Software Process Modelling and Technology, Research Studies Press Ltd., Taunton, UK

[8] Bergner K, Friedrich J (2010) Using project procedure diagrams for milestone planning. Proc Int Conf on Software Process

[9] Boose ER, Ellison AM, Osterweil LJ, Clarke LA, Podorozhny R, Hadley JL, Wise A, and Foster DR (2007) Ensuring reliable datasets for environmental models and forecasts. Ecological Informatics 2(3): 237-247

[10] Buettner DJ (2009) A system dynamics model that simulates a significant late life cycle manpower increase phenomenon. Proc Int Conf on Software Process '09

[11] Cain BG, Coplien J (1993) A role-based empirical process modeling environment. Proc Second Int Conf on the Software Process

[12] Campbell RH, Habermann AN (1974) The specification of process synchronization by path expressions. Symp on Operating Systems

[13] Canals G, Boudjlida N, Derniame J-C, Godart C, Lonchamp J (1994) ALF: a framework for building process-centered software engineering environments, Software Process Modelling and Technology, Research Studies Press Ltd., Taunton, UK

[14] Cass AG, Lerner BS, Sutton SM Jr., McCall EK, Wise A, Osterweil LJ (2000) Little-JIL/Juliette: a process definition language and interpreter. Proc 22nd Int Conf on Software Engineering

[15] Cass AG, Osterweil LJ (2005) Process support to help novices design software faster and better. Proc 20th IEEE/ACM Int Conf on Automated Software Engineering

[16] Cass AG, Sutton SM Jr, Osterweil LJ (2003) Formalizing rework in software processes. Proc 9th Int Workshop on Software Process Technology (EWSPT 2003)

[17] Chen B, Avrunin GS, Clarke LA, Osterweil LJ (2006) Automatic fault tree derivation from Little-JIL process definitions. Proc Int Software Process Workshop and Int Workshop on Software Process Simulation and Modeling (SPW/ProSim 2006)

[18] Chen B, Avrunin GS, Henneman EA, Clarke LA, Osterweil LA, Henneman PL (2008) Analyzing medical processes. ACM SIGSOFT/IEEE 30th Int Conf on Software Engineering (Reprinted as Chapter 21)

[19] Chen W, Ying Q, Xue Y, Zhao C (2005) Software Testing Process Automation Based on UTP - A Case Study. Proc Int Software Process Workshop (SPW 2005)

[20] Clarke LA, Osterweil LJ, Avrunin GS (2010) Supporting human-intensive systems. Proc FSE/SDP Workshop on Future of Software Engineering Research (FoSER '10)

[21] Cobleigh JM, Clarke LA, Osterweil LJ (2000) Verifying properties of process definitions. ACM Sigsoft 2000 Int Symp on Software Testing and Analysis (ISSTA 2000)

[22] Cohen D (1988) AP5 manual. Univ. of Southern California, Information Sciences Institute

[23] Conradi R, Hagaseth M, Larsen J-O, Nguyên MN, Munch BP, Westby PH, Zhu W, Jaccheri ML, Liu C (1994) EPOS: object-oriented cooperative process modelling, Software Process Modelling and Technology, Research Studies Press Ltd., Taunton, UK

[24] Cook JE, Wolf AL (1999) Software process validation: quantitatively measuring the correspondence of a process to a model. ACM Trans. Softw. Eng. Methodol. 8(2):147-176

[25] Deiters W, Gruhn V, Schäfer W (1989) Process programming: a structured multi-paradigm approach could be achieved. Proc 5th Int Software Process Workshop (ISPW 1989)

[26] Demeure IM, Osterweil LO (1987) What we learn about process specification languages from studying recipes. Tech Rept, Univ of Colorado, Boulder, Comp Sci Dept, CU-CS-373-87

[27] Ellison AM (2010) Repeatability and transparency in ecological research. Ecology 91: 2536-2539.

[28] Ellison AM, Osterweil LJ, Clarke L, Hadley JL, Wise A, Boose E, Foster DR, Hanson A, Jensen D, Kuzeja P, Riseman E, Schultz H (2006). Analytic webs support the synthesis of ecological data sets. Ecology 87.6 (2006): 1345-1358.

[29] Emmerich W, Bandinelli S, Lavazza L, Arlow J (1996) Fine grained process modelling: an experiment at British Airways. Proc Fourth Int Conf on the Software Process (ICSP 1996)

[30] Fernstrom C (1993) Process weaver: adding process support to UNIX. Proc Second Int Conf on the Software Process (ICSP 1993)

[31] Gamalel-din SA, Osterweil LJ (1988) New perspectives on software maintenance processes. Proc Conf on Software Maintenance

[32] Garousi V (2009) Evidence-based insights about issue management processes: an exploratory study" Proc Int Conf on Software Process (ICSP 2009)

[33] Gruhn V (1990) Managing software processes in the environment MELMAC, Proc fourth ACM SIGSOFT Symp on Software Development Environments.

[34] Harada A, Awane S, Inoya Y, Ohno O, Matsushita M, Kusumoto S, Inoue K (2005) Project Management System Based on Work-Breakdown-Structure Process Model. Proc Int Software Process Workshop (SPW 2005)

[35] Harel D, Lachover H, Naamad A, Pnuelli A, Politi M, Sherman R, Shtull-Trauring A, Trakhtenbrot M (1990) Statemate: a working environment for the development of complex reactive systems. IEEE Trans Software Eng 16(4):403-414

[36] Heimbigner D (1989) P4: a logic language for process programming. Proc 5th Int Software Process Workshop (ISPW 1989)

[37] Heimbigner D (1992) The process wall: a process state server approach to process programming. Proc. 5th ACM SIGSOFT Symp on Software Development Environments

[38] Henneman EA, Avrunin GS, Clarke LA, Osterweil LJ, Andrzejewski C, Merrigan K, Cobleigh R, Frederick K, Katz-Bassett E, Henneman PL (2007) Increasing patient safety and efficiency in transfusion therapy using formal process definitions. Transfusion Medicine Reviews 21.1: 49-57

[39] Henneman EA, Cobleigh R, Avrunin GS, Clarke LA, Osterweil LJ, Henneman PL (2008) Designing property specifications to improve the safety of the blood transfusion process. Transfusion Medicine Reviews 22.4:291-299

[40] Huff KE, Lesser VR (1988) A plan-based intelligent assistant that supports the software development. Proc Third ACM SIGSOFT/SIGPLAN Software Engineering Symp on Practical Software Development Environments

[41] Humphrey W (2005) The software process: global goals. Proc Int Software Process Workshop (ISPW 2005)

[42] Iida H, Mimura K-I, Inoue K, Torii K (1993) Hakoniwa: Monitor and navigation system for cooperative development based on activity sequence model, Proc 2nd Int Conf on the Software Process

[43] Jeffery DR (2005) Achieving software development performance improvement through process change. Proc Int Software Process Workshop (SPW 2005)

[44] Jensen D, Dong Y, Lerner BS, McCall EK, Osterweil LJ, Sutton Jr. SM, Wise A (1999) Coordinating agent activities in knowledge discovery processes. Work Activities Coordination and Collaboration Conference (WACC 1999)

[45] Junkermann G, Peuschel G, Schäfer W, Wolf S (1994) MERLIN: supporting cooperation in software development through a knowledge-based environment. In: Software Process Modelling and Technology, Anthony Finkelstein, Jeff Kramer, and Bashar Nuseibeh (Eds.). Research Studies Press Ltd., Taunton, UK

[46] Kaiser GE, Barghouti NS, and Sokolsky MH (1990). Experience with process modeling in the MARVEL software development environment kernel. In: B. Shriver, editor, 23rd Annual Hawaii Int. Conf on System Sciences

[47] Kaiser GE, Popovich SS, Ben-Shaul I (1993) A bi-level language for software process modeling. Proc 15th Int Conf on Software Engineering (ICSE 1993)

[48] Katayama T (1989) A hierarchical and functional software process description and its enaction. 11th Int Conf on Software Engineering (ICSE 1989)

[49] Katayama T (1990) Proc Sixth Int Software Process Workshop (ISPW 1990)

[50] Katsh E, Osterweil LJ, Rainey D, Sondheimer NK (2006) Experimental application of process technology to the creation and adoption of online dispute resolution (DG o2006): The National Conference on Digital Government Research

[51] Katsh E, Osterweil LJ, Sondheimer NK, Rainey D (2005) Early lessons from the application of process technology to online grievance mediation. Proc 2005 National Conference on Digital Government Research (dg.o '05)

[52] Kellner MI (1991) Multiple-paradigm approaches for software process modeling. Proc Seventh Int Software Process Workshop (ISPW 1991)

[53] Kellner MI, Feiler PH, Finkelstein A, Katayama T, Osterweil LJ, Penedo MH, Rombach HD (1991) ISPW6 software process example. Proc 1st Int Conf on the Software Process

[54] Kiebusch S, Franczyk B, Speck A (2006) Process-family-points. LNCS 3966, 2006:314-321

[55] Klingler CD (1993) A case study Process definition. Proc conference on TRI-Ada '93

[56] Koudri A, Champeau J (2010) MODAL: A SPEM extension to improve co-design process models. Proc Int Conf on Software Process (ICSP 2010)

[57] Lerner BS, Christov S, Osterweil LJ, Bendraou R, Kannengiesser U, Wise A (2010) Exception handling patterns for process modeling. IEEE Trans Software Engineering 36.2:162-183

[58] Li M, Boehm B, Osterweil LJ (2006) Unifying the Software Process Spectrum—Proc Int Software Process Workshop (ISPW 2005)

[59] Madhavji NH (1991) The process cycle. Softw. Eng. J. 6, 5 (September 1991), 234-242.

[60] McCall EK, Clarke LA, Osterweil LJ (1998) An adaptable generation approach to agenda management. Proc 20th Int Conf on Software Engineering (ICSE 1998)

[61] Mertens WC, Chrostov S, Avrunin GS, Cassells LB, Chen B, Brown DE, Parisi R, Clarke LA, Osterweil LJ. (2008) Chemotherapy ordering and delivery: Rigorously defining and analyzing a complex process employing software engineering techniques. Journal of Clinical Oncology, 2008 ASCO Annual Meeting Proceedings (Post-Meeting Edition). Vol 26, No 15S (May 20 Supplement), 2008: 17514.

[62] Mi P, Scacchi W (1991) Articulation: supporting dynamic evolution of software engineering processes. Proc Seventh Int Software Process Workshop (ISPW 1991)

[63] Münch J, Yang Ye, Schäfer W (Eds.) (2010) New Modeling Concepts for Today's Software Processes--Proc Int Conf on Software Process (ICSP 2010)

[64] Navascués J, Ramos I, Toro M (2009) A hybrid model for dynamic simulation of custom software projects in a multiproject environment. Proc Int Conf on Software Process

[65] Osterweil L (1986) Software process interpretation and software environments. Tech Rept, Univ of Colorado, Boulder, Comp Sci Dept, CU-CS-324-86.

[66] Osterweil L (1986) A process-object centered view of software environment architecture. Advanced Programming Environments. LNCS 244:156-174.

[67] Osterweil LJ (1987) Software processes are software, too. 9th Int Conf on Software Engineering (ICSE 1987) (Reprinted as Chapter 17)

[68] Osterweil LJ (1997) Software processes are software too, revisited. 19th Int Conf on Software Engineering (ICSE 1997) (Reprinted as Chapter 18)

[69] Osterweil LJ (2006) Ubiquitous process engineering: Applying software process technology to other domains. Proc Int Software Process Workshop and Int Workshop on Software Process Simulation and Modeling (SPW/ProSim 2006)

[70] Osterweil LJ (2011) Personal communication on the feasibility of using commercial process support systems as vehicles for process research.

[71] Osterweil LJ, Avrunin GS, Chen B, Clarke LA, Cobleigh R, Henneman EA, Henneman PL (2007) Engineering medical processes to improve their safety. Situational Method Engineering: Fundamentals and Experiences 244:267-282.

[72] Osterweil LJ, Clarke LA (2001) Frameworks for reasoning about agent based systems. Int Workshop on Infrastructure for Agents, Multi-Agent Systems, and Scalable Multi-Agent Systems 1887

[73] Osterweil LJ, Clarke LA, Ellison AM, Boose ER, Podorozhny R, Wise A (2010) Clear and precise specification of ecological data management processes and dataset provenance. IEEE Trans on Automation Science and Engineering 7(1):189-195

[74] Osterweil LJ, Wise A (2010) Using process definitions to support reasoning about satisfaction of process requirements. Proc Int Conf on Software Process (ICSP 2010)

[75] Osterweil LJ, Wise A, Clarke LA, Ellison AM, Hadley JL, Boose E, and Foster DR (2005) Process technology to facilitate the conduct of science. Proc Int Software Process Workshop

[76] Pennsylvania, Commonwealth of, Patient Safety Authority (2010) Improving the safety of the blood transfusion process. Pa Patient Saf Advis 2010 Jun;(2)33-40

[77] Perry, D (1994) Enactment Control in Interact/Intermediate. 3rd European Workshop on Software Process Technology

[78] Podorozhny RM, Lerner BS, Osterweil LJ (1999) Modeling resources for activity coordination and scheduling. In Ciancarini P, Wolf AL (eds): Proc 3rd Int Conf on Coordination Languages and Models (COORDINATION 1999)

[79] Podorozhny RM, PerryDE, Osterweil LJ (2005) Automatically analyzing software processes: experience report. Proc Int Software Process Workshop (SPW 2005)

[80] Podorozhny RM, Osterweil LJ (1997) The criticality of modeling formalisms in software design method comparison: experience report. Proc 19th Int Conf on Software Engineering

[81] Raunak RM, Chen B, Elssamadisy A, Clarke LA, and Osterweil LJ (2006) Definition and analysis of election processes. Proc Int Software Process Workshop and Int Workshop on Software Process Simulation and Modeling (SPW/ProSim 2006)

[82] Raunak MS, Osterweil LJ (2005) Process definition language support for rapid simulation prototyping. Proc Int Software Process Workshop (SPW 2005)

[83] Raunak MS, Osterweil LJ, Wise A, Clarke LA, Henneman PL (2009) Simulating patient flow through an emergency department using process-driven discrete event simulation. Int Conf on Software Engineering Workshop on Software Engineering for Health Care

[84] Saeki M, Kaneko T, Sakamoto M (1991) A method for software process modeling and description using LOTOS. Proc First Int Conf on the Software Process (ICSP 1991)

[85] Schäfer W, Broekman P, Hubert L, Scott J (1990) ESF and software process modeling. Proc 5th Int Software Process (ISPW 1990)

[86] Shen B (2008) Support IT service management with process modeling and analysis. Proc Int Conf on Software Process (ICSP 2008)

[87] Shu F, Li Q, Wang Q, Zhang H (2010) Measurement and analysis of process audit: a case study. Proc Int Conf on Software Process (ICSP 2010)

[88] Simidchieva B, Engle SJ, Clifford M, Jones AC, Peisert S, Bishop M, Clarke LA, Osterweil LJ (2010) Modeling and analyzing faults to improve election process robustness. Proc 2010 Electronic Voting Technology Workshop/Workshop on Trustworthy Elections

[89] Simidchieva BI, Osterweil LJ (2010) Categorizing and modeling variation in families of systems: a position paper. Proc Fourth European Conf on Software Architecture: Companion Volume (ECSA 2010)

[90] Simidchieva BI, Osterweil LJ, Wise A (2009) Structural considerations in defining executable process models. Proc Int Conf on Software Process (ICSP 2009)

[91] Sondheimer N, Osterweil L, Billmers M, Sieh J, Southard B (2003) e-government through process modeling: a requirements field study. IADIS Int Conf e-Society 2003

[92] Song X, Osterweil LJ (1994) Engineering software design processes to guide process execution. 3rd Int Conf on the Software Process (ICSP 1994)

[93] Song X, Osterweil LJ (1989) Debus: A software design process program. Arcadia Tech Rept UCI-89-02, Dept of Information and Computer Science, University of California,

[94] Song XP and Osterweil LJ (1994) Experience with an approach to comparing software-design methodologies. IEEE Trans on Software Engineering 20(5):364-384

[95] Soto M, Ocampo A, Münch J (2009) Analyzing a software process model repository for understanding model evolution. Proc Int Conf on Software Process (ICSP 2009)

[96] Sutton Jr. SM (1990) A flexible consistency model for persistent data in software-process programming languages. In Shaw GM, Zdonik SB (Eds) Implementing Persistent Object Bascs, Principles and Practice, Proc Fourth Int Workshop on Persistent Objects

[97] Sutton Jr. SM (1990) A process-program in APPL/A for the software-process modeling problem. Proc Sixth Int Software Process Workshop (ISPW 1990)

[98] Sutton Jr. SM (1991) Accommodating manual activities in automated process programs. Proc 7th Int Software Process Workshop

[99] Sutton Jr. SM, Heimbigner DM, Osterweil LJ (1990) Language constructs for managing change Process-centered environments. 4th ACM SIGSOFT Symp on Software Development Environments (SIGSOFT 1990) (Reprinted as Chapter 19)

[100] Sutton Jr. SM, Heimbigner DM, Osterweil LJ (1995) APPL/A: A language for software process programming. ACM Trans Softw Eng Methodol 4(3):221-286

[101] Sutton Jr. SM, Osterweil LJ (1996) Product families and process families. 10th Int Software Process Workshop (ISPW 1996)

[102] Sutton Jr. SM Jr, Osterweil LJ (1997) The design of a next-generation process language. Software Engineering – (ESEC/FSE 1997)

[103] Sutton Jr. SM, Ziv H, Heimbigner D, Yessayan HE, Maybee M, Osterweil LJ, Song X (1991) Programming a software requirements-specification process. Proc First Int Conf on the Software Process

[104] Suzuki M, Iwai A, Katayama T (1993) A formal model of re-execution in software process. Proc Second Int Conf on the Software Process (ICSP 1993)

[105] Tarr PL, Sutton Jr. SM (1993) Programming heterogeneous transactions for software development environments. Proc 15th Int Conf on Software Engineering

[106] Taylor RN, Belz FC, Clarke LA, Osterweil L, Selby RW, Wileden JC, Wolf AL, and Young M. (1988) Foundations for the Arcadia environment architecture. SIGSOFT Softw. Eng. Notes 13(5):1-13

[107] Terwilliger RB, Maybee MJ, Osterweil LJ (1989) An example of formal specification as an aid to design and development. Proc 5th Int Workshop on Software Specification and Design (IWSSD '89)

[108] Thomas I (ed) (1991) Proc Seventh Int Software Process Workshop (ISPW 1991)

[109] Valetto G, Kaiser GE (1996) Enveloping sophisticated tools into process-centered environments. Automated Software Engineering, 3(3):309-345

[110] Wang Q, Pfahl D, Raffo DM, Wernick P (Eds.) (2006) Software Process Change—Proc Int Software Process Workshop and Int Workshop on Software Process Simulation and Modeling (SPW/ProSim 2006)

[111] Wang Q, Pfahl D, Raffo DM (Eds.) (2007) Software Process Dynamics and Agility--Proc Int Conf on Software Process (ICSP 2007)

[112] Wang Q, Pfahl D, Raffo DM (Eds.) (2008) Making Globally Distributed Software Development a Success Story--Proc Int Conf on Software Process (ICSP 2008)

[113] Wang Q, Garousi V, Madachy R, Pfahl D (Eds.) (2009) Trustworthy Software Development Processes--Proc Int Conf on Software Process (ICSP 2009)

[114] Warboys BC (1989) The IPSE 2.5 project: process modelling as a basis for a support environment. Proc First Int Conf on System Development Environments and Factories (SDEF1)

[115] Wise A (1998) Little-JIL 1.0 language report. Tech Rept. Univ of Massachusetts, Amherst, Dept of Comp Sci, UM-CS-1998-024

[116] Wise A (2006) Little-JIL 1.5 language report. Tech Rept. Univ of Massachusetts, Amherst, Dept of Comp Sci, UM-CS-2006-51

[117] Wise A, Cass AG, Lerner BS, McCall EK, Osterweil LJ, Sutton SM Jr (2000) Using Little-JIL to coordinate agents in software engineering. Automated Software Engineering Conference (ASE 2000) (Reprinted as Chapter 20)

[118] Wolf AL, Rosenblum DS (1993) A study in software process data capture and analysis. Proc Second Int Conf on the Software Process (ICSP 1993)

[119] Xu B, Huang L, Koolmanojwong S (2009) Incremental process modeling through stakeholder-based hybrid process simulation. Proc Int Conf on Software Process (ICSP 2009)

[120] Young, PSC (1994) Customizable Process Specification and Enactment for Technical and Non-Technical Users. Dissertation, Information and Computer Science, University of California, Irvine

[121] Young PS, Taylor RN (1994) Human-executed operations in the Teamware process programming system. Proc Ninth Int Software Process Workshop

[122] Zhang H, Kitchenham B, Pfahl D (2010) Software process simulation modeling: an extended systematic review. Proc Int Conf on Software Process (ICSP 2010)

[123] Zhang H, Shu F, Yang Y, Wang X, Wang Q (2010) A fuzzy-based method for evaluating the trustworthiness of software processes. Proc Int Conf on Software Process (ICSP 2010)

[124] Zhu L, Osterweil LJ, Staples M, Kannengiesser U, Simidchieva BI (2007) Desiderata for languages to be used in the definition of reference business processes. Int Journal of Software and Informatics 1(1):37-65

The Mechatronic UML Development Process

Joel Greenyer, Jan Rieke, Wilhelm Schäfer, and Oliver Sudmann

Software Engineering Group, Heinz Nixdorf Institute,

Department of Computer Science, University of Paderborn

Warburger Str. 100, 33098 Paderborn, Germany

(jgreen|jrieke|wilhelm|oliversu)@upb.de

Abstract The advanced functions of mechatronic systems today are essentially realized by software that controls complex processes and enables the communication and coordination of multiple system components. We have developed MECHATRONIC UML, a comprehensive technique for the model-based development of hybrid real-time component-based systems. MECHATRONIC UML is based on a well-defined subset of UML diagrams, formal analysis and composition methods. Vital for the successful development with MECHATRONIC UML, however, is a systematic development process, on which we report in this paper.

Keywords: Mechatronic UML, software development process, real-time systems, mechatronic systems

1. Introduction

From household machines to medical devices and transportation systems, we find mechatronic systems everywhere around us today. These systems are often required to fulfill advanced functions that are essentially enabled by software. Software controls the complex processes and realizes the communication and collaboration of components in what are typically distributed and dynamic systems.

One kind of advanced mechatronic systems are *self-optimizing* systems, which are the focus of the Collaborative Research Center 614 (CRC 614), an interdisciplinary, large-scale research project at the University of Paderborn. Self-optimizing systems are systems that can autonomously monitor their performance, assess current optimization objectives, and adapt their behavior or structure to changing environmental conditions in order to fulfill their optimization objectives. An example of such a self-optimizing system is the RailCab system[1], a rail-based transport

---

[1] http://www-nbp.upb.de/en

system where small, autonomous vehicles transport passengers and goods on demand. In order to reduce the wind resistance, RailCabs can form convoys when driving in the same direction. The vision of the RailCab project is to provide the comfort of individual transport concerning scheduling and on-demand availability of transportation on the one hand, and the cost and resource effectiveness of public transport on the other hand. The modular railway system combines sophisticated undercarriages with the advantages of innovative linear-drive technology to increase passenger comfort while still enabling high-speed transportation and (re)using the existing railway tracks.

Mechatronic systems like the RailCab are highly safety-critical. The software must fulfill many real-time requirements, and discrete software must be combined with control functions that are of continuous nature. Furthermore, these systems are often highly *dynamic*, which means that the number of components in the system, and communication relationships between these components, may change over time. When RailCabs form convoys, for example, this changes the communication relationships between the RailCabs. In addition, RailCab software may be required to change the structure of its control functions, depending on certain operating states. In a convoy, for example, the function controlling the RailCab's speed is different from the control function that is used when the RailCab is not in a convoy. We call changes in the structure of software components *reconfiguration*.

All these aspects induce an enormous complexity in the development of the software for these systems. During the past years, we have developed a comprehensive, model-based technique for developing software for advanced mechatronic systems, called MECHATRONIC UML. MECHATRONIC UML provides software engineers with different methods for modeling and verifying component-based software, with a special focus on real-time behavior, hybrid software components, and dynamic systems. The modeling and verification methods are all prototypically implemented within the FUJABA Real-Time tool suite.

Our work applies and expands Osterweil's original software process ideas [13] into a completely different domain than he anticipated. Vital for a successful application of MECHATRONIC UML is a systematic and partially automated development process, as hypothesized by Osterweil. The notion of a formal process definition, which is automated and analyzable by computer programs, is not well-known in the engineering domain, despite the fact that engineers use semi-formal notations and guidelines a lot. Taking this next step forward is certainly an outcome of work in the software process area. Our approach is in keeping with results that also demonstrate the usefulness of formal process definitions in other areas [4].

In this paper, we present the MECHATRONIC UML *development process*, describing how the MECHATRONIC UML methods are systematically applied in the development of advanced mechatronic systems. In the following, Section 2 overviews the MECHATRONIC UML process and describes how this process is embedded in the overall system development process. Section 3 presents the major steps in the MECHATRONIC UML process, using an example from the context of the RailCab project. We finally conclude in Section 4 and present future work.

2. Overview of the Development Process

Most system development lifecycles follow some variant of the V-model. For mechatronic systems, the VDI 2206 "Design Methodology for Mechatronic Systems" [14] was developed. This lifecycle model is, however, only a very first and coarse-grained approach to foster joint development across the different disciplines required to produce mechatronic systems, to define a joint development process, a joint modeling formalism, and a joint use of tools. It does not, therefore, sufficiently address the problems in today's interdisciplinary development settings. Worse, many industrial organizations still follow the traditional "throw-it-over-the-wall" approach, which means that mechanical engineering department finishes the mechanical design using CAD (Computer-Aided Design) tools, hands it over to the electrical engineers, who do the wiring, and finally, the software engineers have to build the software with the restrictions they inherit from the first two groups of engineers.

In an ongoing effort within the CRC 614, we have refined the V-Model of the VDI 2206 to facilitate the development of self-optimizing mechatronic systems, with a focus on improving the collaboration of the different disciplines throughout the development of the system. The macro structure of the development process of the CRC 614 consists of the *interdisciplinary conceptual design*, the parallel *discipline-specific development*, and finally, the *system integration*.

The top of Fig. 16.1 shows the first two phases of this macro structure. During the interdisciplinary conceptual design, a team of interdisciplinary experts specifies the *principle solution*, a first system model which captures all interdisciplinary relevant aspects of the system. The purpose of the principle solution is to form a common basis for the subsequent parallel development of the discipline-specific parts of the system. The principle solution includes the system's requirements, its logical and physical structures, and its spatial properties (shape). Relevant from a software engineering point of view, a first model of the software architecture can be derived from the system structure that is described in the principle solution [6]. The principle solution also contains a scenario-based specification of the interactions among the software components and their environment. These interactions are described by *Modal Sequence Diagrams* (MSDs) [9], a formal interpretation of UML sequence diagrams for describing interactions that may, must, and must not occur. During the conceptual design, the consistency of the scenario-based specification is checked by simulation and formal synthesis techniques [8].

Based on the principle solution, the software is developed using MECHATRONIC UML in three phases, starting with an initial software specification that is derived from the principle solution, and resulting in generated source code for the software components.

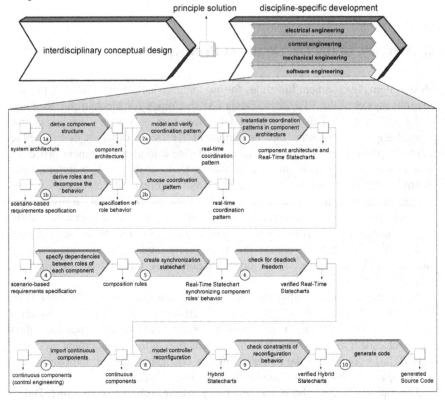

Fig. 16.1. The MECHATRONIC UML process and its integration into the overall development process for the development of advanced mechatronic systems.

In the first phase (steps 1 to 3), the component architecture is created and the communication between the components is defined. More specifically, an initial version of the component architecture can be derived from the system architecture in the principle solution (step 1a). This can be done semi-automatically with a model transformation approach, as described by Gausemeier et al. [6]. If necessary, the component architecture can be extended by adding further software components or connectors that represent communication relationships. In step 1b, the behavioral specification of the components as given in the principle solution is analyzed and decomposed. In the principle solution, the behavior is typically specified in a use case-centric manner, by scenarios that describe many interdependent interactions of many components and their environment. This specification, which we call the *global specification*, can often be decomposed into smaller specification parts that only span smaller sets of components. For these interaction specifications, which we call *protocols*, the behavior can be implemented more easily and verified more effectively than attempting to develop and verify an implementation of the global specification of the system.

Based on the given component architecture and the decomposed behavior specification, protocols either need to be implemented and verified (step 2a), or existing protocols can be reused (step 2b). More specifically, in MECHATRONIC UML, protocols are implemented by *Real-Time Statecharts*, a variant of UML state machines with a formal semantics based on Timed Automata [2]. To implement a protocol, Real-Time Statecharts are modeled for each participant in the protocol. The resulting interacting Real-Time Statecharts can be formally verified to fulfill the requirements of the protocol.

The protocol implementations can be parameterized to allow for flexible reuse in other contexts. The behavior is then also no longer implemented for concrete components. Instead, the behavior of the participants in the protocol is described for abstract *roles* that can later be instantiated in a specific component architecture. These reusable protocols are then called *real-time coordination patterns*, or *coordination patterns* for short [7]. Each new protocol is implemented (step 2a) as a reusable coordination pattern and added into a library for later reuse. Making a coordination pattern reusable in a wide variety of applications typically requires additional design efforts, such as parameterizing time intervals or adding foreseeable alternative flows of events in the form of non-determinism. Over the last few years, we have collected a number of reusable coordination patterns.

Once a set of communication protocols is collected or created for the system, the coordination patterns are instantiated in the component architecture (step 3). The effect of this instantiation is that the roles of the coordination patterns are associated with ports of the components in the component architecture.

The result of step 3 is a set of components where each component behavior consists of the independent parallel composition of the Real-Time Statecharts. These statecharts describe the behavior of the roles corresponding to the component's ports. This independent parallel composition, however, does not incorporate dependencies that usually exist between the different roles within a component. In the second phase (steps 4 to 6), the internal behavior of the components is refined. First, the dependencies between the different roles within a component are extracted from the principle solution and formally specified in the form of *composition rules* (step 4). Composition rules are a combination of timed automata [2] and Boolean logic formulae that are used to specify behavior that must happen in a component or states that are forbidden [5].

These composition rules specify that the previously independent role statecharts of a component have to be synchronized in a specific manner. This synchronization of the role behavior can be done automatically or manually (step 5). We have developed an automated synthesis technique that can automatically "find" an implementation of the component that correctly refines and synchronizes the role behavior and satisfies the composition rules [5]. It may be that the synthesizer cannot find an implementation of the component, which implies that the role behavior and the composition rules are *inconsistent*, i.e., there does not exist any implementation of the component that satisfies the composition rules while still correctly refining the role statecharts. In this case, the composition rules or the coordination patterns that are applied to the component must be changed.

Due to the inherent complexity of this synthesis, this technique sometimes cannot be applied to components that are involved in many complex interactions. In this case, the roles can be synchronized manually, by introducing an additional statechart in the component that synchronizes certain transitions in the role statecharts. This additional statechart is called the *synchronization statechart*. When implementing this synchronization manually, the developer must check that the resulting implementation is still a valid refinement of the role behavior. This guarantees that the synchronized behavior does not violate the safety properties that were proven for the coordination patterns. Giese et al. suggest an approach to guarantee valid refinements of the role statecharts by construction [7]. Furthermore, the developer must ensure that the behavior is free of deadlocks (step 6). The result of the second phase is the component architecture and the discrete behavior for all software components.

In mechatronic systems, the discrete behavior is often tightly coupled with continuous control functions: changes in continuous variables may trigger changes of discrete states and vice versa. In particular, it may be necessary to reconfigure the continuous control functions when the system is switching between certain operating states. To incorporate this behavior in the discrete software model, the continuous control functions are embedded in the discrete software components (step 7). From a software engineering point of view, continuous controllers are black-box components with continuous ports. Continuous controller structures are extracted from the principle solution. Mostly, however, the controller structures are obtained from control engineering, where the controllers are extended and refined by the parallel development of the control engineers. If different configurations of controllers are active in different operating states, this is modeled formally in step 8. The controller configurations are associated with the states in which they are active. For this purpose, the real-time statecharts are extended to *hybrid statecharts* [3]. The hybrid statecharts in MECHATRONIC UML are based on the theory of hybrid automata [1], and they are similar to the timed and hybrid statecharts proposed by Kesten and Pnueli [12].

Because of discipline-specific restrictions, the controller reconfiguration may take a certain amount of time. Therefore, it is necessary to check whether these time restrictions contradict the deadlines that are annotated in the discrete behavior (step 9). Finally, the source code is generated (step 10).

3. Mechatronic UML Example

In this section, we discuss the software development process for MECHATRONIC UML in more detail. The RailCab system serves as an example. We focus on the

convoy scenario that was briefly described in Section 1. To reduce wind resistance, RailCabs can form convoys when driving in the same direction. If one
RailCab closes in on another RailCab, the first RailCab may propose to form a
convoy with the second. Due to the close distance, the coordination of the Rail-
Cabs' acceleration control becomes a safety-critical aspect, as the RailCabs must
not collide. One critical requirement is that one RailCab must not believe that it is
part of a convoy while the other RailCab believes that no convoy was formed.
Furthermore, a RailCab that follows another within a convoy must reconfigure its
acceleration controller. The follower RailCab in a convoy must control its acceleration based on a desired distance that it must keep from the leader RailCab. If
RailCabs are operating independently, the acceleration is controlled instead according to a target velocity that is determined elsewhere in the RailCab. Thus, a
reconfiguration between a distance-based acceleration and a velocity-based acceleration controller is required whenever a RailCab joins or leaves a convoy as a
follower RailCab. For the scope of this paper, only convoys of two RailCabs are
considered.

As described above, such communication scenarios are identified during the interdisciplinary conceptual design, and they are described in the principle solution
in a scenario-based manner. The software engineers then implement this behavior
in the form of *coordination patterns* (step 2).

The bottom of Fig. 16.2 shows a coordination pattern, "convoy coordination",
which implements, using Real-Time Statecharts, the behavior of forming and
breaking up a convoy for the roles *leader* and *follower*. In the middle, the figure
shows how this coordination pattern is mapped to the component structure (step
3). UML component diagrams are used for the specification of the component architecture in MECHATRONIC UML. In this case, we only consider a single component, the RailCab component. This component has two ports, to which the roles of
the coordination pattern are mapped. In a situation where two RailCabs form a
convoy, as illustrated on the top of the figure, two instances of RailCab components communicate via a communication connector from one component instance's *follower* port to the other component instance's *leader* port.

Let us consider the behavior described by the Real-Time Statecharts in Fig.
16.2 in more detail. Initially, the statecharts are in the state noConvoy::default.
The follower role can non-deterministically choose to send a convoyProposal
message to the leader role. The leader role can accept or reject the proposal within
1000 time units. This decision is also not deterministic. (This non-determinism
will be eliminated by refinement later on.) If the leader accepts the convoy proposal, the leader role sends a message startConvoy to the follower role. After the
follower role receives this message, both roles switch to the convoy::default
state. While the RailCabs drive in a convoy, the follower can non-
deterministically decide to leave the convoy, sending a breakConvoyProposal
message to the leader role. The leader role can either accept or reject the proposal.
If it accepts the proposal, both roles switch to the noConvoy::default state. It can

be shown that the described behavior contains no deadlocks and that the leader role is always in convoy mode when the follower role is in convoy mode.

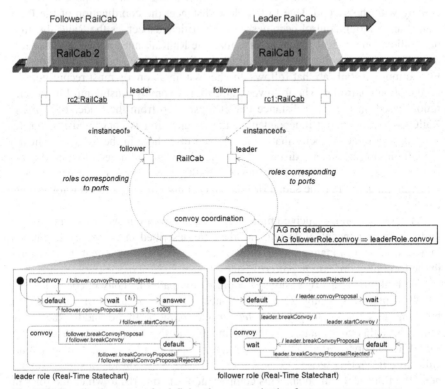

Fig. 16.2. Coordination pattern for defining the communication for convoy management.

Step 3 produces a set of components where the behavior of each component consists of an independent parallel composition of the component's role state-charts; the dependencies between the different interactions in which the component is involved are not yet specified. The next step (step 4) is to specify these dependencies formally. As described above, these dependencies are described by composition rules, a combination of timed-automata or Boolean formulae. It is not always necessary to use both timed-automata and Boolean formulae. For instance, the following simple formula is sufficient to describe that a RailCab cannot be the leader of a convoy and a follower in another convoy at the same time (effectively only allowing convoys of two RailCabs, to simplify this example):

$$\neg(\text{followerRole.convoy} \wedge \text{leaderRole.convoy})$$

The component behavior now has to be refined to satisfy the dependencies among the behaviors of the roles. As explained above, this refinement can be constructed by automatic synthesis or manually. In the following, let us inspect a manually created synchronization statechart and the refined roles' statecharts that implement the RailCab component (see Fig. 16.3).

The behavior of the RailCab component is described by a statechart with one top-level state that has three orthogonal (parallel) regions: LeaderRole, FollowerRole and Synchronization. The regions LeaderRole and FollowerRole contain internal statecharts that refine the behavior of the respective role in the convoy coordination pattern. Synchronization coordinates the communication such that the composition rules are fulfilled. For instance, the RailCab is never in the states LeaderRole::convoy and FollowerRole::convoy at the same time.

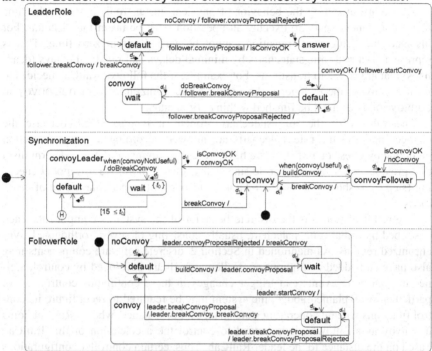

Fig. 16.3. Internal behavior of the RailCab component.

If a RailCab approaches another RailCab, the follower RailCab can decide to start a convoy. To reduce the complexity of this example, we omit an additional "decider" component, which decides whether a convoy is useful. Whenever this decider component in the follower RailCab sends a when(convoyUseful) message, the follower RailCab initiates the communication to the leader RailCab by sending a convoyProposal message through the port "leader". In doing so, it switches into the states Synchronization::convoyFollower and FollowerRole:noConvoy::wait (in the parallel regions Synchronization and FollowerRole).

Next, the convoyProposal message is received by the leader RailCab, which accepts the convoy proposal if it is not yet participating as a follower in another convoy. This is ensured in the Synchronization region: if the leading RailCab is in state Synchronization::convoyFollower, the result of an isConvoyOK message is always a noConvoy message. If the leader RailCab is in the state Synchronization::noConvoy, it accepts the proposal to form a convoy and it replies to the follower RailCab with a startConvoy message. In so doing, it changes to the states LeaderRole::convoy::default and Synchronization::convoyLeader::default.

The communication to break up the convoy is very similar to the initiation of the convoy, so we will not elaborate this behavior.

As we are modeling the behavior of physical, mechatronic systems, the time that a component needs to execute an operation must be taken into account. For instance, the firing of a transition cannot be carried out in zero time. This is represented in real-time statecharts by minimal delays and maximal delays (deadlines) that are added to transitions. For example, if the follower RailCab decides to form a convoy, the change in the region Synchronization from noConvoy to convoyFollower must be finished within d_1 time units.

The validity of the role statechart refinement is guaranteed, because the changes made to the role statecharts are allowed according to the construction guideline by Giese et al. [7], as we have basically eliminated the non-determinism that previously existed in the role statecharts. Furthermore, we use model checking (step 6) to show that the Real-Time Statechart in the example is free of deadlocks.

The result of step 6 is the discrete behavior of the system's components, each described by a real-time statechart, usually consisting of several orthogonal, synchronized regions. As mentioned in Section 2, discrete software components may also have embedded continuous controllers, which are developed by control engineering. Discrete events can trigger changes in these continuous controllers. In particular, as explained above, the system may be required to reconfigure its control functions when its operating state changes. For instance, when a RailCab joins a convoy as a follower, it is crucial to control the acceleration of this RailCab based on the distance to the leader RailCab. Thus, certain controller configurations must be associated with discrete states (step 8). To model this reconfiguration behavior adequately, we have developed *hybrid statecharts*, an extension to statecharts where the states additionally show the configuration of internal components that is associated with the state [3].

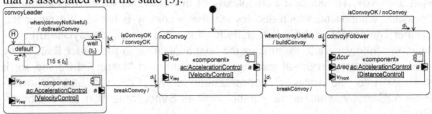

Fig. 16.4. Hybrid statechart for modeling the reconfiguration of continuous controllers.

In Fig. 16.4, the acceleration controller is embedded in the synchronization sta-techart of Fig. 16.3. As described above, it operates in two different modes. When the RailCab is traveling alone or is leading a convoy, i.e., it is in the states Synchronization::noConvoy or Synchronization::convoyLeader, the AccelerationControl works in VelocityControl mode. In this mode, it calculates the acceleration based on a given target velocity. When the RailCab is following in a convoy, i.e., it is in the state Synchronization::convoyFollower, the AccelerationControl works in DistanceControl mode. In this case, its acceleration is calculated using the current and the required minimum distance to the leader RailCab and the velocity of the leading RailCab. This extension of the synchronization statechart to a hybrid statechart now shows that the state change also implies a reconfiguration of the embedded AccelerationControl, ensuring that the RailCab's acceleration is always controlled correctly in the different convoy modes.

When embedding the continuous controllers and their reconfigurations in the software components, it may turn out that the time required to perform certain reconfigurations contradicts deadlines that were specified in the statecharts. The reconfiguration of a controller may take time, because controllers often cannot be directly switched between one controller configuration and another. Typically, some sort of "fading" must take place for smoothing the transition between controller configurations. For example, when switching the configuration of the acceleration controller, the passengers may feel an unpleasant jolt if the reconfiguration is abrupt. Therefore, the developer must check whether the hybrid statechart with the embedded AccelerationControl and the time restrictions that are implied by its reconfiguration is still a valid refinement of the role behavior (step 9).

4. Conclusion

In the past, we have developed MECHATRONIC UML, a comprehensive technique for model-based development of hybrid, real-time, component-based systems. MECHATRONIC UMLis based on a formal subset of UML diagrams and formal analysis and composition methods. At this point, MECHATRONIC UML comprises a range of methods that must be applied in a systematic way. In this paper, we have presented the MECHATRONIC UML *development process* and illustrated this process based on an example from the RailCab project.

We plan to extend the presented process to incorporate other analysis methods that we have developed within the scope of MECHATRONIC UML, such as hazard analysis and hazard reduction techniques [10], and methods for integrating legacy components [11]. Within the CRC 614, we are already integrating the software development process with the development processes of the other disciplines, which take place in parallel. In practice, the different disciplines often have to coordinate discipline-spanning changes that may be necessary during development, and the consistency between the development artifacts of the different disciplines must be ensured. In order to validate the process model, we plan to evaluate it in case studies.

Not all development methods in MECHATRONIC UML are seamlessly integrated by automated techniques yet. In the future, we plan to elaborate in more detail how to synthesize automatically coordination patterns and composition rules from the scenario-based behavior specifications in the principle solution.

Acknowledgments This contribution was developed and published in the course of the Collaborative Research Center 614 "Self-Optimizing Concepts and Structures in Mechanical Engineering" funded by the German Research Foundation (DFG) under grant number SFB 614. Jan Rieke is supported by the International Graduate School Dynamic Intelligent Systems.

References

[1] Alur R, Courcoubetis C, Halbwachs N, Henzinger TA, Ho PH, Nicollin X, Olivero A, Sifakis J, Yovine S (1995) The algorithmic analysis of hybrid systems. Theor. Comput. Sci. 138:3-34
[2] Alur R (1999) Timed Automata. Theor. Comput. Sci. 126:183-235
[3] Burmester S, Giese H, Oberschelp, O (2006) Hybrid UML components for the design of complex self-optimizing mechatronic systems. In: Informatics in Control, Automation and Robotics I
[4] Chen B, Avrunin GS, Henneman EA, Clarke LA, Osterweil LJ, Henneman PL (2008) Analyzing medical processes. In: Proc. 30th International Conference on Software Engineering
[5] Eckardt T, Henkler S (2010) Component behavior synthesis for critical systems. In: Proceedings of the First International Symposium of Architecting Critical Systems
[6] Gausemeier J, Schäfer W, Greenyer J, Kahl S, Pook S, Rieke J (2009) Management of cross-domain model consistency during the development of advanced mechatronic systems. In: Proceedings of the 17th International Conference on Engineering Design
[7] Giese H, Tichy M, Burmester S, Schäfer W, Flake S (2003) Towards the compositional verification of real-time UML designs. In: Proc. 9th European Software Engineering Conf./11th ACM SIGSOFT International Symp. on Foundations of Software Engineering
[8] Greenyer J (2010) Synthesizing Modal Sequence Diagram specifications with Uppaal-Tiga. Technical Report tr-ri-10-310, University of Paderborn
[9] Harel D, Maoz S (2008) Assert and negate revisited: Modal semantics for UML sequence diagrams. Software and Systems Modeling 7(2):237-252
[10] Henke C, Tichy M, Schneider T, Böcker J, Schäfer W (2008) System architecture and risk management for autonomous railway convoys. In: Proc. 2nd Annual IEEE Intl. Systems Conf.
[11] Henkler S, Meyer J, Schäfer W, Nickel U, von Detten M (2010) Legacy component integration by the Fujaba Real-Time Tool Suite. In: Proc. 32nd ACM/IEEE Intl. Conf. on Software Engineering
[12] Kesten Y, Pnueli A (1991) Timed and hybrid statecharts and their textual representation. In: Proc. 2nd Intl. Symp. on Formal Techniques in Real-Time and Fault-Tolerant Systems
[13] Osterweil LJ (1997) Software processes are software too, revisited: an invited talk on the most influential paper of ICSE 9. In: Proc. 19th Intl. Conf. on Software Engineering (Reprinted as Chapter 18)
[14] VDI, Verein Deutscher Ingenieure (2004) VDI Guideline 2206, Design Methodology for Mechatronic Systems

Software Processes are Software Too

Leon Osterweil

University of Colorado Boulder, Colorado USA

The Nature of Process

The major theme of this meeting is the exploration of the importance of process as a vehicle for improving both the quality of software products and the way in which we develop and evolve them. In beginning this exploration it seems important to spend at least a short time examining the nature of process and convincing ourselves that this is indeed a promising vehicle.

We shall take as our elementary notion of a process that it is a systematic approach to the creation of a product or the accomplishment of some task. We observe that this characterization describes the notion of process commonly used in operating systems—namely that a process is a computational task executing on a single computing device. Our characterization is much broader, however, describing any mechanism used to carry out work or achieve a goal in an orderly way. Our processes need not even be executable on a computer.

It is important for us to recognize that the notion of process is a pervasive one in the realm of human activities and that humans seem particularly adept at creating and carrying out processes. Knuth [Knuth 69] has observed that following recipes for food preparation is an example of carrying out what we now characterize as a process. Similarly it is not difficult to see that following assembly instructions in building toys or modular furniture is carrying out a process. Following office procedures or pursuing the steps of a manufacturing activity are more widely understood to be the pursuit of orderly process.

The latter examples serve to illustrate an important point—namely that there is a key difference between a process and a process description. While a process is a vehicle for doing a job, a process description is a specification of how the job is to be done. Thus cookbook recipes are process descriptions while the carrying out of the recipes are processes. Office procedure manuals are process descriptions, while getting a specific office task done is a process. Similarly instructions for how to drive from one location to another are process descriptions, while doing the actual navigation and piloting is a process. From the point of view of a computer scientist the difference can be seen to be the difference between a type or class and an instance of that type or class. The process description defines a class or set of objects related to each other by virtue of the fact that they are all activi-

Leon J. Osterweil, "Software processes are software too," Proceedings of the 9th international conference on Software Engineering (ICSE 1987). © 1987 IEEE

P.L. Tarr, A.L. Wolf (eds.), *Engineering of Software*,
DOI 10.1007/978-3-642-19823-6_17, © Springer-Verlag Berlin Heidelberg 2011

ties which follow the dictated behavior. We shall have reason to return to this point later in this presentation.

For now we should return to our consideration of the intuitive notion of process and study the important ramifications of the observations that 1) this notion is widespread and 2) exploitation of it is done very effectively by humans. Processes are used to effect generalized, indirect problem solving. The essence of the process exploitation paradigm seems to be that humans solve problems by creating process descriptions and then instantiating processes to solve individual problems. Rather than repetitively and directly solving individual instances of problems, humans prefer to create generalized solution specifications and make them available for instantiation (often by others) to solve individual problems directly.

One significant danger in this approach is that the process itself is a dynamic entity and the process description is a static entity. Further, the static process description is often constructed so as to specify a very wide and diverse collection of dynamic processes. This leaves open the distinct possibility that the process description may allow for process instances which do not perform "correctly." Dijkstra makes this observation in his famous letter on the GOTO statement, [Dijkstra 69] observing that computer programs are static entities and are thus easier for human minds to comprehend, while program executions are dynamic and far harder to comprehend and reason about effectively. Dijkstra's point was important then and no less significant now. Processes are hard to comprehend and reason about, while process descriptions, as static objects, are far easier to comprehend. Finally it is important to also endorse Dijkstra's conclusion that our reasoning about process descriptions is increasingly useful in understanding processes as the descriptions are increasingly transparent descriptions of all processes which might be instantiated.

In view of all of these dangers and difficulties it is surprising that humans embark upon the indirect process description/instantiation/execution approach to problem solving so frequently. It is even more startling to observe that this approach is successful and effective so often. This suggests that humans have an innate facility for indirect problem solving through process specification. It is precisely this innate ability which should be able to propel us to become far more systematic and effective in the development and evolution of computer software. What currently stands most directly in our way is our failure—to date—to understand our most central and difficult problems in terms of the process description/instantiation/execution paradigm.

Computer Software Processes

It has become increasingly popular to characterize software development as a manufacturing activity in which the final delivered software should be considered to be a manufactured product. Efforts to consider software development analogous to other manufacturing activities such as auto assembly or parts fabrication have considerable intuitive appeal, although they have not been entirely satisfactory. From our perspective it seems clear that the set of activities carried out in order to effect the development or evolution of a software product should be considered to be a process. There seems to be a clear analogy between this sort of process and the process by which airplane wings are built, gourmet meals are prepared and autos are assembled.

The analogy seems to be relatively weaker in that 1) the product produced by a software process is intangible and invisible and 2) there seems to be no tangible process description from which our software processes are instantiated.

The former difficulty has been observed and discussed before. It is certainly true that we are hindered in our work by the fact that we cannot see our product and by the fact that we are neither guided nor constrained by the laws of physics, biology or chemistry in creating it and reasoning about it. Our product is a pure information product, being a structure of information and relations upon that information. Curiously enough, people in other disciplines emulate our situation, fashioning abstract models of their more concrete problems and systems in order to render them more analyzable and manipulable. The difference here is that their information structures are created to represent key aspects of their more concrete realities, while our information structures are our final products and our realities. They can use the five human senses to grasp and reason about their product—we cannot use these same senses to help us with our product. Accordingly we have difficulty reasoning about software products, and difficulty in thinking of them as real and tangible.

The latter difficulty is the main subject of this presentation—namely the paradoxical lack of process descriptions which are appropriate for the specification of the processes which we use in developing and evolving software. The paradox here is that elaborate and careful descriptions of our processes would seem to be most appropriate in view of the fact that our products are so difficult to grasp and so large and complex. Contemporary software products would have to be considered very large and complex by any objective measure. Our large systems may contain millions of lines of source code, but also contain volumes of documentation, enormous quantities of design information, specifications, testcases and testing results, as well as user manuals, maintenance manuals, and so forth. Further each of these software objects must have been integrated and correlated within themselves and with each other in surprisingly intricate ways. Our early attempts to define and characterize even relatively simple software products have lead to the conclusion that, while we were expecting these products to be large and complex, they are far larger and more complex than we had expected.

In view of the fact that our products are so large and complex, and in view of the compounding effect of the intangibility and invisibility of these products it is all the more surprising that we generally go about the job of developing and evolving them by employing processes which are rarely if ever guided by appropriately sharp, detailed and understood process descriptions. It is even more astounding that we are generally rather successful with these processes. This suggests that our innate process description/instantiation/execution capabilities are powerful indeed. They seem to be sufficiently powerful that we are able to improvise effective process descriptions on the fly, maintain them in our heads, modify them as necessary and guide others in their effective execution. Just think how much we might be able to achieve were we able to externalize these process descriptions, express them rigorously, promulgate them publicly, store them archivally, and exploit computing power to help us in guiding and measuring their execution.

This talk suggests a specific approach to doing this. We suggest that it is important to create software process descriptions to guide our key software processes, that these descriptions be made as rigorous as possible and that the processes then become guides for effective application of computing power in support of the execution of processes instantiated from these descriptions.

Our specific approach is to suggest that contemporary "programming" techniques and formalisms be used to express software process descriptions.

Software Process Programming

By now many will doubtlessly be observing that the idea of describing software processes is not new and has been done before. Certainly software "program plans," "development plans," even "configuration control plans," are examples of externalized software process descriptions. Further, industrial processes are routinely expressed by means of such formalisms as Pert charts and flow diagrams. Office procedures are often described in written procedures manuals. In view of this it is reasonable to question what new is being proposed here and to ask why we believe that we should expect dramatic improvement in the way in which we develop and evolve software in view of the fact that we are emulating techniques which have not been completely successful in other disciplines.

Our optimism springs from the fact that we have evolved powerful and disciplined approaches to handling intangibles as products, where other disciplines have not. We have dealt with the fact that our products are procedures for creating and managing invisible information structures. While our solutions are far from perfect, they are, at least, direct attempts to manage the invisible and intangible. By contrast the efforts of other disciplines seem less direct, less powerful and less effective. As computer scientists we have long ago embraced the use of rigorously defined languages as vehicles for describing complex and intricate information creation and management processes. We have evolved systems and procedures for studying these process descriptions, for analyzing them, and for applying them to the solution of specific problems. This whole realm of activities is what we have come to loosely describe as "programming." As computer scientists we have developed programming languages, have had some success in formally describing them and their effects, have encoded enormously complex descriptions of information manipulation processes, and have had success in instantiating such processes to carry out such impressive jobs as guiding the landing of people on the moon, switching myriads of telephone calls in a second and navigating airplanes and rockets at high speeds. In doing all this, we as a community have developed considerable instincts, talents and tools for treating processes as tangibles. It seems most natural and most promising to harness these instincts, talents and tools to the job of describing software development and evolution processes just as we approach classical "programming."

Our suggestion is that we describe software processes by "programming" them much as we "program" computer applications. We refer to the activity of expressing software process descriptions with the aid of programming techniques as *process programming*, and suggest that this activity ought to be at the center of what software engineering is all about. In succeeding remarks we shall attempt to briefly outline why we have this opinion.

A Rudimentary, but Instructive, Example

In this section we will present a very small example of a process program and use it to illustrate some of the benefits of the process programming approach. Before giving the example it seems worthwhile to make some basic observations about the strong analogy between a classical application program and a process program.

Perhaps the most basic observation is that both programs should be viewed as descriptions of processes whose goal is the creation or modification of a complex information aggregate. Each is used by instantiating the description into a specific product template, binding specific data values to it, and then allowing the process to transform those values into software objects and aggregate those objects into a final software product. In the case of an application program we generally think of the size of the input data objects as being relatively small—perhaps single numbers or short character strings—although we are all familiar with application programs in which the input data values are large and complex data aggregates. The inputs to software process programs will generally be of this latter kind, typically being source code statements or procedures, design information, test cases, or blocks of documentation. In both cases, however, the input data is examined, stored, and transformed into output software objects and products.

Further, in both cases the problem at hand, be it the solution of an application data processing problem or the conduct of a software process, is effected by instantiation of the process description, binding of values to the instance and evolution of problem specific solution elements. In the case of the application program, the embodiment of the problem solution description is executable code. In the process programming case, the problem solution is the process program itself. Later we shall discuss the sense in which we believe that process programs should be considered to be executable. For now, however, we can think of them as being expressed in a comfortable high level language.

In the following example, the process programming language is taken to be Pascal-like. The reader should not be misled into thinking that such a language is the preferred medium in which to express process programs. Research into appropriate process programming language paradigms is needed. We are convinced, for example, that rule-based languages will be effective vehicles for expressing certain software process descriptions, while algorithmic languages may be preferable in other areas. Thus, the following example is offered only in the spirit of lending definition and specificity to this discussion.

The Example

Here is an example of a process program which describes a very straightforward type of process for testing application software. As such it is offered as an example of how to describe one small but important part of a larger software development process.

```
Function All_Fn_Perf_OK(executable, tests);
        declare executable executable_code,
        tests testset,
        case, numcases integer,
        result derived_result;
--Note that executable_code, testset, and derived_result
--are all types which must be defined, but are not defined
--here.
  All_Fn_Perf_OK := True;
  For case := 1 to numcases
--This is the heart of the testing process, specifying
--the iterative execution of the testcases in a
--testset array and the comparison of the results with
--expected behavior.
    derive (executable,
        tests[case].input_data,
        result)
    if ~resultOK (result,
        testcase[case].req_output)
      then All_Fn_Perf_OK := False;
      exit;
--Note that the process specified here mandates that
--testing is aborted as soon as any test execution does
--not meet expectations. This is an arbitrary choice
--which has been made by the process programmer who
```

--designed this testing procedure.
    end loop;
  end All_Fn_Perf_OK;

While this process program is quite short it exemplifies some important aspects of process programs. First it should be noted that it highlights the key aspects of the testing process, while hiding lower level details. As such it is a reasonable example of the use of modularity, and of its application to the hard and important task of conveying software process information clearly. In this case we see that the testing process is an iterative loop which ends when a testcase fails. Further we see that the essence of testing is the evolution of test results and the evaluation of them. Details of how the results are evolved and how they are evaluated are left for elaboration in lower level process program procedures. It turns out that these details depend upon the fine-structure of objects of types testset and derived_result. It is important in itself that such entities as testsets, testcases, and derived results are treated as typed objects, requiring rigorous specification, and dealt with as operands to key operators in the process.

We may be interested in evaluating test results either for functional correctness or for adequate performance, or both. We may wish to determine acceptable functionality by comparing two simple numbers, by comparing two information aggregates, or by applying some complex function to the derived result and the expected result. The process program we have just shown is equally descriptive of all of these types of processes. It can be specialized to meet any specific testing need by the proper elaboration of the types and procedures which it uses.

For example, the following procedure specifies that a testing result is to be considered acceptable if and only if 1) the the functional result computed and the functional result needed cause the function "fcnOK" to evaluate to True, and 2) the observed execution time for the testcase is less than or equal to the execution time needed.

In order to understand this procedure and the way in which it elaborates upon All_Fn_Perf_OK, it is important to have the following type descriptions. It should be assumed that these definitions have been made in some outer scope of the process program in such a way that they are visible and accessible to the procedures we are specifying here.

  declare testset array of
    testcase[1..numcases];
  --
  declare testcase record of
    (input_data real,
    req_output record of
     (fcn_tol predicate,
     time_tol predicate,
     fcn real,
     time real));
  --

```
declare derived_result record of
  (fen_output real,
   observ_timing real);
```

We can now specify key lower level process program procedures.

```
Function resultOK (result, needed);
  declare result derived_result,
      needed req_output;
  if fcnOK (result.fcn_output,
      needed);
--Did the test compute an acceptable functional result
   OR
  (result.observ timing >
   needed.time)
--Did the test run fast enough
    then resultOK := False;
    else resultOK := True;
  endif;
  end resultOK;
--
--
Function derive (pgm, test, result);
  Declare pgm executable_code,
      test testcase,
      result derived_result;
--start by resetting the testing timer to zero
  reset_clock
--derive the functional output result and set it in the
--right field of the derived_result object
  result.fcn_output := execute (pgm, test.input_data);
--stop the testing timer and store the execution time
--of the testcase in the right field of the
--derived_result object
  result.observ_timing := read_clock;
  end derive;
--
--
Function fcnOK (result, needed);
  Declare result derived_result,
      needed req_output;
--NB It is assumed here that the process programming
--language allows for the inclusion of a function which
--has been specified as the value of a typed object
```

```
--and for the application of that function as part
--of the execution of a process program procedure.
   fcnOK := needed.fcn_tol (needed.fcn, result.fcn_output);
   end fcnOK;
```

In the interest of saving space, this example is left incomplete. Some lower level procedures and some types have not been completely specified. We believe that this lack of completeness should not interfere with a basic understanding of process programming. We hope that the reader sees that these algorithmic expressions can be used to effectively capture and convey details of a software development procedure clearly, but in a phased, gradual way which is familiar to software engineers. It is not important that the particular details of this example either agree or disagree with the reader's experiences or opinions on how testing should be carried out, but rather that the reader understand that the process programming vehicle has been used to unequivocally describe a specific procedure in terms that software practitioners should have little trouble understanding and reasoning about. Similarly it is believed that this mechanism could be used to clearly and unequivocally express whatever other testing procedure a software practitioner might wish to specify. In particular, if a given process program is not deemed suitable, then it becomes an appropriate centerpiece for sharp, focused discussions of how it should be modified to make it more suitable.

Further, this example is intended to suggest that the specified testing process might well be imbedded in a higher level process which describes the broader development contexts within which testing is to be carried out. In general we see no limits on the level at which software processes might be described by process programs. Process programs have been used to express entire software lifecycle models and have been elaborated down to very low level details. When process programs are written at a high level, but are not elaborated to low levels of detail, they become general prescriptions for how software work is to be done. When process programs describe lower levels of detail they become tools for substantive discussions of exact procedure. Each type of activity in its own way seems useful in assuring effective software development.

We believe it is significant that the example is longer and more complex than might be expected. What is described above is a rather straightforward testing loop, yet there are surprisingly many details to be specified. There is an unexpectedly large hierarchy of types needed to clearly and accurately express exactly what this testing process entails. This suggests to us that the processes which we intuitively carry out are more complex than might be expected and explains why it is often so difficult to explain them to others, so easy to overlook unexpected consequences, and so hard to estimate the effort needed to carry them out. These observations lead us to some important conclusions about the potential benefits of process programming.

Advantages of Process Programming

In general we believe that the greatest advantage offered by process programming is that it provides a vehicle for the materialization of the processes by which we develop and evolve software. As noted above, it is startling to realize that we develop and evolve so large, complex, and intangible an object as a large software system without the aid of suitably visible, detailed and formal descriptions of how to proceed. In that process programs are such descriptions they offer an enormous advantage. Through a process program the manager of a project can communicate to workers, customers and other managers just what steps are to be taken in order to achieve product development or evolution goals. Workers, in particular, can benefit from process programs in that reading them should indicate the way in which work is to be coordinated and the way in which each individual's contribution is to fit with others' contributions.

Finally, in materializing software process descriptions it becomes possible to reuse them. At present key software process information is locked in the heads of software managers. It can be reused only when these individuals instantiate it and apply it to the execution of a specific software process. When these individuals are promoted, resign or die their software process knowledge disappears. Others who have studied their work may have anecdotal views of the underlying process descriptions, but these descriptions themselves vanish with the individual who conceived them. Obviously such process knowledge is a valuable commodity and ought to be preserved and passed on. Materializing it is a critical necessity.

The preceding discussion simply emphasizes that any vehicle for capturing software process knowledge is far better than no vehicle at all. As observed earlier, however, Pert charts and procedures manuals are such vehicles. We believe that process programming is superior to these other approaches, however, in that it enables far more complete and rigorous description of software processes. By defining a process programming language in which data objects, data aggregates and procedural details can be captured and expressed to arbitrary levels of detail we make it possible to express software processes with greater clarity and precision than has previously been possible. Further, as the process descriptions are to be expressed in a programming language, both the act of creating the descriptions and the act of reading and interpreting them should be comfortable for software professionals.

Thus process programs written in a suitable process programming language should be expected to be particularly effective media for communicating arbitrarily large and complex software processes between software professionals. This should not be surprising, as all languages are supposed to be media for communication. Going further, the fact that software process programs are to be expressed in a computer programming language suggests that this language should also be an effective medium for communicating these process descriptions to computers as well. Specifically, we proposed that another important reason for writing software process programs is so that they can be automatically analyzed, compiled and interpreted by computers.

Some readers must certainly have observed that our previous example, replete as it was with type definitions, declarations and non-trivial algorithmic procedures, was likely to contain errors. As it was written in a language with definable syntax and semantics, however, the possibility of parsing it, semantically analyzing it and conveying diagnostic information back to the writer and readers is quite a real one. Clearly as process descriptions grow to contain more detail, and the programming language in which they are written matures to have more semantic content, the process programmer can expect to receive more diagnostic feedback. We see no reason why process programs written in such a rigorously defined language might not be compiled and executed. There would seem to be no reason why the testing process program presented in the previous section could not be executed on a computer once the lowest level procedures are defined. We have written a number of process programs which have been elaborated sufficiently far to suggest that they could be directly executed on a computer. Other process programs, which have not been elaborated down to suitable levels of detail, can still be reasonably thought of as being interpretable, but only if the lowest level procedures are to be "executed" either by software tools or by humans.

This observation suggests that process programs can be thought of as vehicles for indicating how the actions of software tools might be integrated with human activities to support software processes. Thus the process programming viewpoint leads to a novel approach to designing software environments. In this approach, software objects are thought of as variables—or instances of types. Software tools are thought of as operators which transform software objects. Humans are accorded certain well defined roles in creating and transforming objects too. The specification of what they do, when they do it, and how they coordinate with each other and with their tools is embodied in the process program, and is thus orchestrated by the process programmer. It is important to stress that the process programmer, by leaving certain high level tasks unelaborated, thereby cedes to the human software practitioner correspondingly wide latitude in carrying out those tasks. Thus interpretable process programs do not necessarily unduly constrain or regiment humans. The level of control and direction provided to humans is under the control of the process programmer, who exercises this control by providing or withholding details of the tasks assigned.

Further, this seems a suitable time to repeat our earlier observation that we cannot currently be sure of the linguistic paradigm in which software process programs ought to be expressed. This question must be considered to be a research topic. Our example process program was algorithmic. Thus, humans interpreting parts of it would be guided by procedural instructions. Process programs written in a rule-based language would be guided by prescriptive rules and would presumably feel more free and unconstrained.

Processes as Software

The foregoing discussion indicates why we believe that software process descriptions should be considered to be software. They are created in order to describe the way in which specific information products are to be systematically developed or modified. In this respect they are no different than a payroll program or a matrix inversion program. Further, our early work indicates that process programs can be written in compilable, interpretable programming languages which might bear a striking similarity to the languages in which conventional applications programs are written.

We believe that the primary difference between the process programs which we are suggesting and conventional programs is that process programs represent programming in a non-traditional application domain. This domain is distinguished first by the fact that its objects are perhaps larger, less well defined and more poorly understood than those in traditional application areas. Second, and more important, the product in this application area is not simply passive data, but includes yet another process definition (ie. an executable program for a traditional application area). Thus process programming is a more indirect activity. Its goal is the creation of a process description which guides the specification and development of an object which in turn guides the specification and development of another object which solves problems for end users. This doubly indirect process must be considered to be particularly tricky and error prone. It seems, however, to be the essence of software engineering. It is remarkable that we do it as well as we do. It seems self-evident that we could do it far better if process program software was materialized and made as tangible as the application software whose creation it guides.

The doubly indirect nature of software process programming is illustrated in the accompanying set of figures. Fig. 17.1 shows an end-user's view of how an application program is used to solve a problem by creating information as a product. Here we see that the user's problem is solved through the instantiation of a process description (an executable application program), the binding of that instance to specific data which the user supplies, and the execution of a process which is defined by the process description (the application program). The effect of this process is to create information products, some of which are temporary and internal to the process and some of which are externalized and aggregated into the user's final product. Control of how this is done resides with the process which has been instantiated. It is worthwhile to observe that the process description which has been instantiated for this user is presumably available for instantiation for the benefit of other users. In such a case, these other instances are bound to different input information and carry out somewhat different processes to create different products. The end-user may be only dimly aware of the way in which the process description came into existence or the way in which it works.

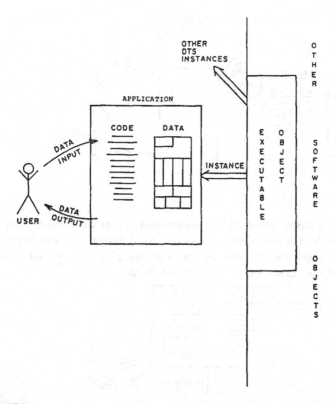

Fig. 17.1

Fig. 17.2 shows a larger context in which the situation depicted in Fig. 17.1 operates. In Fig. 17.2 we see that the process description which has been instantiated for the benefit of the end-user is actually a part of a larger information aggregate, and that this information aggregate is the domain of an individual whom we refer to as a software practitioner. We refer to this larger information aggregate as a Software Product and see that it is the product which the software practitioner is responsible for creating. The software product contains such information objects as specifications, designs, documentation, testcases, test results, source code, object code, and executable code (the end-user's process description). Some of these objects are received as input directly from the software practitioner (just as some of the end-user's information product is received directly from the end-user). Additionally, however, much of the rest of the Software Product is derived by the action of a process (just as the end-user's process derives some information).

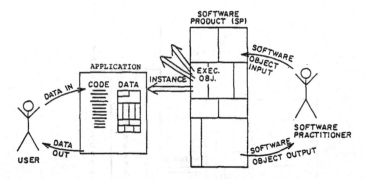

Fig. 17.2.

In both of these cases humans effect the creation of a product which is an information aggregate. The end user's product is derived through a process which is instantiated from a description created by someone else. Fig. 17.2 does not make it clear how the software practitioner's product is derived.

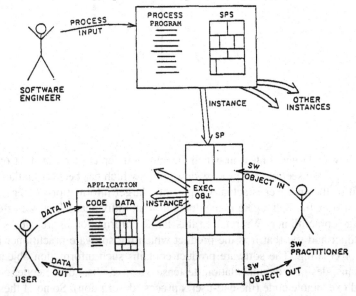

Fig. 17.3.

Fig. 17.3 suggests how we believe this should be done. In Fig. 17.3 we indicate that the Software Product should be viewed as an instance of a Software Product Structure (which we can think of as a very large template) and that the evaluation of the instance should be thought of as having been guided by the execution of a process program. We suggest that, just as the end-user may have only a dim understanding of the process which guides the creation of the end-user information product or where it came from, the software practitioner may also have only a dim understanding of the process program or where it came from. In each case the user is to be prompted from needed information, while the process accepts that information, uses it to derive more information, assembles that information, find produces the user's final information product. Certainly, at least for now, we expect that the level of involvement of the software practitioner in the process of creating the Software Product will be much higher than the usual level at which end-users are involved in the creation of their information products. This need for more involvement will result from the inability or reticence of the software process programmer to fully elaborate software process programs down to the level of directly executable code.

In that Fig. 17.3 strongly suggests the underlying similarity of applications programs and process programs, it thereby strongly invites the question of whether process programs might themselves be considered to be instances of some higher level process description. In Fig. 17.4 we indicate our belief that this is the case. Because software process programs are programs in what we now see to be the classical sense of this term, we should expect that they are best thought of as being only a part of a larger information aggregate. This information aggregate contains such other software objects as requirements specifications (for the process description itself), design information (which is used to guide the creation of the process description), and test cases (projects which were guided by processes instantiated by the process description).

There are a number of satisfying implications of the perspective that process program descriptions are themselves developed software. One such implication is that it is reasonable for there to be many different process descriptions that might be used to create similar software products. As process descriptions are developed to meet process requirements which may be expected to vary, clearly the design and implementation of these process descriptions should also be expected to vary. Thus it should be clear that there is no "ideal software process description." Software process descriptions should be created by software development processes which should take due regard of specialized requirements and constraints. In this sense software process programming is a true programming discipline. We believe that expert software managers have intuitively understood this for quite some time and have become adept at tailoring their processes to their needs. They do not seem to have appreciated their activities as programming activities, but it seems likely that the realization will be something of a relief.

Another satisfying implication of the view that software process descriptions emerge as part of a development lifecycle is that software process descriptions should undergo testing and evaluation. In fact this evaluation is carried out as the process description guides the evolution of individual software products. Successful process descriptions tend to get used again. Unsuccessful ones tend to be changed or discarded. The weakness of testing as the sole mechanism for software evaluation has been remarked upon before [Osterweil 81]. An integrated approach to evaluation incorporating static analysis and verification is clearly indicated.

Once software process descriptions have been materialized as code it becomes quite reasonable to consider such other forms of evaluation. The result should be software processes which should be far more trustworthy.

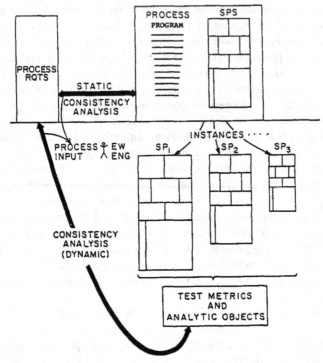

Fig. 17.4.

The previous paragraph sketches some of the characteristics of what we might describe as a "process development process." We have begun to examine what a description of such a process might be like. It is also reasonable to consider "process evolution processes" as well. We have begun to consider what the nature of a software process evolution process description might be as well. These considerations have shed light upon the nature of what has been dubbed "maintenance."

There has been some fear that these considerations might lead to an ever-rising hierarchy of processes which produce processes, which produce processes which eventually actually produce end-user software. This fear seems groundless, as process programs and end-user programs do not seem to be essentially different. This leads to optimism that processes which we employ to develop and evolve end-user software products should also be applicable to the development and evolution of process program descriptions. This premise is a very important one and is being explored.

We have concluded that the notion of software process programming is a generalization, or extension to a new domain, of classical applications programming. The disciplines, techniques and tools of classical applications programming apply to process programming and can rapidly lead to the effective materialization of the descriptions of the processes which we use and their rapid improvement, maturation and archival storage for reuse.

Future Directions

It should be clear that we believe that important contributions to software engineering can be made by pursuing the notion of process programming in any of a number of directions. In this section we indicate some of these directions, summarizing early work which has been done and continuations which seem indicated.

Software Process Studies

We believe that great strides can be made in understanding software processes once they have been materialized. Materializing them in the form of process programs offers great hope because such programs are rigorous and comfortable for both readers and writers. Discussion and evaluation of such software processes as testing [Howden 81] and design [JeffTPA 81] have been going on for quite some time. In addition debates about software development lifecycle models have been proceeding for well over a decade. We believe that these discussions have not been nearly as substantive and effective as they could and should be, largely because they have not been carried out in a rigorous and agreed-to form of discourse. Adoption of the idiom of process programming has the potential to precipitate rapid and significant advances in understanding the software lifecycle and the various of the subprocesses which comprise it, as process programming supplies a natural idiom in which to carry out these discussions.

At the University of Colorado we have begun to develop a variety of process programs and have found that these activities have almost invariably led to interesting insights into the processes under study. Much of this work has been done by graduate students who have had only a brief exposure to the idea of process programming. Their success in producing cogent and compelling process programs leads one to believe that this technique is rather easily motivated and rather easy to embark upon. These early experiences suggest that our instincts and experiences as programmers tend to lead us to worthwhile questions when they are applied to programming software processes.

We have written and compared process program definitions describing testing and evaluation. We believe that such process program definitions are best viewed as rigorized test plans. As such they elucidate both the test planning and the testing processes which we carry out. We have also written software requirements as elaborate data specifications. This exercise suggests some interesting ways in which requirements might be captured more rigorously. Again, our instincts and experiences seem to tend to guide us to interesting and worthwhile questions, suggesting new formalisms which seem to have much promise. We have also tried to capture some software lifecycle models as process program definitions. Glaring weaknesses in such well-known models as the "Waterfall" manifest themselves in the form of trivial and incomplete code.

Experimental process program description writing should continue. It seems certain to shed important light on the nature of our software processes. It also holds promise of providing a vehicle for sharply accelerated progress towards consensus on some processes, providing this formalism is adopted widely as a medium of discourse.

Process Programming Language Studies

It is clear that the rapid progress which we have just described cannot be achieved until and unless there is some consensus about a language in which software processes and software products can be defined. In our earliest work we attempted to use simple language constructs in familiar linguistic paradigms. While quickly indicating the power of the process programming approach, these efforts also quickly served to show that powerful linguistic primitives are essential if process programs are to be sufficiently precise and powerful.

Software products can only be described as very complex data aggregates. Thus powerful type definition and data aggregation mechanisms must be included in any process programming language. A full range of control flow mechanisms also seems needed if the language is to be capable of conventional algorithmic expressions. Alternation and looping are clearly crucial parts of familiar software processes. We were surprised to observe, moreover, that these processes could not be expressed effectively without the use of concurrency specifications. On reflection this should be no surprise. Human processes are clearly highly concurrent, thus they can best be expressed using concurrency primitives. In addition, it seems that the scoping and accessing rules for a process programming language must be sophisticated. Our early work has shown that classical hierarchical scoping rules are not adequate to describe the complex ways in which software subprocesses must communicate with each other. Rigid message-passing mechanisms have also been shown to be unequal to the stringent information sharing requirements of actual software processes.

All of these early results indicate that significant research is needed to produce the definition of a suitable language. As observed earlier, this research cannot be restricted to an examination only of algorithmic languages. We have produced some very provocative process programs using informal languages which borrowed freely from the rule-based, object-oriented and applicative linguistic paradigms. It seems likely that only a mixed paradigm or wide spectrum language will prove adequate for comfortably expressing software process programs.

Software Environment Architecture Research

As noted earlier, one of the more exciting consequences of this work is that it has suggested a novel architecture for a software environment. We now believe that a software environment is best viewed as a vehicle for the specification of process programs, and for their compilation and interpretation. In such an environment tools would be treated as operators, or lowest level software processes, whose jobs were defined in terms of the need to create and transform software objects which would be treated as instances of types. These types would correspond to different types of intermediate and final software products. Humans would participate in executing such software processes by serving as the execution devices for subprocesses which were not elaborated to sufficient levels of detail to enable interpretation by either tools or the host computing system execution environment.

One of the more powerful suggestions of this work is that software processes can themselves be treated as software objects by an environment. We believe that development and evolution processes can be produced in such a way that they specify how both application programs and process programs are created and maintained. As software processes are software objects, and our environment architecture treats all software objects as instances of types, this suggests that software processes might well be organized by some sort of type hierarchy. We have begun pursuing the notion that various software processes can be organized into such a hierarchy and can, perhaps, be characterized by the operational characteristics that they inherit and/or mix in. We propose to explore these hypotheses by experimentally building and using a process programming environment. Arcadia is a project to create just such an environment [Arcadia 86]. The first prototype environment, to be called Arcadia-1, will provide a testbed for the evaluation of many of our environment architectural ideas, as well as a vehicle for experimenting with process programming.

Software Metrics

One of the most gratifying aspects of our exploration of the notion of process programming is that it has led to insights and research directions which were not expected outgrowths of the work. Once such outgrowth has been some promising ideas about software metrics. It seems clear that in materializing software process descriptions we are creating a natural subject for measurement. If a software process such as testing or development is to be thought of as the execution of a process program, it seems reasonable to measure the size of the product in terms of the size of the objects declared within the process program, and to measure the degree of completion of the process in terms of the position of the execution pointer in the process program code. Static analysis of process programs could likewise lead to promising measures of the complexity of the corresponding software processes.

We make no claims that such software metrics are necessarily superior to existing metrics, but we do suggest that comparison of such new metrics to more classical ones warrants research attention.

Implications for Software Reuse

Another unexpected outcome of this line of inquiry has been a somewhat different understanding of the nature of software reuse and the problems in effectively achieving this important goal. We believe that the goal of software reuse is the successful integration into an evolving software product of software object(s) which were developed as part of a different development process. That being the case, reuse entails the careful assimilation of the reused objects into the new product. Given that software products are notorious for their intricate interconnectivity, it seems evident that only a complex process will suffice for assuring that the reused objects are properly interwoven into their new context, and properly evaluated in that new context. Thus effective reuse can only be achieved through the execution of a suitable process which should be defined by means of a suitable reuse process program. It is interesting to note that managers often observe that reuse "must be planned for." From our perspective that means that reuse processes must have been previously programmed. Further, these programs must be executed only at the proper points in the larger process of developing the reusing software. We conjecture that software reuse can only be expected to be a realistic prospect when the structure of the reused software closely matches the structure of the reusing software, and when the process by which the reused software was developed closely matches the process by which the reusing software is being developed.

Finally, it seems important to repeat our observation that perhaps the most important benefit of process programming is that it offers the hope that software processes themselves can be reused. We believe that effective software process descriptions are one of the most valuable resources which we as a society have. The realization that these resources are never effectively preserved beyond the working lifetime of the people who execute them is a sobering realization. We look forward to the prospect that process programs which have been shown to be effective can one day be captured rigorously and completely and made part of libraries of reusable software process programs. Such reusable process programs would then become the modular parts out of which new process definitions could be fashioned or adapted. We expect that early process programs will be produced from scratch by software engineering researchers, but that in the future process programs will be customized by working engineers out of standard process programs.

Conclusion

In this paper we have suggested that the notion of a "process program"—namely an object which has been created by a development process, and which is itself a software process description—should become a key focus of software engineering research and practice. We believe that the essence of software engineering is the study of effective ways of developing process programs and of maintaining their effectiveness in the face of the need to make changes.

The main suggestions presented here revolve around the notion that process programs must be defined in a precise, powerful and rigorous formalism, and that once this has been done, the key activities of development and evolution of both process programs themselves and applications programs can and should be carried out in a more or less uniform way.

This strongly suggests the importance of devising a process programming language and a software environment capable of compiling and interpreting process programs written in that language. Such an environment would become a vehicle for the organization of tools for facilitating development and maintenance of both the specified process, and the process program itself. It would also provide a much needed mechanism for providing substantive support for software measurement and management.

We are convinced that vigorous research directed towards 1) the creation of a process programming language, 2) the construction of a compilation and interpretation system for programs written in it and 3) the use of these tools in the careful description of key software processes will surely be of enormous value in hastening the maturation of software engineering as a discipline.

Acknowledgments The author gratefully acknowledges that this work was made possible by the generous support of the National Science Foundation, through Grant #DCR 1537610, the US Department of Energy through Grant #1537612, and The American Telephone and Telegraph Company. In addition the author wishes to thank Professor John Buxton of King's College, University of London, Professor Manny Lehman of Imperial College, University of London, and Dr. Brian Ford of Nag, Ltd., Oxford, England, for their help, encouragement and numerous challenging conversations during Academic Year 1985-86, while the author formulated these ideas while on leave of absence in England. In addition numerous stimulating conversations and interchanges with Stu Feldrnan, Dick Taylor, Bob Balzer, Geoff Clemm, Lori Clarke, Dennis Heimbigner, Stan Sutton, Shehab Gamelel-Din, Brigham Bell, Steve Krane, Steve Squires, Bill Scherlis, Frank Belz and Barry Boehm also helped to shape these ideas significantly. Finally the author thanks the students in Computer Science 582, Fall 1986, for their patience in trying to understand process programming and their energy and enthusiasm in producing an impressive base of process programs.

References

[Arcadia 86] R.N. Taylor, L.A. Clarke, L.J. Osterweil, R.W. Selby, J.C. Wileden, A. Wolf and M. Young, Arcadia: A Software Development Environment Research Project, *ACM/IEEE Symposium on Ada Tools and Environments*, Miami, Florida, April 1986.

[BoehmMU 75] B. Boehm, R. McClean, D. Urfrig, "Some Experiments with Automated Aids to the Design of Large Scale Reliable Software," *IEEE Trans. on Software Eng.*, SE-1, pp. 125-133 (1975).

[Dijkstra 68] Dijkstra, Edsger W., "Go To Statement Considered Harmful," *CACM 11* pp. 147-148 (March 1968).

[Howden 85] Howden, W.E., "The Theory and Practice of Functional Testing," *IEEE Software*, 2 pp. 6-17 (Sept. 1985).

[JeffTPA 81] R. Jeffries, A. Turner, P. Polson, M. Atwood, "The Processes Involved in Designing Software," in *Cognitive Skills and Their Acquisition* (Anderson, ed.) Lawrence Erlbaum, Hillsdale, NJ, 1981.

[Knuth 68] Knuth, Donald E., *The Art of Computer Programming, V.1—Fundamental Algorithms* Addison Wesley, Reading, MA 1968.

[Osterweil 81] L. J. Osterweil, "Using Data Flow Tools in Software Engineering," in *Program Flow Analysis: Theory and Application,* (Muchnick and Jones, eds.) Prentice-Hall Englewood Cliffs, N.J., 1981.

[SPW1 84] Proceedings of Software Process Workshop, Runnymede, England, February 1984.

[SPW2 85] Proceedings of Second Software Process Workshop, Coto de Caza, CA, March 1985.

Software Processes Are Software Too, Revisited

An Invited Talk on the Most Influential Paper of ICSE9

Leon J. Osterweil

University of Massachusetts, Dept. of Computer Science, Amherst, MA 01003 USA +1 413
545 2186, ljo@cs.umass.edu

Abstract   The ICSE 9 paper, "Software Processes are Software Too," suggests
that software processes are themselves a form of software and that there are considerable benefits that will derive from basing a discipline of software process development on the more traditional discipline of application software development.
This paper attempts to clarify some misconceptions about this original ICSE 9
suggestion and summarizes some research carried out over the past ten years that
seems to confirm the original suggestion. The paper then goes on to map out some
future research directions that seem indicated. The paper closes with some ruminations about the significance of the controversy that has continued to surround this
work.

Introduction

"Software Processes are Software Too." How many times I have heard that phrase
quoted back to me in the past ten years! And how many times it has been (sometimes amusingly) misquoted too. Often I have been flattered to have had the
ICSE9 paper [15] and its catchy title referred to as being "classic" and "seminal".
But often I have also been asked, "what does that really mean?" The idea is, alas,
still misunderstood and misconstrued in some quarters. But amazingly, and grati-
fyingly, the phrase is still used, and the discussion of the idea still continues, even
after ten years. The suggestion that software, and the processes that deal with it,
might somehow be conceptually similar remains a powerfully appealing one that
seems to have led to a considerable body of investigation. The suggestion was
immediately controversial, and continues to be argued. Subsequently I discuss
why I believe this discussion indicates a pattern of behavior typical of traditional

Leon J. Osterweil, "Software Processes Are Software Too, Revisited:
An Invited Talk on the Most Influential Paper of ICSE 9,"
19th International Conference on Software Engineering, ACM, 1997.
DOI: 10.1145/253228.253440, © 1997 ACM, Inc. Reprinted with permission

P.L. Tarr, A.L. Wolf (eds.), *Engineering of Software*,
DOI 10.1007/978-3-642-19823-6_18, © Springer-Verlag Berlin Heidelberg 2011

scientific inquiry, and therefore seems to me to do credit to the software engineering community.

But what of the (in)famous assertion itself? What does it really mean, and is it really valid? The assertion grew out of ruminations about the importance of orderly and systematic processes as the basis for assuring the quality of products and improving productivity in developing them. Applying the discipline of orderly process to software was not original with me. Lehman [13] and others [18] had suggested this long before. But I was troubled because I had started to see the development of a whole new discipline and technology around the idea of software process, and to notice the emergence of many notions and tools that seemed eerily familiar. I was starting to see the creation of a software process universe parallel to the universe of notions and tools surrounding application software development. The more I looked, the more similarities I saw. Processes and applications are both executed, they both address requirements that need to be understood, both benefit from being modelled by a variety of sorts of models, both must evolve guided by measurement, and so forth. Thus it seemed important to suggest that software process technology might not need to be invented from scratch (or reinvented), but that much of it might be borrowed from application software technology.

I have often been reminded that application software technology is still badly underdeveloped and that using it as a model for software process technology might be of dubious value. This, however, overlooks clear evidence that, while we have not mastered application software technology, we have, nevertheless, created a powerful assortment of tools, principles, and techniques in this domain. Thus, there is much to be gained from using obvious parallels to hasten the maturation of software process technology. It seemed important to suggest that the community should look to the more traditional and better-developed disciplines of application development to see what might be borrowed or adapted. It seemed clear that there were strong similarities, but likely that there were differences as well. Investigation of the extent of each seemed to be in order. The ICSE 9 talk invited community investigation of how processes and application software are the same and how they differ, so that relevant findings, approaches, and tools of one could be of use to the other. It has been gratifying to see that this invitation has been taken up and that these explorations are still ongoing.

Conversely it has been disappointing to see the way in which the suggestion has continued to be misconstrued in some quarters. Subsequent sections will deal with these misconceptions in more detail, but the following brief summary seems in order here.

Software is not simply code. Neither are software processes. Application software generally contains code. This suggests that software processes might also contain code. Coding software processes thus seems to be an interesting possibility. Research has borne this out.

Programming is not the same as coding, it entails the many diverse steps of software development. Software process programming should, likewise, not simply be coding, but seemed to entail the many non-coding steps usually associated with application development. Process modelling, testing, and evolution research seems to have borne that out.

There are many examples of application code that are not inordinately prescriptive, authoritarian, or intolerable to humans (eg. operating systems). Thus, there should be no presumption that process code must be overly prescriptive, authoritarian, or intolerable either. Process programs need not treat humans like robots unless that is the intention of the process programmer. Process modelling and coding languages demonstrate this.

Finally, good software code is written at all levels of detail. Code contains fine scale details, but they emerge at lower levels, after high level code addresses larger issues. Similarly process code contains details that are nested below higher abstract levels. Process code, like application code, can demonstrate that precise implementation of broader notions in terms of lower level engineering details. Contemporary process coding languages demonstrate this too.

The following section summarizes some research that suggests continued and broadened research into these issues.

Parallels Between Software Processes and Application Software

Much work seems to demonstrate the existence of significant parallels between software processes and application software, although not all of this work was intended to do so. This section briefly surveys what has been learned.

Process Modelling

There has been a great deal of study of how well various application software modelling formalisms model software processes. For example, Petri Nets [l], [5], Finite State Machines [6], [11], and data flow diagrams [19] have been used to model software processes. These activities have clearly demonstrated that application software modelling approaches can be strong aids in conceptualizing processes, in helping people to communicate about processes and collaborate in their execution, and in raising intuition about processes.

As with application software modelling, different types of process models are good for different things. Petri Net models, for example, are quite useful in elucidating parallelism and concurrency, but are less useful in modelling artifacts. Petri Nets process models seem to have very similar properties. They help to identify parallelism in processes, but have generally required augmentation in order to effectively elucidate the flow of software artifacts through processes. Other similar examples could readily be pointed out.

In general, models, by their nature, abstract away details in order to focus on specific narrow issues, which are thereby made correspondingly clearer and more vivid. Thus, Petri Net models depict parallelism clearly in part because depictions of other less relevant details are specifically omitted. Thus, any particular model should be expected to be useful in some contexts, but less helpful in others. To support understanding of various aspects of a software product different models are generally needed. Thus, a number of modelling systems (eg. [6]) support the development and coordination of multiple models of application software. Experience in the software process domain has been similar. Statemate was used as a process modelling tool [11], and its support for multiple models was useful precisely because the different models supported understanding and reasoning from a variety of aspects. In the application software domain there is a growing understanding of which modelling tools and formalisms best elucidating which issues. We expect similar understandings to emerge in the software process domain.

But, as with application software modelling, it has also become clear in process modelling that there are reasons why models, even multiple models, are sometimes inadequate. The very lack of certain types of details in models means that models inevitably lack specifics that can be very important. In addition, many modelling formalisms (eg. graphical models) are based upon weak and shallow semantics. Because of this it is usually impossible or unsafe to reason about such models. Models expressed in a formalism with a weak semantic base may convey an intuitive impression, but they usually cannot support precise, reliable reasoning. For example, many modeling notations (especially graphical notations) can indicate parallel activities, but offer no semantics for defining the precise nature of the parallelism. This lack of semantics leaves human interpreters free to suppose whatever form of parallelism they like. Inevitably this leads different interpreters to different conclusions about what the model represents. The result is often miscommunication and misunderstanding. Where the intent of the model was presumably clarity, the effect will have been quite the opposite. Even where the semantics of such constructs as parallelism are incorporated in the modelling formalism, it is unusual for there to be much variety in the sorts of parallelism. This semantic sparseness usually causes such formalisms to be inadequate to depict the full range of parallel constructs needed to represent the full range of parallelism that process modelling seems to require. Thus, there seems to be a growing understanding that models of processes meet some needs (eg. raising one's intuition about processes), but that there are more needs that are unlikely to be met by single process models, or even combinations of process models.

Process Coding

While there is good evidence that processes need to be represented by executable code, as well as by models, as in the case of application code, it is difficult to draw a sharp distinction between coding languages and modelling languages. Certain coding languages are imprecise about the execution semantics of certain constructs, and certain modelling languages have very precise execution semantics. There are often disputes about whether particular application languages should be considered to be coding or modelling languages. The process community has experienced similar disputes and disagreements about process languages during the past years.

Such disputes are unproductive. The important distinctions among these languages are the nature, depth, and scope of the semantic details that they provide. As noted in the previous sections, modelling formalisms tend to offer relatively weak, shallow, or narrow semantics. Thus, while a strong modelling formalism may support deep and reliable reasoning about a narrow aspect of the software it models, such formalisms are at best helpful only in narrow contexts. When broad categories of powerful precise, reliable reasoning is required stronger, broader semantics and greater detail are essential. In reasoning, for example, about the presence or absence of deadlocks and race conditions in processes it is essential for the process to be defined in a formalism that supports precise definition of parallelism and shared access to data and resources. The semantics needed to support such reasoning must be quite precise and powerful, and are generally consistent with semantics found in full coding languages, rather than in modelling languages. Processes, like applications, at times benefit from the existence of codelike representations that offer a wide range of semantic power and definition detail. At some times the detail will be undesirable, interfering with clarity and intuition. But at other times it will be essential as the basis for effective reasoning and actual execution.

There are other reasons why it is important to reduce software to code. Application developers know that, until software has been coded, it is unknown whether the possibly myriad models that have preceded it can actually be reduced to practice. Similarly a set of software process models may depict an enticing view, but can still leave open to question just how a process consistent with all of those views will actually work. It is the interplay of all of the details, both present and absent, from all of the models that characterizes and defines the actual application or process. Only a language that can specify and interrelate all of these details can support definitive demonstrations of the realizability of the desired product. In short, real code provides real assurances; models mostly provide enticements.

The original ICSE 9 paper emphasized yet another reason for defining processes in coding languages. That paper suggested that processes should be viewed as prescriptions for the synergistic coordination of the efforts of humans, computers, and software tools. Process code was suggested as the vehicle for specifying the precise details of this coordination. Because coding languages have executable semantics, the paper suggested that computers could execute such code and could, in doing so, supervise the integration of the efforts of people, machines and tools.

This point has been the subject of much unfortunate misinterpretation and caricature. Careless reading of this point has taken it to suggest that all processes could, or should, be reduced to computer executable instructions. This was neither the intent nor the proposal of the original paper. Indeed, the paper stated that software development processes should refrain from elaborating the details of how humans should carry out their tasks. Human tasks should be represented as functions or procedures for which the definition is omitted, thereby leaving the human free to execute the task as he or she sees fit. The level to which any human task is elaborated by the process code is the choice of the process coder, who, in doing so, specifies the extent to which the process is authoritarian and prescriptive, or permissive and relaxed. The vehicle of process code is thus not a device for dictating what a human must do, but rather a vehicle for specifying the degree to which human activities are to be circumscribed by the defined process. The act of defining the process by executable code does not necessarily unduly restrict the human, although the nature of the code may do so. Indeed, the JIL [23] language, is an example of a process coding language that supports considerable latitude in the degree of specificity of process definition.

Here too, experience suggests that a wide range of process coding languages and coding styles seem to be of value. Less detailed process code is preferable, for example when the process is to be performed by seasoned experts who can exercise good judgment in devising sequences of process steps to carry out a task. More detailed and precise process code is of value in other circumstances, for example in restricting and regulating the work of software developers who are novices, or whose actions may eventually be subject to careful scrutiny (as, for example in the case where an organization wishes to provide protection against possible subsequent legal claims of carelessness in software development).

As suggested above, detailed process code specifications are also of particular importance in specifying how tools and automated procedures are to be integrated into processes, and how the activities of humans are to be coordinated with them. This requires precise specifications of how various software artifacts are to be fed into tools and extracted from their outputs, precise specification of how such artifacts are to be made available to the right humans at the right time, and how human development artifacts are to be channeled to the right colleagues and tools. All of this requires a great deal of precise specification that is consistent with the levels of detail and precision found in the executable semantics of coding languages.

Experimental research of the past few years seems to confirm that coding languages are particularly adept at expressing the specifics of the interactions of process steps and software artifact operands, while modelling languages tend to be particularly ineffective at this. Modelling languages tend to focus on either activity or artifact modelling, thereby failing to support the choreography of artifacts through tools and humans. Coding languages tend to be superior in this regard. Thus there seems to be considerable evidence that software processes require and benefit from both modelling and coding for very much the same reasons that software applications benefit from both of these activities.

Process Evaluation

There is also considerable evidence that software processes are amenable to evaluation using approaches that bear important similarities to the approaches used in evaluating application software. Indeed, the past ten years have witnessed explosive growth in work on the evaluation of software processes. Most of this work has grown out of the proposal of Humphrey and his colleagues at the Software Engineering Institute, of the Capability Maturity Model (CMM) [7] [16]. The aim of the CMM is to provide an evaluation vehicle for determining the quality of an organization's software development processes. Organizational software process evaluation is done by a variety of means, but is usually based upon questionnaire-based surveying, and by examination of the artifacts produced by past software development projects.

Although the CMM does not take the explicit position of viewing software processes as software, it seems useful for us to do so. Taking the position that an organization has a process that it executes in order to develop its products leads to the conclusion that such products are reasonably viewed as the outputs of the execution of that process. If the quality of the process is evaluated through examination of such outputs, then doing so is essentially a testing activity. This leads us to conclude that the CMM establishes the structure for a process testing regimen, and that such instruments as the CMM-based questionnaires function as process test plans.

These observations demonstrate that testing and evaluation of software processes has been a prevalent activity over the past several years, even despite the fact that explicit process representations may not have been available. The lack of explicit process definitions forces the process evaluator to examine output artifacts, and to take a testing-like approach to process evaluation. From our perspective of viewing processes as software, we suggest that this is analogous to testing quality into the software process. Experience in such fields as manufacturing suggests that it is preferable to build quality in, rather than test it in. Building quality into processes seems to require the explicit representation and definition of the processes. We view this as yet another key reason why processes should be precisely defined using formalisms with strong semantics.

Indeed, going one step further, we observe that carrying out a CMM-based evaluation or assessment is in fact the execution of a process-testing process. As such, this sort of process too should be amenable to specification by process formalisms. Such formally specified process-testing processes are examples of higher-order processes that should be developed for the evaluation of processes and the feeding back of such evaluations as part of larger process improvement processes.

Formal specifications of such higher-order processes should facilitate more precise and sure reasoning about these key processes. These ideas are developed more fully in [14].

Process Requirements

The observed parallels between modelling, coding, and evaluating application software and software processes might suggest that similar parallels have been demonstrated between application requirements specification and process requirements specifications. It is startling to note that such parallels have not been demonstrated yet due to an apparent lack of interest in studying software process requirements.

Especially in view of the intense interest in supporting the modelling, coding, and evaluation of processes, it seems almost bizarre that there has been virtually no work in supporting the specification of process requirements. Indeed early suggestions that more attention be focussed on process requirements sometimes brought disbelief in the very existence of process requirements. The enterprise of process modelling should instantly raise in trained software engineers important questions about the validation of such models. That, in turn should suggest that the models are there in large measure to demonstrate that a particular process approach is effective in addressing certain process problems, as enunciated in a set of requirements.

Software processes generally have clear (albeit unstated) performance requirements, (eg. deadlines for completion of the entire process or various of its steps). Further, these requirements function very much in the way that application software requirements do, often influencing important choices about what steps to parallelize, in which way, and to what degree. Similarly processes often have robustness requirements, specifying how processes must react to such adverse situations as the loss of key personnel or artifacts. Replication, redundancy, and backups are the standard application software approaches to addressing these requirements, and they are also process architecture approaches to similar process requirements. Processes also have functional requirements, for example specifications of the range of software artifacts to be produced as the final output of the process, and the nature of the required demonstrations of internal consistency.

Despite these rather obvious types of process requirements, and the fact that they should function as essential baselines against which to measure both process models and process test plans, there has been virtually no interest in developing and using process requirement formalisms. Thus, although the parallelism between application software requirements and software process requirements seems apparent, there has been scant research to demonstrate it. This seems to be an area that is very much in need of considerably more investigation.

Looking Ahead

It seems increasingly clear that the weight of evidence is supporting the hypothesis that software processes are indeed very much like application software in many important ways. That being the case, we should expect to be able to exploit the similarities in a number of ways. The previous section has suggested some of these ways. In this section we suggest some others.

Programming Key Processes

It seems clear that it is time to get on with the important work of developing models and code of key software development processes. There are important benefits to be gained from this. Software engineering (indeed any sort of engineering) has as two of its key objectives the reduction of costs and the improvement of the quality of products. Processes play a key role in both of these. As software costs derive almost exclusively from the cost of human labor, cost reduction must come from reduction in labor. Explicit software process representations can be analyzed to identify needless and unproductive human labor, and to identify process steps that might be performed by automated devices. Both then lead to reductions in labor costs. Further, as noted above, quality is generally understood to be built into products through periodic careful testing and analysis of the product as it evolves through the development process. Here too, explicit process representations should be effective bases for identifying where and how to carry out these periodic tests and analyses.

Thus, the development, demonstration, and reuse of demonstrably superior software processes still remains the goal that it was as enunciated in the original ICSE 9 paper. However, now, ten years later, we should have greater assurance that this goal is achievable, and a weight of experimentation suggesting how to proceed. We have demonstrated a variety of modelling formalisms (largely borrowed from application software technology). We have also begun to understand the demanding requirements of process coding languages. But, here application software coding languages have proven less useful. Experimentation has demonstrated the value of various programming paradigms, such as the procedural programming paradigm (eg. with the APPL/A language [22]), the rule based programming paradigm (eg. with MSL, the Marvel Specification Language [8]), and real-time programming approaches (eg. with Adele [2]). But this experimentation has also shown the inadequacy of each of these by itself. Experience has shown that representing in a clear and straightforward way all of the details and complexities of software processes by means of a language with executable semantics is far more difficult and challenging than was expected ten years ago. Second generation languages such as JIL [23], which enable the blending of the benefits of various programming language paradigms, seem to hold promise. More experimentation and evaluation of such languages is clearly indicated.

In order for the cost and quality improvements mentioned above to be realized, execution engines for such languages will have to be developed. Recent research is leading to understandings that such engines must have highly flexible distributed architectures. The Amber project [9], and the Endeavors project [3] offer good examples of such architectures. These projects should provide encouragement to believe that the superior process code to be written in the new generation of process coding languages will be effectively executable to provide the sort of strong support needed to reduce costs and improve quality in developed software.

Once these languages and execution engines are in place the development of exemplary software processes should begin. Some examples of processes that should greatly benefit from such encodings are: processes for collaborative design, processes for integrated testing and analysis, processes for configuration management, processes for tracking bug fixing, and processes for effecting successful reuse. Indeed, the last ten years has seen a growing awareness of the broad range of processes that are executed in the course of developing software. As these processes have been more clearly identified, they have become increasingly important targets for understanding and improvement. Detailed encodings should support reliable analyses and detailed dynamic monitoring of these processes that should then lead to the kinds of deep understandings that are needed in order to effect improvements reliably.

Creating a practice of software process engineering that will lead to reliable techniques for systematic improvements to processes through engineering of process program artifacts is clearly some distance off. But the progress of the past ten years seems to indicate that it is still a worthy goal, and to justify greater belief in assertions that it is definitely achievable than could have been justified ten years ago.

Scientific Classification and Comparison of Software Processes

While most of the process technology research of the past ten years has focussed on supporting the synthesis of new processes, there has also been an important demonstration of the use of process technology to support the analysis of existing processes. As noted above, there has been a growing recognition of the number and diversity of processes in use to support software development. Thus, designing, debugging, requirements specification, and configuration management have come to be recognized as key software development processes. In some of these areas, for example software design, there has been a long history of suggested approaches to performing the process. These suggestions have all too often taken the form of imprecise and/or incomplete prose articles, courses, and books, often consisting largely of examples. Attempts to compare and contrast these suggested software design approaches have been reduced to similarly informal, often anec-dotal, treatments of the various approaches. The lack of definitive, precise charac-terizations and comparisons of these design approaches frustrates practitioners who must choose from among them, and impedes progress towards the establish-ment of a scientific discipline of software engineering.

Regarding software design as a process that can be expressed in precise model-ling and coding formalisms seems to help considerably. This perspective suggests that the writings about various software design approaches might be considered to be specifications of requirements and/or architectures of contrasting software de-sign processes. It further suggests that detailed models and encodings of these processes, using formalisms based on precise and deep semantics, can be bases for correspondingly precise characterizations, classifications, and comparisons.

A series of papers published over the past five years demonstrates the viability of this approach [20, 21, 17]. In these papers popular software design methods (SDM's) are modelled using popular software process modelling formalisms (eg. HFSP [10] and Slang [1]). Comparison frameworks are hypothesized to guide clas-sification of SDM features. A carefully defined SDM comparison process is ex-ecuted to extract comparison results from the classifications of the models of the SDM's. The papers demonstrate that this approach can be used to produce classi-fication and comparison results that agree with and extend classifications and comparisons arrived at based on informal models and comparison techniques. The precision and specificity of both the models and the comparison process itself (it is a process programmed in process modelling and coding languages) suggest that these classification and comparison results are reproducible by different human comparators.

Work in this area is just now beginning to proliferate, and it seems that this kind of work could be most critical to fostering the maturation of software engi-neering. If software engineering is to mature into an orderly discipline it seems that it must develop a core set of well understood, well-supported standard processes, and a cadre of practitioners who understand what the processes are and how to use them. Certainly the older, better established engineering disciplines, such as Chemical Engineering and Industrial Engineering, exemplify this sort of use of process. In order for such a core set of standard processes to emerge there must be a considerable amount of differentiation and sorting out of the processes that are currently in existence, and an orderly way of dealing with the steady flow of new process proposals, especially in such active areas as software design.

The work just described seems particularly promising because it suggests that structures and processes can be put in place that will serve to support standardized comparisons and evaluations of the processes that must form the core of discip-lined software engineering practice. It is unfortunate that debates about the relative merits of different approaches to such key activities as software design are cur-rently argued in the advertising pages of *IEEE Software*, rather than in the scholar-ly works of *IEEE Transactions on Software Engineering* or *ACM Transactions on Software Engineering Methods*. If our discipline is to mature satisfactorily that must change. The frameworks and processes suggested in the papers referred to above are suggested initial starting points, and it can only be hoped that the community will take them as such and work collaboratively to develop them into agreed upon standards. With such standards in place it should then be possible for objective evaluators to produce specifications and descriptions that characterize clearly and understandably the merits of competing methods. Such evaluations should also be usable in estimating costs and results of applying these methods.

This suggests a line of experimental research that focuses on performing software engineering process classifications and comparisons, but with an eye towards evaluating the standard classification frameworks, the standard process modelling formalisms, and the standard comparison process. Evolution of all of the above is to be an expected outcome of this experimentation. A steadily growing and improving stream of classifications, characterizations, and comparisons should also result. This line of research seems to be converging interestingly with research being done by the Method Engineering community (see, eg. [4]).

Beyond Software Engineering

In examining the hypothesis that software processes are software, there seems to be nothing particularly special about *software* processes. This suggests a hypothesis that processes in general are also software. Confirmation of that hypothesis would be of particular interest as it would suggest that application software technology can also help support the development and evolution of all kinds of processes. In particular it suggests that software engineers might have something of particular value to offer those who engineer manufacturing systems, management systems, classical engineering systems, and so forth. A variety of private conversations and preliminary investigations seem to confirm that these systems often have (or should have) architectures, that they are intended to satisfy understood requirements, and that their implementations are generally on virtual machines consisting of people, devices, and computers. In addition, these systems are usually continuously being evaluated and evolved. All of this suggests that they are software in the same sense in which we believe that software processes are software. That being the case, it suggests that software process researchers ought to widen their sights and study the applicability of the emerging software process technology to manufacturing, management, and allied disciplines.

Conclusions

The foregoing sections of this paper have been intended to suggest that there are numerous technological benefits from considering software processes to be software, and that examining them should lead to a considerable amount of worthwhile research. But there is yet another aspect of this work that seems worth remarking upon, and that is its contribution to the scientific underpinnings of software engineering. It was clear from the moment I concluded the original talk at ICSE 9 that the suggestion that software processes might be software had initiated a type of discussion that was different from other discussions following other papers that I had given. The substance of the discussions and debates that have followed has rarely been at the level of technical details, but rather at more philosophical levels. There were debates about whether it was seemly or possible to use the rigorous semantics of programming languages to describe what people did or should do. There were debates about whether processes were a subtype of application software, or vice versa. There were debates about whether processes have a different character than applications.

The distinguishing characteristic of most of these debates has been the fact that there did not, and still does not, seem to be much possibility that these debates and questions can be resolved definitively. One reason is that there is no agreed upon definition of what software is. Likewise there is no firm agreement on what programming is, or what a process is for that matter. Thus, the debates and discussions that have swirled around the original suggestion have been largely philosophical, and the opinions expressed have been based largely upon personal aesthetics. The suggestion that software and processes are made out of basically the same stuff sets well with some people, not so well with others. The suggestion implies that what we know and can learn about one transfers to some extent over to the other. This suggestion has obvious importance for the technologies in these two areas, but this has been met with skepticism and reticence in some quarters.

Skepticism, reserve, and the impossibility of definitive adjudication of these questions, however, should not be allowed to obscure what seems to be the most significant implication of the suggestion, namely its potential to shed some light on the nature of software itself. If it is shown that software is highly akin to something else about which we can have a variety of new and different insights, then those insights illuminate the nature of software. Thus, in the debates about the relationship between process and software I see the reflections of a broader debate about the nature of software. In that software engineering purports to be a discipline devoted to the effective development of software, it seems essential that we as a community have a shared view of what software is. Debates such as these, that help lead to that shared view, are critically important.

In his renowned book, *The Structure of Scientific Revolutions* [12], the historian of science, Thomas S. Kuhn, suggests that progress in a scientific discipline is discontinuous, progressing incrementally within the bounds circumscribed by the current paradigms, but then lurching forward occasionally when a new paradigm is agreed to account better than the old paradigm for natural phenomena or to provide more assistance in solving practical engineering problems. Kuhn argues that the old and new paradigms are generally mutually incompatible and that, therefore, it is impossible to use either to prove the falsity of the other. Thus shifts from an older paradigm to a newer paradigm generally take place over a period of time during which there is considerable intellectual ferment and philosophical dispute. If the new paradigm is to supplant the older paradigm it will happen only after careful research has demonstrated that the new paradigm is more robust and successful than the old paradigm. After the shift has occurred, the shape of the science, its view of its problems, and the manner of its approaches and explanations will have been substantively changed. Most practitioners will accept the paradigm shift, but adherents to the old paradigm may persist.

It seems just possible that what we have been witnessing is a slow paradigm shift to a view of software and software development that is rooted in the centrality of the notion of process as a first-class entity whose properties are very much like those of software itself. The nature of the debates that we have been witnessing are consistent with what would be expected if this were the case, being essentially discussions that are based more on aesthetics than upon the ability to perform definitive demonstrations. As the accretion of evidence of the power of a process-centered view of software grows it seems conceivable that we are seeing the establishment of a new paradigm. The preceding discussions in this paper do seem to suggest that grasping the importance of process, and exploiting its relation to software, does help deal more effectively with important technological and conceptual issues. Pursuing the research agenda outlined in the previous section should go a long way towards confirming this suggestion or to demonstrating its inadequacy. In either case it seems most encouraging to observe that the intense debates and discussions of the premise that "software processes are software too," seems to be quite consistent with the behavior of a responsible community of scientists doing real science. Ultimately this affirmation of our growing maturity as a scientific community may be the most important outcome of the proposal and ensuing discussions.

Acknowledgments My ideas and work on software processes has been greatly helped and influenced by many people, indeed too many to mention here. The earliest impetus for the ideas of process programming arose out of meetings and conversations with Watts Humphrey and his team at IBM in the early 1980's. The specific proposal of the notion of process programming was honed and sharpened through many conversations with Manny Lehman at Imperial College and John Buxton at Kings College, London in 1985 and 1986. Confidence in the idea was built through intense conversations with many people, but most notably with Dennis Heimbigner. Over the past ten years I have been fortunate to have been able to collaborate with Stan Sutton and Dennis Heimbigner on process programming language design and implementation and Xiping Song on software method comparison formalization. Numerous conversations with Dick Taylor, Bob Balzer, Gail Kaiser, Alex Wolf, Dewayne Perry, Mark Dowson, Barry Boehm, Wilhelm Schafer, Carlo Ghezzi, and Alfonso Fuggetta have also shaped this work in important ways. I would also like to thank the (Defense) Advanced Research Projects Agency for its support of this work, and particularly Bill Scherlis, Steve Squires, and John Salasin for their support, even while these ideas were formative and while they continue to be controversial.

References

[1] S. Bandinelli, A. Fuggetta, and S. Grigolli. Process modeling in-the-large with SLANG. In *Proc. of the Second International Conference on the Software Process*, pages 75 - 83, 1993.

[2] N. Belkhatir, J. Estublier, and Walcelio L. Melo. Adele 2: A support to large software development process. In *Proc. First Intl. Conf. on the Software Process*, pages 159 - 170, 1991.

[3] G. A. Bolcer and R. N. Taylor. Endeavors: A process system integration infrastructure. In *Proc. Fourth International Conference on the Software Process*, pages 76 - 85, Dec. 1996.

[4] S. Brinkkemper, K. Lyytinen, and R. J. Weike. *Method Engineering*. Chapman & Hall, 1996.

[5] V. Gruhn and R. Jegeika. An evaluation of FUNSOFT nets. In *Proc. of the Second European Workshop on Software Process Technology*, Sept. 1992.

[6] D. Harel, H. Lachover, A. Naamad, A. Pnueli, M. Politi, R. Sherman, A. Shtull-Trauring, and M. Trakhtenbrot. STATEMATE: A working environment for the development of complex reactive systems. *IEEE Trans. on Software Engineering*, 16(4):403 - 414, Apr. 1990.

[7] W. S. Humphrey. *Managing the Software Process*. Reading, MA. Addison-Wesley, 1989.

[8] G. E. Kaiser, N. S. Barghouti, and M. H. Sokolsky. Experience with process modeling in the MARVEL software development environment kernel. In B. Shriver, editor, *23rd Annual Hawaii Intl. Conf. on System Sciences*, volume II, pages 131- 140, Kona HI, Jan. 1990.

[9] G. E. Kaiser, I. Z. Ben-Sham, S. S. Popovich, and S. E. Dossick. A metalinguistic approach to process enactment extensibility. In *4th Intl. Conf. on the Software Process*, Dec. 1996.

[10] T. Katayama. A hierarchical and functional software process description and its enaction. In *Proc. of the 11th International Conference on Software Engineering*, pages 343 - 353, 1989.

[11] M. I. Kellner. Software process modeling support for management planning and control. In *Proc. of the First International Conference on the Software Process*, pages 8 - 28, 1991.

[12] T. S. Kuhn. *The Structure of Scientific Revolutions*. University of Chicago Press, 1962.

[13] M. M. Lehman. The Programming Process. In *IBM Res. Rep. RC 2722*, IBM Res. Center, Yorktown Heights, NY 10594, Sept. 1969.

[14] Leon J. Osterweil. Improving the quality of software quality determination processes. In *The Quality of Numerical Software: Assessment and Enhancement*. Chapman & Hall, 1997.

[15] L. J. Osterweil. Software Processes are Software Too. In *Proceedings of the Ninth International Conference on Software Engineering*, pages 2-13, Monterey CA, March 1987. (Reprinted as Chapter 17)

[16] M. C. Paulk, B. Curtis, M. B. Chrisis. Capability maturity model for software, version 1.1. Technical Report CMU/SEI-93-TR, Carnegie Mellon University, Feb. 1993.

[17] R.M. Podorozhny, L.J. Osterweil. The Criticality of Modeling Formalisms in Software Design Method Comparison. Technical Report TR-96-049, University of Massachusetts, Computer Science Department, Amherst, MA, Aug. 1996.

[18] Potts C. (ed). Proc. of the softw. process worksh. In *IEEE cat. n. 84CH2044-6, Comp. Soc.*, Washington D. C., Feb. 1984. order n. 587, 27 - 35.

[19] Richard J. Mayer et al. IDEF family of methods for concurrent engineering and business re-engineering applications. Technical report, Knowledge Based Systems, Inc., 1992.

[20] X. Song and L. Osterweil. Toward Objective, Systematic Design-Method Comparisons. *IEEE Software*, pages 43 - 53, May 1992.

[21] X. Song and L. J. Osterweil. Experience with an approach to comparing software design methodologies. *IEEE Trans. on Software Engineering*, 20(5):364 - 384, May 1994.

[22] S. M. Sutton, Jr., D. Heimbigner, and L. J. Osterweil. APPL/A: A language for software-process programming. *ACM Trans. on Soft. Eng. and Methodology*, 4(3):221 - 286, July 1995.

[23] S. M. Sutton, Jr. and L. J. Osterweil. The design of a next-generation process language. Technical Report CMPSCI Technical Report 96-30, University of Massachusetts at Amherst, Computer Science Department, Amherst, Massachusetts 01003, May 1996.

Language Constructs for Managing Change in Process-Centered Environments

Stanley M. Sutton, Jr., Dennis Heimbigner, and Leon J. Osterweil

Stanley M. Sutton, Jr. and Dennis Heimbigner are at Department of Computer Science, University of Colorado, Boulder, CO 80309-0430

Leon J. Osterweil is at Department of Information and Computer Science, University of California, Irvine, CA 92717

Abstract   Change is pervasive during software development, affecting objects, processes, and environments. In process centered environments, change management can be facilitated by software-process programming, which formalizes the representation of software products and processes using software-process programming languages (SPPLs). To fully realize this goal SPPLs should include constructs that specifically address the problems of change management. These problems include lack of representation of inter-object relationships, weak semantics for inter-object relationships, visibility of implementations, lack of formal representation of software processes, and reliance on programmers to manage change manually.

APPL/A is a prototype SPPL that addresses these problems. APPL/A is an extension to Ada. The principal extensions include abstract, persistent relations with programmable implementations, relation attributes that may be composite and derived, triggers that react to relation operations, optionally-enforcible predicates on relations, and five composite statements with transaction-like capabilities.

APPL/A relations and triggers are especially important for the problems raised here. Relations enable inter-object relationships to be represented explicitly and derivation dependencies to be maintained automatically. Relation bodies can be programmed to implement alternative storage and computation strategies without affecting users of relation specifications. Triggers can react to changes in relations, automatically propagating data, invoking tools, and performing other change management tasks. Predicates and the transaction-like statements support change management in the face of evolving standards of consistency. Together, these features mitigate many of the problems that complicate change management in software processes and process-centered environments.

Stanley M. Sutton Jr., Dennis Heimbigner, and Leon J. Osterweil, "Language Constructs for Managing Change in Process-Centered Environments," In Proceedings of the 4th ACM SIGSOFT Symposium on Software Development Environments, 1990.
DOI: 10.1145/99277.99296, © 1990 ACM, Inc. Reprinted with permission

P.L. Tarr, A.L. Wolf (eds.), *Engineering of Software*,
DOI 10.1007/978-3-642-19823-6_19, © Springer-Verlag Berlin Heidelberg 2011

1. Introduction

Change is pervasive in software development processes. During development all components of a software product undergo changes: requirements, design, code, test cases, etc. The development process can change, for example, by the addition of new testing and analysis phases or the incorporation of prototype development. The supporting environment can also change, for example, new tools may be added, and major components such as the underlying storage system may be replaced. Often change management is relegated to the maintenance phase of software development, but in practice "maintenance" (as a synonym for managing change) occurs throughout the software life cycle [12].

One major difficulty in managing change is in detecting and propagating the effects of a change to other components of the environment. A change to one object often requires changes to other objects that are derived from it or that must be kept consistent with it, and changes to those objects must be propagated in turn. A change in the development process must be implemented consistently and correctly in the face of existing practices, tools, and products. A change to the environment can force adaptations in processes and object management, with the potential for errors and inconsistencies in those areas.

In a process-centered software environment, some representation of the software process can serve as a focal point and integration mechanism for development activities and the supporting technologies. One important class of process-centered environments are software-process programming environments. In software-process programming, the software process is represented by programs written in a formal process programming language [20]. Examples of environments which are intended to support process programming or which are driven by process programs include Arcadia [33], E-L [10, 7], ASPECT [16], and the software factory system described in [17].

Software-process programming has the potential to make the change-management problem tractable by formalizing the structure of software products and the processes by which they are constructed. By making this structure explicit, a process program can enable the tracking of changes. Moreover, it offers the possibility that the process of change propagation can be automated. With respect to change management, process programming is somewhat similar to software configuration management [11, 8, 14]. However, process programming languages can, in principle, represent a wider range of objects and processes than can conventional configuration-management systems.

The realization of the potential of software-process programming depends on the availability of software process programming languages (SPPLs) with appropriate constructs and capabilities. Requirements for SPPLs are difficult to determine *a priori*. It seems reasonable to assume that SPPLs must subsume the capabilities of conventional programming languages. However, we also expect that SPPLs will include extensions and specializations that reflect the distinctive aspects of software processes and products, including constructs relevant to change management.

APPL/A [32] is a prototype process programming language based on Ada [34]. It is designed to support change management as an intrinsic part of software processes. This paper describes some of the kinds of change that can be expected during software development and shows how APPL/A can be used to manage those kinds of change. APPL/A research is one part of the process programming research that is taking place in the Arcadia project [33].

This paper is organized as follows. Section 2 presents a scenario that illustrates several common kinds of change in a software environment. On the basis of this scenario we draw some conclusions about what makes change management difficult and recommend language capabilities to make it easier. Section 3 provides an overview of the APPL/A programming language. Some examples that illustrate APPL/A and address issues raised in the scenario are provided in Section 4. Section 5 discusses APPL/A in light of the requirements in Section 2. The paper concludes with a summary of the status of work.

2. A Scenario of Change

Many changes in software environments can be considered to fall into three categories:

- Changes to objects in the environment
- Changes in the process for using the environment
- Changes to the environment itself, including tools, support systems, and hardware

The following scenarios illustrate changes of these kinds and problems that may result. The examples have been kept simple, but the problems they illustrate are nevertheless fundamental and widespread in software development.

The hypothetical system in which the scenarios are set is a simple development environment consisting of several tools in a UNIX-like operating system. The tools initially include a compiler, a loader, and a dataflow analyzer capable of detecting anomalies such as uninitialized variables, unused variables, etc. [19, 18].

The development process is informal. Programmers write source code, compile this to object code, link object code to executable code, then test the resulting executable code for bugs. If bugs are found the source code is revised and the process repeated. The dataflow analyzer may be used occasionally during the writing of source code (in an attempt to avoid errors) or when debugging (in an attempt to identify the source of errors).

This scenario is, of course, simplistic. Many projects would use tools such as Make [11] or SCCS [24] to help manage changes to code. However, such tools help to manage certain kinds of change but not others; for example, they rely on a fixed storage system, they focus on derivation relationships, they use a fixed evaluation and caching strategy, and they provide limited inferencing capabilities.

2.1 A Scenario of Change to Objects

The normal course of development in this environment involves repeated additions, updates, and deletions of source modules. Suppose a programmer adds a new source module. He or she must then determine how to proceed. There are few constraints on the process. The programmer may first invoke either the dataflow analyzer or compiler; the use of either may or may not be conditioned on the results of the other. The dataflow analyzer may be ignored altogether, perhaps because the programmer does not care to use it or is simply unaware of it. Once a plan for tool invocation is determined it must be carried out manually. For example, the programmer may apply the dataflow analyzer to the source code, evaluate the results of the analysis, and then apply the compiler if the analysis is acceptable. Note that both the compiler and the dataflow analyzer create new objects with types distinct from the type of the source code and that the application of these tools creates an implicit consistency relationship between the source code and the new objects.

The programmer must also iterate this process for new objects derived from the source code. In this scenario it is necessary to check whether the compilation was successful and, if so, link the resulting object module into the executable modules to which it belongs. The effects of these changes also need to be propagated further, for example, to the rederivation of test results. In a more realistic scenario there may be still more tools that apply to any new derived object.

A similar situation occurs if an existing source module is updated. The applicable tools must be identified and invoked, and the resulting changes to derived objects must be propagated. In this case, however, the programmer is also responsible for identifying and removing previous versions of various kinds of objects (either deleting or archiving them) and for maintaining the consistency of system configurations that combine versions of various modules.

2.2 A Scenario of Change in Process

The process used to develop software is subject to change for many reasons. For example, suppose that the project manager institutes a policy requiring that all source modules must meet certain criteria with respect to data flow before they can be compiled. This implies that the dataflow analyzer and compiler should be applied to the source modules in sequence and that the application of the compiler is conditional on the results of the analysis. In order to implement this policy, programmers must be aware of the sequence and must understand the conditions under which compilation is allowed. They must also manually carry out the prescribed process.

The availability of tools to implement a given development process does not guarantee that it will be carried out consistently or correctly, however. The potential for problems is compounded when the process is changed. In this scenario the change of process is small and the resulting process is simple. However, there may still be errors since the control and execution of the process is manual. Moreover, this potential increases as the complexity of the process and the magnitude of change increase. Similar problems can result whatever the cause of a change in process.

2.3 Scenarios of Change to the Environment

Environments can change in many ways, each with consequent problems in change management. Two examples are presented below.

2.3.1 Adding a Tool

One common change to software environments is the addition of a new tool. For example, suppose the environment above is extended to include a "word-count" tool similar to the UNIX "WC" tool (which counts the number of lines, words, and characters in given files). In this scenario the addition of the tool is simple because there are no restrictions on how and when it can or should be used.

At first this new tool may not be widely or effectively used. Programmers may not be aware of it, they may not understand its function and relationship to existing tools and objects (admittedly simple in this case), or they may not see any need for it. Eventually some programmers may begin to use it occasionally, possibly to measure their productivity or to obtain information on the size of modules as an aid in managing program complexity. Even so the tool may still not be used consistently or comprehensively. Finally, the project manager may promulgate a new policy that requires the size of all source code modules to be within certain limits. The word-count result for each source module is to be saved along with the source modules for subsequent review by management. This makes the role of the tool more specific, but it requires programmers to change their work habits (with potential problems as indicated above). It also requires management of a new type of object, the word-count results, which must be stored and kept consistent with the source modules.

2.3.2 Changing the Underlying Storage System

It is assumed for the above scenarios that the host file system is used to store all persistent data. However, a large development project is likely to include multiple storage systems, and these may change over time. For example, suppose that a commercial database is added to the environment described above. It is to be used to store project-management data and also the word-count data. Programmers now must work with two storage systems: the file system in which they store their code, and the database in which they store the word-count data. Moreover, they are personally responsible for managing the word-count data. They must extract the data from the files output by the tool and insert them into the database, and they must maintain consistency between the output files and the database (in addition to maintaining consistency between the source modules and the word-count data). Further complications may arise if some of the data for project management must be imported from a separate and distinct company-wide database, or if some of the code must be imported from other projects or libraries that use other file systems.

2.4 Causes and Consequences of Change-Management Problems

The scenarios presented here are not exhaustive. Many other kinds of changes can occur: changes to hardware, resources, and personnel, among others. But the features of these scenarios are representative of the kinds of problems that can result from change.

These problems are attributable to several fundamental and interdependent causes:

- **Manual implementation of change management**. Depending on programmers for change management entails the potential for human error. This may result in incomplete, incorrect, inconsistent, and inefficient response to changes.
- **Lack of explicit representation of dependency relationships between objects**. When one object is changed, it is difficult to identify which other objects are affected. Consequently, the direction and extent of change propagation are difficult to determine, and changes may not be propagated completely. (Interobject relationships include, but are not limited to, those established by automated derivations.)
- **Lack of semantic information associated with objects and relationships**. Without some form of constraints and specification of derivation processes, it may be difficult to understand the consequences of any given change and therefore difficult to propagate its effects correctly and efficiently.
- **Lack of abstraction of the development process from implementation factors**. Although the development process in the abstract should be independent of implementation factors, changes in supporting systems can nevertheless force changes in the development process. These in turn may lead to problems in the process and resulting product.

- **Lack of explicit representation of the development process.** Developers may lack a clear, correct, and consistent understanding of the process. Consequently the process of managing change to objects and to the process itself may be prone to errors, inefficiencies, and inconsistencies.

2.5 Recommendations for SPPLs

It is our contention that an appropriately designed software-process programming language can alleviate many problems in change management. Certainly, the programming of processes in an SPPL directly addresses the issue of explicit representation of the development process. Additionally, the use of appropriate language constructs in formalizing the processes and products can help with the other problems associated with change. We believe that SPPLs should support the following:

- Explicit representation of both objects and inter-object relationships.
- Explicit representation of the semantics of objects and relationships, including constraints and derivations.
- Automation of as much of the change process as is feasible, including propagation of data, maintenance of consistency, and invocation of tools.
- Abstraction of processes, objects, and relationships from the underlying implementation system. At the logical level change management should be independent of the implementation, and changes to the implementation should not affect the abstract representation of development processes and products.

We believe that these items comprise a set of basic SPPL requirements in the area of change management. In the next sections we present an overview of APPL/A and show how its features can address these requirements.

3. APPL/A

APPL/A is a prototype process-programming language [29]. It is defined as an extension to Ada [34]. Ada provides the general-purpose capabilities that we believe any SPPL must include. APPL/A includes additional features to address the special characteristics of software process, including change management, and also data modeling, derived data, persistent data, consistency management, and accommodation of inconsistency.

The principal extensions that APPL/A makes to Ada include programmable persistent relations, triggers on relation operations, optionally-enforcible predicates on relations, and several composite statements that provide a variety of transaction-like capabilities.

- Relations can be used to store persistent and/or shared data, to encapsulate derivations and represent relationships among objects, to represent objects, to store constrained data, and to store data to be triggered on.
- Triggers can be used to propagate updates from one relation to other relations, to send messages in response to changes in data, to perform computations, to maintain logs, and to respond concurrently to operations on relations for any purpose.
- Predicates express conditions on the state of relations (and, hence, on whatever the relations represent). Predicates can be used like functions, and, when enforced, they can serve as constraints or assertions.
- The transaction-like statements can be used to assure serializable and (optionally) recoverable access to relations. They can also be used to control the local enforcement of predicates. They can be combined to create higher-level transaction constructs including conventional and nested transactions, repair operations, cooperative transactions, etc.

Relations and triggers most directly address the particular problems of change management raised in Section 2.4. The use of APPL/A constructs to support change management is discussed further below and illustrated in the example of Section 4.

3.1 Relations

Relations are a special kind of program unit in APPL/A that provides for the persistent storage of data. Abstractly, APPL/A relations represent the mathematical notion of a relation, i.e. a subset of the cross-product over a list of object domains. However APPL/A relations have several important differences from the relations of conventional databases. APPL/A relations can have composite and abstract attribute types, they support derived attributes, and they have programmable implementations. These adaptations of the relational model make it more appropriate for software-object management and for change management in particular. Some other recent projects in which relations are used include the advanced data-management system Postgres [25,28] and AP5, which extends Common Lisp with relations [9].

Each APPL/A relation has a specification and a body. A typical specification, for relation Word_Count, is shown in Fig 19.1. This relation represents the derivation relationship between text objects and the number of lines, words, and characters in those objects computed by a word-count tool wc. The features of APPL/A relations are explained below in terms of this example.

```
with WC; -- separate "word-count" tool
with text_def; use text_def;
Relation Word_Count is
    type wc_tuple is tuple
        text: in text_type;
        lines, words, characters: out natural;
    end tuple;
    entries
        entry insert(text: in text_name);
        entry delete(text: text_type;
            lines: natural;
            words: natural;
            characters: natural);
        entry find(iterator: in out integer := 0;
            found: out boolean;
            first: boolean;
            t: out wc_tuple;
            select_text: boolean;
            text: text_type;
            select_lines: boolean;
            lines: natural;
            select_words: boolean;
            words: natural;
            select_characters: boolean;
            characters: natural);
        dependencies
            determine lines, words, characters
                by wc(text, lines, words, characters);
    End Word_Count;
```

Fig 19.1. Specification for the Relation Word_Count

Each relation has a defining tuple type that determines the names and types of attributes for the relation. A tuple type is similar to a record type, but the attributes have modes like Ada parameters. The attribute modes indicate the way in which attributes may take on values. Attributes of mode **in** must be given values directly. Attributes of mode **out** must take on computed values. Attributes of mode **in out** may take on given and computed values in turn. Thus, attributes of modes **in out** and **out** represent derived data.

The operations on a relation are represented by entries analogous to task entries. The entries for a relation must be some non-empty subset of insert, update, delete, and find. The insert entry takes parameters for attributes of mode **in** and **in out** and implements the insertion of a tuple with those parameters into the relation. The update entry enables a tuple with given attribute values to be assigned new values for attributes of mode **in** and **in out**. The delete entry deletes a tuple with given attribute values. The find entry iteratively returns tuples selected by given attribute values.

The specification of any relation with derived attributes may also contain a *dependency specification*, which indicates how the derived attributes are to be computed. In Word_Count the dependency specification states that for each tuple the attributes lines, words, and characters are to be computed by a call to the procedure WC given the corresponding value of attribute text as input. In this way Word_Count represents the derivation relationship established by the WC tool between text objects and the counts of lines, words, and characters computed by this tool. It is the responsibility of the body of the relation to automatically carry out the computations necessary to assign values to derived attributes. If a relation has a dependency specification then the computation of attributes must be carried out according to that specification. In any case the computed values must be kept up-to-date with respect to the given values from which they are derived.

It is the responsibility of the body of a relation to implement the semantics of that relation. This means that the relation body must

- provide persistent storage
- implement the relation entries
- compute and assign values for derived attributes

However, the details of the implementation of a relation can be left up to the programmer of the relation (although a default implementation mechanism will be available). In this respect APPL/A relations are *programmable*. Apart from the requirements listed above, the implementation of a relation is *not* constrained with respect to

- the persistent storage system
- the derivation strategy for computed attributes (e.g. eager or lazy)
- the caching strategy for computed attributes (e.g. cached when computed or re-computed when needed)

The implementor of a relation can program the body in any appropriate way that satisfies the required semantics, and the implementation can change over time without affecting users of the relation. In this way APPL/A allows tremendous flexibility in the makeup and use of the underlying environment.

In providing a persistent data type, APPL/A can be regarded as a "persistent" programming language. Other such languages include PS-Algol [2], Adaplex [27] (which extends Ada with a functional data model), E [23] (the database implementation language of the EXODUS [5] extensible DBMS and an extension of C++), and Owl [26] (the object-oriented language of the Trellis environment). However, these languages as a group are diverse, and APPL/A differs from each of them in many particulars.

3.2 Triggers

Triggers are like tasks in that they represent concurrent threads of control. However, triggers differ from tasks in that triggers lack entries. Instead, triggers *react* indirectly and automatically to operations on relations.

A trigger has a simple specification, comparable to an Ada task's but without the entries. A trigger body comprises a loop over a *selective trigger* statement. A selective trigger statement is like an Ada selective wait statement, except that it has *upon* alternatives instead of accept alternatives. Each upon alternative consists of an *upon* statement followed by a (possibly empty) sequence of statements. The upon statements identify the relation operations to which a response is to be made. The statements within and immediately following the upon statement encode the trigger's response to the relation operation.

```
with Source_to_Object, Word_Count;
with Code_Types; use Code_Types;
trigger body Maintain_Source_WC is
begin
    loop
        select
            upon Source_to_Object.insert
                (scr: source_code)
            completion do
                Word_Count.insert(src);
            end upon;
        or
            upon Source_to_Object.delete
                (src: source_code; obj: object_code)
            completion do
                for t2 in Word_Count where
                    t2.text = t.src
                loop
                    Word_Count.delete(t2);
                end loop;
            end upon;
        end select;
    end loop;
end Maintain_Source_WC;
```

Fig 19.2. Trigger Maintain_Source_WC.

The body of trigger Maintain_Source_WC is shown in Fig 19.2. The goal of the trigger is to automatically collect and maintain up-to-date word-count data for source-code modules. This trigger responds to operations on relation

`Source_to_Object` (Fig 19.4). The trigger propagates changes in `Source_to_Object` to the relation `Word_Count`. When a new source-code object is inserted into `Source_to_Object`, the trigger automatically inserts that object into `Word_Count`; the trigger makes an analogous response to delete operations on `Source_to_Object`. (For simplicity, this example assumes that source modules are stored in `Source_to_Object`, so the trigger responds to operations on that relation. In a more realistic system source modules would probably be stored in a separate `Source_Code` relation, along with additional information such as author, permissions, timestamps, etc. In that case a trigger could be defined to respond to operations on the `Source_Code` relation.)

Trigger `Maintain_Source_WC` includes two upon statements, one each for the insert and delete entries of `Source_to_Object`. Each of these upon statements is for a *completion* event, i.e. a response is to be triggered only upon the successful completion of the corresponding entry call. (Upon statements can also designate *acceptance* events, in which case a response would be triggered by the acceptance of the relation entry call.) Each upon statement also includes a list of formal parameters. For an acceptance event these comprise the **in** parameters for the relation entry call; for a completion event these comprise both the **in** and **out** parameters for the call. Through these parameters the actual values given to and returned from the relation entry call are made available to the trigger. Although it is not shown in the example, upon declarations may also be given priority values. When an event occurs (i.e. a relation entry call is accepted or completed), a signal is sent to each trigger that designates that event in an upon statement. This signal includes the identity of the event and the corresponding actual parameters. Event signals are queued at the trigger in order of priority and responded to in turn.

It should be noted that a trigger can make both "synchronous" and "asynchronous" responses to events. The body of an upon statement (within the **do ... end** block) is executed synchronously with the event signal in the same sense that an accept statement is executed synchronously with an entry call. While the upon statement is executing the execution of the corresponding relation is suspended at the point at which the signal is generated (either acceptance or completion of the rendezvous for the relation entry). However, the trigger does not execute a full rendezvous with the relation, and no parameters or exceptions are returned from the trigger to the relation. Once the upon statement completes the synchronization with the relation is released and the trigger and relation proceed in parallel. A sequence of statements immediately following an upon statement thus executes asynchronously with the relation and can be used to provide an asynchronous response to relation operations.

It should also be noted that triggers can be used to propagate changes in both an eager and a lazy way. For example, whenever an insertion or deletion is performed on relation `Source_to_Object`, the trigger `Maintain_Source_WC` directly propagates the effects of that operation to relation `Word_Count`. This illustrates the eager propagation of changes between relations. An alternative approach could be obtained through a trigger `Get_Source_for_WC` (not shown), which would respond synchronously upon acceptance of calls to `Word_Count.find`. In response to such calls, the trigger would search `Source_to_Object` for (selected) source code modules for which word-count results were desired. These modules would be propagated to `Word_Count` and made available for return by the `find` entry. Propagation would occur only when the modules were requested, thus implementing a lazy evaluation strategy.

3.3 Predicates and Transaction-Like Statements

APPL/A provides two other principal extensions to Ada which are supportive of change management. These are optionally-enforcible predicates and five transaction-like composite statements. These constructs are addressed primarily to issues of consistency maintenance and accommodation of inconsistency. A more complete explanation is given in [30, 31, 29].

3.4 Predicates

Predicates are named boolean expressions over relations. The expression language includes existentially and universally quantified forms and conditional expressions. An example predicate is shown in Fig 19.3. This predicate refers to two relations introduced in Section 4 (Fig 19.5). The predicate states that for every tuple `t1` in relation `Executable_Systems` there is some tuple `t2` in relation `Link_Map` such that the name attribute of `t1` equals the `exe_name` attribute of `t2`. In the context of the example in Section 4 this means that every executable module is constructed from a known set of object modules.

```
predicate enforced
    Executable_Systems_Dangling
is return
    every t1 in Executable_Systems satisfies
        some t2 in Link_Map satisfies
            t1.name = t2.exe_name
        end some
    end every;
end Executable_Systems_Dangling;
```

Fig 19.3. Predicate **Executable_Systems_Dangling**.

Predicates are optionally enforcible. If a predicate is enforced in a program then no operation by that program on a relation designated by the predicate may leave the predicate violated. Each predicate has an associated boolean "attribute" (in the

Ada sense) `enforced`. If this attribute is true, then predicate is enforced by default; otherwise, it is not. This attribute is assignable; thus the enforcement of a predicate can, in effect, be turned on and off.[1] An exception is a predicate declared with the keyword enforced (as in Fig 19.3); in this case the predicate is always enforced by default.

3.5 Transaction-Like Statements

The ability to enforce predicates only at some times means that a process may find that the relations on which it operates are either over- or under-constrained. Some mechanism is needed to allow a process to cope with these situations. The transaction-like statements of APPL/A provide such a mechanism, as well as supporting control over serializability and atomicity. The statements include the serial, atomic, suspend, enforce and allow statements. The serial, atomic, suspend, and allow statements provide serializable access to relations. The suspend, allow, and enforce statements also affect the enforcement of predicates (the suspend and allow statements locally suspending enforcement, the enforce statement locally imposing enforcement). The atomic and suspend statements also support atomicity, i.e. rollback (for exception propagation in the atomic, and for predicate violation in the suspend).

These statements allow processes to operate on data that are more or less constrained than desired. By providing serializable access they assure that interference by other processes can be precluded. By enabling predicates to be locally enforced or suspended they allow a process to establish just the needed enforcement regime. By supporting rollback they enable erroneously incomplete or inconsistent work to be voided. These statements are more specialized in their effect than conventional database transactions, but in various combinations they can represent conventional transactions, nested transactions, "assertion" constructs, and more.

4. An Example APPL/A System

This section presents an example system of APPL/A relations and triggers. Together with the relation `Word_Count` (Fig 19.1) and trigger `Maintain_Source_and_Word_Count` (Fig 19.2), the relations and triggers pre-

---

[1] It is possible to make data inconsistent by turning on a predicate that was not previously enforced. However, statements such as the suspend and enforce (Section 3.5) can then be used to operate on the data even though they are inconsistent and to make them consistent if desired. In this way inconsistency is accommodated as a natural rather than exceptional condition.

sented here represent and implement many of the relationships and process steps described in the scenario of Section 2. This example has somewhat the flavor of configuration management. Configuration management is one area in which many automated systems for change management have been developed; thus it provides a natural starting point for process programming. However, as noted elsewhere, process programming should be applicable (and has been applied) to other development activities.

Relation Source_to_Object (Fig 19.4) represents the derivation relationship between source modules and the object modules compiled from them. In this relation the object modules are automatically derived and the relationship between source and object modules is automatically kept consistent and up-to-date. As described in Section 3, relation Word_Count relates text objects to the counts of lines, words, and characters they contain. The text objects include source code from Source_to_Object. Like the computed values in Source_to_Object the computed values in Word_Count are automatically derived and kept up-to-date. These relations facilitate the management of changes to objects in that they explicitly represent the derivation relationships between objects and automate the computation and maintenance of the derived objects.

```
with compile; -- separate compiler
with code_defs; use code_defs;
Relation Source_to_Object is
    type src_to_obj_tuple is tuple
        src: in source_code;
        obj: out object_code;
    end tuple;
    entries
        entry insert (src: source_code);
        entry delete (src: source_code;
            obj: object_code);
        entry find (iterator: in out integer;
            first: boolean;
            found: out boolean;
            t: out src_to_obj_tuple;
            select_src: boolean; src: source_code;
            select_obj: boolean; obj: object_code);
    dependencies
        determine obj by compile(src, obj);
end Source_to_Object;
```

Fig 19.4. Specification of Relation Source_to_Object.

The trigger Maintain_Source_and_WC automatically maintains inclusion dependencies between the two relations. For example, if a new source module is inserted into Source_to_Object, then the trigger automatically inserts that module into `Word_Count`. The word-count data are recomputed as necessary in `Word_Count` whenever a source file is inserted. Thus the word-count data are automatically obtained and kept up-to-date for all source modules. The trigger provides further automation of the propagation of changes to objects. In terms of the scenario, it also represents and implements the policy that word-count data must be obtained for all source modules.

Relation `Link_Map` relates the names of object modules to the names of executable modules of which they are part. Relation `Executable_Systems` stores executable modules by name. These relations are sketched in Fig 19.5. A trigger, `Maintain_Link_and_Executable` (Fig 19.6), automatically maintains dependencies between `Link_Map` and `Executable_Systems`. This trigger also automatically (re)computes executable modules whenever the link map is changed. A similar trigger (not shown) can be used to maintain consistency between relations `Source_to_Object` and `Link_Map`.

```
Relation Link_Map is
    type link_map_tuple is tuple
        obj_name: in name_type;
        exe_name: in name_type;
    end tuple;
    entries
        . . .
End Link_Map;


Relation Executable_Systems is
    type executable_systems_tuple is tuple
        name: in name_type;
        exe: in executable_code;
    end tuple;
    entries
        . . .
End Executable_Systems;
```

Fig 19.5. Sketch of Specifications for Relations Link_Map and Executable_Systems.

A variety of predicates could be defined to characterize and constrain the relations in this example. One predicate is shown in Fig 19.3. Another could require, for example, that all source modules named in `Link_Map` have line counts in `Word_Count` of less than 50; this would help to enforce managerial policies about the size of source modules.

Although it is not directly shown in these examples, the use of these relations also helps in managing changes to the environment. For example, when the word-count tool is added, it can be encapsulated in the relation `Word_Count` and linked into user programs. If the compiler is changed, the body for `Source_to_Object` can be rewritten without affecting users of the relation. If a new database is introduced, it can be used to store the word-count data without affecting users who access the data through Word_Count. Changes in derivation strategy and storage strategy are also hidden from users.

```
with Source_to_Object, Link_Map,
Executable_Systems;
with Link; -- separately defined linker
trigger Maintain_Link_and_Executable is
-- Maintain desired inclusion dependencies between
-- relations Link_Map and Executable_Systems
begin
  loop
    select
      upon Link_Map.insert(...) completion do
        -- Save obj_name and exe_name for use
        -- outside of the upon statement
      end upon
      -- Update Executable_Systems asynchron-
      -- ously: Compute (recompute) the named
      -- executable module and store in Execut-
      -- able_Systems.
      upon Link_Map.delete(...) completion do
        -- Save the deleted tuple for use
        -- outside of the upon statement
      end upon
      -- Update Executable_Systems asynchrony-
      -- ously: If the tuple deleted is the last
      -- in the named executable module then
      -- delete the corresponding tuple from
      -- Executable_Systems. If not, then
      -- relink the executable module and store
      -- it in Executable_Systems.
    or
      upon Executable_Systems.delete(...)
      completion do
        -- Save the deleted tuple for use
        -- outside of the upon statement
      end upon
      -- Delete corresponding tuples from
      -- Link_Map.
    end select;
  end loop;
End Maintain_Link_and_Executable;
```

Fig 19.6. Sketch of Trigger Maintain_Link_and_Executable.

5. Discussion

The constructs in APPL/A support change management in several ways. APPL/A relations combine several capabilities that are recommended for change management in Section 2.5:

- They provide a data structure for the explicit representation of relationships among objects. Relations can be used to determine the direction and extent of propagation of changes to objects.
- They encapsulate derivation processes. Derivation dependencies are represented explicitly and maintained automatically. Thus relations free developers from the need to track and maintain derivations manually.
- They are abstract types with programmable implementations. Consequently, they serve to isolate logical from implementation issues. The implementation can be varied without affecting users of the abstract interface, and processes can be programmed in terms of the interface without regard for implementation details.

Each of these capabilities is illustrated or discussed in the example (Section 4). Their integration in relations makes relations an especially powerful tool for change management.

Triggers support change management by further automating the response to change. Triggers react to operations that can change relations. They can be used to propagate data, invoke tools, log changes, and perform other tasks. Thus triggers can assume many of the roles of change management performed by programmers in the scenario of Section 2.

Predicates and transaction-like statements also facilitate change management, albeit in respects that are not emphasized in this paper. The turning on and off of predicate enforcement allows the consistency of relations to evolve over time. Enforcement of predicates restricts the kinds of changes and responses that can be made, while suspension of enforcement relaxes these restrictions. The transaction-like statements enable processes to operate on relations free of interference by other processes. They also enable processes to respond to changes in predicate enforcement and relation consistency by establishing their own predicate-enforcement regime locally.

These constructs as a group allow for the explicit representation of relationships, constraints, and processes that are essential to change management. They can be incorporated into programs that automate software processes. Concomitantly they reduce the reliance on programmers to understand and execute change management processes manually. In light of these observations we believe that the constructs introduced in APPL/A generally meet the recommendations presented in Section 2.5. Thus they should generally facilitate change management in process programs and process-centered environments.

6. Status and Future Work

APPL/A is defined as an extension to Ada [29]. The APPL/A definition includes a formal syntax and English semantics with examples in a style similar to that of the Ada manual [34].

An automatic APPL/A to Ada translator, called "APT", exists in prototype form. It is a modification of a partial Ada compiler which is a component of existing Arcadia [33] Ada language technology. For technical and historical reasons, the language translated by APT is a subset of the full APPL/A language. APT can automatically translate relation specifications, relation bodies, triggers (with global event signaling) and predicates. APT can recognize the transaction-like statements, but it cannot translate them because of lack of run-time support capabilities. Support for predicate enforcement and non-global event signaling is also lacking. However, we have developed designs for the implementation of all of these features, and the automatic translation of the complete language is conceptually feasible. A practical problem at this time is that most of the features which are not yet translated depend on the ability to trace the execution of a (concurrent) program through its call stack. This information is difficult to obtain from current Ada compilers (without being able to modifying them), and the development of an alternative approach, while possible, is costly.

We recognize that for many users it is a burden to construct the bodies of relations. In light of that, we are designing default implementations for APPL/A relations based on some existing database systems. These database systems provide persistence and some form of data model into which APPL/A relations are mapped. Our original process programs used Cactis [15]. Current work is making use of Triton [13], a persistent object system built on top of the EXODUS [6] storage manager. It is now possible to generate default bodies, which use Triton, for simple stored relations (i.e. relations lacking derived attributes).

A goal for the APPL/A project is to code process programs covering a complete software life cycle. At least partial code exists to support requirements (the REBUS program) and design (DEBUS). REBUS is an executable system which supports the specification of software requirements in a functional hierarchy. REBUS stores data about requirements in APPL/A relations which are constrained by APPL/A predicates and maintained by APPL/A triggers. REBUS is translated by APT and makes use of Triton. DEBUS, a design support system, is under construction in APPL/A. DEBUS is based on the Rational Design Methodology of Parnas [21] and the IEEE design standard [3]. An early version of APPL/A was also used to code DataFlow⋈Relay, which integrates dataflow and fault-based testing and analysis [22]. REBUS and DEBUS were also initially coded using early versions of APPL/A. In the case of REBUS, the APPL/A code was translated by hand into an executable Ada program. The early version of REBUS also included extensions based on RSL/REVS [1, 4] which will be incorporated into the current version. The experience gained with the earlier process programs contributed greatly to our understanding of SPPL requirements. That experience enabled us to refine APPL/A in significant ways, resulting in the definition described here.

Future work will continue the development and implementation of APPL/A and the coding of process programs to support the complete software life cycle. One area of concentration is representation and automation of change processes, including the propagation of changes. From this experience we hope to learn more about managing change and software development generally in process-centered environments.

Acknowledgments This research was supported by the Defense Advanced Research Projects Agency, through DARPA Order #6100, Program Code 7E20, which was funded through grant #CCR-8705162 from the National Science Foundation. Support was also provided by the Naval Ocean Systems Center and the Office of Naval Technology. The authors wish to thank Deborah Baker, Roger King, Shehab Gamalel-din, Mark Maybee, and Xiping Song for their advice. The comments of the members of the Arcadia consortium were also important in clarifying the issues surrounding APPL/A.

References

[1] Mack W. Alford. A requirements engineering methodology for real-time processing requirements. *IEEE Trans. on Software Engineering*, SE-3(1):60 - 69, January 1977.

[2] Malcolm P. Atkinson, Peter J. Bailey, K. J. Chisholm, W. P. Cockshott, and Ronald Morrison. An approach to persistent programming. *The Computer Journal*, 26(4):360-365, 1983.

[3] Jack H. Barnard, Robert F. Metz, and Arthur L. Price. A recommended practice for describing software designs: IEEE standards project 1016. *IEEE Trans. on Software Engineering*, SE-12(2):258 - 263, February 1986

[4] E. Bell, Thomas, David C. Bixler, and Margaret E. Dyer. An extendable approach to computer-aided software requirements engineering. *IEEE Trans. on Software Engineering*, SE-3(1):49 - 59, January 1977.

[5] Michael J. Carey, David J. Dewitt, Daniel Frank, Goetz Graefe, M. Muralikrishna, Joel E. Richardson, and Eugene J. Shekita. The architecture of the exodus extensible dbms. In *Proc. of the International Workshop on Object Oriented Database Systems*, pages 52 - 65, 1986.

[6] Michael J. Carey, David J. Dewitt, Daniel Frank, Goetz Graefe, Joel E. Richardson, Eugene J.Shekita, and M Muralikrishna. The architecture of the EXODUS extensible DBMS: a preliminary report. Technical Report Computer Sciences Technical Report #644, University of Wisconsin, Madison, Computer Sciences Department, May 1986.

[7] Thomas E. Cheatham. Process programming and process models. In *5th International Software Process Workshop - Preprints*, October 1989. Kennebunkport, Maine, October, 1989.

[8] Geoffrey M. Clemm and Leon J. Osterweil. A mechanism for environment integration. Technical Report CU-CS-323-86, University of Colorado, Department of Computer Science, Boulder, Colorado 80309, 1986.

[9] Don Cohen. *AP5 Manual*. Univ. of Southern California, Information Sciences Institute, March 1988.

[10] Cheatham, Jr. Thomas E. The E-L software development database - an experiment in extensibility. In *Proc. 1989 ACM SIGMOD Workshop on Software CAD Databases*, pages 21 - 25, 1989. Napa, California, February.

[11] Stuart I. Feldman. Make - a program for maintaining computer programs. *Software— Practice and Experience*, 9:255 - 265, 1979.

[12] Shehab A. Gamalel-din and Leon J. Osterweil. New perspectives on software maintenance processes. In *Proceedings of the Conference on Software Maintenance*, pages 14 - 22. IEEE, October 1988.

[13] Dennis Heimbigner. Triton reference manual. Technical Report CU-CS-483-90, University of Colorado, Department of Computer Science, Boulder, Colorado 80309, August 1990.

[14] Dennis Heimbigner and Steven Krane. A graph transform model for configuration management environments. In *Proc. Third ACM SIGSOFT/SIGPLAN Symposium on Practical Software Development Environments*, pages 216 - 225, November 1988. Special issue of SIGPLAN Notices, 24(2), February, 1989.

[15] Scott E. Hudson and Roger King. The Cactis project: Database support for software environments. *IEEE Trans. on Software Engineering*, 14(6):709-719, June 1988.

[16] Lech Krzanik. Enactable models for quantitative evolutionary software processes. In Cohn Tully, editor, *Proc. 4th International Software Process Workshop*, pages 103 - 110, Moretonhampstead, Devon, U.K., May, 1988, 1988. ACM SIGSOFT Software Engineering Notes, v. 14, n. 4, June 1989.

[17] Yoshihiro Matsumoto, Kiyoshi Agusa, and Tsuneo Ajisaka. A software process model based on unit workload network. In *5th International Software Process Workshop - Preprints*, October 1989. Kennebunkport, Maine, October, 1989.

[18] K. M. Olender. *Cecil/Cesar: Specification and Static Evaluation of Sequencing Constraints*. PhD thesis, University of Colorado, 1988.

[19] Leon J. Osterweil. Using data flow tools in software engineering. In Muchnick and Jones, editors, *Program Flow Analysis: Theory and Application*. Prentice-Hall, Englewood Cliffs, N. J., 1981.

[20] Leon J. Osterweil. Software processes are software too. In *Proc. Ninth International Conference on Software Engineering*, 1987. (Reprinted as Chapter 17)

[21] David L. Parnas and Paul C. Clements. A rational design process: How and why to fake it. *IEEE Trans. on Software Engineering*, SE-12(2):251 - 257, February 1986.

[22] Debra J. Richardson, Stephanie Leif Aha, and Leon J. Osterweil. Integrating testing techniques through process programming. In *Testing, Analysis, and Verification (3)*, pages 219-228, Key West, December 1989. SIGSOFT.

[23] Joel E. Richardson and Michael J. Carey. Programming constructs for database system implementation in EXODUS. In *Proc. ACM SIGMOD Conf.*, pages 208-219, 1987.

[24] Mark J. Rochkind. The source code control system. *IEEE Trans. on Software Engineering*, SE-1:364 - 370, December 1975.

[25] Lawrence A. Rowe and Michael R. Stonebraker. The POSTGRES data model. In *Proc. of the Thirteenth International Conf. on Very Large Data Bases*, pages 83 - 96, 1987.

[26] Craig Schaffert, Topher Cooper, Bruce Bullis, Mike Kilian, and Carrie Wilpolt. An introduction to Trellis/Owl. In *OOPSLA '86 Conf. Proc.*, pages 9-16, 1986. Available as ACM SIGPLAN Notices 21, 11, November 1986.

[27] John M. Smith, Steve Fox, and Terry Landers. Reference manual for ADAPLEX. Technical Report CGA-83-08, Computer Corporation of America, May 1981.

[28] Michael Stonebraker and Lawrence A. Rowe. The design of POSTGRES. In *Proc. of the ACM SIGMOD International Conf. on the Management of Data*, pages 340 - 355, 1986.

[29] Stanley M. Sutton, Jr. *APPL/A: A Prototype Language for Software-Process Programming*. PhD thesis, University of Colorado, August 1990.

[30] Stanley M. Sutton, Jr. FCM: A flexible consistency model for software processes. Technical Report CU-CS-462-90, University of Colorado, Department of Computer Science, Boulder, Colorado 80309, March 1990.

[31] Stanley M. Sutton, Jr. A flexible consistency model for persistent data in software-process programming languages. In *Proc. of the Fourth International Workshop on Persistent Object Systems*, 1990. Martha's Vineyard, Massachusetts.

[32] Stanley M. Sutton, Jr., Dennis Heimbigner, and Leon J. Osterweil. APPL/A: A prototype language for software process programming. Technical Report CU-CS-448-89, University of Colorado, Department of Computer Science, Boulder, Colorado 80309, October 1989.

[33] Richard N. Taylor, Frank C. Belz, Lori A. Clarke, Leon J. Osterweil, Richard W. Selby, Jack C. Wileden, Alexander Wolf, and Michal Young. Foundations for the Arcadia environment architecture. In *Proc. ACM SIGSOFT/SIGPLAN Software Engineering Symposium on Practical Software Development Environments*, pages 1-13. ACM, November 1988. (Reprinted as Chapter 13)

[34] United States Department of Defense. *Reference Manual for the Ada Programming Language*, 1983. ANSI/MIL-STD-1815A-1983.

Using Little-JIL to Coordinate Agents in Software Engineering

Alexander Wise, Aaron G. Cass, Barbara Staudt Lerner, Eric K. McCall, Leon J. Osterweil, and Stanley M. Sutton Jr.

Alexander Wise, Aaron G. Cass, and Leon J. Osterweil are at Department of Computer Science, University of Massachusetts, Amherst, MA 01003-4610 USA, {wise, acass, ljo}@cs.umass.edu

Barbara Staudt Lerner is at Department of Computer Science, Williams College, Williamstown, MA 01 267 USA, lerner@cs.williams.edu

Eric K. McCall is at HP Laboratories, Palo Alto, CA 94304 USA, emccall@hpl.hp.com

Stanley M. Sutton Jr. is at IBM T. J. Watson Research Center, Hawthorne, NY 10532 USA, suttonsm@us.ibm.com

Abstract Little-JIL, a new language for programming the coordination of agents is an executable, high-level process programming language with a formal (yet graphical) syntax and rigorously defined operational semantics. Little-JIL is based on two main hypotheses. The first is that the specification of coordination control structures is separable from other process programming language issues. Little-JIL provides a rich set of control structures while relying on separate systems for support in areas such as resource, artifact, and agenda management. The second is that processes can be executed by agents who know how to perform their tasks but can benefit from coordination support. Accordingly, each step in Little-JIL is assigned to an execution agent (human or automated): agents are responsible for initiating steps and performing the work associated with them. This approach has so far proven effective in allowing us to clearly and concisely express the agent coordination aspects of a wide variety of software, workflow, and other processes.

1. Introduction

Software engineering activities often involve many human agents and tools that must coordinate to produce a complex artifact such as the design of a large software system. The formalized specification and automated execution of these software engineering activities has been the goal of previous research on process programming. However, to support the complex coordination that must be achieved

Alexander Wise, Aaron Cass, Barbara Lerner, Eric McCall, Leon J. Osterweil, and Stanley M. Sutton Jr., "Using Little-JIL to Coordinate Agents in Software Engineering," Proceedings of the 15th IEEE international conference on Automated software engineering (IEEE), 2000. © 2000 IEEE in software engineering processes, a coordination language has to provide constructs to support a wide variety of process abstractions such as organizations, activities, artifacts, resources, events, agents, and exceptions, which can easily make a language large and complex. In this paper we present Little-JIL, a process language that attempts to resolve the apparently conflicting objectives of supporting this wide variety of abstractions and creating a language that is easy to use and understandable by non-programmers.

Little-JIL is strongly rooted in our past research on process programming languages [27, 28], but it makes some important breaks with this earlier work. Of primary importance for this paper is the focus on the *coordination* of activities and agents. Coordination, as defined by Carriero and Gelernter is "the process of building programs by gluing together active pieces" and is a vehicle for building programs that "can include both human and software processes" [7]. From this perspective, it can be seen that coordination is a logically central aspect of process semantics.

As with Linda [7], in Little-JIL we have separated coordination from other language elements. Unlike Linda, which is made up of a set of common primitives for the construction of multiple coordination paradigms and removes all computational elements, in Little-JIL we have selected a single higher-level coordination paradigm that we believe fits naturally with the domain of process and workflow specification and included a small set of computational constructs to allow the programmer to further refine the ways in which the major computational elements interact. Furthermore, the paradigm we have selected serves as a natural focus to which other elements of the process such as artifacts and resources can be related, and their use orchestrated.

Little-JIL is primarily a graphical language. This helps to promote understandability, adoption, and ease of use. However, Little-JIL language constructs are still defined using precise operational semantics as textual languages typically have.

We believe that focusing on coordination, and allowing the process program to add additional layers of program complexity incrementally can lead to benefits in many areas, including process analysis, understanding, adaptation, and execution. In this paper, we present the design of Little-JIL and evaluate our experience with it. We illustrate Little-JIL's features using an example process for solving the familiar problem of trip planning. While this process is not as complex as the software engineering processes for which Little-JIL is designed, it serves as an effective vehicle for demonstrating the language features.

2. Design Principles

Little-JIL draws on the lessons of our earlier work [28] by retaining the "step" as the central abstraction and scoping mechanism but refines the features in terms of which a step is defined. The design of Little-JIL features was guided by three primary principles:

Simplicity: To foster clarity, ease-of-use, and understandability, we made a concerted effort to keep the language simple. We added features only when there was a demonstrated need in terms of function, expressiveness, or simplification of programs. To help make the language accessible to both developers and readers, we adopted a primarily visual syntax.

Expressiveness: Subject to (and supportive of) the goal of simplicity, we made the language highly expressive. Software and workflow processes are semantically rich domains, and a process language, even one tightly focused on coordination, must reflect a corresponding variety of semantics. We wanted the language to allow users to speak to the range of concerns relevant to a process and be able to express their intentions in a clear and natural way.

Precision: The language semantics are precisely defined. This precision contributes to several important goals. First, it enables automatic execution of process programs. Second, precision supports the *analyzability* of process programs. Analysis is key to assuring that process programs indeed have properties that are desirable for process safety, correctness, reliability, and predictability (or, conversely, for showing that those properties cannot be guaranteed). Analysis also contributes to process understanding and validation.

We also followed many other software and language design criteria, such as hierarchic decomposition, scoping, and so on, but the three principles described were the primary concerns for Little-JIL. These concerns are related, however, so the design of Little-JIL has also involved balancing tradeoffs. For example, adding a control construct may increase expressiveness, but it may also increase complexity in terms of the number of language features. Some additional complexity may be warranted if new features will be widely used or they result in a simplification of programs. We believe that such decisions must be made through experimentation.

3. Coordination Paradigm

A coordinated activity consists of the following elements:

- A collection of agents each capable of carrying out one or more tasks in support of the activity,
- A communication mechanism enabling the agents to share information,
- A distribution mechanism enabling the agents to operate on separate machines,
- An assignment of tasks to agents, and
- A coordinating process that glues the agents and their tasks together in a manner conducive to accomplishing the coordinated activity.

The coordination paradigm of Little-JIL is one in which independent agents are coordinated in their ability to share information as well as being proactively assigned tasks. All communication between the process and the individual agents takes place via the agent's agenda, which can migrate from machine to machine. A new task is assigned to an agent by placing it on the agent's agenda along with data required to complete the task. The agent informs the Little-JIL interpreter when it has begun a task so that the interpreter can acquire resources on the agent's behalf to assist with the task. The agent also informs the interpreter when it has completed a task, reporting back information to the process such as updated data or exceptional situations that prevented satisfactory completion of the task.

The binding between agents and tasks is done dynamically. In particular, the process program contains declarations of the capabilities the agent must have. Just before assigning a task to an agent, the interpreter uses these declarations of required capabilities to select an agent who has those capabilities and is also available to do the task.

Agents may either be human or software. Little-JIL does not distinguish between them. In particular, both human and software agents have agendas. The distinction lies in how the agents connect to their agendas. Specifically, human agents use a GUI which interacts with the interpreter via a well-defined API, while software agents use this API directly.

Decisions on how a process should proceed may be based upon the following information:

- Whether an individual task was successfully completed or not,
- Which agents and resources are available to support future tasks,
- Decisions made dynamically by the intelligent agents participating in the process. In particular, agents are responsible for making context-specific decisions based upon the data within the process as well as criteria that is external to the process.

Little-JIL's coordination paradigm allows for a range of strictness or flexibility in the execution of the process. This is controlled by the process programmer's choice of constructs and the specificity in the agent capability requirements. These are explained more fully below.

4. Language and Illustrative Example

Capturing the coordination in a process as a hierarchy of steps is the central focus of programming in Little-JIL. A Little-JIL program is a tree of steps whose leaves represent the smallest specified units of work and whose structure represents the way in which this work will be coordinated. Steps provide a scoping mechanism for control, data, and exception flow and for agent and resource assignment.

As a process executes, steps go through several states. Typically, a step is *posted* when assigned to an execution agent, then started by the agent. Eventually either the step is successfully *completed* or it is *terminated* with an exception. Many other states exist, but a full description of all states is beyond the scope of this paper.

There are six main features of the Little-JIL language that allow a process programmer to specify the coordination of steps in a process. Due to space constraints, we can only give an overview of the language. Detailed operational semantics are provided by the Little-JIL 1.0 Language Report [29].

The main features of the language and their justifications are the following:

- Four non-leaf *step kinds* provide control flow. These four kinds are "sequential," "parallel," "try," and "choice." Non-leaf steps consist of one or more substeps whose execution sequence is determined by the step kind. A sequential step's substeps are all executed in left to right order. A parallel step's substeps can be simultaneously executed. A try step's substeps are executed in left to right order stopping when one completes successfully. Exactly one of a choice step's substeps is executed; the agents dynamically decide which step to execute. It is important to note how the parallel and choice step kinds accord to agents the power to exercise their judgment and to make choices about the order in which the substeps of a step should be performed or how a particular item of work is to be done. While the language can be used to constrain the alternatives, the agent is left free to make the choices.

- *Requisites* are a mechanism to add checks before and after a step is executed to ensure that all of the conditions needed to begin a step are satisfied and that the step has been executed "correctly" when it is completed. A prerequisite is a step that must be completed before the step to which it is attached. Similarly, a postrequisite must be completed after the step to which it is attached. While requisites decrease the simplicity of the language, we have found them necessary to allow process programmers to naturally describe common step contingencies. The need for pre- and post-requisites appears common enough in process programs and requisite step semantics seem different enough from other kinds of sequential steps that a special notation was introduced.

- *Exceptions and handlers* augment the control flow constructs of the step kinds. Exceptions and handlers are used to indicate and fix up, respectively, exceptional conditions or errors during program execution and provide a degree of reactive control that we believe allows a process programmer to simply and accurately codify common processes.

The exception mechanism in Little-JIL has been designed to be simple yet remain expressive. It is based on the use of steps to define the scope of exceptions and handlers. Exceptions are passed up the step decomposition tree (call stack) until a matching handler is found.

Our experience has indicated that it is necessary to allow different exception handlers to work in a variety of ways. After handling an exception, a continuation badge determines whether the step will continue execution, successfully complete, restart execution at the beginning, or rethrow the exception. Detailed semantics are provided in [29].

- *Messages and reactions* are another form of reactive control and greatly increase the expressive power of Little-JIL. The greatest difference between exceptions and messages is that messages do not propagate up the step decomposition tree, being global in scope instead—any executing step can react to a message. Thus, messages provide a way for one part of a process program to react to events without being constrained by the step hierarchy. Because messages are broadcast, there may be multiple reactions to a single message. The semantics of messages are still undergoing evaluation and evolution, but experience so far has convinced us that a process language must be both able to drive execution forward through proactive mechanisms, and be able to react to events from the environment.
- *Parameters* passed between steps allow communication of information necessary for the execution of a step and for the return of step execution results.
- *Resources* are representations of entities that are required during step execution. Resources may include the step's execution agent, permissions to use tools, and various physical artifacts.

What's missing from the above feature list is also important to note. Little-JIL does not specify a data type model for parameters and resources. It also omits expressions and most imperative commands. Little-JIL relies on agents to know how the tasks represented by leaf steps are performed: Little-JIL is used to specify step coordination, not execution. These typical language features have been excluded in order to focus the process program on coordination. We believe this makes the language more applicable to domains in which the agents are primarily autonomous.

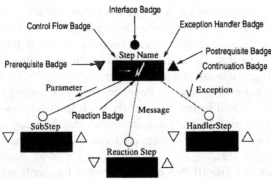

Fig. 20.1. Legend

The graphical representation of a Little-JIL step is shown in Fig. 20.1. This figure shows the various badges that make up a step, as well a step's possible connections to other steps. The interface badge at the top is a circle to which an edge from the parent may be attached. The circle is filled if there are local declarations associated with the step, such as parameters and resources, and is empty otherwise. Below the circle is the step name, and to the left is a triangle called the prerequisite badge. The badge appears filled if the step has a prerequisite step, and an edge may be shown that connects this step to its prerequisite (not shown). On the right is another similarly filled triangle called the postrequisite badge to which a postrequisite step may be attached. Within the box (below the step name) are three more badges. From left to right, they are the control flow badge, which tells what kind of step this is and to which child steps are attached, the reaction badge, to which reaction steps are attached, and the exception handler badge, to which exception handlers are attached. These badges can be omitted if there are no child steps, reactions, or handlers, respectively. The edges that come from these badges can be annotated with parameters (passed to and from substeps), messages (to which reactions occur), and exceptions (that a handler should handle). It is possible for an exception to have a null handler, in which case the continuation badge alone determines how execution proceeds.

To better motivate each of these language features and to illustrate their use, we present in Figs. 20.2, 20.3, and 20.4 a trip planning process, coded in Little-JIL. The process is based on one presented in [5]. Our version involves four people: the traveler, a travel agent, and two secretaries. The basic idea is to make an airline reservation, trying United first, then USAir. If (after making the plane reservation) the traveler has gone over budget, and a Saturday stayover was not included, the dates should be changed to include a Saturday stayover and another attempt should be made. After the airline reservation is made and travel dates and times are set, car and hotel reservations should be made. The hotel reservations may be made at either a Days Inn or, if the budget is not tight, a Hyatt, and the car reservations may be made with either Avis or Hertz.

The separation of the semantic issues into separate graphical components, as described above, allows Visual-JIL (our editor for Little-JIL programs) to selectively display information relevant to a particular aspect of a Little-JIL program. Indeed, we illustrate this approach to visualization in the subsequent figures to highlight various language features.

4.1. Step Kinds

Fig. 20.2 depicts the overall structure of the Little-JIL trip planning process program. Each of the four step kinds are used where appropriate:

- A sequential step is used to make plane reservations before car and hotel reservations,
- A try step is used to try United first, then USAir,

- A parallel step is used to allow two secretaries to make car and hotel reservations simultaneously, and
- Choice steps are used to allow a secretary to choose which hotel chain or car company to try first.

Note that the process program is relatively resilient to many expectable sorts of changes. For example, changing the process program to express a preference in hotel or car rental companies or deciding to attempt all reservations in parallel, i.e., changing the way in which these activities are coordinated, can be accomplished with a straightforward change of step kind.

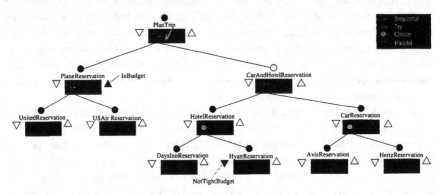

Fig. 20.2. Reservation process showing proactive control: step kinds, requisites.

4.2. Requisites

There are two cases in the example (Fig. 20.2) where requisite steps have been used. A postrequisite has been attached to the **PlaneReservation** step to check that the airfare hasn't exceeded the budget. This means that after the travel agent has successfully made an airline reservation, the traveler should complete the **In-Budget** step. A prerequisite for the **HyattReservation** step is also shown. This prerequisite could be considered an optimization that is based on the assumption that staying at a Hyatt depletes one's travel budget more than staying at a Days Inn. If a secretary chooses to reserve a room at the Hyatt and the budget is too tight, that step aborts immediately because it will definitely cause costs to exceed the budget.

While the English description of the process does not specify who should check the budget, the Little-JIL program specifies that the traveler is responsible for this task. Postrequisite steps help clarify how the delegation of work can be done. For example, a subordinate can be assigned to do the work associated with a step, but the subordinate's supervisor could be responsible for the postrequisite of the step to check the acceptability of the work done by the subordinate. This is shown in the PlaneReservation step. If, for example, the travel budget were sensitive information, the execution agent for PlaneReservation could assign the UnitedReservation and USAirReservation steps to other agents without divulging the budget.

4.3 Exceptions and handlers

If the agent determines that the budget has been exceeded, the agent throws the NotInBudget exception to the parent. The parent step's handler, IncludeSaturdayStayover (in Fig. 20.3[1]), would check to see if a Saturday stayover was already included, and if not, it would change the travel dates and restart the PlanTrip step with the new travel dates. If there was already a Saturday stayover, the handler could throw another exception (not shown) that would be propagated higher up the process tree or would terminate the program.

Just as different step executions result from the different step kinds, different executions result from different continuation badges. If, for example, IncludeSaturdayStayover were rewritten to make alternative plans, the continuation badge would be changed to "complete," indicating that the exception step had provided an alternative implementation of PlanTrip.

4.4. Messages and reactions

An example of a reaction, the "handler" for a message, appears in Fig. 20.3. Here, when the MeetingCancelled message is generated, the CancelAndStop substep of PlanTrip is assigned to the traveler. In this case, there may be very little information associated with that step; it is assumed that the agent will take appropriate action (e.g., phoning the travel agent and secretaries and asking them to abort).

4.5 Parameters

In the example, it is clear that information must be passed from step to step. For example, the PlaneReservation step must pass the trip dates and times to the other reservation steps so that a hotel room and car are reserved for the correct times. Information is passed between steps via parameters. Parameter passing is

---

[1] In the figures, ellipses indicate where substeps have been omitted for clarity. Visual-JIL elides information at the user's request

indicated by annotations made on the step connections, shown in Fig. 20.4. Three parameter passing modes are defined in Little-JIL. Arrows attached to the parameters indicate whether a parameter is copied into the substep's scope from the parent, copied out, or both.

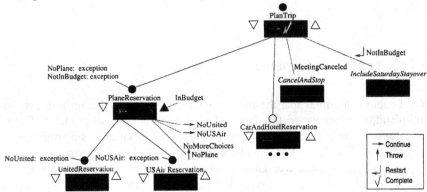

Fig. 20.3. Reservation process showing reactive control: exceptions, messages.

Because Little-JIL is focused on coordination, a process specifies at what points during execution parameter values should be copied to and from steps without specifying the computations to be performed on them. Thus, it is assumed that the agents executing those steps understand the meanings of the parameter values. For example, the use of InBudget as a postrequisite provides guidance about when to check the budget, but doesn't dictate any particular computation for doing so.

4.6. Resources

Resource requirements for a step are indicated by annotations on the step's interface specification and resources play a central role in the execution of Little-JIL programs. By identifying and acquiring resources at run time, a resource management component enables a Little-JIL program to adapt to different environments, allowing more dynamism during process execution. Because the resource model is external to any one process and may be shared by multiple processes, the details of the resource model are not represented in the process program.

In Fig. 20.4 execution agent resources are specified as annotations on the interface badge. The steps for HotelReservation and CarReservation specify a secretary as the agent responsible for the task. We allow for the possibility that these tasks could be done in parallel by two different secretaries—but in an environment with only a single secretary, we also allow for the dynamic assignment of both of these tasks to the same secretary who might interleave the activities or perform them sequentially.

In the example, only the agents are being managed as resources, however, re-sources can be any artifact for which the resource manager's ability to identify ar-tifacts and avoid usage conflicts would be an asset.

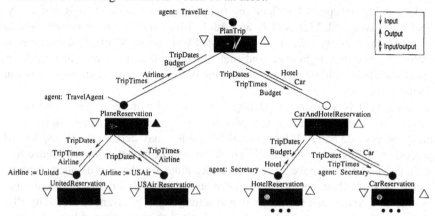

Fig. 20.4. Reservation process showing data flow.

5. Related Work

In our research, we have constructed a richly-featured process language including agent coordination, resource dependencies, proactive control constructs, both broadcast and scoped reactive control, data flow specification and pre- and post-requisites. These features are used to specify the set of tasks required, and the ways in which a collection of agents can cooperate to achieve a goal, but still offer the agents flexibility in the way the tasks are performed. This top-down approach contrasts with most work in coordination (e.g., [14, 3, 17, 22, 7]) in which coordi-nation is specified from the perspective of the individual agents, and as such, our work is most directly comparable to workflow systems and other process pro-gramming languages. A notable exception is the 'set-plays' in [26]. Set-plays are multi-step multi-agent plans, and as such are similar to our approach of specifying the interactions between the agents from an integrated perspective.

While our use of high-level, process-oriented abstractions and a focus on the "step" as the unit of work separates us from process languages based on general-purpose programming languages or Petri-Nets, such as APPL/A [27], AP5 [11], and SLANG [2], many process or workflow languages have focused on process steps (variously also called tasks or activities). For example HFSP [20], EPOS [12], Teamware [30], and APEL [13]. None of the features in Little-JIL are unique, but the way we have combined proactive and reactive control and resource and artifact management into a single consistent abstraction is. For example, while

ALF [6] "MASPs" include an object model (parameters), tools (with pre/postconditions), ordering constraints on operators (path expressions), rules (reactions) and "characteristics" (postconditions on the MASP as a whole), ALF lacks explicit exception handlers and treats human agents and tools separately. ProcessWeaver [16], Merlin [19], and Adele-Tempo [4], focus on notions related to "work contexts" (which may be correlated with steps). Work contexts are generally assigned only to humans and such languages treat tools and humans differently thereby requiring process programmers to determine agent assignments at design time.

APEL [13] is a process modeling formalism with many of our same goals, namely to provide a high-level, expressive, yet executable language suitable for many process domains. While the APEL project has defined many aspects of process modeling in great detail (such as the artifact model, which we leave to a separate model), we have chosen to concentrate on the coordination aspects. APEL's control flow mechanisms are similar to Little-JIL's in that both proactive and reactive control can be specified, and activities can be arranged hierarchically. However, the reactive control in APEL is limited to an un-scoped broadcast mechanism similar to Little-JIL's reaction mechanism. As such, Little-JIL's scoped exception handling has no direct analog in APEL. This scoped exception mechanism allows a flexible, yet careful way to deal with exceptional behaviors at runtime.

6. Experience and Conclusions

We have implemented several tools to support the definition and execution of Little-JIL programs. The tools are written in Java and have been used both on Linux and Windows platforms. The tools include a graphical editor, an interpreter [9], a distributed object substrate, an agenda management system [24], and a resource manager [25].

6.1. Process programs

We have applied Little-JIL to problems ranging from data mining [18], to electronic commerce [8], to the high-level coordination of teams of robots [1]. In the software engineering domain, we have written process programs for coordinating the actions of multiple designers doing Booch Object Oriented Design [23] and the assignment and tracking of bug reports from submission through regression testing. These processes have focussed on programming coordination among programmers, and also on how to assure that the processes provide support to humans, while not appearing to be too prescriptive or authoritarian. We have also written process programs for guiding the use of the FLAVERS dataflow analysis toolset [15]. In this work we have been particularly interested in using Little-JIL to provide guidance both novice and expert users in being more effective in using several tools in this complex toolset. We have also written process programs for guiding the application of formal verification methods and tools, but here our experience has been rather limited. Finally, we have also used Little-JIL to program the ISPW 6 software development process [21].

6.2. Language extensions

To maintain its simplicity, we have resisted impulses to add features to the language, but our experience indicates that it may be necessary to add several new language features to improve expressiveness. For example, we have encountered several idioms that simplify the design and understanding of processes for which a formalism might be useful. The most common of these is *resource-bounded recursion* which allows a step to be repeated multiple times executing with a different resource on each iteration and ceasing when there are no more resources. *Resource-bounded parallelism* is similar to resource-bounded recursion except that in this case the iterations are allowed to happen in parallel. While we can express these idioms currently, introducing appropriate constructs would allow much more concise and understandable representation of the idioms. In particular, we have found that we currently need to use exceptions to terminate the resource-bounded recursion and parallelism. This is an inappropriate use of exceptions since those termination conditions are not exceptional but an essential piece of the idioms.

We have also begun to explore the role of timing in a process program and are developing constructs to support the definition of timing criteria. We intend to use that information to support deadlines for tasks and also to enable scheduling analyses of processes.

6.3. Analysis

Complex processes typically involve a great deal of concurrent activity being performed by multiple agents. We want to reason about common concurrency problems, such as ordering of activities, possibilities for deadlock or starvation, and so on.

Thus far most of our static analysis has been limited to manual evaluation of processes, but Little-JIL is precise enough to allow application of static analysis technology, especially to the analysis of issues directly related to the coordination of step execution. In recent work we have begun to demonstrate success in applying the FLAVERS static dataflow analyzer to Little-JIL process programs [10].

This work has been very revealing. We have succeeded in demonstrating the presence of specific bugs in some Little- JIL process programs, and the absence of bugs in others. We have also discovered that apparently simple and intuitive Little-JIL constructs such as the parallel and choice steps (especially when used in conjunction with recursion) often conceal considerably semantic complexity. This buttresses our contention that these language constructs are important additions to process programming languages, as they are intuitively clear, yet represent substantial semantic content.

Much of the detailed behavior of a process is left unspecified in Little-JIL process programs. Rather it is left to the agents because we believe micromanagement of an agent's activities is inappropriate. Because this and many other aspects of the process are not completely represented in Little-JIL, it will be interesting to discover what the practical limits of analysis are. It will likely be necessary to perform analysis across the boundaries separating the process and the software agents to prove certain desirable characteristics of our processes.

Acknowledgments The authors would like to thank Rodion Podorozhny for his early contributions to Little-JIL and the resource management system, and Yulin Dong, Hyungwon Lee, and Marcia Zangrilli for programming in and providing feedback about many versions of the language. This research was partially supported by the Air Force Research Laboratory/ IFTD and the Defense Advanced Research Projects Agency under Contract F30602-97-2-0032. The views and conclusions contained herein are those of the authors and should not be interpreted as necessarily representing the official policies or endorsements, either expressed or implied, of the Defense Advanced Research Projects Agency, the Air Force Research Laboratory/IFTD, or the U.S. Government.

References

[1] E. Araujo, D. Karuppia, Y. Yang, R. Grupen, P. Deegan, B. Lemer, E. Riseman, and Z. Zhu. Software mode changes for continuous motion tracking. In *Int'l Workshop on Self Adaptive Software*, Apr 2000.

[2] S. Bandinelli, A. Fuggetta, and S. Grigolli. Process modeling in-the-large with SLANG. In *Proc. of the Second Int'l Conf. on the Software Process*, pages 75-83. 1993.

[3] M. Barbuceanu and M. S. Fox. COOL: A language for describing coordination in multi agent systems. In *Proc. of the First Int'l Conf on Multi-Agent Systems*, 1995.

[4] N. Belkhatir, J. Estublier, and M. L. Walcelio. ADELE-TEMPO: An environment to support process modeling and enaction. In A. Finkelstein, J. Kramer, and B. Nuseibeh, editors, *Software Process Modelling and Technology*, pages 187 - 222. John Wiley & Sons Inc., 1994.

[5] E. Bertino, S. Jajodia, L. Mancini, and I. Ray. Multiform transaction model for workflow management. In *Proc. of the NSF Workshop on Workflow and Process Automation in Information Systems*, May 1996.

[6] G. Canals, N. Boudjlida, J.-C. Demiame, C. Godart, and J. Lonchamp. ALF: A framework for building process-centred software engineering environments. In *Software Process Modelling and Technology*, John Wiley & Sons Inc., 1994.

[7] N. Carriero, D. Gelernter. *How to Write Parallel Programs A First Course*. MIT Press, 1990.

[8] A. G. Cass, H. Lee, B. S. Lerner, and L. J. Osterweil. Formally defining coordination processes to support contract negotiations. Technical Report 99-39, University of Massachusetts at Amherst, Jun 1999.

[9] A. G. Cass, B. S. Lerner, E. K. McCall, L. J. Osterweil, and A. Wise. Logically: central, physically distributed control in a process runtime environment. Technical Report 99-65, University of Massachusetts at Amherst, Nov. 1999.

[10] J. M. Cobleigh, L. A. Clarke, and L. J. Osterweil. Verifying properties of process definitions. Technical Report 99-63, University of Massachusetts at Amherst, Nov. 1999.

[11] D. Cohen. *AP5 Manual*. Univ. of Southern California, Information Sciences Institute, 1988.

[12] R. Conradi, M. Hagaseth, J.-O. Larsen, M. N. Nguyên, B. P. Munch, P. H. Westby, W. Zhu, M. L. Jaccheri, and C. Liu. EPOS: Object-oriented cooperative process modelling. In *Software Process Modelling and Technology*, pages 33 - 70. John Wiley & Sons Inc., 1994.

[13] S. Dami, J. Estublier, and A. Amiour. APEL: A graphical yet executable formalism for process modelling. *Automated Software Engineering*, Mar. 1997.

[14] K. S. Decker and V. R. Lesser. Designing a family of coordination mechanisms. In *Proc. of the First Int'l Conf. on Multi-Agent Systems*, 1995.

[15] M. B. Dwyer and L. A. Clarke. Data Flow Analysis for Verifying Properties of Concurrent Programs. In *Proc. 2nd ACM SIGSOFT Symp. on Foundations of Software Engineering*, 1994.

[16] C. Femström. PROCESS WEAVER: Adding process support to UNIX. In *Proc. of the Second Int'l Conf. on the Software Process*, pages 12 - 26, 1993.

[17] T. Finin, Y. Labrou, and J. Mayfield. Kqml as an agent communication language. In *Software Agents*. MIT Press, 1997.

[18] D. Jensen, Y. Dong, B. S. Lerner, E. K. McCall, L. J. Osterweil, S. M. Sutton Jr., and A. Wise. Coordinating agent activities in knowledge discovery processes. In *Int'l Joint Conf. on Work Activities Coordination and Collaboration*, July 1998. submitted.

[19] G. Junkermann, B. Peuschel, W. Schafer, and S. Wolf. MERLIN: Supporting cooperation in software development through a knowledge-based environment. In *Software Process Modelling and Technology*, pages 103 - 129. John Wiley & Sons Inc., 1994.

[20] T. Katayama. A hierarchical and functional software process description and its enaction. In *Proc. of the 11th Int'l Conf. on Software Engineering*, 1989.

[21] M. I. Kellner, P. Feiler, A. Finkelstein, T. Katayama, L. J. Osterweil, and M. H. Penedo. ISPW-6 software process example. In *Proc. of the First Int'l Conf. on the Software Process*, pages 176 - 186, 1991.

[22] K. Kuwabara, T. Ishida, and N. Osato. Agentalk: Coordination protocol description for multi-agent systems. In *Proc. of the First Int'l Conf. on Multi-Agent Systems*, 1995.

[23] B. S. Lerner, S. M. Sutton, Jr., and L. J. Osterweil. Enhancing design methods to support real design processes. In *9th IEEE Int'l Workshop on Software Specification and Design*, pages 159-161. IEEE Computer Society Press, Apr. 1998.

[24] E. K. McCall, L. A. Clarke, and L. J. Osterweil. An Adaptable Generation Approach to Agenda Management. In *Proc. 20th Int'l Conf. on Software Engineering*, 1998.

[25] R. M. Podorozhny, B. S. Lerner, and L. J. Osterweil. Modeling resources for activity coordination and scheduling. In *Proc. Coordination 1999*.

[26] P. Stone and M. Veloso. Task decomposition, dynamic role assignment, and low-bandwidth communication for realtime strategic teamwork. *Artificial Intelligence*, 1999.

[27] S. M. Sutton, Jr., D. Heimbigner, and L. J. Osterweil. APPL/A: A language for software-process programming. *ACM Trans. on Software Engineering and Methodology*.

[28] S. M. Sutton, Jr. and L. J. Osterweil. The design of a next-generation process language. In *Proc. of the Joint 6th European Software Engineering Conf. and the 5th ACM SICSOFT Symp. on the Foundations of Software Engineering*, pages 142-158. Springer-Verlag, 1997.

[29] A. Wise. Little-JIL 1.0 Language Report. Technical Report 98-24, University of Massachusetts at Amherst, Apr. 1998.

[30] P. S. Young and R. N. Taylor. Human-executed operations in the teamware process programming system. In *Proc. of the Ninth Int'l Software Process Workshop*, 1994.

Analyzing Medical Processes[1]

Bin Chen, George S. Avrunin, Elizabeth A. Henneman, Lori A. Clarke, Leon J. Osterweil, and Philip L. Henneman

Bin Chen, George S. Avrunin, Lori A. Clarke, and Leon J. Osterweil are at Dept. of Computer Science, University of Massachusetts, Amherst, MA 01003, {chenbin, avrunin, clarke, ljo}@cs.umass.edu

Elizabeth A. Henneman is at School of Nursing, University of Massachusetts, Amherst, MA 01003, henneman@nursing.umass.edu

Philip L. Henneman is at Tufts-Baystate Medical Center, Springfield, MA 01199, philip.henneman@bhs.org

Abstract This paper shows how software engineering technologies used to define and analyze complex software systems can also be effective in detecting defects in human-intensive processes used to administer healthcare. The work described here builds upon earlier work demonstrating that healthcare processes can be defined precisely. This paper describes how finite-state verification can be used to help find defects in such processes as well as find errors in the process definitions and property specifications. The paper includes a detailed example, based upon a real-world process for transfusing blood, where the process defects that were found led to improvements in the process.

1. Introduction

This paper describes how software engineering techniques that have been successfully applied in analyzing software systems can be effectively employed to detect problems in medical processes. This paper builds upon earlier work demonstrating that healthcare processes can be defined precisely using the Little-JIL process definition language [28]. Here, we describe our experiences in applying finite-state verification to precisely defined medical processes to identify process defects and then to confirm the effectiveness of corrections to those processes. Although described with respect to human-intensive, safety-critical medical processes, this

[1] Research partially supported by the National Science Foundation under awards CCF-0427071, CCR-0205575, and CCF-0541035, and by the U.S. Department of Defense/Army Research Office under awards DAAD19-01-1-0564 and DAAD19-03-1-0133.

work also suggests the applicability of these and related technologies to processes in other problem domains.

Medical errors are a major cause of death in our society. A 1999 report from the Institute of Medicine (IOM) [31] estimated that approximately 100,000 people die each year in US hospitals from preventable medical errors. There is ample anecdotal evidence that the complexity of the processes used to administer health-care is a significant source of the problem. The healthcare literature is replete with documented evidence of such errors as administration of blood of the wrong type, misidentification of patients, and incorrect dosages of potentially lethal medications.

The medical community is aware of these problems and has approached them in a number of ways. One principal approach has been to devise mandated procedures for carrying out many healthcare activities, especially those identified as being particularly high-risk. Mandated procedures are generally described in considerable detail, sometimes in documents that are dozens of pages long. These documents consist largely of natural language text, often supplemented by diagrams. These documents are the basis for both the training of medical professionals and the actual processes performed in hospitals. Despite the care that went into the creation of such documents, as well as other safety measures, a subsequent IOM study [39] revealed that error rates in hospitals had not declined significantly in the five-year period following the initial IOM report.

Examination of documents used to describe medical processes suggest several reasons why such documents have proven to be inadequate. Documents describing such processes as blood transfusion (e.g., [50], [51]) provide good examples of the problem. Despite attempts to be complete, they contain terms that are poorly defined and inconsistently used, and important details are often missing, especially details for handling special cases that might arise. Recognizing such limitations, the medical community has tried to employ a number of modeling representations, but these are usually based upon such formalisms as data flow graphs that make it relatively cumbersome to represent the handling of exceptional cases or complicated concurrency and synchronization. As a result, these representations generally fail to represent the full complexity of these processes.

Indeed, the many diverse circumstances under which activities like blood transfusions must take place require processes of considerable complexity. Moreover, blood transfusion, like many other medical activities, requires coordinating the efforts of many different parties, often performing their activities in parallel. The complexity of a process, such as this one, increases the risk of defects. Software engineers will readily note that the software development community already deals with the creation of complex procedures (e.g., complex software systems) that present a range of difficulties analogous to those found in medical processes. This suggests that the approaches used in software engineering to build and analyze complex, distributed systems might be effective in defining and analyzing medical processes.

This paper describes our work on using finite-state verification to identify defects in actual medical processes. The example described in this paper is based on a blood transfusion process being studied by the nursing community and commonly used in hospitals. In our project, software engineers collaborated with healthcare professionals to define key parts of the processes and their desired properties in rigorous formalisms, and then applied finite-state verification to determine whether the process definition satisfied the properties. In doing so, process defects were detected and subsequently repaired. The verification also uncovered inaccuracies in our process definition and our property specifications. Since we use, or intend to use, these artifacts in a wide range of evaluation activities, detecting and correcting these problems is also vitally important.

In a broad sense, this work demonstrates the feasibility of medical process improvement, carried out in ways that are strongly analogous to software improvement approaches. It suggests the applicability of this approach to other domains as well as consideration of other software engineering tools. In the next section of this paper, we provide a high-level description of the technologies that we employed, and Section 3 presents a detailed example. Section 4 discusses observations about this approach, and Section 5 outlines related work. The conclusion summarizes the contributions of this work and describes some areas of future research.

2. An Overview of the Techniques and Methodology Used

To evaluate the applicability of software engineering technologies to medical process definitions and analysis, we have used the Little-JIL process definition language [10], the PROPEL property elucidation system [17], and two finite-state verification systems, FLAVERS [22] and SPIN [29].

Modeling Processes Using Little-JIL: To analyze medical processes, it is important to develop precise, rigorous definitions of those medical processes first. The process definitions need to capture not only the standard cases, but also the exceptional situations. They also need to precisely specify the communication and coordination between medical professionals. In our approach, we use the Little-JIL language to define processes.

Little-JIL was originally developed to define software development and maintenance processes. A Little-JIL process definition consists of three components, an *artifact specification*, a *resource specification*, and a *coordination specification*. The artifact specification contains the items that are the focus of the activities carried out by the process. The resource specification specifies the agents and capabilities that support performing the activities. The coordination specification ties these together by specifying which agents and supplementary capabilities perform which activities on which artifacts at which time(s). A Little-JIL coordination specification has a visual representation, but is precisely defined using finite-state automata, which makes it amenable to definitive analyses. Among the features of Little-JIL that distinguish it from most process languages are its 1) use of abstraction to support scalability and clarity, 2) use of scoping to make step parameterization clear, 3) facilities for specifying parallelism, 4) capabilities for dealing with exceptional conditions, and 5) clarity in specifying iteration.

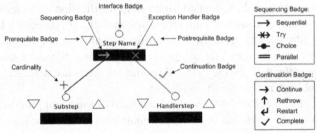

Fig. 21.1. Little-JIL steps

A Little-JIL coordination specification consists of hierarchically decomposed steps (see Fig. 21.1), where a step represents a task to be done by an assigned agent. Each step has a name and a set of badges to represent control flow among its sub-steps, its *interface* (a specification of its input/output artifacts and the resources it requires), the exceptions it handles, etc. A step with no sub-steps is called a *leaf step* and represents an activity to be performed by an agent, without any guidance from the process.

Little-JIL steps may be decomposed into two kinds of substeps, *ordinary substeps* and *exception handlers*. Ordinary substeps define how the step is to be executed and are connected to their parent by edges that may be annotated by specifications of the artifacts that flow between parent and substep and also by cardinality specifications. *Cardinality specifications* define the number of times the substep is instantiated, and may be a fixed number, a Kleene *, a Kleene +, or a Boolean expression (indicating whether the substep is to be instantiated). *Exception handlers* define how exceptions thrown by the step's descendants are handled.

A non-leaf step has a *sequencing badge* (an icon on the left of the step bar; e.g., the right arrow in Fig. 21.1) that defines the order of substep execution. For example, a *sequential step* (right arrow) indicates that substeps execute from left to right. A *parallel step* (equal sign) indicates that substeps execute in any (possibly interleaved) order, although the order may be constrained by such factors as the lack of needed inputs. A *choice step* (circle slashed with a horizontal line) indicates a choice among alternative substeps. A *try step* (right arrow with an X on its tail) indicates the sequence in which substeps are to be tried as alternatives.

A Little-JIL step can be optionally preceded or succeeded by a *pre-requisite*, represented by a down arrowhead to the left of the step bar, or a *post-requisite*, represented by an up arrowhead to the right of the step bar. Pre-requisites check if the step execution context is appropriate before starting execution of the step, and post-requisites check if the completed step execution satisfied its goals. The failure of a requisite triggers an exception.

Channels are message passing buffers, directly connecting specified source step(s) with specified destination step(s). Channels are used to synchronize and pass artifacts among concurrently executing steps.

Specifying Properties Using PROPEL: A property is a specification of the requirements for some aspect of the behavior of a process. In the medical domain, properties are often specified as policies in natural language so that they can be easily understood by the medical professionals. Such informal descriptions, however, are often vague and ambiguous and need to be translated into rigorous mathematical formalisms such as automata or temporal logics that can be used as the basis for verification. This is a surprisingly difficult task. Even experienced developers may overlook subtle, but important, details. In our approach, we use PROPEL to support specifying formal properties.

PROPEL guides users through the process of creating properties that are both accessible and mathematically precise. PROPEL provides users with a set of property templates, each of which can be viewed as an extended Finite-State Automaton representation, a Disciplined Natural Language representation, or a Question Tree. Each representation contains options (or questions) that explicitly indicate the variations that must be considered, thereby ensuring that users do not overlook important subtle details. In addition, the Question Tree can be used to guide the user in selecting the appropriate template. All three representations are views of a single underlying representation so that a change in any representation is reflected automatically in the others.

Verifying Processes Using FLAVERS and SPIN: Finite-state verification (FSV) techniques, such as model checking [15], involve the construction of a finite model that represents all possible relevant executions of a system with respect to the property to be evaluated. Then algorithmic methods are employed to determine whether the particular property holds for the model. A number of FSV tools have been proposed; for this work, we have used FLAVERS and SPIN. We chose these tools because we were familiar with them (FLAVERS was developed in our laboratory), they represent distinct modeling and checking approaches, and we could build on existing technology to construct models for them.

To construct models of Little-JIL processes, we first translate the Little-JIL into the Bandera Intermediate Representation (BIR) [30]. BIR is a guarded-command language for describing state-transition systems and was intended to support translation into the input languages of a variety of model checkers. A translator from BIR to the Promela language used by SPIN was constructed by the Bandera team, and we have built a translator for FLAVERS. Medical processes entail substantial amounts of concurrency and exception handling. This leads to very large state spaces, making scaling an important issue. Therefore, we use several optimizations and abstractions to reduce the size of the generated model. Most of these are performed during the Little-JIL to BIR translation to take advantage of the scoping and hierarchy in Little-JIL. All the transformations are conservative for the property and process definition. This means that a process will not be reported to be consistent with a property unless that is indeed the case. Spurious violations, property violations in the model that do not correspond to any real trace through the process, could be introduced by these optimizations, but this problem arises rarely, and when it does can often be dealt with by using various model refinement techniques.

Methodology: To evaluate the effectiveness of this approach, we are engaged in three case studies, the blood transfusion case study described in more detail here, as well as a case study on emergency room patient flow and one on an outpatient chemotherapy process for treating breast cancer.

For each case study, a small team of computer scientists meets regularly with a group of medical professionals to elicit the process definition and the properties. The medical professionals are responsible for describing the processes and their requirements and for reviewing the material created by the computer scientists. The computer scientists are responsible for defining the process in Little-JIL, the properties in PROPEL, and for doing the analysis, as well as enhancing the tools as needed. The procedure that we follow is to first focus on the process definition. The benefits of capturing the blood transfusion process formally from the perspective of the nursing profession is described in [28].

While the process is being defined, it is not unusual for goals or high-level requirements to be mentioned, and these are recorded by the computer scientists. After the process definition has begun to stabilize, meetings are then held to elicit a more complete set of requirements. The requirements are first stated informally in natural language. The computer scientists then work with the medical professionals to agree on a glossary of terms that are used to more systematically describe the requirements, still in natural language. After agreement is reached on these statements, computer scientists work closely with the medical professionals to develop the detailed property specifications using PROPEL.

It is after this point that the computer scientists apply the FSV tools to evaluate whether the process definition is consistent with the stated formal properties. As with programs, it is often the case that the FSV tools find problems in the process definition and in the property specifications as well as in the process. Our long-range plans include using the process definitions to support fault tree analysis, simulations, and even process-guidance in the clinical setting. Thus, it is extremely important that the process definition accurately reflects the process and, of course, it is important that the process does not violate correctly formulated properties.

3. An Example

Blood transfusion, although a common procedure, involves considerable risk to the patient, and experts believe that adverse events involving transfusion are significantly underreported. Indeed, transfusion medicine professionals were among the first to develop classification schemes for medical errors, but most of the work in this area has focused on the handling of blood products in the laboratory rather than at the point of care where the actual transfusion occurs [28].

One of us (E. Henneman) is involved in the development of guidelines regarding the safe administration of blood and blood products. As part of this work, she identified a checklist [51] from a standard nursing reference [50] as a good example of a description of the standard transfusion process from the standpoint of the nurse administering the transfusion. This checklist has 40 items (some of which have a number of sub-items) ranging from "Administers pretransfusion medication as prescribed" and "Obtains IV fluid containing normal saline solution and a blood transfusion administration set" to "Compares the patient name and hospital identification number on the patient's identification bracelet with the patient name and hospital identification number on the blood bank form attached to the blood product" and "Using aseptic technique, attaches the distal end of the administration set to the IV catheter." To support her evaluation of such descriptions of the clinical transfusion process, we modeled the process described by the checklist in Little-JIL, and composed it with a model of the process that the hospital blood bank performs. The process model focuses particularly on representing the blood bank's interactions with the nurse, and abstracts away most of the details of the complex activity that the blood bank performs to prepare blood products for administration to patients.

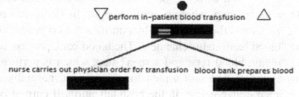

Fig. 21.2. Root of the transfusion process

In our Little-JIL model, shown in Fig. 21.2, the root of the transfusion process is a parallel step (note the equal sign in the lefthand side of the step bar), "perform in-patient blood transfusion," whose children are the steps "nurse carries out physician order for transfusion" and "blood bank prepares blood." This root step begins after a physician orders a transfusion, and each of its substeps is further elaborated in separate Little-JIL diagrams, shown in Figs. 21.3 and 21.4.

The substeps of the root step in Fig. 21.3, which are numbered to show the correspondence with the items in the checklist, are carried out in order from left to right (note the right arrow in the lefthand side of the step bar). Although its interface specification is elided from the figure to reduce clutter, the step "verify informed consent has been obtained" may throw the exception "NoPatientConsent" if the nurse cannot verify that consent has been obtained.

The root step has an exception handler whose purpose is to obtain this consent. Similarly, "verify physician's order" may throw an exception if the order is incomplete. The step "notify blood bank to prepare blood" puts a message with the order into the "order blood" channel (here, too, the actual specification of this use of the channel has been elided; a yellow documentation annotation serves as a visual reminder), from which it is to be retrieved by a step performed by the blood bank. The steps "obtain infusion materials," "obtain blood product from blood bank," and "perform transfusion" are themselves elaborated in additional diagrams that are not included here. In the "obtain blood product from blood bank" diagram the nurse repeatedly checks the "blood bank status" channel for a "blood product ready" message, modeling the behavior of the nurse who calls the blood bank repeatedly to see if the blood product is ready yet, and then picks up the blood product once it is ready.

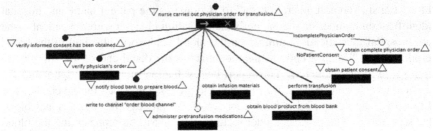

Fig. 21.3. Elaboration of "nurse carries out physician order for transfusion"

As shown in Fig. 21.4, the blood bank's process begins with execution of the "receives notification from nurse" step, whose execution begins by taking an order from the "order blood" channel and then continues by putting a "blood product not ready" message into the "blood bank status channel." The blood bank process continues by executing the "obtain blood type and screen" step, which is performed by checking the lab for a current type and screen for this patient, normally obtained from a blood specimen drawn earlier in the hospitalization. If current type and screen are not available, the process indicates that an exception is thrown. In that case, the blood bank puts a "blood type and screen unknown" message into the "blood bank status" channel and waits for the specimen. Once the blood bank has prepared the blood (represented by the "prepares blood" step), the process specifies that the blood bank replace the "blood product not ready" message in the "blood bank status" channel with a "blood product ready" message. The process concludes with execution of the "gives blood to nurse" step.

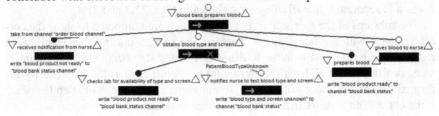

Fig. 21.4. Elaboration of "blood bank prepares blood"

Although we have elicited and formalized more than 60 properties that should be satisfied by a safe blood transfusion process, we focus here only on the property that, once the nurse notifies the blood bank to prepare the blood product, the nurse will eventually pick up the blood product. When we attempt to verify that our process satisfies this property, the verification tool reports a violation and produces as a counterexample a path through the process in which the patient's type and screen are not available and the blood bank is then unable to prepare the blood. Indeed, our model of the nursing process reflects the assumption in the checklist that the type and screen have been obtained prior to the transfusion order, an assumption that usually, but not always, holds. This analysis has thus identified a problem with the process specified by the checklist, namely that it has failed to deal with this exceptional situation. Our experience has indicated that such problems are often found in existing natural language process descriptions. It is particularly interesting that, as we noted earlier, this checklist is unusually detailed and complete, and yet it does not carefully specify the required behavior of the nurse in a number of exceptional cases, such as this one.

Upon discovering this process defect, medical professionals suggested improving the process by inserting a step mandating that the nurse respond to the "blood type and screen unknown" message by drawing a blood specimen for determining type and screen. Verification of the modified process then showed that blood would always be prepared, though the sample for type and screen might not be drawn until after all of the other preparations for the transfusion have taken place and the nurse has called the blood bank (represented in the process by reading from the "blood bank status" channel) to see if the blood is ready for pickup. This can involve significant delay and risk to the patient, and such errors are not uncommon in clinical practice. To address this process defect, we next modified the nursing process to have the nurse check for the availability of the type and screen *before* notifying the blood bank of the transfusion order and, if necessary, drawing the specimen for type and screen at that time. By making this process modification, the possibility of this delay is eliminated.

For those hospitals using electronic order entry, another concern is whether the nurse will see a transfusion order promptly. In about 10% of US hospitals, orders for transfusions are entered at a computer terminal by the physician and sent electronically to the blood bank and nurse. In such situations the nurse will see the transfusion order only when viewing a particular "task list" page in the patient's electronic record. To evaluate whether the nurse will respond to such an order promptly, we adapted the corrected version of the nursing and blood bank processes and introduced an abstract model of the physician's activities. In this model, the processes performed by the physician, the nurse, and the blood bank are defined to execute in parallel with each other and the nurse's process is defined to repeatedly make a choice between performing other nursing tasks or checking for a transfusion order. The resulting process specifies that if the nurse checks for a transfusion order and finds that one has been issued by the physician, the nurse then follows a process that is similar to the one previously described, but modified to indicate that the blood bank has received the order electronically from the physician rather than from the nurse. Fig. 21.5 shows the top-level diagram of this process.

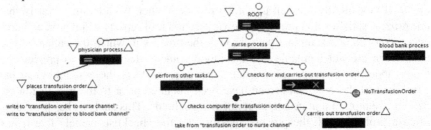

Fig. 21.5. Process model for hospitals with electronic transfusion orders

We then tried to verify the property that, if a physician orders a transfusion and certain exceptions (such as the patient refusing consent) do not occur, then the nurse will see the order. The verifier reported that the property does not hold in the case where the nurse never checks for the transfusion order. We understand that, in actual practice, the press of other urgent tasks may indeed cause a nurse to consult the task list only at the start and end of a shift, when the nurse going off duty reviews cases with the nurse coming on. Unlike other pages in the electronic patient record, such as those to order and record the administration of medication, the task list page is not frequently referenced during typical nursing procedures. A few large research hospitals or groups of hospitals with the resources to write their own systems have modified those systems so that the nurse sees an alert indicating that the transfusion has been ordered whenever the patient's record is accessed, and the alert remains visible until it is acknowledged. Hospitals that use commercial electronic order systems are often unable to get such changes made. (Some hospitals have resorted to entering transfusion orders on the medication page of the record since that page is consulted frequently by the nurse, even though this causes other difficulties with the electronic order system.)

We modified the process to reflect such an alert by explicitly distinguishing nursing activities that use the computer from those that do not and adding a prerequisite to the steps representing activities involving the computer. That prerequisite is a check for the existence of a transfusion order, representing an alert that informs the nurse of the existence of the order. We then tried to verify the property under the assumption that at least one activity involving use of the computer occurs after the physician orders the transfusion. With this assumption, which, as noted above, reflects the fact that many nursing activities in hospitals with electronic order systems do involve interaction with the computer system, the property holds. The important point is that the original problem with the process could be detected using FSV and the effectiveness of the modification could be subsequently evaluated, including the assumptions that were needed to make it valid.

Verification of each of the properties we have examined for the blood transfusion process takes about 10 seconds or less on a 1.86 GHz Pentium M processor and uses a few megabytes of memory.

4. Discussion

This project has helped the medical professionals understand and improve their processes in a variety of ways. In this section we discuss the impact of FSV on process understanding and improvement and some of the issues that have arisen in applying FSV techniques to medical processes.

Impact of Verification on Process Definition: Specifying properties for verification and attempting to verify them identified a number of problems in our process definitions. In some cases, simply trying to formulate properties precisely pointed out gaps in the formal process definitions, for instance because there simply were no steps that could be bound to the events used to specify those properties. In some cases, this was because the part of the process intended to address the issue being captured by a property was simply missing and had to be added. In other cases, the problem was that certain steps needed to be further decomposed in order to identify the substeps that should be bound to the property events.

Verification efforts also helped us to find several subtle errors in the formal process definitions that had remained undiscovered despite careful inspection by both software engineers and domain experts. For example, the blood transfusion process definition specified that if discrepancies occur during the "verify blood product" step, then "verify blood product" is to be terminated and a "Failed Blood Product Check" exception is to be thrown. The handler "handle failed blood product check", which refers to a step defined in other diagrams (not shown here due to lack of space), requires the nurse to send the blood product back to the blood bank and obtain a replacement blood product. The exception continuation badge of this handler was specified to be "continue", which implied that, after this exception has been handled in this way, the process continues with the nurse signing the blood bank form after obtaining the replacement product. This process thus violated the property "The nurse must verify the blood product before it is transfused to the patient", where the event "verify the blood product" is bound to completion of the step "verify blood product". It is clear that this would introduce the potential for serious medical error, and in the actual process the nurse verifies the patient identification and the product identification again after obtaining the replacement product. Thus, attempting to verify this property indicated that the exception's continuation badge was wrong and needed to be changed to "restart".

The accuracy of the formal process definitions is, of course, critical to the utility of the analysis—verifying properties of a model that does not reflect the real process provides no information about the real process and may in fact lead to dangerous overconfidence in the safety of the process. Furthermore, our process models are also intended to be used for other types of analysis, simulation, and possibly even guidance in the clinical setting, so detecting and correcting errors in the models is important for other reasons as well.

Impact of Verification on Processes: The analysis of the processes described in this paper identified problematic defects in the processes, helped determine the causes of the problems, and subsequently provided some assurance that the modified processes were indeed improvements. This was the case with other processes from our case studies as well.

Perhaps the greatest direct benefit of verification, however, is the assurance it provides that the revised process satisfies the previously violated property as well as other previously verified properties. In practice, modifications to the processes are usually made incrementally, with changes introduced to address some perceived problem. Sometimes this problem is a "sentinel event," an occurrence in the execution of the existing process where a patient has been put at risk, and thus changes are introduced to prevent the recurrence of that event. In other cases, changes are introduced to increase efficiency or make the process more convenient for the medical professionals or more comfortable for patients. But the medical professionals have very few methods for assessing the impact of such changes, and it is hard for them to determine whether the changes really do address the intended problem and do not introduce new problems. For example, our analysis of a chemotherapy process detected a deadlock that was introduced by a change that was intended to prevent ill patients from having to make an extra trip to the chemotherapy site. When this deadlock arose in practice, the medical professionals involved in the process broke the deadlock by ad hoc means. It took some additional process modifications and further analysis to be sure that this would not lead to any reductions in the number of safety checks in the process. For life-critical processes, the ability to evaluate proposed changes in the process without having to first put them in place is very significant.

Issues in Applying FSV to Medical Processes: There are a number of obstacles to applying FSV techniques to complex, human-intensive processes. First, it is hard to get the formal definitions of the processes right. The amount of effort invested by both the medical professionals and the computer scientists involved in our project is considerable. The computer scientists have to learn enough of the medical terminology and context to understand what the medical professionals are saying and the medical professionals have to think very hard about the details of their processes and the possible exceptions. This is itself a complex, human-intensive activity. As we have described above, aspects of the modeling and verification process help detect errors in the formal definitions, but getting the right formal definitions at a suitable level of detail for verification of the properties related to medical safety is not easy.

A second obstacle is that specifying properties for verification is also hard. Domain experts often had problems being precise about the high-level properties that they wanted their processes to obey. In addition, these high-level statements were often incorrect. This frequently occurred because the domain experts did not consider possible exceptional situations that could impact the property. For example, the property "The nurse must verify patient's identification bracelet matches patient's stated name and birth date before infusing blood product" requires that the event "verify patient's identification bracelet matches patient's stated name and birth date" must occur on every execution of the process. In attempting to verify this property, however, the verifier reported a violation, identifying the possibility that if the patient refuses to sign the consent form, the process cannot proceed, and hence the event "verify patient's identification bracelet matches patient's stated name and birth date" will not occur. The actual property should have taken this constraint into consideration and instead have stated that "After the patient signs the consent form, verify patient's identification bracelet matches patient's stated name and birth date."

Once the abstract statements of the desired properties have been chosen, the events in those statements must be bound to specific events in the formal process definitions for verification. It can be quite difficult to determine which step or steps should be bound to which events. We encountered problems with this because the sources for the property specifications (i.e., medical guidelines) were sometimes different from the sources for the process definition or because the two descriptions were at very different levels of abstraction; sometimes both problems arose. The property specifications frequently had to be broken down from a high, abstract level (e.g., "the right drug to the right patient at the right time") to lower-level specifications that could be mapped to the process step names (e.g., the patient's name and date of birth as given by the patient match the name and date of birth in the chart). Sometimes high-level abstract specifications were mapped to several low-level properties, stated in the terminology of the step names, and sometimes property events needed to be represented by more than one process step name. Similar problems occur for software systems when high-level system requirements need to be mapped to lower level properties stated with respect to the details in the system design or implementation.

Because errors in the formal process definitions and property specifications were often not detected until the first rounds of verification, the verification process could be very lengthy. This, of course, is also the case with verification of software systems—much of the early effort of verification is devoted to finding problems in the model and the properties. For human-intensive processes, like many medical processes, however, this may be even more significant since the initial artifacts from which process definitions and properties are derived are less concrete and precise than, say, source code.

Finally, one expects problems of scale in FSV. For the sorts of processes that we have analyzed so far, these have not been serious. In particular, some of our optimizations are able to take advantage of aspects of the structure of Little-JIL process definitions to reduce the size of the models. But our examples have largely been restricted to very small configurations, such as one nurse performing one transfusion on one patient. As we extend this work to consider processes involving many medical professionals carrying out many activities to treat many patients, we expect that the time and memory resources required for verification may begin to limit the applicability of our methods. As for verification of software systems, we will look for new abstractions to reduce the size of the models and new domain-specific verification techniques that take advantage of special features of these processes.

5. Related Work

Process Definition: Many languages and diagrammatic notations have been evaluated as vehicles for defining processes. For example, APPL/A [44] used a procedural language, MARVEL/Oz [8] used a rule-based language and SLANG [5] used modified Petri Nets to define processes. More recently, the workflow [36] and electronic commerce [27] communities have pursued similar research. In the medical domain, several languages, such as Asbru [41], GLARE [33], and PROforma [43], have been especially designed for representing clinical protocols and guidelines using an AI-based linguistic paradigm. Noumeir has also pursued similar goals, but using a notation like UML to define processes [34]. Others (e.g., [40]), view medical processes as workflows and use a workflow-like language to define processes and drive their execution. None of these process definition approaches, however, seems able to support process definitions that are both sufficiently clear and sufficiently broad and precise to support analysis of the sort described in this paper. The main problems with these approaches include inadequate specification of exception handling, weak facilities for controlling concurrency, lack of resource management, and inadequate specification of artifact flows. We believe that the Little-JIL language addresses these problems relatively more successfully, although it still has inadequacies, such as the lack of good support for specifying timing constraints and transactions.

Property Specification: There are many property specification approaches that aim to provide both accessibility and precision. The Attempto Controlled English (ACE) project [24] uses a natural language processing technique to translate natural language (NL) property specifications into first-order logic. It also provides annotated NL templates for non-expert users. Ambriola and Gervasi [1] have developed the CARL and CICO/CIRCE tools to translate NL property specifications into propositional logic and back again. One limitation of these approaches is that the translator and the user may have different interpretations of NL specifications due to the ambiguity in those NL specifications. Interpretation alternatives like the options in PROPEL might help in improving the accuracy of the resulting formal property representations. Unlike these approaches, PROPEL does not attempt to understand NL, even in restricted domains. Some other approaches, including the Dwyer et al. property patterns work [21], and Drusinsky's (N)TLCharts [20], simply annotate the formal model with NL comments. Unlike the DNL representation in PROPEL, the NL comments are not in themselves intended to function as property specifications, but instead are just a means of conveying the basic gist of what the property is meant to express.

FSV: There has been a great deal of work on the analysis of software artifacts. Most of this work has been focused on analysis of code or models of systems. Finite-state verification, or model checking, techniques (e.g., [15], [13], [29]), work by constructing a finite model that represents all possible relevant executions of the system and then analyze that model algorithmically to detect executions that violate the particular property. Our team has been involved in the analysis and evaluation of various finite-state verification approaches [3], and the development of verifiers such as FLAVERS [22] and INCA [18]. Our work seems to be among the first that has applied FSV approaches to process definitions [16], [12], [32]. As noted above, one of the major concerns of these techniques is controlling the size of the state space, while maintaining precision in the analysis result. Many abstraction and reduction techniques (e.g., [19], [14], [26]) have been used to tackle this problem. The optimization and abstraction approaches we have taken in this work are not new. They are however, effective, since they can take advantage of Little-JIL's scoping and hierarchy to achieve important reductions.

Improving Medical Processes: To our knowledge, there has been very little work on using formal methods to improve medical procedures. In [45], a medical protocol is modeled in the Asbru [41] language. To analyze the protocol, the model is automatically translated to a formal representation for the interactive theorem prover KIV [4]. This approach was applied to two real-life medical protocols, a jaundice protocol and a diabetes mellitus protocol. In [7], the Asbru model is translated into the input language of the SMV model checker and a simple abstraction is used to reduce the model. This work also used the jaundice protocol as an example and found errors in it. The blood transfusion process that we analyzed seems to be notably more complex than the protocols analyzed in these two papers. The Little-JIL model of the blood transfusion process consists of about 120 steps (some of which are essentially invocations of previously defined steps) while the Asbru model of the jaundice protocol has only about 40 plans (a plan is the counterpart of a step in Little-JIL). And unlike the Asbru model, which only defines the normal procedure, our blood transfusion process models specify real-world exception handling that could greatly change the control-flow of the normal process. Our blood transfusion processes also define the interactions among various medical professionals, making the models even more complex. In [46], the clinical guideline defined in GLARE [33] is translated to a Promela [29] representation and verified by SPIN. However, no details of the evaluation are presented in the paper.

There have been other approaches to improving medical safety, as well, but much of the emphasis of this work has been targeted towards quality control measures [49], [23], error reporting systems [6], and process automation in laboratory settings [25], such as those where blood products are prepared. In other work, Bayesian belief networks have been used as the basis for discrete event simulations of medical scenarios and to guide treatment planning (e.g., [47]).

6. Conclusions and Future Work

This project has demonstrated some of the benefits of applying selected software technologies to improve healthcare processes. We found, for instance, that the very act of using technologies that support process and property elicitation was effective in identifying defects in medical processes. For example, Little-JIL's facilities for exception management invite process eliciters to inquire about exceptional behavior as a routine part of their interviewing of domain experts. In doing so exception management issues are brought forward. Similarly PROPEL's interactive questioning about the details of properties has also proven to be effective in causing domain experts to confront property details that otherwise are typically overlooked.

It is true that addressing all of these details carefully, as invited by these technologies, causes the process and property elicitation processes to be lengthy. Typically the process and property elicitations and reviews took place through weekly meetings over a period of several months. While this cost is admittedly high, we believe that it is more than repaid by the quality of the processes and properties obtained and by the improvements achieved.

Indeed, we believe that these costs will be further amortized as we use these process definitions and property specifications as the basis for further types of analysis. In preliminary work we outlined how our process definitions can be used to automatically generate Fault Trees [11] that can then be used as the basis for Fault Tree Analysis (FTA) and Failure Mode and Effects Analysis (FMEA) [42, 48]. Such analyses seem likely to be effective in supporting such diagnoses as the presence of single points of failure and how faulty performance of a process step may impact subsequent process executions. We have also begun working on the automatic generation of simulations from Little-JIL process definitions. As these process analysis efforts proceed, we hope to discover that they are mutually supportive, and that the combined value of such analyses richly repays the costs of elicitation of processes and properties.

The processes studied in the project have all been human intensive. As noted, the underlying technologies were first developed for software systems and have been considered for combined hardware/software systems. We envision expanding the scope of this project to include medical devices and the human processes involved in employing those devices. We believe that it is important to not only verify the device but to evaluate it in the context in which it will be employed. We have shown in preliminary work [2] that the properties can be quite different in different contexts.

Ultimately we envisage the development of a process environment in which process definition tools are smoothly integrated with a spectrum of process analysis capabilities. Such a support environment would hopefully lead to a systematic and well-reasoned approach to process improvement. Our primary focus is on processes in the healthcare community, but in other work we are also exploring processes in use in such other diverse domains as labor-management dispute resolution [35], ecological data processing [9], and elections [37].

Finally we would like to emphasize that the benefits of this work are not restricted to effecting improvements only in the application domains. Our work has also resulted in improvements to our process definition language and in our requirements engineering and analysis capabilities. Little-JIL's semantic capabilities, for example, have been broadened and sharpened in response to needs that became manifest as we defined processes in the healthcare domain. Our understanding of the difficulty of defining resources and the ways in which processes specify needs for them was also sharpened considerably by our work on healthcare processes. This is leading to challenging new directions in resource specification and management [38]. Other needs are continually being recognized, leading to a range of research challenges, most of which have direct relevance to software engineering.

We regard the project described in this paper as only an early indication of the many possible ways in which software engineering technologies can be applied to new domains. Doing so offers the strong prospect of benefit to those domains and also to the further development of the software technologies themselves.

Acknowledgments The authors gratefully acknowledge the work of Sandy Wise, Barbara Lerner, and Aaron Cass, who made major contributions to the development of Little-JIL, to Heather Conboy and Jamieson Cobleigh, who made major contributions to the development of FLAVERS, to Rachel Cobleigh, who developed PROPEL, and to Houng Phan, who helped to elicit the blood transfusion process and properties.

References

[1] V. Ambriola and V. Gervasi. On the systematic analysis of natural language requirements with circe. *Automated Software Eng.*, 13(1):107-167, 2006.

[2] G. S. Avrunin, L. A. Clarke, E. A. Henneman, and L. J. Osterweil. Complex medical processes as context for embedded systems. *ACM SIGBED Rev.*, 3(4):9-14, 2006.

[3] G. S. Avrunin, J. C. Corbett, and M. B. Dwyer. Benchmarking finite-state verifiers. *Software Tools for Technology Transfer*, 2(4):317-320, 2000.

[4] M. Balser, W. Reif, G. Schellhorn, K. Stenzel, and A. Thums. Formal system development with kiv. In T. Maibaum, editor, *Fundamental Approaches to Software Engineering*, 2000.

[5] S. C. Bandinelli, A. Fugetta, and C. Ghezzi. Software process model evolution in the SPADE environment. *IEEE Trans. on Softw. Eng.*, 19(12), December 1993.

[6] J. Battles, H. Kaplan, T. van der Schaaf, and C. Shea. The attributes of medical event-reporting systems: experience with a prototype medical event-reporting system for transfusion medicine. *Arch. Pathology Laboratory Medicine*, 122:231-238, 1998.

[7] S. Bäumler, M. Balser, A. Dunets, W. Reif, and J. Schmitt. Verification of medical guidelines by model checking - a case study. In A. Valmari, editor, *SPIN*, 2006.

[8] I. Z. Ben-Shaul and G. E. Kaiser. A paradigm for decentralized process modeling and its realization in the oz environment. In *16th Intl. Conf. on Software Engineering*, 1994.

[9] E. R. Boose, A. M. Ellison, L. J. Osterweil, L. Clarke, R. Podorozhny, J. L. Hadley, A. Wise, and D. R. Foster. Ensuring reliable datasets for environmental models and forecasts. In *Ecological Informatics*, volume 2, pages 237-247, 2007.

[10] A. G. Cass, B. S. Lerner, E. K. McCall, L. J. Osterweil, J. Stanley M. Sutton, and A. Wise. Little-jil/juliette: A process definition language and interpreter. In *22nd Int. Conf. on Softw. Eng.*, pages 754-757, Limerick, Ireland, 2000.

[11] B. Chen, G. S. Avrunin, L. A. Clarke, and L. J. Osterweil. Automatic fault tree derivation from little-jil process definitions. In *SPW/ProSim*, volume 3966 of LNCS, 2006.

[12] S. Christov, B. Chen, G. S. Avrunin, L. A. Clarke, and L. J. Osterweil. Rigorously defining and analyzing medical processes: An experience report. In *1st International Workshop on Model-Based Trustworthy Health Information Systems*, September 2007.

[13] A. Cimatti, E. Clarke, E. Giunchiglia, F. Giunchiglia, M. Pistore, M. Roveri, R. Sebastiani, and A. Tacchella. NuSMV version 2: An opensource tool for symbolic model checking. In *Proc. Int. Conf. on Computer-Aided Verification*, volume 2404 of LNCS, July 2002.

[14] E. M. Clarke, O. Grumberg, and D. E. Long. Model checking and abstraction. *ACM Transactions on Programming Languages and Systems*, 16(5):1512-1542, September 1994.

[15] E. M. Clarke, O. G. Jr., and D. A. Peled. *Model Checking*. MIT Press, 2000.

[16] J. M. Cobleigh, L. A. Clarke, and L. J. Osterweil. Verifying properties of process definitions. In *ACM SIGSOFT Int. Symp. on Software Testing and Analysis*, 2000.

[17] R. L. Cobleigh, G. S. Avrunin, and L. A. Clarke. User guidance for creating precise and accessible property specifications. In *14th ACM SIGSOFT Int. Symp. on Foundations of Software Eng.*, pages 208-218, Portland, OR, November 2006.

[18] J. C. Corbett and G. S. Avrunin. Using integer programming to verify general safety and liveness properties. *Formal Methods System Design*, 6(1):97-123, 1995.

[19] P. Cousot and R. Cousot. Abstract interpretation: a unified lattice model for static analysis of programs by construction or approximation of fixpoints. In *4th ACM Symposium on Principles of Programming Languages*, pages 238-252, Los Angeles, 1977.

[20] D. Drusinsky. Visual formal specification using (n)tlcharts: Statechart automata with temporal logic and natural language conditioned transitions. In *International Workshop on Parallel and Distributed Systems: Testing and Debugging*, April 2004.

[21] M. B. Dwyer, G. S. Avrunin, and J. C. Corbett. Patterns in property specifications for finite-state verification. In *21st Int. Conf. on Softw. Eng.*, pages 411-420, Los Angeles, May 1999.

[22] M. B. Dwyer, L. A. Clarke, J. M. Cobleigh, G. Naumovich (2004) Flow analysis for verifying properties of concurrent software systems. *ACM Trans. Softw. Eng. Methodol.*, 13(4).

[23] M. Foss and S. Moore. Evolution of quality management: integration of quality assurance functions into operations, or "quality is everyone's responsibility". *Transfusion*, 43(9):1330-1336, September 2003.

[24] N. E. Fuchs, U. Schwertel, and R. Schwitter. Attempto controlled english - not just another logic specification language. In P. Flener, editor, *8th International Workshop on Logic Programming Synthesis and Transformation*, number 1559 in LNCS, pages 1-20, 1998.

[25] S. Galel and C. Richards. Practical approaches to improve laboratory performance and transfusion safety. *American Journal of Clinical Pathology*, 107(4):S43-S49, 1997.

[26] S. Graf and H. Saïdi. Construction of abstract state graphs with pvs. In *9th Int. Conf. on Computer Aided Verification*, number 1254 in *LNCS*, pages 72-83, 1997.

[27] B. N. Grosof, Y. Labrou, and H. Y. Chan. A declarative approach to business rules in contracts: courteous logic programs in XML. In *ACM Conf. on Electronic Commerce*, 1999.

[28] E. A. Henneman, G. S. Avrunin, L. A. Clarke, L. J. Osterweil, C. Andrzejewski, Jr., K. Merrigan, R. Cobleigh, K. Frederick, E. Katz-Bassett, and P. L. Henneman. Increasing patient safety and efficiency in transfusion therapy using formal process definitions. In *Transfusion Medicine Review*, volume 21, pages 49-57, January 2007.

[29] G. J. Holzmann. The SPIN Model Checker. Addison-Wesley, 2004.

[30] R. Iosif, M. B. Dwyer, and J. Hatcliff. Translating java for multiple model checkers: The bandera back-end. *Formal Methods in System Design*, 26(2):137-180, March 2005.

[31] L. T. Kohn, J. M. Corrigan, and M. S. Donaldson, editors. *To Err Is Human: Building a Safer Health System*. National Academy Press, Washington, D.C., 1999.

[32] B. S. Lerner. Verifying process models built using parameterized state machines. In *ACM SIGSOFT Int. Symp. on Software Testing and Analysis*, 2004.

[33] G. Molino, P. Terenziani, S. Montani, A.Bottrighi, and M. Torchio. Glare: a domain-independent system for acquiring, representing and executing clinical guidelines. In *J. of the Amer. Medical Informatics Association (JAMIA) Symposium supplement*, 2006.

[34] R. Noumeir. Radiology interpretation process modeling. *J. of Biomedical Informatics*, 39(2):103-114, 2006.

[35] L. J. Osterweil, N. K. Sondheimer, L. A. Clarke, E. Katsh, and D. Rainey. Using process definitions to facilitate the specification of requirements. Technical report, Department of Computer Science, University of Massachusetts Amherst, 2006.

[36] S. Paul, E. Park, and J. Chaar. Rainman: a workflow system for the internet. In *USENIX Symp. on Internet Technologies and Systems*, Berkeley, CA, 1997.

[37] M. S. Raunak, B. Chen, A. Elssamadisy, L. A. Clarke, and L. J. Osterweil. Definition and analysis of election processes. In *SPW/ProSim 2006*, volume 3966 of *LNCS*, 2006.

[38] M. S. Raunak and L. J. Osterweil. Effective resource allocation for process simulation: A position paper. In *6th Intl. Workshop on Software Process Simulation and Modeling*, 2005.

[39] P. P. Reid, W. D. Compton, J. H. Grossman, and G. Fanjiang, editors. *Building a Better Delivery System: A New Engineering/Health Care Partnership*. National Academy Press, 2005.

[40] M. Ruffolo, C. Information, and R. Curia. Process management in health care: A system for preventing risks and medical errors. In *Business Process Management*, pages 334-343, 2005.

[41] Y. Shahar, S. Miksch, and P. Johnson. The asgaard project: a task-specific framework for the application and critiquing of time-oriented clinical guidelines. *Artificial Intelligence in Medicine*, 14(1-2):29-51, 1998.

[42] D. H. Stamatis. Failure Mode and Effect Analysis: FMEA from Theory to Execution. *Amer. Society for Quality*, March 1995.

[43] D. R. Sutton and J. Fox. The syntax and semantics of the proforma guideline modeling language. In *Journal of the American Medical Informatics Association*, 10, Sep-Oct 2003.

[44] J. S. M. Sutton, D. Heimbigner, and L. J. Osterweil. Appl/a: a language for software process programming. *ACM Trans. on Software Engineering and Methodology*, 4(3):221-286, 1995.

[45] A. ten Teije, M. Marcos, M. Balser, J. van Croonenborg, C. Duelli, F. van Harmelen, P. Lucas, S. Miksch, W. Reif, K. Rosenbrand, and A. Seyfang. Improving medical protocols by formal methods. *Artificial Intell. in Medicine*, 36(3):193-209, 2006.

[46] P. Terenziani, L. Giordano, A. Bottrighi, S. Montani, and L. Donzella. Spin model checking for the verification of clinical guidelines. In *ECAI 2006 Workshop on AI techniques in healthcare: evidence-based guidelines and protocols*, August 2006.

[47] L. van der Gaag, S. Renooij, C. Witteman, B. Aleman, and B. Taal. Probabilities for a probabilistic network: a case study in oesophageal cancer. *Artificial Intelligence in Medicine*, 25(2):123-148, June 2002.

[48] W. Vesely, F. Goldberg, N. Roberts, and D. Haasl. Fault Tree Handbook (NUREG-0492). U.S. Nuclear Regulatory Commission, Washington, D.C., Jan. 1981.

[49] D. Voak, J. Chapman, and P. Phillips. Quality of transfusion practice beyond the blood transfusion laboratory is essential to prevent abo-incompatible death. *Transfusion Medicine*, 10(2):95-96, June 2000.

[50] J. M. Wilkinson and K. V. Leuven. *Fundamentals of Nursing*. F. A. Davis Company, 2007.

[51] J. M. Wilkinson, K. V. Leuven. Procedure checklist for administering a blood transfusion. http://davisplus.fadavis.com/wilkinson/PDFs/Procedure_Checklists/PC_Ch36-01.pdf, 2007.